Making Sense of Education

Making Sense of Education provides a contemporary introduction to key issues in educational philosophy and theory. Exploring major past and present conceptions of education, teaching and learning, this book aims to make philosophy of education relevant to the professional practice of teachers and student teachers, as well as of interest to those studying education as an academic subject.

The book is divided into three parts:

- Education, teaching and professional practice: issues concerning education, the role of the teacher, the relationship of educational theory to practice and the wider moral dimensions of pedagogy.
- Learning, knowledge and curriculum: issues concerning behaviourist and cognitive theories of learning, knowledge and meaning, curriculum aims and content and evaluation and assessment.
- Schooling, society and culture: issues of the wider social and political context of education concerning liberalism and communitarianism, justice and equality, differentiation, authority and discipline.

This timely and up-to-date introduction should assist all those studying and/or working in education to appreciate the main philosophical sources of and influences on present day thinking about education, teaching and learning.

David Carr is Professor of Philosophy of Education at the University of Edinburgh. He is author of *Educating the Virtues* (Routledge 1991), *Professionalism and Ethical Issues in Teaching* (Routledge 2000) and of numerous philosophical and educational articles.

Making Sense of Education

An introduction to the philosophy and theory of education and teaching

David Carr

RoutledgeFalmer
Taylor & Francis Group

LONDON AND NEW YORK

First published 2003
by RoutledgeFalmer
11 New Fetter Lane, London EC4P 4EE

Simultaneously published in the USA and Canada
by RoutledgeFalmer
29 West 35th Street, New York, NY 10001

RoutledgeFalmer is an imprint of the Taylor & Francis Group

Typeset in Baskerville by Taylor & Francis Books Ltd
Printed and bound in Great Britain by Biddles Ltd, Guildford and
King's Lynn

British Library Cataloguing in Publication Data
A catalogue record for this book is available from the British
Library

Library of Congress Cataloging in Publication Data
Carr, David.
Making sense of education: an introduction to the philosophy and
theory of education/David Carr.
Includes bibliographical references and index.
1. Education–Philosophy. I. Title.

LB14.7 .C366   2002
370'.1–dc21   2002069876

ISBN 0–415–27486–9 (hbk)
ISBN 0–415–23074–8 (pbk)

Contents

Preface

Some years ago, it occurred to me that the days of fairly frequent introductions to philosophy of education seemed to have gone, and that there seemed to be something of a need in the contemporary literature for an updated work of this kind, still in the broad analytical tradition of previous introductory works, which might nevertheless attempt to take account of recent developments in the field for the possible benefit of a professional or wider readership. The present work is an attempt, following a struggle of some three years with what proved to be a rather harder task than I originally anticipated, to provide just such an introduction.

In prospect of this goal, at all events, the work has three broad aims. First, it sets out to provide the reader with some understanding of the crucial relevance of such past great philosophers as Plato, Aristotle, Descartes, Locke, Hume, Kant, Mill, Frege and Wittgenstein to contemporary philosophy of education. Secondly, it attempts to deal with some of the more recent developments in educational philosophy under the influence of what are sometimes (perhaps misleadingly) called 'non-analytical' or 'post-analytical' philosophical traditions. In this respect, there is appreciable critical engagement in this work with neo-idealist and communitarian perspectives on moral and social theory, pragmatist conceptions of epistemology, structuralist approaches to learning and under-standing, neo-Marxist and post-structural (and hence, at least by implication, postmodern) hegemonic analyses of society and education – though I have also chosen to focus here only on what seem to me to be the most educationally significant of such developments. Thirdly, however, I have considered it impor-tant at all stages and in all parts of this work to maintain close contact with those key issues and problems of professional policy and practice that are to a great extent the *raison d'être* of educational philosophy. From this viewpoint, not only is the author of the present work an academically trained philosopher who has over the years published in many leading mainsteam philosophical as well as educational journals, but he is also a former primary and secondary school teacher who has been professionally involved with the preparation and supervi-sion of classroom teachers for over a quarter-century. Indeed, a good deal of my previously published work on teaching and learning has been a direct result of first-hand experience and observation of on-site professional practice.

The work itself consists of three parts of five chapters each. The three parts observe a fairly arbitrary separation of educational concerns into (i) questions of teaching and professional practice, (ii) problems of learning and knowledge, and (iii) issues of wider social and cultural context – although it will also be evident that these matters inevitably overlap, and that other possible ways of dividing the conceptual territory might well have been adopted. Unlike some previous introductions to philosophy of education, in which key ideas have been treated more or less separately in relatively self-contained essays, I have tried in this work to develop a fairly continuous narrative in which each new chapter attempts as far as possible to develop or build upon the arguments of preceding chapters. At the same time, each part is sufficiently self-contained to be used as a companion to more specifically focused academic or professional courses on *either* teaching and professionalism *or* learning, knowledge and curriculum *or* education, society and culture. Above all, however, it should be clear that this work is throughout concerned to develop a consistent set of arguments towards what is ultimately, I hope, a generally coherent perspective on problems of education, teaching and learning. If these arguments are not consistent or coherent, I would also see it as the principal task of any readers of this work to try to show why and in what respects this is so.

At all events, the first part, on general issues of pedagogy, professionalism and the role of the teacher, begins with a chapter focused on the concept of education as such. Commencing with some exploration of the basic idea that education is profoundly implicated in the essentially normative task of promoting *personal* formation, the chapter proceeds to defend a version of the postwar analytical account of education as a matter of the acquisition of human characteristics of more than merely instrumental or utilitarian value. That said, the discussion also proceeds via examination of some possible confusions in the liberal traditional assimilation of the distinction between education and training to that between intrinsically versus extrinsically worthwhile forms of knowledge, and it also traces the closely related liberal idea of the school curriculum as essentially concerned with knowledge of the former kind to some evident conflation of education and schooling. Whereas the first chapter is concerned with the pedagogical enterprise in the broader sense of education, however, the second chapter is the first of two concerned to interrogate the nature of teaching as a more specific human project, occupation or profession. Indeed, that chapter is concerned to explore the nature of teaching as a particular kind of *activity* in which one might be held to engage for this or that measurable period of time. However, it is the main purpose of this examination to show that despite a contemporary trend towards construing any and all aspects of teaching in terms of technical skill, effective teaching is implicated in a range of human capacities, personality traits, dispositions and qualities of character, not all of which are reasonably appreciable as technical skills, or as apt for acquisition in the manner of such skills.

While the second chapter is concerned to show that there is more to teaching as an activity than the acquisition of skills, the third chapter aims to explore the complexities inherent in understanding teaching as a particular type of *occupation* or mode of professional practice. In fact, chapter 3 argues that teaching has often been liable to construal in a wide variety of ways and via comparison with an extraordinary range of other more or less skilled human occupations, vocations and professions. Moreover, since any claim that teaching is indeed a profession or professional activity is mostly held to depend upon its relationship to a distinctive body of theoretical or principled knowledge, chapter 4 turns to a consideration of the deeply vexed educational theory–practice relationship. On this basis, it is argued that teaching as a profession or vocation is a form of principled moral practice, which – contrary to the views of some opponents of educational theory – needs to be informed by a wider understanding of the moral, social and political context of education. Insofar as that is so, it is here held to be a mistake to regard so-called 'educational theory' as applicable to practice in any straightforward technical sense. The fifth and final chapter of part I, however, follows fairly hard on the heels of the first four by giving more precise attention to the particular moral educational implications of the broader, less technicist and more professional view of teaching defended in previous chapters. This chapter also seeks to advance beyond the first four, by opening up some of the fairly intractable ethical issues about educational formation destined to receive rather fuller treatment in part III.

Part II is mainly concerned with central educational issues of learning, knowledge acquisition, curriculum and assessment: to this end, chapters 6 and 7 are devoted to a philosophical critique of the various empirical psychological theories that have deeply influenced latter-day approaches to education. First, chapter 6 sets out to locate behaviourist and cognitivist theories of learning in a broader philosophical context of issues about the relationship of mind to the world, and proceeds to examine some of the key difficulties of both empirical scientific perspectives on mental life. In particular, it is argued that while the failure of behaviourism to account for the semantic aspects of learning undercuts its prospects of appreciating the nature of education as meaningful understanding, cognitivists' more 'internalist' conceptions of mind as mental structure also fail in their own way to account for the public or social character of human meaning. In consequence, chapter 7 goes in search of an alternative socio-cultural or 'interpersonal' conception of meaning via a brief exploration of (various forms of) philosophical idealism. Ultimately, however, this chapter seeks to address the problem of the social character of meaning via attention to the important twentieth-century work on language, concept formation and understanding of Frege and Wittgenstein. In focusing on the problem of knowledge and its educational significance, moreover, chapter 8 is at pains to distance any general thesis of the social character of meaning from idealism, to argue for an essentially *realist* version of the Platonic idea that knowledge is justified true belief, and to insist that any serious confidence in the educational value of knowledge must be deeply compromised by non-realist views. Chapter 9 explores a range of basic problems about curriculum aims and content via attention to certain allegedly fundamental curriculum principles of breadth, balance, coherence, continuity and progression, and argues that these should be construed as essentially *evaluative* notions, and hence as more normative than technical problems of curriculum design. In addressing more procedural problems of curriculum implementation and the assessment of learning, chapter 10 concludes part II by examining some of the key conceptual difficulties of both behavioural objectives and 'process' models of curriculum, before proceeding to look critically at a recent important educational philosophical debate about the nature and status of assessment.

The third and final part of this work undertakes to explore a range of issues concerning the larger socio-cultural context of education and schooling – and, to this end, chapters 11 and 12 set out to examine the nature and educational relevance of an important recent debate between so-called 'liberal' and 'communitarian' approaches to understanding moral, social and political life. However, before proceeding to a critical consideration of liberal conceptions of society, state and education, chapter 11 takes some care to distinguish between importantly different senses in which communitarian thinking may be contrasted with more liberal or individualist thinking. In turn, the distinctions made in chapter 11 are put to work in the fuller discussion of communitarianism in chapter 12, where it is once more suggested that the key communitarian thesis of the social character of meaning needs dissociating politically and educationally from the dangerously relativistic implications of idealism or non-realism. Chapter 13 connects with the communitarian theme of respect for diversity by exploring a key problem of the extent to which educational policies should be based on recognition or celebration of individual and/or social differences – for, although recognition of difference is often demanded by communitarians in the interests of justice, certain forms of discrimination (on grounds of ability, race and gender) have clearly been regarded by liberals and others as themselves deeply unjust. In chapter 14, however, another form of diversity – of approaches to educational authority and discipline – is examined via attention to the time-honoured distinction between traditional and progressive education. Developing a basic claim that the traditional–progressive dichotomy has often been fatally misinterpreted as a distinction between different types of educational method, this chapter proceeds to argue that it should properly be understood as marking a moral or evaluative distinction between different conceptions of authority and freedom in education. Finally, the last chapter of this work sets out to explore the political dimensions of education, and to distinguish more from less interesting senses of a common claim to the effect that all education is political. In particular, this chapter focuses on questions of the extent to which tensions between political and professional educational imperatives are inevitable, and upon issues concerning the precise educational implications of particular party politics.

In conclusion, I should also say that although this work inevitably draws on ideas developed in previous publications of the author, I have not lifted any material (apart from a couple of sentences) from elsewhere, and all the following chapters have been freshly written for this volume. That said, although it seems unfair to single out particular individuals for special mention, there are so many people who have over the last three decades contributed immeasurably to the development of the ideas in this work. In this regard, I shall simply extend a general heartfelt thanks to all those friends and colleagues who have over the years helped to make my professional life so socially and intellectually stimulating and pleasurable. A similar expression of general but profound gratitude is also due to all at RoutledgeFalmer for their unfailing patience and understanding at the missed deadlines, and above all for the peerless quality of help with the final production of this and previous works that I have now come to expect from them.

David Carr
Faculty of Education
University of Edinburgh
April 2002

Part I

Education, teaching and professional practice

Chapter 1

Education, persons and schooling

The concept of education

It has often been claimed that the concept of education is essentially *contested*.[1] On this view, different socio-cultural consituencies and interest groups are inclined to endorse or canvass their own distinctive conceptions of education, and one may not expect to find any generally agreed definition of the term 'education'. To whatever extent this is so, it is also reasonable to suppose that our best educational efforts depend upon *some* rationally coherent and defensible interpretation of the term, and that insofar as some educational endeavours are less rationally defensible than others, not all rival perspectives can be of equal value. From this viewpoint, one basic problem for any rational account of education is that of holding together two separately plausible ideas that appear nevertheless to be in some tension. The first is the professionally important point that there are different (often opposed) ideas about education, and that the prospects of professional development and progress stand to be enhanced by an educated appreciation of a range of diverse and perhaps logically incompatible educational possibilities. Hence, one key task of professional education and training is to shake the established educational prejudices of trainee teachers – to help them see that the way in which education has been hitherto or conventionally conceived is not necessarily either the only or the best way of operating. However, real educational progress also depends upon recognising that coherent practice is ultimately answerable to certain rational criteria that professional practitioners ignore only at their peril: that therefore not all rival conceptions of education are equally worthy of serious rational consideration. In short, any sensible account of education needs to steer a course between reasonable pluralism and indiscriminate relativism. Following some exploration of the reasons for supposing that education cannot but be a contested concept, this chapter will nevertheless proceed to indicate some of the groundfloor conceptual considerations and distinctions that might nevertheless be said to underlie any and all coherent conceptions of educational practice.

Educational philosophers and theorists have adopted a variety of approaches to understanding the concept of education. For example, one time-honoured strategy has been to examine possible etymological derivations of 'education' from such Latin terms as 'educere' and 'educare'. Eschewing such well-worn and not notably promising leads, however, I shall here and elsewhere in this work try to see what basic light might be shed on the nature of education by exploring its links with some other closely associated notions. First, there is a clear enough relationship between education and *learning*: whatever is learned in the course of education or related enterprises could hardly be other than a matter of the *acquisition* of skills, capacities, dispositions or qualities not previously possessed – although it may also be a matter of the development of already given (innate) qualities or potentialities. Secondly, and consequently, any learning surely presupposes *learners*: thus, insofar as there have to be subjects *of* education as well as education *in* subjects (or whatever), it seems worth asking what kinds of agencies these are, and what benefits we would expect them to derive from education. Thirdly, there are apparent links between education, learning and *teaching*: learning is often assumed (rightly or wrongly) to be a causal or other consequence of teaching, and the terms 'education' and 'teaching' are sometimes used interchangeably. Fourthly, there is a fairly common association between education and *schooling*: indeed, there is a significant tendency, not least in modern civil societies, to associate education with the sort of institutions in which education is held to occur – though the very idea of schools as sites of education has also been seriously questioned in recent times (in my view, coherently if not necessarily justifiably).[2] Since a large portion of part I of this work is devoted to different aspects of teaching, and the issue of learning and its educational significance will occupy most of part II, I shall not say much more about these issues in the present chapter. However, some preliminary examination in this first chapter of the learner or subject of learning, and of the vexed relationship between education and schooling, should serve to provide significant insights into the basic formal character of education as a human practice.

Education and persons

Let us therefore begin with a brief examination of the learner as the subject or recipient of education. In this connection, we should first observe that the class of educated or educable agencies is not obviously coextensive with that of those who can learn. Since most biologically constituted forms of life – for example, bats, rats, cats and amoebas – are capable of some degree of learning, the category of learners is obviously larger than that of educated or educable beings: whereas we may speak perfectly coherently of teaching dogs to do things, or of their learning this or that, it seems absurd or solecistic to speak of educated mice or of educating rabbits. Should we only then talk of educating human beings? In fact, I think that insofar as humans are themselves only a biological species – a kind of animal – there is probably something also rather inexact or misleading about regarding humans as the subjects of education. A rather different uptake on any inquiry about who or what qualifies for education might reflect the consideration that education concerns the initiation of human agents into the rational capacities, values and virtues that warrant our ascription to them of the status of *persons*. This, in turn, presupposes an important distinction between

human beings and persons. Human beings conceived as evolutionarily continuous with other animal species may be the objects of biological or
anthropological study. Persons, however, are not primarily *objects* of scientific
study, but *subjects* of criminal prosecutions, *parties* to marriage contracts, *members*
of clubs and associations, *actors* on stages, *characters* in novels, and so on. From this
viewpoint, we should also note that (biological) humanity might not be necessary
for personhood: non-human extra-terrestrial or alien intelligent life forms might
well be regarded as persons (as hence as educable) – and, of course, many religious believers regard gods, angels and demons as non-human persons. More
controversially, however, there may be some case for denying (at least complete)
personhood to some human beings: we do not readily regard – other than in a
somewhat courtesy sense – newborn infants as (more than potential) persons,
and we may also be inclined to deny the status of person to those in irretrievable
comas whose mental life no longer exceeds bare sentience.[3]

In short, the idea of person – as distinct from human being – is more or less
that of a bearer of rational and practical capacities, values and traits of character, which are themselves inconceivable apart from complex networks of
interpersonal association and/or social institution. To this extent, there seems to
be a large grain of truth in the famous (or notorious) doctrine of the great
French founding father of modern philosophy, René Descartes,[4] known as
Cartesian dualism – basically the idea that minds or souls are non-physical or
immaterial entities or substances that are metaphysically or ontologically distinct
from the physical bodies with which they are associated (as well as separable
from them, in principle, upon death). The significant truth in this idea is that
human *persons* are indeed not identical with the biologically constituted bodies of
human beings, and that features of human personality, character and value do
seem resistant to explanation and understanding in the natural scientific terms of
physics, chemistry or biology. At this point, to be sure, one might well insist that
there *are* something like natural sciences of persons as well as of human being:
do not such statistical sciences as sociology, psychology and economics take
persons as their objects, as those of biology and anthropology take human
beings as objects? But this is in itself to beg, in a peculiarly post-Cartesian way, a
question that this work is concerned to raise – not least in part II. The key point
here is that it is in fact an *open* question whether it is appropriate to regard
psychology as a statistical science in the manner of physics or chemistry: as we
shall see, there may be reasons for doubting whether different forms of empirical
psychology can afford insight into those features of personal agency of particular
interest to educationalists. To be sure, to raise questions about the status of
psychology as an empirical science is not to say that it cannot be regarded as a
valid form of human inquiry; it is rather to say that if someone is intent upon
understanding the minds of other people, he or she might do better to study
history, biography or the works of Shakespeare than 'scientific' psychology. From
this viewpoint, there may be reasons to be sympathetic to Descartes's denial of
any complete reduction of 'soul', mind, biography or history to the causal and
statistical discourses and categories of natural science.

The real trouble with Descartes's mind–body dualism, of course, follows from his conclusion that the minds or souls not liable for such scientific reduction are individual and 'inner' ghostly entities, inaccessible to observation, and in principle detachable from their corporeal vehicles.[5] First, if many of the psychological characteristics we attribute to persons have inherently *public* and *practical* features and associations, it is difficult to see how these might be properties of anything even potentially disembodied: how could I be described as a courageous person or a talented pianist apart from the contexts of embodied agency and skill that give substance to such attributes? Thus, some form of embodiment – terrestrial or other – seems presupposed to many if not most personal attributes. Secondly, if the mentality of personhood cannot be defined apart from certain public institutions and practices, then it can hardly be possessed by essentially *disassociated* individuals: how, for example, can I attribute criminal responsibility to a person in the absence of *socially* constituted legal institutions? None the less, it is the Cartesian idea of a person as an inner, private and dissociated psychological entity that continues to haunt Descartes's rationalist and empiricist heirs – Leibniz, Locke, Berkeley and Hume and others – well into the twentieth century. It even survives in Kant's heroic attempt to reconcile the basic insights of empiricism and rationalism in his great *Critiques of Pure and Practical Reason*.[6] Indeed, a particularly virulent form of Cartesianism seems deeply implicated in Kant's idea of the moral agent as a non-empirical subject of an other-worldly moral law. For Kant there can be no genuine personhood without the freedom of rational autonomy or self-determination – but, in turn, no such self-determination apart from the rational disinterest and impartiality that characterises the moral law: hence, the real personhood of pure practical reason has to be significantly independent of the world of familiar self-referenced (if not self-interested) drives and motives. For Kant the *real* person is not the empirical self of familiar everyday association, but rather the metaphysical *noumenal* self of transcendent practical rationality.

At all events, two important consequences may be observed to follow from this brief exploration of the conceptual relationship between education and personhood – from, indeed, the suggestion that education primarily concerns the promotion of personhood. The first is that ideas of person and education are essentially *normative* notions: from this viewpoint, personhood is best understood as a function of the initiation via education and other processes of socialisation into the values, habits, practices, customs and institutions constitutive of peculiarly human *culture*. What may be considered peculiar about human culture, of course, is that it is the free creation or product of *rational* agents who are able to plan and direct their lives in the light of reasons not entirely (if at all) explicable in the statistical terms of natural science: there is the problematic gap, noted by philosophers from the time of Plato, between causal and normative explanation and understanding.[7] However, although modern educational philosophers have sometimes expressed much this point by claiming that education is about the development of *mind*, we have seen that this way of putting things is also liable to misconstrual if the mind is conceived in Cartesian terms as something purely subjective or exclusively 'inner'. On the contrary, regarding personhood as a function of educational initiation into the norms of human culture enables us to appreciate more clearly the essentially practical, public and social character of human mental or spiritual life: this has the significant consequence of leaving open the possibility – a bone of contention in modern educational philosophy – that the values and practices into which persons may be initiated in the name of education are at least as much *practical* as theoretical.

All the same, the claim that education is a matter of initiation into the values, habits, practices, customs and institutions of (human) culture does not yet get us very far. For a start, the term 'culture' is notoriously ambiguous. With respect to the 'sociological' sense of culture, which means the entire sum of customs and practices that characterise a given social constituency, it should be clear enough that education could not concern itself with all of these: aside from the fact that any such comprehensive initiation must be (logistically) beyond the scope of education, it is also clear that many human practices are morally or otherwise unsuitable for educational consumption. However, a narrower *evaluative* conception of culture as what is most humanly worthwhile – in the famous words of Matthew Arnold, 'the best that has been thought and said in the world'[8] – confronts us with the central educational question of deciding *which* of the numerous forms of learning encountered in human culture(s) are to be considered crucial for the personal development of young people. This, of course, is a large question upon which much ink has been spilt in educational philosophy – and which will, in one way or another, concern us throughout the rest of this work. For the rest of this chapter, however, we shall try to prepare the ground for subsequent inquiries by focusing on a number of fairly elementary (albeit not unproblematic) distinctions.

Education, culture and value

How then should we reasonably conceive the overall aims and content of education and schooling? A rather unhelpful response in line with the story so far is that the main task of education is to prepare young people for adult personal and social functioning: a little more precisely, to equip individuals with the knowledge, understanding and skills apt for a personally satisfying, socially responsible and economically productive life. Once again, however, the trouble is that it is not obvious where these banalities – the kind of rhetorical flourishes that often find their way into party political speeches about education (education, education[9]) – precisely get us in any useful practical terms. Indeed, it is not obvious that all of these alleged educational goals would always sit comfortably together. On the one hand, a life given over to tedious factory routine might well be considered economically productive, but it is not obviously personally satisfying; on the other, the life of drug abuse and sexual promiscuity that this person finds personally satisfying could hardly be thought socially responsible. Thus, at the very least, such generalities require considerable further specification in the interests of some resolution of potential tensions. Indeed, it may well be thought that some of these tensions are actually *irresolvable*. Some such suspicion may be reinforced by those public disputes between so-called 'educational traditionalists' and proponents of so-called 'progressive' or 'child-centred' education – or (a different distinction) between those who emphasise the responsibilities of education to economic goals and those who stress its importance for personal growth and fulfilment – which may seem (literally) interminable. More profoundly, however, such suspicion also seems supported by the kind of reflection about the normativity of ideas of person, education and culture on which we have already briefly touched: given the diverse purposes of knowledge, and the different ways in which it can be valued in human life and experience, it ought not to occasion much surprise that there is serious disagreement about educational aims and goals.

Furthermore, on an even superficial view, the standard school curriculum seems to contain forms of knowledge, understanding and skill of rather diverse human significance and value. First, many of the subjects and skills that have found their way into past and present schools would appear to have been included on grounds of simple *usefulness*. Some subjects may have been included because they were considered personally useful for post-school individual functioning – for example, the home economics and woodwork that used to figure prominently (and usually respectively) in the education of British secondary school girls and boys. Others may have been included as indispensible to the *vocational* training of certain types (again often defined by ability) of learner – for example, auto-repair techniques or (especially in pre-information and communication technology eras) secretarial skills. However, it is usually possible to discover many other activities and skills in school curricula that are not in any of these senses *useful* – for example, the skills and activities of physical education and dance that feature on most school curricula. Of course, it is often insisted that such activites are *instrumentally* useful insofar as they can claim to be conducive to the general level of health and fitness of those who pursue them. But since the time allocated to physical education in most school curricula is seldom sufficient to improve health and fitness significantly, and it is anyway unclear why physical educationalists would not choose more fitness-efficient activities than hockey and ballet if that was all they were interested in, such arguments are not especially persuasive. The truth is that people often live long and full lives without engaging in physical activity of any kind (indeed, sport and games may actually damage the health) and that the main reason why people dance or play games is that they find them personally fulfilling – or, less pretentiously, just *fun*.

Just as clearly, however, educational curricula are bristling with subjects that are not only of little direct practical utility, but also not just matters of personal bent or predilection (nor even, for that matter, much fun). To be sure, some of these may be pursued as personal interests or passions in much the same way as sport or dance: just as some people may want to spend their leisure time, or even their entire lives, playing golf or engaging in creative dance, so others may devote themselves to reading great literature, writing poetry or performing in amateur or professional opera or theatre. All the same, one might also observe a significant difference between an interest in creative fiction, poetry and drama (in which category we might well include dance) and an interest in golf or football. Indeed, to put a finer point on it, it might be held that whilst it hardly affects one's standing as educated that one has never wielded a golf club or kicked a football, it surely would count against regarding someone as educated that he or she had never read a great novel or had no knowledge of drama or poetry. The point here would be that there is an internal or *conceptual* connection between educatedness and some knowledge of (more or less quality) literature that there is not between education and golfing skills. In this light, one might regard the arts in general as promoting the kind of civilised sensibilities that enable deeper insight into the human cultural, social and psychological condition and better understanding of ouselves, the world and our relations with others. To be sure, this point is not easy to state. For one thing, although the matter is sometimes put by saying that education in this sense is a route to human improvement, it is not always clear that such deeper insight makes people *morally* better – and physical educationalists have sometimes claimed an intrinsic connection between the playing of sports and moral development of a kind that (if it held) would yield more *fair* cricketers than poets.[10] But in one familiar sense of educational improvement – that which focuses on development of *understanding* of ourselves and our condition – we may, on the face of it, be better served by a single reading of *King Lear* than by a thousand holes in one.

But, of course, there are yet clearer cases of time-honoured educational content – disciplines such as history, geography and biology – that have no obvious or direct practical utility for the great majority of those who study them. It is not obvious that we teach geography to young people so that they can find their way around – as we might, to be sure, teach them arithmetic and measurement so that they can count and measure things – and few of those to whom we teach the basics of biology or physics will be destined to enter the medical, technical or educational fields in which the knowledge and skills of these subjects are likely to be matters of routine employment. It is sometimes said that we need to teach history in order to avoid in the future the mistakes of the past, but this is to put a rather impossibly strained utilitarian gloss on such teaching – which probably owes more to the instrumentalist logic of many latter-day curriculum planners that requires us to say what a subject is *for*, than to any real sane and sensible appreciation of the human value of history. Indeed, it is far from clear that a keen appreciation of history has been particularly effective in preventing either nations or individuals from repeating their mistakes – but even if it was so effective, it could hardly be our best reason for teaching history. Despite this, there is surely a strong intuitive case for including history – perhaps along with literature – in the education of *all* young people. Thus, though it is not implausible to conceive an education without hockey or golf, or not easy to defend compulsory advanced biology or higher mathematics beyond the stages of basic nature study and numeracy, it is arguable that some form of history should continue to be part of a young person's education throughout their formal schooling. History, extending more broadly into social, modern and human studies, seems crucial to educated sensibility – and so if education is a *lifelong* process, as often alleged, it must also be of enduring interest to the educated and self-educating adult. But what grounds could one have for claiming the educational significance for all pupils of a subject that has only clear practical utility for the handful of pupils who are likely to become history teachers? If history is not useful in this readily intelligible sense, what is it *for*?

The purposes of education and learning

It would be hard to exaggerate the difficulties that confusion over the meaning of the simple preposition 'for' – particularly the failure to appreciate that there is a significant non-instrumental use of 'for' – has created for educational philosophy in general and for the business of curriculum planning in particular. The chief confusion is a muddling of what might be called *instrumental* and non-instrumental or *teleological* senses of 'for'. It is not uncommon, even in mainstream philosophy, to find these senses run together – perhaps partly because one of the most famous ethical theories (utilitarianism) is *both* a teleological and an instrumental theory: utilitarians *define* goodness in terms of the beneficial outcomes or consequences of actions.[11] But the teleological and instrumental senses in which A may said to be *for* B are nevertheless distinct and separable. Suppose, in asking what creative dance is for, one is told that it concerns the symbolic expression of feelings or ideas in patterns of human movement. However, a famous dancer asked the same question replies that creative dance is for him a means of making easy money, enjoying a comfortable lifestyle and achieving many sexual conquests. Do these different replies express different (and rival) answers to the same question about what dance is for? Of course not: for they are clearly different answers to effectively *different* questions. The first answers the question about what dance is for by indicating what the *purpose* of dance is: it constitutes a *teleological* justification. The second answer addresses a question about individual motives for personally pursuing dance: it offers an instrumental *justification*. This, by the way, is a site of widespread confusion in other areas of philosophy – for example, sexual ethics. Some defenders of traditional moral objections to homosexuality – or, for that matter, heterosexual promiscuity or non-reproductive sexual practices – defend this position on the grounds that sexuality is essentially *for* reproduction.[12] Now whether or not this is an ethically defensible view, it is crucial to see the irrelevance of any reply to the effect that people engage in sexual activity for all sorts of reasons *besides* reproduction (pleasure, love, control or whatever) – since it rests on the same *equivocation* over the word 'for'. Since the sexual conservative is expressing a teleological (and biologically accurate enough) point about what sexuality is for, any (sociological) observation to the effect that this is not why many people engage in it is largely beside the point. In the same vein, if I say that cricket bats are meant for hitting cricket balls, but you insist that you use them for bludgeoning people to death in dark alleys, we are responding to quite different questions about what cricket bats are *for*.[13]

This distinction between teleological and instrumental justifications is related to, though not coextensive with, the not entirely fortuitous distinction of postwar pioneers of analytical educational philosophy between *intrinsic* and *extrinsic* value.[14] Basically, that distinction aimed to show that there are reasons for the pursuit of activities and projects that focus more on intrinsic features of those enterprises than on considerations of individual or social benefit and/or motive. Whereas some activities are chosen and pursued for the instrumental and perhaps contingent benefits they confer on the pursuer – I opt to specialise in business studies because I can see a lucrative career in the offing – others are pursued because we discern a value in them that relates more to a non-instrumental view of their worth. But on what could this sense of value rest and why would it be non-instrumentally compelling? One attraction of the distinction between extrinsic or instrumental value and intrinsic value (or value for its own sake) is that it seems to have real *motivational* bite: no human agent could live his or her entire life on the basis of instrumental motivation, since any chain of instrumental justifications must *logically* end somewhere with something I do for its own sake rather than for that of a further thing.[15] However, the difficulty is not just that the idea of intrinsic value does not on the face of it offer us a *common* human motivation – since people value widely differing things for their own sake – but that many of the interests and activities that people do value for their own sake are not the sort of things that would be educationally desirable. From this viewpoint, the trouble with the distinction between extrinsic and intrinsic value is that it is ambiguous between the teleological and instrumental justification or *purpose* distinction, and that between intrinsic and extrinsic *motivation*. Having (rightly) recognised that we have motives for action that are linked to an appreciation of non-instrumental purposes of activities – expressed in the distinction between intrinsic and extrinsic value – it is tempting to seek a form of intrinsic motivation invariably associated with what is of intrinsic worth. Postwar analytical philosophers of education located this in a general human commitment to *rationality* – the idea that as rational agents we cannot without self-contradiction reject what we see as educationally valuable forms of knowledge and understanding.[16] The trouble is, of course, that rational agents can and do evade commitment to such knowledge – and that confusion of intrinsic worth with intrinsic motivation issues in an attempt to prove too much.

The important kernel of truth in the alleged connection between intrinsic value and education is that the capacity to value things for their own sake is arguably a *necessary* condition of educatedness. However, it is equally obviously *neither* a necessary *nor* a sufficient condition of the *educational value* of a subject or activity that it is valued for its own sake – for one can intrinsically value activities that have no educational significance (such as gin-soaked sun worshipping), and a subject or activity can have educational value without being valued for its own sake. In what, then, does educatedness more fully reside? The best we can so far say is that to be educated is to come to appreciate or value for their own sake the non-instrumental or teleological (intrinsically valuable) features of those forms of knowledge, understanding and skill for which a reasonable educational case has or can be made. At first sight, of course, this seems hopelessly question begging: the definition (if such it is) quite blatantly assumes what it is supposed to be defining. However, if we recall that we have already said a good deal about the key role of education in the initiation of young people into identity or person-constitutive aspects of the best of human culture, there may be more conceptual mileage here than immediately meets the eye. For, in this light, education is clearly both more and less than equipping young people with the knowledge, understanding and skills that may be useful (vocationally, healthfully or therapeutically) to them in adult life: it is *more* because young people could come to master and exercise such skills without ever valuing them for their own sake, and it is *less* because at least some of the subjects and activities that are acquired for their instrumental value have few or no non-instrumental person-constitutive features.

On this view, education concerns the pursuit for their own sake of a range of personally formative modes of knowledge, understanding and skill of which history provides as good an example as any other – though other arts and sciences provide equally plausible examples. One should recognise that any of these forms of knowledge might be valued *other than* educationally – for example, as means to technical achievement, for vocational purposes, or for the winning of cash prizes on game shows. Hence any *educational* appreciation of such forms of knowledge or activity would be a matter of relating to them in ways not entirely reducible to considerations of practical utility. In essence, it is coming to see that such forms of knowledge, understanding or skill are more *constitutive* features of personhood than contingent or disposable commodities of individual and social consumerism. From this viewpoint, nothing worth calling an historical *education* could be just an initiation into a body of historical facts – as, to be sure, the history we learn at school is all too often just a body of remote facts – but would need to be a *meaningful* engagement with those aspects of our cultural heritage and traditions without which we could hardly understand who we are or might aspire to be. Moreover, in the absence of appreciation of such non-instrumental person-constitutive dimensions of knowledge, understanding and skill – those features that enable us to understand ourselves, the world around us and our relations with others – it must remain well nigh incomprehensible why so many artistic and scientific subjects and activities with little or no ultimate practical utility to the the majority of learners have found a time-honoured place in most past and present school curricula.

Education, schooling and curriculum

All that has so far been said, of course, may be taken as a reconstruction of that admittedly rarified concept of education of early postwar analytical philosophy, which was grounded in a recognition of the difference between educational and such other processes of human development as socialisation, vocational training and (psycho)therapy.[17] The defence of certain forms of knowledge and understanding as educationally valuable in and of themselves rests mainly on appreciation of the different goals of these diverse enterprises, and of the different roles that knowledge plays in the course of their pursuit. On this view, it is usually claimed that one cannot readily ask for an external or extrinsic justification of education in the same way that one might seek for an extrinsic justification – in terms of house training, economic growth or mental heath – of socialisation, vocational training and (psycho)therapy. In short, it is tantamount to bad logical grammar to ask what one has been educated *for*, as one might coherently ask what someone has been (vocationally) trained or (psychologically) treated for. This is also what gives substance to the idea that *if* education *is* valued (and, of course, it may not be), it will have to be valued non-instrumentally or for its own sake, rather than for some external goal – and fits neatly with the point that what education in itself *is* is what (teleologically) distinguishes its purposes and goals from those of such other processes as socialisation, training or (psycho)therapy. However, on this view, it seems as odd to claim that the *aim* of education is to develop knowledge and understanding for its own sake as it is to say that the aim of fishing is try to catch fish – because just as trying to catch fish is not something we aim to do by means of fishing, but just what fishing *means*, so developing knowledge and understanding (in the idenity-constitutive sense lately identified) is not something we aim to do by means of education, but just what education means.[18]

All the same, any such rehabilitation of the postwar analytical conception of education as the non-instrumental pursuit of knowledge and understanding may appear to be not without problematic consequences or implications. One of these that has indeed proved troublesome follows from the thought that if the prime purpose of the school curriculum is to *educate* pupils and education is a matter of initiation into forms of knowledge and understanding that can be valued for their own sake, then there can be little place in the curriculum for subjects and skills that cannot be so conceived. This is not inconsistent with the idea that many of the non-instrumentally valuable forms of knowledge and understanding to be found in the school curriculum might *also* be valued as instrumentally (vocationally or therapeutically) worthwhile – but it does greatly reinforce a tendency towards what I shall here call *non-instrumentalism* in educational theorising. Non-instrumentalist educational theorising, indeed, has distinguished precedents in the work of past educational philosophers. For example, Matthew Arnold, who might fairly be considered the founding father of modern liberal traditionism, strongly argued against the *instrumentalism* of his nineteenth-century utilitarian contemporaries, which held that the fundamental purpose of even popular education should be to equip individuals with the values, virtues and sensibilities of civil and civilised association.[19] From this viewpoint, he was greatly inclined to reverse the standard utilitarian estimate of literature, the arts and other culturally significant studies as of secondary educational importance to economically productive scientific and technical skills. For Arnold, insofar as the subjects with the best claim to non-instrumental value should form the core of education, they would also have a privileged claim to inclusion in the school curriculum – though, of course, he did not entirely deny the importance of vocational training for socio-economic ends.

However, the modern form of this educational non-instrumentalism, developed some three decades ago by analytical philosophers of education, seems to have been even more radically non-instrumentalist than its nineteenth-century precedent. Thus, on one highly influential version of this new non-instrumentalism[20] it was argued that the heart of education is *intellectual* and that the school curriculum should be primarily concerned to promote rational initiation into a number of fundamental 'logically distinct' forms of knowledge and understanding (sometimes identified as the logical and/or mathematical, the scientific, the aesthetic and/or artistic, the moral, the religious, the human or social scientific and the philosophical). Yet more tellingly, insofar as education ought to be 'based on the nature and significance of knowledge itself, and not on the predilections of pupils, the demands of society, or the whims of politicians',[21] the task of determining the educational content of the curriculum would be exclusively a matter for professional educationalists. Hence, although the authors of this conception also did not deny the socio-economic importance of vocational training, the message was clear enough: the curricular content of schooling is not significantly answerable to the non-educational socio-economic, therapeutic or other interests of non-professional private or public agencies. Moreover, given the considerable professional and even political influence that this conception of education for a time wielded, the literature of curriculum justification that proliferated in the wake of such philosophising bears witness to the paranoia that such non-instrumentalism generated among teachers of subjects not so easily justifiable in non-instrumental terms. Many teachers of activities whose non-instrumental educational value was not notably transparent – not least in such fields as physical education, which could not claim much instrumental and/or vocational worth either – felt under some political and professional pressure to demonstrate, in sometimes rather improbable ways, that their subjects were intrinsically valuable intellect-enhancing forms of knowledge and understanding.[22]

But such non-instrumentalist thinking has also been seen as a wildly improbable view of the proper purposes and content of schooling. Indeed, despite the objections of Matthew Arnold and his modern-day heirs to the view that vocational and socio-economic concerns should always play a secondary educational fiddle, it should occasion little surprise that state educational policy making in most competitive past and present economies has more often been dominated by a utilitarian or *instrumentalist* mindset. Thus, in postwar Britain, non-instrumentalism flourished mainly during a relatively brief period of social optimism and economic expansion – marked also by the construction of the British welfare state – which rapidly came to be regarded as very much outwith what the nation could afford. It might therefore have been predicted that the eventual overstretching (in Britain and elsewhere) of welfare provision, and the onset of postwar economic downturn, would usher in more hard-headed perspectives on the accountability or otherwise of schooling and education to socio-economic goals: if any economy was going to operate effectively in an increasingly competitive global market, then it needed a skilled workforce that it was surely the prime duty of schools and other educational institutions to provide. Indeed, well in advance of these events, the new educational non-instrumentalism had already come under attack from different educational theoretical directions. First, advocates of popular education and sociologists of knowledge (despite their other differences) held that the new liberal traditionalism was too elitist and/or middle-class and that forms of knowlege curricula unreasonably exalted the intellectual or academic over the practical and useful.[23] Secondly, new educational philosophical utilitarians[24] argued that there was no such thing as knowledge and understanding for its own sake, and that the acid test of fitness for inclusion of any subject or activity in the school curriculum should be social or economic utility: education should be seen as a *means* to an end, not as an end in itself.

However, on a critical view of this rather polarised debate between educational instrumentalism and non-instrumentalism, it is hard to avoid an impression of serious confusion and cross-purposes: indeed, I believe that this debate perfectly exemplifies the sort of issue that stands to benefit from some good old-fashioned clarification of basic terms. Where, then, should we look for the confusions? First, the basic non-instrumentalist claim – that education, as a matter of initiation into intrinsically valuable forms of rational knowledge and understanding, is an end in itself – seems right enough. However, the instrumentalist counter-claim that schools, as institutions supported by the taxpayer, are publicly and politically accountable to larger socio-economic concerns seems equally hard to gainsay. But if both these claims are true, they can hardly be in conflict. In order to see what generates the appearance of conflict, we have only to suppose someone claiming – as people can sometimes be heard to claim – *either* that schooling is a matter of initiation into forms of knowledge and understanding for their own sake, *or* that education is a means to the promotion of socio-economic growth. But in fact anyone who made *these* claims would be mistaken on *both* counts: just as it is not (at all) the purpose of education to serve economic ends, so it is not the (exclusive) function of schools to promote a love of knowledge for its own sake.

In short, the key muddle in which debates between instrumentalists and non-instrumentalists are embroiled – an error that constantly reoccurs in various guises in a great deal of public, political and professional debate about the purposes of education – is basically a confusion between *education* and *schooling*.[25] Schooling is, of course, a social institution that is provided for out of public funds, and is to that extent accountable to the desires of taxpayers and their democratically elected political representatives. Among the many things that the average taxpaying parent will require from schools is that they equip their offspring with the sort of skills that will enable them to become responsible, productive and financially successful members of society. However, what will also be desired by many parents is that their offspring acquire the sort of educated understanding of themselves, the world and their relations with others that enables autonomous recognition and pursuit for their own sake of interests and projects of intrinsic satisfaction and value: for what would be the point of capacities to earn a comfortable living in the absence of those aesthetic, scientific, spiritual or social and political interests and passions that can provide reasons for living? But education thus construed is not a social institution or a process like schooling that we undergo for a period of time in a particular location. Thus, in one sense, education is *more* than schooling: we can speak meaningfully of lifelong education or learning, but not so sensibly of lifelong schooling. From this viewpoint, the relationship between education and schooling is comparable to that between religion and church, or justice and the legal system. Indeed, just as someone might claim to be religious without being a churchgoer, it makes perfect sense for someone to claim that he or she is educated despite never having been to school (as it is also not unintelligible to claim that wherever religion is encountered it is not in churches, or that justice is not to be found in the law courts). In fact, such shortfall between education and schooling has often been emphasised by radical critics of conventional schooling: the so-called 'deschoolers' of three or more decades ago precisely attacked the conventional state schooling of advanced economies on the grounds that it was indoctrinatory rather than educational.[26] But, in another sense, education (even in schools) is rather *less* than schooling. It can only be *part* of the business of the institution of schooling to initiate young people into an appreciation of the flower of worthwhile human literary, artistic and other achievements *for its own sake*: at the very same time as it renders unto God, schooling must render unto Caesar by equipping pupils with vocationally relevant skills – and the economy with the productive workforce – that conduce wealth-creation in a competitive market.

Education, theory and practice

All the same, it should be conceded that the distinction we have just observed between education and schooling – not least the distinction between education and (vocational or other) training that it seems to presuppose – would not be warmly received in many contemporary educational philosophical quarters. The main reason for this turns upon what we earlier in this chapter identified as the general 'practical' or anti-Cartesian turn in modern philosophy. In this connection, three apparent dialectical manoeuvres of early postwar educational philosophical analysis have attracted persistent criticism. The first is the already noted tendency to identify the difference between the educational and the non-educational with a distinction between activities and skills valuable in themselves and activities and skills valuable only as a means to an end. The second identifies the difference between activities and skills valuable in themselves and activities and skills valuable only as a means to an end with a distinction between the theoretical and the practical. The third identifies the theory–practice dichotomy with a distinction between the vocational and the non-vocational. However, it is clear that these crude conflations[27] will not do, and it is easy to find subjects and activities with a legitimate place in the school curriculum that do not at all fit this analysis. Initiation into morality and the arts is often as much a practical as a theoretical matter, but the educational potential of such initiation can hardly be doubted. Theoretical physics and archaeology may be vocational without being practical – or even especially useful. Hockey and football are pursuable for their own sake, but they are not obviously educational in the sense of (say) history or botany. Home economics, woodwork and aspects of health education are variously useful, but may be of little vocational use. And so on and so forth. Thus, in the light of the modern rejection of Descartes and the recognition that the normative aspects of human personhood are best understood in terms of initiation into complex human practices,[28] would it not be best to jettison all outdated distinctions of the above kind and simply regard education as a matter of initiation into any generally morally acceptable activities conducive to the pursuit of a person's purposes or projects?

I believe, however, that any such conclusion is both premature and mistaken. In the first place, it should be clear that abandonment of the distinctions is self-undermining – since, despite the criticisms to which certain received versions of them are vulnerable, it should be clear that any such criticism would itself be hardly possible without their employment: the task of the educational philosopher is not therefore to abandon such distinctions, but to sharpen them for more precise use. But, in the second place, we should recognise at least one important reason for observing some difference between education and other forms of principled understanding or practice – not least because some of the lately considered dualisms and distinctions have recently been opposed in the name of morally suspect conclusions about what is educationally suitable for some young people. Again, the argument seems to rest mainly on a rejection of any distinction of education from vocational training on the grounds that (i) since theory (principled reflection) is invariably implicated in practice, and (ii) practice is frequently a significant route to the understanding of theory, (iii) practically focused forms of vocational and other training may properly provide, for at least some young people, a valid 'practical education' that is equal to any 'academic' education.[29] On this view, it is little more than elitist prejudice to regard some forms of intelligent practice – woodwork or cuisine – as less educationally valuable than science or classic literature simply because they are practical and useful.

Since this argument ignores significant ambiguities in the idea that practice can be a source of theoretical understanding in the education of young people, however, it is simply fallacious. On the one hand, if it means that one effective way to teach pupils science is to engage them in practical experimentation rather than in the memorisation of laws and theorems, this, while true, indicates only another way of theoretical learning that does not support any substitution of hands-on practical experience for a proper intellectual appreciation of scientific principles. On the other hand, if it means that there are ways of learning skills that focus more (or as much) upon the acquisition of those principles that inform intelligent practice than upon the rote learning of practical procedures, this point also fails to license the substitution of such principled skill learning for more intellectual forms of understanding. In short, any such critique of the education–training distinction succeeds only by ignoring the very different roles which that principled understanding (however practically acquired) that constitutes scientific knowledge, and the grasp (however 'intellectual') of any principles that inform (say) effective hairdressing, play in personal formation. One cannot 'liberalise' home economics or invest volleyball with educational significance by a more precise articulation of the principles that enable us to engage in such activities intelligently, because they are simply not the right kind of principles. Moreover, it is surely the royal road to elitism or worse to argue that we might reasonably substitute a critical appreciation of cookery for a critical understanding of history in the education of some (usually less able) pupils.

This should serve to remind us, as I think the architects of modern liberal traditionalist non-instrumentalism were very anxious to show, that there is a cultural inheritance to which all young persons are entitled – irrespective of differences of ability, social background and vocational destiny – and into which it is therefore the sacred duty of schools to acquaint each and every child. Thus, although there are going to be skills and activities (such as literacy and numeracy) that *all* need to acquire because no modern person can adequately function without them, as well as skills (of auto-repair and secretarial work) that some but not all individuals will require for particular vocations, the different vocational destinies of children should not be allowed to undermine their common entitlement to proper initiation into the 'best that has been thought and said'. From this viewpoint, it is arguable that there are forms of human understanding that constitute universal educational requirements, and reasonable to suppose that although not all young people may possess the abilities required to pursue higher mathematics or quantum mechanics, all should – in the interests of the cultivation of civilised personal sensibilities – be afforded significant exposure to serious literary, historical, cultural and moral appreciation. This is not to deny that differences of individual ability, interest and background circumstances must have a bearing upon questions about how the design of the school curriculum should go, and on whether the same sort of educational exposure is ultimately suitable for all. These are questions, however, to which we shall need to return in subsequent chapters.

Possible tasks

(1) In the light of a distinction between education and schooling, identify a range of goals of individual development and social preparation that you think schooling might be reasonably concerned to achieve, as well as some of the curriculum areas or subjects conducive to the achievement of such goals

(2) Identify the reason or reasons you might give for including the following subjects or activities in the school curriculum, and consider whether you would want to include them for all or only some young people: (i) geography; (ii) algebra; (iii) woodwork; (iv) cookery; (v) netball; (vi) biology; (vii) dance; (viii) IT skills; (ix) English literature; (x) business studies.

Chapter 2

The complex character of teaching

Senses of teaching

Although education does not necessarily involve teaching, and there can be forms of teaching that are not especially educational, teaching is nevertheless clearly enough a strongly educationally implicated notion. In this respect, of course, we should first observe that the term 'teaching' is ambiguous, and that in order to get clearer about the relationship of teaching to education, we may therefore need to distinguish rather different uses of the expression. For example, insofar as 'Has she been in teaching long?' and 'Has she been long in education?' are in *some* contexts much the same question – as, again, are the questions 'Where was she educated?' and 'Where was she taught?' – senses of 'teaching' and 'education' may sometimes coincide. All the same, there are other contexts in which such terms do not appear at all synonymous: for example, whereas it seems natural enough to say 'Please don't bother me while I'm teaching' or 'I must try to improve my teaching', it seems less appropriate to say 'Please don't interrupt me while I'm educating' or 'I must brush up my educating'. Even these nuances of usage, moreover, are sufficient to yield *three* fairly distinct senses of 'teaching'. First, then, to ask 'Where was she taught?', in the sense of 'Where was she educated?', is to regard teaching as more or less identical with the *practice* of education as discussed in the previous chapter. However, to ask 'Has she been in teaching long?', in the sense of 'Has she been long employed in education?', is to conceive teaching more as a particular sort of occupation or *role* – a profession or vocation perhaps – which might or *might not* be conducive to the goals of education as we have so far characterised these. Finally for now (for this is not to deny the possibility of other further significant senses of teaching), in saying 'Please don't bother me while I'm teaching', teaching would appear to be regarded as a particular datable episode or *activity* in which it is possible for me to engage for a particular period of time – with or without interruption.[1]

Furthermore, although these different *practice*, *role* and *activity* senses of teaching may often go hand in hand – as a member of the teaching profession, I may indeed be concerned to promote the ends of teaching *qua* education via the activity or processes of teaching – they may also come apart in significant ways. First, for example, a quite small child might teach her young sister to perform a simple skill – tying her own shoelaces perhaps – without being either much concerned with the practice of education (at any rate, in the more special sense of this term aired in the previous chapter), or (obviously enough) a member of the teaching profession. In short, she is a teacher in the activity sense, but the role and practice senses hardly seem to come into it. Secondly, a certificated teacher in the role sense, who is also concerned with overall promotion of the educational enterprise, might be little occupied with teaching as an activity. On the one hand, as either headteacher or head of department, such a teacher may be concerned with administrative or pastoral duties to the virtual exclusion of actual practical teaching. On the other hand, perhaps more controversially, it may be that some practising teachers do not much engage in teaching as an overt *activity* – at least on a narrower but common enough sense of teaching as a matter of explicit instruction. Indeed, some might argue that much good teaching in the practice and role senses is a more a function of judicious *refraining* from direct intervention (facilitating self-directed learning, allowing space for creativity, or whatever) than of up-front communication or demonstration – and it is sometimes complained that such non-intervention is something that teachers as professionals are not particularly good at, to the general educational detriment of those they teach. Thirdly, it would appear that there are professional teachers (at least in the sense that they do it for a living) who engage in teaching activity, but who are nevertheless not much concerned with the promotion of *education* in the broader sense considered in the previous chapter. Many private teachers of piano or coaches of gymnastics, for example, are concerned with instruction in certain fairly narrowly defined skills of a sort that might make us reluctant to regard them as teachers in any more robust educational sense of wider personal formation (although they might still, for all that, merit our proper respect as professionals).

But fourthly, it would appear that there is a fairly common use of the term 'teaching' in something like the *educational* sense, which is not obviously – or only dubiously – connected with either the role or the activity senses. Thus, if we think of the many famous historical figures who have commonly been regarded as great teachers – Jesus, Socrates, Gandhi, Buddha, Confucius, Muhammad, Marx or Freud – few of these would appear to have had any occupational or professional connection with teaching. Indeed, even in the cases of those individuals – Jesus and Socrates are clear enough examples – who do seem to have spent much of their time actually engaged in the activity of teaching, it seems doubtful whether they would have regarded themselves as professional teachers on that account. (In this respect, it seems just as odd to think of Jesus as a teacher because he sometimes taught, as it would be to regard him as a doctor because he sometimes cured the sick.) If anything, indeed, both Jesus and Socrates were inclined to contrast (unfavourably) the work of teachers operating in more official professional or other ccupational capacities with their own more informal pedagogical efforts.[2] But yet more tellingly, we need not suppose that even those past teachers who did engage in the activity of teaching would have had to perform it *well* (although this is also not to say, of course, that they did not do so) in order to have won lasting fame as great teachers. One can also think of actual examples of enormously influential modern thinkers, who are or were indeed teachers by profession, but who nevertheless enjoyed less than enviable reputations as teachers in the performance sense.[3] Moreover, still other great past and present thinkers will have wielded greatest pedagogical influence through their literary works, or through the books about them of their followers, pupils and disciples, rather than through any of their own face-to-face teaching. Thus, to the extent that much great teaching seems to be at least as much, if not more, a matter of *what* someone has to say as of *how* they say it, we might look for good teaching in the *content* no less than in the form of what is taught. At all events, it seems possible to regard some as great teachers in the *educational* sense who are hardly if at all teachers in the *role* or *activity* senses. I also believe that this is a point that needs to be borne firmly in mind, not least in view of enormous contemporary pressure (possibly in the light of a certain latter-day scepticism about the objectivity of human knowledge and values) to conceive teaching more in (the sophistical) terms of activity and process than content.

Teaching as activity and performance

Still, since wider questions about the aims and content of education are revisited throughout this work – and the next chapter will be explicitly concerned with questions of the occupational (professional or other) status of teaching – we shall for the moment focus primarily upon the performative character of teaching. How, then, should we understand the activity or activities in which teachers engage with a view to the proper pursuit of the pedagogical project? In overall strategical terms, we should first notice – as we did in reflecting upon education in the previous chapter – that teaching is a *normative* concept: teaching is apt for appraisal as good or bad, effective or ineffective, according to more or less observable standards of success. From this viewpoint, any general question about what teaching as an activity *means* might be recast as an inquiry into what are ordinarily regarded as the *criteria* of *good* or practically effective, as opposed to not so good or ineffective, teaching. In order to address this issue, however, it might first seem reasonable to try to identify the main goals of teaching, as well as the sorts of failures that might lead us to question the efficacy of any teaching methods adopted to secure such goals. In this light, indeed, we might well begin by characterising teaching – as educational philosophers have fairly routinely characterised it – as an intentional or deliberate attempt to bring about *learning*.[4] So, on the face of it, standards of good teaching would appear to be indexed fairly directly – if not, indeed, in straightforward causal or *productive* terms – to the production of effective learning: on this view, successful teaching would simply be whatever issued in successful learning. However, I believe that a question of some importance here – one that is all too rarely raised in discussions of this issue – is whether the respects in which one's teaching is liable to fail are of all of a normative piece: more specifically, we might ask, is pedagogical success or effective teaching always measurable by the standards of causal or technical effectiveness?

This might be regarded as rather an odd question. Indeed, it might appear difficult to *conceive* how standards of good teaching could be anything other than the standards of causal or technical effectiveness – and, in fact, I suspect that this has been the position of many professional educational theorists and policy makers for much of the recently departed century. This viewpoint, moreover, has a certain simple (if specious) lucidity. Suppose that it is our intention to bring about a particular piece of learning – for example, a child's mastery of a headstand. What is a headstand? Effectively, it is a behavioural skill analysable as a sequence of physical events. Moreover, we can (roughly) identify the main constituent events as: (a) positioning the (fore)head on the mat; (b) placing the hands to form a triangle with the head; (c) raising the body from the floor; (d) vertical elevation of the body. What then would it be to teach a headstand effectively? Arguably, it amounts to little more than having ensured that a proper appreciation of this causally ordered sequence of events is logically or coherently reflected in one's instruction. Indeed, it would appear at least necessary for any effective learning of this skill that one's teaching embraces a sequence of instruction (saying or showing) of roughly the form: do (a), do (b), do (c), now do (d). In short, insofar as learning may be understood in terms of the acquisition of this or that more or less complex skill – which it obviously can be for much of the time – then teaching can *itself* be understood as a skill: namely, as a skill that is productive of other skills. On this view, moreover, it is a skill that can itself be *taught* and learned like other skills, and it is the main if not the sole purpose of any professional training of teachers to be concerned with the promotion and acquisition of such skills (via, one supposes, the practice of certain higher-order or meta-skills of teaching the skills of teaching).[5]

One obvious appeal of this instrumental or technicist conception of teaching as a 'skill-promoting skill' is that it seems often to be linked to a basically natural scientific conception of learning as the acquisition of adaptive behaviour. From this viewpoint, indeed, the development of behavioural theories of learning in the early twentieth century was warmly welcomed by some very famous educational names[6] precisely because it finally seemed to offer the possibility of placing education on a respectable scientific footing: it was held that if human learning could be construed as just another matter for scientific inquiry, then it might be but a short further step to empirical testing of the effectiveness of those pedagogical processes through which we promote learning. On this view, learning and teaching are not just behavioural processes, they are also processes that can be identified, modified and refined in the light of scientific research and experiment: educational theory is also thereby conceivable as a branch of empirical scientific theory. Another consequence of this, we should note, is that authority or expertise with regard to what is to count as good teaching shifts from the realms of professional practice to the academy. On the face of it, it is educational researchers in universities rather than field professionals who are best placed to determine effective educational method – and, on this view, the teaching of even experienced teachers is subject to the 'external' authority of experts. Moreover, there can be no doubt of the potential political implications of this explicitly top-down technocratic view of teaching expertise – and it is no accident that such conceptions have been grist to the mill of politically centralist attempts to control the activities of teachers in schools. In this connection, the currently fashionable *competence* models of professional preparation, which have had much influence on recent policy making in relation to teacher education, have two noteworthy features. First, such models are clearly traceable to the sort of scientific approaches to pedagogy just considered: they are predicated (however much this is denied) on the idea that professional expertise is reducible to a set of discrete experimentally testable behaviours. Secondly, the promotion of such models has mostly been politically rather than professionally motivated: precisely, they have been supported mainly by those whose interest lies in securing the accountability of teachers to centrally prescribed norms.[7]

Teaching and skill

Whatever difficulties some may have had in conceiving pedagogical expertise in other than such scientific-technical terms, however, such a conception might also appear to be ill-starred from the outset. Indeed, there are so many possible objections to the scientific-technical conception of pedagogy as skill-acquisition that it is rather hard to know quite where to begin. Still, it may be useful to start with an initial distinction between: (i) those who would agree with technicists that pedagogy is essentially a matter of skill-acquisition – but disagree that the skills in question are primarily technical abilities identified on the basis of scientific inquiry or research; and (ii) those who would be disinclined to regard the activity of teaching as primarily or necessarily – or, at the very least, as exhausted by – the acquisition of skills as such at all. The first sort of position is probably more common. Indeed, in this connection (if not perhaps in both connections) one might first observe that the pedagogical reputation and/or expertise of many historically renowned teachers – again we might mention Jesus, Socrates or Gandhi – could hardly have rested upon their training in scientific research-validated skills. Hence, at the very least, even if it were to be insisted that such individuals were *innately* endowed with skills that *might* nevertheless be scientifically validated, it would not appear that any such scientific-technical training would be *necessary* for their acquisition, mastery or exercise. But, of course, if we were asked to guess what made Jesus and Socrates great teachers (divine inspiration aside), we might also want to deny that it was primarily a matter of their systematic deployment of *any* skills or strategies of the sort usually held to be disclosed by empirical research.

There are of course various respects in which the practical teaching methods or procedures of memorable teachers might be considered at odds with any general research-based approach to the systematic understanding of pedagogical method. First, on the basis of much recent work on professional pedagogical expertise,[8] it would seem that any research into teaching by 'external' educational researchers rather than field professionals faces something of a dilemma. The basic trouble is that if such research seeks to be of *universal* value to any and all practitioners, it must aim for a level of generality that considerably prescinds from the specificities of particular contexts of practice. In so doing, however, any conclusions about teaching to which such research gives rise are likely to be of an order of abstraction or banality that can have little or no useful application to actual classroom practice. This would seem to be so even of any general advice to teachers that they should employ a mixed economy of teaching approaches or styles (rather than a single preferred one). It is all very well advising teachers that they need to vary their teaching approaches between direct instruction, inquiry, discussion and activity (or whatever): the trouble is that – beyond these common-places (which all professionals worth their salt may fully appreciate) – what teachers really need to know is how to balance these teaching modes appropri-ately for precise deployment in particular contexts of learning – and this must surely depend upon the kind of judgements that only situated professionals could be in a proper position to make. Indeed, this point has lately been fairly strongly made.[9] It has precisely been insisted that since the pedagogical and other exper-tise of teachers is context-specific, *only* field professionals could be in a position to appreciate the precise nature of their own or their pupils' practical needs in this or that particular context, and so only such professionals could be well placed to research teaching. Hence the dilemma: on the one hand, insofar as the generali-ties of professional educational researchers ignore particular contextual features, they can be of little or no use to practitioners; on the other, if they are sensitive to the context, then they can have no very general professional relevance.

On this view, it is in the very nature of teaching expertise to be indexed to *particular* circumstances, and there is hardly anything of *general* interest that we can say about teaching method as such. Thus, good teachers are not those who apply off-the-peg strategies of pedagogy or management for the quasi-technical manipulation of this or that impersonal learning process, but those whose approach is characterised from the outset by sensitive interpersonal engagement with the unique needs and interests of particular human persons: the very best teachers are invariably remembered for their human touch, and their transac-tions with pupils are better conceived as *relationships* grounded in genuine care and concern for the particular interests and needs of others. Indeed, one might well picture the ideal teacher–learner interaction (whilst appreciating that any such ideal may be harder to acheive in some contexts than others) as a form of *conversation* in which pupils are encouraged to make sense of some aspect of their experience with the help of wiser or more experienced associates. This point, however, brings us to other respects in which a scientific or technological approach to the study of pedagogy apparently fails to capture the spirit of good or memorable teaching.

It seems to be another presupposition or dogma of scientific or technological approaches to understanding educational method that pedagogical research should disclose techniques that are not just *generally* but also *systematically* appli-cable in ways that conduce to the setting and attainment of pre-specifiable learning objectives. On this view, the aim would be to remove each and every margin of hazard and uncertainty from the business of learning by the optimal logical and/or causal ordering of this or that process of knowledge- or skill-acquisition. But beyond the relatively 'closed' processes involved in the learning of simple physical skills, it seems questionable whether it is possible to identify any such optimal learning strategies with respect to many if not most significant forms of knowledge and understanding. Is it really plausible to suppose that we could approach the learning of a particular period of British history as we might well approach the learning of a forward roll – by reducing it to a set of epistemic components into which a learner might be quasi-causally conditioned? To be sure, one fairly conspicuous problem with this strategy is that – in the case of historical knowledge – the most obvious candidates for any such componential analysis and/or causal conditioning are the *facts* of historical information; but any thought that historical (or other) *education* might proceed by way of such fact acquisition seems variously objectionable.

First (and it may nowadays be important to say this), although one cannot doubt that there *are* historical facts (for example, that the Battle of Hastings occured in 1066 or that Henry VIII had six wives), an *education* in history is just as obviously not a matter of mere memorising, but of *understanding* such facts. Moreover, in the case of historical understanding, we should appreciate that even hard facts are open to rival interpretation or explanation. But now, if historical education is a matter of understanding and interpretation, it is also a matter of *meaningful* learning – and it remains a persistent danger that such learning may be utterly sidelined by precisely the kind of analysis that reduces knowledge to such atomic elements as facts. Indeed, I have previously argued that even reductive analyses of apparently skills-based activities can fatally bypass meaningful appreciation:[10] thus, as we shall see more clearly in the next section, it is possible for physical activities to be taught as mere sequences of movement in the absence of any appreciation of the social, artistic or other ends and purposes that would normally give sense to their performance. However, there can just as clearly be meaningless teaching of the facts of history or religious knowledge that is no less educationally sterile than the meaningless teaching of physical activities. Someone might now complain, of course, that this only shows that there *can* be meaningless teaching on the basis of such reductive analysis – not that there *has* to be: might we not argue that although teaching that faithfully mirrors such componential analysis is certainly not a sufficient condition of educational learning, it is all the same a *necessary* one? There are reasons, however, for suspecting that it may not actually be necessary either.

First, leaving aside the evident chronological order of historical facts – after all, one can hardly deny that events happen before or after one another – it is not obvious with respect to many other academic subjects that there is any determinate order in which the *facts* as such would have to be learned: since the facts are just what require to be explained, there is no reason to suppose that this fact would as such have logical or causal priority over that one. What one might more plausibly claim with regard to some academic subjects is that there are relations of logical or causal priority between different levels of explanation, or approaches to making the facts more meaningful, and that insofar as education is about *explaining* or making sense of the world, any meaningful teaching of a subject would have to respect these explanatory considerations. But this is not entirely clear either. It is a commonplace of contemporary philosophy of science that even the apparently descriptive theories and hypotheses of natural science are in fact deeply interpretative, and often trade in suggestive but contestable metaphors and analogies: on this view, since there is much that is figurative and expressive at the heart of even scientific explanation, teachers may need to introduce students to scientific perspectives in a variety of imaginative and not unequivocally ordered ways. Moreover, if this is so even of empirical or (arguably) objectively descriptive inquiries, how much more will it not be so of more overtly evaluative and expressive inquiries? From this perspective, affording insight into history, religion or literature may be more a matter of constructing imaginative pictures, models and metaphors than of routinely following the prescribed pedagogical procedures of the learning maintenance manual. In this connection, indeed, what is most striking about such past great teachers as Jesus and Socrates is their deployment – not least in connection with understanding such complex and profound issues as the nature of justice and salvation – of not especially systematically connected parables, myths and fables in their efforts to enhance the understanding of their pupils and disciples. Thus, although we also need to be careful not to overstate this point – since there is also a real enough distinction between imaginative and incoherent teaching – it is not obvious that good teaching ever does, should or could proceed according to some single scientifically grounded pattern of correct pedagogical procedure.

These points should not, of course, be taken to undermine any claim that good teachers are possessors and utilisers of teaching *skills* – of, for example, clear communication and imaginative presentation: the point is more that it may be an error to construe such skills as the universally generalisable and technically systematic products or deliverences of scientific research. Rather, on this view, we may be better to regard such teaching skills as creative responses to the contextually defined demands of actual professional experience. Thus, insofar as we must speak generally, it might be nearer the mark to regard such responses more as *artistic* than technical skills: just as a good jazz musician is not someone who simply reproduces sounds with horn or keyboard in blind obedience to fixed and externally prescribed rules, but one whose techniques adapt and evolve in constant sensitive response to the needs of the musical moment, so a good teacher may be regarded as someone whose expertise is a matter of constant creative interplay with the needs and challenges of this or that particular pedagogical occasion. In that case, however, just as it seems absurd to set about the training of jazz musicians by attempting to establish empirically what makes jazz playing effective or meaningful, it may be no less mistaken to suppose that what makes good teaching effective or meaningful is something upon which we need to await the findings of objective scientific inquiry. Thus, although regarding teaching as an art is consistent with regarding it as a matter of *skill* – and hence as something that depends in a large part upon learning and experience for its effective cultivation – it is not to suppose that it would be learned in the manner that science-based techniques are learned. One significant consequence of any extreme version of this view, moreover, would seem to be that such skills are better acquired in the *field* rather than in the academic contexts of training institutions: indeed, the view that teaching is an art developed more through practical experience than research-based theory raises some rather awkward questions about the precise role of the academy in professional training.

How not to conceive teaching as a skill

However, a more radical objection would be that it is a mistake to think of the key features of good teaching in terms of *any* kind of skills. It might be suggested that the most striking pedagogical characteristics of such great teachers as Jesus and Socrates are a function more of authority, character and/or personality – perhaps of that hard-to-define quality that is sometimes referred to as *charisma*. From this viewpoint, indeed, authority seems as much related to *content* as process – mainly, in short, to having something of substance or importance to say – and therefore its importance, at most levels of education, can hardly be overstated. Indeed, at the levels of higher learning to which those of some academic and intellectual ability and/or maturity are drawn with a view to exploring the cutting edges of this or that branch of human inquiry, it might be considered enough for teaching to be regarded as exemplary that it just *is* cutting-edge. From this viewpoint, although we might understand what someone meant by saying, after having actually attended (for example) a Wittgenstein lecture, 'Well, he wasn't much of a teacher', there is another perfectly proper sense in which we could hardly consider him to have been other than among the finest philosophical teachers of all time. Moreover, we should not unduly worry over any incongruity between these different appraisals. What qualifies Wittgenstein as one of the greatest teachers just *is* the depth and seriousness of his philosophical achievement, and his extraordinarily widespread philosophical influence: in this light, it would be absurd to dismiss him as a teacher on the grounds that he often stammered or failed to use overheads. His students attended his lectures not to be entertained by his lively style, but to gain better philosophical insight from his revolutionary exploration of the issues. This is worth mentioning, because I think that some contemporary initiatives designed to improve the professional quality of teaching and learning in higher education have fallen foul of essentially this confusion – precisely by supposing that the quality of university teaching ought to be judged by the same sort of performance criteria that would certainly be relevant to the assessment of teaching in infant or primary schools.[11] This, however, is not obviously so. Thus, whilst conceding that there may always room for some improvement of the pedagogical performance of many university professors, one could scarcely sympathise with any attempt to remove a great scholar from his teaching post, merely on the basis of his or her expressive or communicational shortcomings.

Still, in addition to the sort of authority that derives from mastery of a given topic or discipline, there are clearly other dimensions of authority – of what is precisely called *charisma* – that are related more to character and personality, and hence more to the *process* than to the content of teaching and learning. Indeed, it would be hard to deny that character and personality are often of enormous significance for effective or successful teaching. A lively and colourful personality can make a large difference to the level of pupil interest and motivation, and force of character may be vital to maintaining good order and discipline in the often straitened educational circumstances of much compulsory state schooling: hence, however delicate the matter may be, teachers may be liable to criticism on grounds of either less than lively personality or less than forceful character. That said, the place of character and personality in teaching performance, and the relation of such qualities to teaching skill and technique, are evidently complex and sensitive issues. For a start, although it is no doubt best to construe either or both of character and personality as rough mixtures of nature and nurture, there are clearly professionally and educationally significant differences between these aspects of human demeanour. Indeed, although character and personality are undoubtedly connected, they are nevertheless also clearly separable: we can speak of someone as having much character but little or no personality – or vice versa.

Teaching, personality and character

First, let us consider personality. A generally open and optimistic outlook, or a deficient sense of humour, would seem to be features of personality rather than traits of character – and one mark of this is that it may well be futile, if not actually presumptuous, to criticise a teacher for lacking certain qualities of liveliness and expression in his or her presentation. Many perfectly admirable and well-intentioned people may be ineffective teachers, *precisely* because they are by nature or formation dull, humourless or lethargic people – or, perhaps, because they have irritating and/or readily imitable mannerisms. Among the most difficult situations that teaching supervisors are liable to face are those in which student teachers are clearly burning the midnight oil to achieve worthwhile educational results, but are patently failing to engage the cooperation of pupils on account of this or that feature of personality. It is at such points that teacher trainers will desperately resort to hoary old analogies between teaching and treading the boards in invariably vain attempts to give lifeless or uninspiring students some insight into how to enliven excruciatingly dull personal presentations. But however tempting it may be to address the problem of personally dull or lifeless teaching by appeal to such thespian analogies, the trouble is that teaching is *not* ultimately acting, but more a matter – arguably at this point more than any other – of being just who we are. Indeed, it is not clear that encouraging student teachers in the inauthenticity of pretending to be other than who they are is either a wise or potentially successful strategy: it may be both vain and hazardous to try to encourage the introvert teacher to be extrovert, or the lifeless teacher to be more animated. How, for example, might we advise a person who lacks humour to be more humorous? Indeed, it is not just that any such advice seems liable to dilemma: if those to whom we offer such advice really *do* lack a sense of humour, they can hardly appreciate the advice; but if they are able to take the advice, they should not really need it. The key point is surely more that a sense of humour – no less than an optimistic or charitable outlook – is *not* a *skill,* and is therefore not likely to be learned by (for example) practising the telling of jokes. Rather, it is a matter of understanding or appreciating the world and/or one's relations with others in a particular light (perhaps with some degree of ironic detachment). To this extent, although someone's personality can and may change – a gloomy or depressed person might well suddenly become a very different joyful or upbeat one – this is usually a matter of 'inside-out' personal (perhaps, in a real sense, religious) conversion, and less often a consequence of professional or other 'outside-in' training. Moreover, as already noticed, there is something rather invidious about criticising people for their lack of wit, sparkle or *joie de vivre* – in part because they may not be able to do much about it, but also partly because they are in a genuine sense *entitled* to their lack of optimism or wit, and it is really no-one's business but their own if they do so lack it. To be sure, I might well tell a close friend to snap out of it if she is depressed without any apparent cause – but I should also be prepared for her to tell me what to do with my advice. But even worse, criticising others for their colourlessness of personality is uncomfortably like telling them that they are physically unattractive – involving, as it does, much the same sort of *aesthetic* judgement – and it is therefore hard to envisage circumstances in which it might be done without some real offence.

Matters seem significantly otherwise with qualities of character. Admittedly, insofar as there may be no cut-and-dried answer to the question whether patience or dourness is a feature of personality or a trait of character, character may well be continuous with personality; but there are nevertheless positive character traits – temperance, courage, a sense of justice – where the difference is clear enough. Generally, indeed, character seems to be more a product of conscious or deliberate formation than personality: moreover, insofar as it is implicated in issues and considerations of responsibility, praise and blame, its presence or absence, strength or weakness, seems more a *moral* or *ethical* than an aesthetic matter. More particularly, character is usually held to be the seat of *virtues* and/or *vices* – which are proper objects of moral evaluation. In this respect, although not all virtues are necessarily or inevitably moral in and of themselves – there may be morally bad as well as good possessors of courage or endurance – agents are nevertheless regularly praised for their fortitude, charity and truthfulness, as well as routinely blamed for lacking such traits.[12] Moreover, although character is often by maturity a fairly dyed-in-the-wool affair, and there are clearly limits to what agents can do by way of self-modification in this respect, it may yet not be out of place to advise a teacher struggling with discipline to exercise more mettle or backbone: indeed, to insist that 'You must really put your foot down with this bunch' may be no more inappropriate than advising someone to put more effort into lesson preparation. But is this not just another way of saying – is it not, to be sure, one of the things that one might be likely to say in such circumstances – that what a good teacher may need to acquire and exercise for the sake of good order are certain skills of discipline or management?

In fact, it is not obvious that this *is* the most appropriate thing to say. On the one hand, of course, the notion that qualities of character are little more than skills is upheld or reinforced by the consideration that – unlike many features of personality – such qualities seem more *acquired* than innate. Moreover, any recognition that they are implicated in the discourse of responsibility, praise and blame also presupposes that agents who have acted from less than good character ought to have, or might well have, behaved other than they did. In this regard, it is well known that Aristotle compared the acquisition of virtues to skills, insofar as it seems to make some sense to regard the former, like the latter, as at least partly acquired through training and practice.[13] But, on the other hand – through his influential distinction between *phronesis*, or moral wisdom, and the productive reason of *techne* – Aristotle also makes much of the profound differences between virtues and skills.[14] From this perspective, qualities of character like courage and justice seem, like features of personality, to be more constitutive of *personhood* than particular actions or skills. Thus, criticising agents for failures of skill – for example, for making a mess of the plumbing – is not necessarily, if at all, to criticise them as *persons*: indeed, I might well appreciate that they were doing their best and could *not* have done any better. To criticise agents for failures of courage, self-control or fairness, however, is to criticise them personally on the grounds that they *could* and *should* have done better. In his *Nicomachean Ethics*, Aristotle actually expresses more or less this distinction in a rather different way by saying that whereas any *intentional* commission of a mistake in a technical performance is a sign of the *superior* craftsman, any deliberate moral transgression on the part of agent is a sign of an *inferior* moral agent.[15]

Still, it might now be said that although this point calls into question any exhaustive reduction of virtues to skills, it need not undermine any conception of virtues as involving a significant element of skill or *techne*. If we cannot completely reduce a virtue such as steadfastness or resolution to skill, it could still be held that good discipline requires *both* firmness of (moral) character *and* (technical) skills of management: in that case, a teacher failing to maintain discipline might be criticised on grounds of *either* lack of firmness *or* ineffective management – or *both*. But there are considerations – from, as it were, a virtue-ethical perspective – that might persuade us that even this semi-technicist way of thinking about good discipline is barking up the wrong tree. To begin with, it can be argued that since authority and discipline are *inherently* normative (specifically ethical) notions, it is simply mistaken to suppose that we can separate the technical from the moral in any such clear-cut way. I was once told of a teacher in a grammar school for boys who would burst into tears and sob uncontrollably whenever his pupils misbehaved: at that point, so the story goes, the pupils would say to each other in a spirit of deep contrition: 'That's it lads, we've upset him – let's stop it now.' I cannot see the least reason to doubt the veracity of this story – or, at any rate, to suppose that if it did not happen, it could not.

But true or false, the story seems instructive in at least two significant respects. First, this route to class control was or is clearly not a *generalisable* technique: whereas it might well work in some circumstances, one can imagine others in which it would be plain suicide. Secondly, it is not obviously a *technique* as such at all: insofar as the response 'worked', it was more probably because the teacher was expressing *genuine* distress at the misbehaviour and because the liking and respect in which the boys held him meant that they were sincerely moved by the hurt they had caused. Thus, even without denying that class control can sometimes go awry because teachers have not mastered certain pedagogical or organisational strategies, the truth is that: (i) the heart of good discipline is more a matter of 'internal' moral association or ethos than of any such managerial techniques; and (ii) it is not at all clear that we could conceive such relevant strategies independently of the values that constitute the moral ethos or climate.

However, it might be even more strongly suggested that since authority and discipline are inherently moral rather than technical relations, it is not just misleading but dangerously distortive to construe them in the instrumental terms of skill, technique and management. On the face of it, any independently conceived management techniques may be neither necessary nor sufficient for effective discipline: the deployment by teachers of such management skills may do little to improve authority or discipline (indeed, although it is possible that such deployment might make a dire situation better, it is also conceivable that it might make matters worse) and there may be fairly disorganised teachers with little or no interest in such skills who are able to maintain exemplary discipline. Hence, on this stronger view, classroom relations between teachers and pupils – as distinct from (at least some) relations between factory owners and workers or prison guards and inmates – ought to be characterised by interpersonal qualities of respect, care and trust *rather than* by those of impersonal direction, coercion and control. As already noted, it is arguable that good teachers are generally memorable more for their personal qualities of virtue and character than their managerial efficiency: they are invariably those to whom young people can turn with complete confidence, and on whom they can always rely for unfailing academic and personal help and support. From this viewpoint, there are obvious dangers in encouraging young teachers to conceive of classroom discipline more (or worse exclusively) in terms of managerial or organizational skills[16] than of such moral or interrelational virtues or characteristics as care, trust(-worthiness) and respect: indeed, the erosion of appropriate morally grounded educational authority and discipline may be one casualty of some unfortunate modelling of teacher professionalism on inappropriate occupational comparisons from commerce and industry.

Teaching and virtue

But there is an even stronger case for conceiving not just capacities for authority and discipline but *all* aspects of teaching as an activity on the model of *virtues* rather than skills. Indeed, we shall shortly undertake more detailed analysis and exploration of the educational implications of the distinction between the moral or evaluative deliberations of virtue and the technical reasoning of skills. The essential point, however, is that while it would be fool-hardy to deny *any* significant professional role to technical notions of skill in good educational practice, notions of skill and technique – at least on a certain common narrow construal of these as a largely routinised modes of productive instrumentality – cannot even begin to capture what is involved in the complex interplay of cognition and affect, judgement and sensibility, which largely char-acterises teachers' responses to the complex practical challenges of education and teaching. It is in this respect that Aristotle's notion of *phronesis*, or the prac-tical wisdom of virtue, has lately[17] appeared to offer a far better account of the quality of professional reflection and practice – and it is this sense of virtue that is consistent not just with the idea that authority and discipline are more moral than technical matters, but also with the thought that teaching as a profession needs to be understood more in moral rather than technical terms. In this light, it may appear completely mistaken to regard pedagogical and organisational capacities as entirely reducible to specifiable behavioural skills or competences in the manner of many recent policy documents and initiatives. Indeed, this would seem to be so whether we conceive good or effective teaching to be commensurate with some sort of research-based technology of pedagogy – as many twentieth-century apologists for the idea of a science of learning have undoubtedly so tried to conceive it – or whether we construe teaching skills along the lines of more personal and experiential context-specific arts or crafts.

As far as the technological conception of teaching goes, we need not deny that teachers may have something to learn about aspects of lesson presentation, class organization and resource management from more formal social scientific educational or pedagogical research. But although it may be that I stand to benefit from the adoption of this rather than that research-validated organisa-tional technique or presentational device or strategy, such general skills account for relatively little of the 'hands-on' practice of teachers – and a great deal of what makes teachers imposing authorities, interesting presenters or clear communicators would appear to depend on highly context-sensitive responses to the needs of particular pupils on particular occasions. Such responses invariably require very personal signatures and there are serious limits to their general specifiability. That said, as much danger may lie in the currently influential 'particularist' view that we may only properly account for good educational practice in terms of the personal and experiential cultivation of first-hand craft skills to which any general social scientific research has little if anything to contribute. For even subject to the constraints of so-called 'practitioner' or 'action research', this idea may appear dangerously professionally unaccount-able, if not potentially irresponsible. Clearly the idea that there are *no* general professional constraints on what is to count as good practice is as implausible as the idea that *all* such constraints are general. For, if – in response to the objection that what they are doing is just unacceptably brutal or coercive or unaccountably laissez-faire or libertarian – it is acceptable for teachers to reply that this accords with their personal educational philosophy and/or is just what they have found to work with this particular class or type of pupils, there can be no rational basis for professional consensus, and therefore no coherent notion of education profession. If part of what is meant by construing teaching as a normative activity or enterprise is that it should be accountable to certain public standards of productive or other effectiveness, then the practical procedures of teachers must be answerable to more than some personal aesthetic or local prejudice. Thus, without entirely removing all potential for legitimate pedagogical diversity or the possibility of educational experiment, we also clearly need some broad professional conception of what falls within the limits of the pedagogically acceptable.

It might well be maintained that the required professional balance here – the half-way house between personal pedagogical creativity and servile obedience to the officially prescribed – might be sought in some mix of pedagogically general and particular skills. After all, one idea of a good teacher is that of someone who is not just personally inspiring and situationally sensitive to the needs of his or her pupils or audience, but also professionally responsible in his or her conscientious adoption of more conventional resources of state-of-the-art pedagogical research and development. But even if it could be shown that such deployment of first- and second-hand pedagogical skills was necessary for good practice (which I suspect it could not be), it would still not be sufficient. And arguably this, again, is because the norms of good educational practice are not exclusively *technical* norms. To grasp this we have only to see that the above depiction of a good teacher as someone who is both inspirational or charismatic, and who exploits all of the state-of-the-art resources of educational technology, could apply to people – perhaps to such fascist demagogues and crowd manipulators as Hitler and Mussolini – who we may not want to call 'good teachers' in any serious sense of this rather slippery term. Hence, insofar as the standard professional concept of teaching is indexed to some general idea of education as the promotion of human well-being or flourishing, it seems undeniable that even the narrower conception of teaching as a set of occupational procedures has significantly wider ethical implications: as such, the idea of teaching involves that of making people *better* – in some way, one can only suppose, that is at odds with spreading lies, prejudice and intolerance. Moreover, although we should also expect some of the ethical constraints on educational practice to be general moral principles, we have already seen that many others are context-specific virtues, tailored more particularly to the requirements of particular educational occasions and needs. In the next chapter, however, we shall proceed to examine some broader conceptions of the pedagogical enterprise – with particular regard to the question of the precise professional or other occupational status of teaching.

Possible tasks

(1) Identify three – if possible, contrasting – individuals of your past personal acquaintance whom you would regard as having been good or successful teachers. Try, in each case, to identify a range of (if possible contrasting) qualities that seemed to make them good teachers.

(2) Identify a range of qualities that might be jointly held to constitute a generally acceptable model of a good teacher, and for each of these qualities consider the ways in which a programme of professional education and training might assist its cultivation or development. (For example, if these qualities include 'being inspiring' or 'having a sense of humour', what might be done to assist acquisition of such qualities?)

Chapter 3

The complex role
of the teacher

Teaching as an occupation

In the previous chapter we explored the idea of teaching as an activity, project or process in which those who are employed as teachers – as well as those who are not – may engage in a variety of institutional or other contexts. However, any official employment as a *teacher* is likely to involve duties, responsibilities and liabilities that are not confined to the performance of teaching as an activity. Insofar as that is so, we now need to say something about the status of teaching as *occupational role* as well as activity. Moreover, although this might first seem to be a fairly straightforward matter – since we might expect the duties and responsibilities of the teacher to be fairly well defined by, if not directly derivable from, the more basic aim of teaching to promote learning – this issue is also an interestingly complex one. The complexities arise at least partly, once again, from the deeply normative or evaluative (and hence contested) character of received conceptions of education, learning and the social and other functions of schooling: thus, insofar as there are rival views of what is worth learning (or of who is to determine what is worth learning) and of what schools are for (or of who is to decide what schools are for), there will also be be different conceptions of what teachers employed in schools or other pedagogical contexts are in business to accomplish. But such rival conceptions issue not only in different views of what teachers are there to teach, of how they should teach it, and of the basis of their authority with respect to those they are charged with teaching, but also in a surprising variety of different perspectives on teaching as an occupation *per se*. In short, many significant past and present debates about teaching have actually turned on uncertainties about the precise status of teaching as a mode of employment.

A tempting short response to such debates or uncertainties might simply be to maintain that insofar as employed teachers get paid for what they do, they are professionals rather than amateurs, and are hence entitled to be regarded as members of a *profession*. But any such response would simply rest on multiple confusions between significantly different senses of 'profession' and 'professionalism'. First, it does not obviously follow from the fact that the practitioners of a skill, art or trade are professional, in the sense that they get paid for what they

do, that they are to be considered 'professional', in that more substantive normative sense by which we evaluate the conduct of such arts or trades as well or
badly carried out: for example, we may speak of professional footballers
behaving 'unprofessionally', as well as of the professional or unprofessional
quality of the performance of a given task by people who do not get paid for
doing it. Secondly, of course, even regarding those of whom we coherently
speak as having achieved 'professional' standards in some sphere of paid
employment – plumbers, bricklayers, janitors, footballers, perhaps even nurses
and midwives – we are not necessarily committed to regarding them as
belonging to *professions* as such: indeed, the term 'profession' is in one well-established sense precisely reserved to distinguish the activities of cleaners, janitors
and footballers – well executed or otherwise – from those of (say) medical
doctors and lawyers. Moreover, although it is fashionable to hold this distinction
in some contempt (sociologists, for example, are inclined to regard it as symptomatic of little more than outdated status mongering), I believe that it serves to
indicate certain highly significant differences between types of occupation – and
therefore deserves, not least in the present context, serious attention.[1] In this
light, although the routine normative nomenclature of 'professional' and 'unprofessional' – of a job well or badly done – is applicable to *any* occupation, it does
not follow that it is reasonable to regard any occupation as a *profession* as such.
Thus, in the present connection, although we can speak fairly enough of
teaching as an activity conducive to professional or unprofessional performance,
it is an *open question* whether teaching can or should be regarded as a profession.
Indeed, this question is actually more complex than it looks, since although it is
clear enough that if teaching could not be regarded as a profession, it should not
be, it is not so clear that it *should* be regarded as a profession even if it could be –
and it cannot in any case be denied that teaching has not always been so
regarded.

The notion of 'profession' as an occupational category standardly inclusive of
doctors and lawyers is apt for contrast in various ways with such other general
categories of occupation as *trade* (plumbers, electricians, hairdressers), *industry*
(factory hands, shipbuilders, coalminers) and *commerce* (bankers, car salespeople,
shopkeepers). None of these categories is very hard-edged and there is obviously
large scope here for (albeit futile) debate about how properly to categorise this or
that occupation in these taxonomic terms. Still, this rough and ready schema
already suggests several key differences between professions and other occupations. First, as distinct from much industrial work involving straightforward
compliance with the routine demands of the task, or obedience to externally
imposed managerial constraints, the complex challenges of medicine and law
require doctors and lawyers to exercise a good deal of personal initiative and
autonomy: on the face of it, professional conduct *qua* the conduct of professions
requires considerable personal judgement and responsibility. On the other hand,
in contrast with tradespeople – many of whom may well be self-employed individual decision makers – the professional judgements and decisions of members
of professions are implicated in *theoretical* complexities that are not obviously

practically or technically resolvable in the manner of much if not most trade activity: it is a commonplace (if not entirely clear-cut) contrast between the learning of trades and professions that whereas the former are typically focused upon practical 'hands-on' apprenticeship, the latter also usually involve substantial and protracted initiation into forms of theoretical understanding or expertise in the groves of academe.

But what of such commercial services and enterprises as banking, accountancy or auto-sales? On the face of it, these are white-collar occupations demanding considerable personal initiative, and that also in many cases require the acquisition of theoretical knowledge (of, for example, politics and economics) in the context of higher education. Should not these enterprises also therefore be considered professions? The short answer to this question is that the principal obstacle to regarding commercial enterprises as professions in any full sense is their prime concern with financial profit or benefit. There may, of course, be many virtuous accountants and honest bankers (some degree of honesty, after all, goes with the territory), and auto-sales may be conducted in scrupulously fair terms. That said, it may also be that the award for car salesperson of the year goes to the agent who has sold most cars and made the highest profit, rather than to the one who has given greatest consumer satisfaction, and that the contemporary trend towards more ethical business practice has often been a consequence of pressure from consumer organisations, and of commercial recognition that it is not ultimately profitable for banks or car dealers to acquire reputations for unfair dealing. On the other hand, the notion that there are imperatives that override considerations of personal or corporate gain is arguably the key to understanding proper professional practice, construed as the practice of *professions*. Indeed, this basic feature of professional conduct is celebrated in the ancient Hippocratic recognition that improving health and saving lives – rather than wealth or status seeking – should be the foremost concern and duty of medical practitioners.[2]

The moral basis of profession

Moreover, this idea sits very well with the key ethical insight of an enormously influential modern moral theory: for, according to the ethics of Kant, it is the very essence of morality to treat others as ends in themselves rather than as means to ends.[3] Thus, insofar as it seems natural to regard the exercise of medical expertise as a *duty* owed to others in recognition of their compelling needs – needs that, in turn, are better construed in terms of *rights* more than commodities – it also seems proper to regard the profession of medicine as an inherently *moral* enterprise. Indeed, to whatever extent ethical principles and considerations may (by accident or design) be *regulative* of trade and commerce, they would appear to be generally *constitutive* of such professions as medicine: what, in short, is distinctive or definitive of professions is that they are *in principle* moral practices. Indeed, I suspect that some such idea lies at the heart of the oft-cited but otherwise apparently vacuous criterion of professionalism that maintains that the professions are 'important public services'. Although almost any paid human occupation – hairdressing, rubbish collecting, plumbing, fishmongering, catering or whatever – might be regarded as a vital public service in *some* circumstances (and all may be carried on professionally or unprofessionally, ethically or unethically), the professions are arguably key public services by dint of their significant internal relationship to the most basic conditions of civil human flourishing. Thus, to whatever extent there are incompetent doctors, medicine is *inherently* concerned with the promotion of health, good health is a basic precondition of the flourishing of each and every human being, and it must be a prime concern of any civil society to safeguard its members from the evils of illness and disease: in short, to provide medical care as a matter of *right*. Likewise, to whatever extent there are corrupt lawyers, the practice of law is none the less *internally* related to the promotion of justice and freedom, there can be no civilised life in the absence of some protection of individual rights and liberties, and it must be a prime concern of any civil society to protect its citizens from injustice and oppression: to provide legal aid as a matter of *right*. Indeed, insofar as we are inclined to withhold the term 'civilised' from social orders that do not make some systematic institutional and professional provision for the protection of their citizens from the evils of ill-health and injustice, such safeguards may be no less than benchmarks of civil society.

Moreover, the goals of justice and health that the professions of medicine and law aspire to promote are also deeply *normative*: in short, conceptions of health and justice depend upon value judgements, and individuals differ markedly in their views of what is unhealthy or unjust. It is for this reason that interminable political, public and professional debates rage about the proper aims and methods of medical and legal policy, which do not in the same way arise over the aims and methods of those occupations less readily recognised as professions. In short, serious ethical and philosophical disputes are liable to arise about the basic justice of this or that law or medical procedure, of a kind that do not (or not so centrally) occur in connection with catering, bricklaying or pest-control – and while there are many academic journals devoted to the philosophy or ethics of law or medicine, one hardly expects trade journals of plumbing, hairdressing or cookery to be preoccupied with semantic or normative questions of quite the same order. I also believe, by the way, that this consideration provides the key to understanding the important role of 'theory' or principled reflection in the professional deliberations of members of professions – a role that we shall need to examine more closely in relation to education and teaching in the next chapter. For the moment, however, we may observe that any such professional theory is widely misunderstood as mainly required to provide the scientific or other rules that would precisely determine professional practice in any and all circumstances. On the contrary, it seems nearer the mark to observe that insofar as practical questions are amenable to any such straightforward scientific or technical solution, they hardly need reflective professional judgement: it is precisely because many if not most of the central problems of hairdressing, plumbing or auto-repair are resolvable by reference to some book of mechanical rules and procedures that 'hands-on' apprenticeship rather than protracted initiation into the complexities of 'theoretical' debate is largely sufficient for the effective practice of such trades. At heart, genuine professions are moral practices, and hence – even in the case of such professions as medicine that are much concerned with the development of new technologies – professional reflection would appear to require serious engagement with vexed questions about the place of and contribution to ultimate human flourishing of inevitably controversial scientific and other methods.

What, however, are we to say about the occupational status of education and teaching in the light of this brief analysis of some key features of profession? On the one hand, there has been growing contemporary pressure to accord professional status (in the present strong sense of status *as* a profession) to teaching.[4] But, on the other, it would not necessarily follow that this is the best or most appropriate way to regard teaching – if, for example, teaching did not well fit the profile of profession, or if it better fitted some other general occupational description. At all events, we might first consider the pros and cons of regarding teaching as a profession in the sense just delineated. From this viewpoint, the case for according the status of profession to teaching is not insubstantial. To begin with, there is a good case for regarding teaching as a significant public service in the sense in which we have regarded medicine and law as key public services. Just as medical and legal practice may be considered inherently concerned (in principle) with the promotion of such basic aspects of human well-being as health and justice, so the practice of teaching seems internally related to the promotion of education. Indeed, medicine, law and education might well be regarded as the three principal bulwarks against the most basic human evils of pestilence, injustice and ignorance from which any civil society worth its salt will seek to provide some institutional and professional defence for its citizens. Hence, we may reasonably regard health, justice *and* education as universal human *rights* in the absence of which any human life stands to be seriously impoverished or diminished: in this light, mortal illness, injustice and ignorance cannot be considered minor inconveniences, as failures to afford a new car, yacht or meal in an expensive restaurant might be so regarded – for the latter needs are hardly ones to which anyone could seriously claim a human or civil *right*.

But this is also to appreciate: first, that education is – no less than health and justice – an inherently *normative* concept; secondly (and consquently), that teaching is – no less than medicine and law – an essentially *moral* practice. Once again, this is not the patently false claim that teaching, medicine and law are always and everywhere justly or honestly pursued – for there may be as many morally unwholesome teachers as corrupt lawyers and medical malpractitioners; it is rather to recognise that good practice in all these fields is internally related to certain *overriding* moral obligations to address the needs and interests of pupils, patients and clients in professional recognition of their medical, educational and legal rights. It is to appreciate that although a *skilled* tradesperson might still be considered a *good* plumber or car-mechanic, irrespective of an unjust, dishonest or corrupt attitude or character, it is harder to regard someone as a good lawyer, doctor or teacher who fails in such basic ethical respects – since it is logically less easy to separate the practice of medicine, law and education from an explicit moral concern with the well-being of others in this or that relevant respect. In short, whereas a good tradesperson is first and foremost a *skilled* tradesperson, a good teacher or doctor is not *only*, perhaps not even *primarily*, a skilled doctor or teacher – at least in any narrower technical sense of skill. But it is also in virtue of the normative character of education, and the inherently moral quality of good teaching, that questions arise about the proper goals, burdens and benefits of education and teaching that cannot be settled by scientific or technical inquiry or deliberation alone – with the further consequence that initiation into the profession of teaching has not *usually* been regarded as a matter of the 'hands-on' practical apprenticeship characteristic of trades. From this viewpoint, there has been a time-honoured (if also contested) modern presumption in favour of some form of higher academic training and certification (degree, diploma or other) for entry to the teaching profession. To this extent, at any rate, education and teaching would appear to satisfy the general requirements of profession that professional practice should be theoretically and morally as well as technically implicated.

Is teaching a profession?

That said, there are well-rehearsed problems regarding the role and status of theoretical or principled reflection in teacher education and training – which, at the very least, raise doubts about any very precise analogy between teaching and such other more commonly accepted professions as medicine and law. First, at the level of professional curriculum content, although we may not doubt that (at least some) teachers require theoretical knowledge no less than doctors, there may seem to be important differences between the ways in which theoretical knowledge is utilised or implicated in the enterprises of medicine and education. On the face of it, indeed, whereas teachers need more or less advanced theoretical (or other) knowledge in order to have *something* to teach, doctors need knowledge (such as anatomy or physiology) to *enable* them to treat others effectively. Again, whereas the enabling knowledge that doctors need is usually acquired in the professional academy, the content knowledge that teachers need is mostly acquired prior to entry to professional education and training – either through general secondary education (in the case of many primary teachers) or in the course of pre-service university study (in the case of many secondary and some primary teachers). At this point, of course, it may be insisted that teachers need professional courses not so much to know *what* to teach, and more to know *how* to teach: on this view, the knowledge that teachers acquire in the academic contexts of professional training is more like the scientifically informed technical know-how that doctors acquire in medical school than the theoretical knowledge of much other non-vocational university study. But any such suggestion then runs into the second source of difficulty about the place of theory in professional teacher education and training – namely, that the practical knowledge and expertise of teaching is *not* obviously of the scientifically grounded technical kind upon which medical expertise appears to be based. Here, it is not just that so-called 'teaching skills' are not readily subsumable under general scientific laws as efficient causes of learning, but that many alleged 'teaching skills' are probably better regarded as pre-theoretical qualities of ordinary human interpersonal association than as products or deliverances of scientific inquiry or technical training. At all events, such considerations rather serve to reinforce the view of many present-day opponents of theoretical study in teacher education and training that the expertise of teachers is precisely best acquired by 'hands-on' practical apprenticeship in the way of trades.[5]

Nevertheless, in view of recent remarks on the concept of profession, one might object to such doubts about the place and value of theoretical knowledge in the *professional* education of teachers on the grounds that, since teaching is not a technology, one should not expect professional theoretical knowledge to be focused *primarily* upon the development of technical or other *means* to the practice of education. The point would now be that insofar as education, like medicine and law, is conceivable as a *moral* practice, the role of the academy in professional education is less that of advising practitioners what to do, and more that of initiating them into the profound normative or evaluative complexities of professional practice: in short, the academy is needed to equip professionals with the deliberative resources for independent or autonomous judgement in the kind of morally complex circumstances in which there may be no established case law. From this viewpoint, the aim of professional education is to assist the development on the part of each and every professional of his or her own best conception of good practice via principled reflection upon a range of competing conceptions of such practice. Indeed, since many if not most professional issues will be as much moral as technical, some capacity for authentic and intellectually responsible engagement with controversial questions about the ultimate contribution of professional practice to human flourishing must surely be a *sine qua non* of effective professionalism, and the job of the professional academy cannot therefore be merely that of instruction in second-hand or uncontroversial techniques.

That said, it could also be that this apparently plausible case for the legitimate role of normative inquiry in teacher education simply begs the key question about the professional status of teaching. For, of course, it would follow that normative reflection should be a part of the professional equipment of teachers only *if* teaching is a profession; but this is just what is presently in question. However, it may well be denied that teaching is a professional practice of the kind in which it is proper to involve practitioners in debates and decisions about the aims of education or the proper direction of educational policy. In a public arena in which such other social agencies as parents, politicians or employers are important stakeholders, and in which practitioners are (largely in consequence) required to operate in accordance with centrally or officially prescribed policy decisions about management, discipline, curriculum and pedagogy, it might be held that wider normative reflection upon policy is not the legitimate business of teachers, and that their role is more that of the efficient technical transmission of what is considered to be socially and economically useful by those to whom they are politically (albeit democratically) accountable. Although any such viewpoint arguably threatens to 'deprofessionalise' teaching, and to reduce it to something closer to a white-collar trade than a profession in the sense of medicine or law, it has nevertheless been widely influential on contemporary political conceptions of education and teaching. Many, not least those of more right-of-centre political views, have been inclined to blame a wide range of contemporary social and moral evils on the failure of teachers to transmit 'traditional' or 'socially accept-able' values (if not upon the actual espousal and transmission by some teachers of socially subversive ones), and have sought more rather than less restriction of teacher autonomy and independence.[6] Indeed, in the light of an arguably signif-icant causal connection between effective schooling and social and moral cohesion and continuity, it may be tempting indeed to claim that education is far too important to be left to teachers.

All the same, whilst agreeing that education and educationalists are clearly accountable to the democratic will of society – as well as answerable to a compelling social imperative to equip the young with the knowledge and values necessary for the moral and economic survival and continuity of a civilised liberal democratic polity – any such attempt to reduce teachers to mere classroom technicians or tradespeople may well appear both wrong-headed and dangerous. To begin with, although schools are at least partly the agents of social interests and values, and teachers may not be final authorities on what should be taught in the way that doctors or lawyers may be final authorities (at least *vis-à-vis* the views of laypeople) on proper medical treat-ment or legal action, it hardly follows that they are no more than instruments of political, parental or other public will. First, as democratic stakeholders in education themselves, teachers are clearly entitled to at least as much of a say in the formation of public educational policy as others. Secondly, however, it is surely reasonable to expect them to have an authoritative voice in any public debates about education, precisely to the extent that they can claim some first-hand, perhaps expert, occupational experience of the pedagogical and other developmental needs and interests of young people. Moreover, unless we suppose any such authority and expertise to be entirely exhausted by narrow capacities for the routine drilling of information or skills, we might also expect it to extend to some appreciation of how to help children grow in the wisdom and virtue conducive to their living not just skilled or well-informed but also morally worthwhile lives. Indeed, the constant complaints of those right-of-centre or authoritarian educational policy makers that teachers are not properly attending to the task of inculcating correct values[7] makes sense only on the supposition that teachers are both capable of and respon-sible for the transmission of such values (for if they were not, it would make no sense to blame them for failing to do so).

In short, if *education* – conceived as more than just training or drilling – requires capacities to assist others to grow in wisdom and moral discernment, and such wisdom inevitably involves appreciation of and sensitivity to others as ends in themselves more than means to ends, those charged with the promotion of such wisdom would surely need to possess and exhibit some measure of it themselves. But how might one expect those who have themselves been suborned to a conception of good educational practice as docile dependency on externally imposed directives, and who have been encouraged to regard education and teaching as little more than the imposition of information, skills and handed-down values on others, to exhibit the kind of capacities needed to assist children in the growth of moral wisdom? Hence, in view of the sorts of human development in which we would commonly take (school) education and teaching to be implicated, it is arguable that any satisfactory teacher preparation must extend beyond training in prescribed skills to the promotion of the kind of capacities for practical judgement of the sort that defies codification in any simple technical terms. Above all, no claim to the effect that teaching cannot be a professionally autonomous enterprise in the same sense as medical or legal practice should be allowed to mislead us into conceiving it as no more than a collection of routine technical skills, or into supposing that it allows no place for the exercise of significant workplace autonomy: indeed, teaching is clearly enough an occupation that requires considerable independence of context-sensitive judgement, *and* to which significant resources of principled reflection and interpersonal sensibility are therefore presupposed.

Teaching as a vocation

Still, to deny that teachers are more than just classroom technicians or skilled operatives, or even to recognise that the practice of school teaching shares many key features of other moral practices such as medicine and law, is not yet to concede that education and teaching should be regarded with these other occupations as *bona fide* professions. Indeed, reflection upon some further peculiarities of the practical deliberations of teachers may support a case for resisting the inclusion of education among standard professions. Although it is by no means easy to identify any general or easily statable difference between the way in which the theoretical, principled or reflective deliberation and judgement of teachers deviates from common conceptions of professional judgement, it may be that much here turns upon the degree to which any such judgement can have a legitimate *affective* dimension. In brief, it is customary (rightly or wrongly) to construe professional judgement as having a distinctly impartial, disinterested or *impersonal* character. It is usual to construe law and medicine as highly *regulated* occupations in which practice is governed by tightly prescribed rules and guidelines of proper conduct. As we observed with regard to the Hippocratic code, insofar as it rests on impartial recognition of certain universal rights to health, justice or whatever, and upon the disinterested observance of duties with respect to those rights, any ethics of profession seems predominantly *deontological*. On this view, good doctors and lawyers are those whose treatment of patients and clients is governed by a scrupulous regard for distributive justice: hence, to treat people differently in the light of the different personal relations one might have with them, to enter into any kind of personal relationship with them, or to allow personal or affective considerations to influence one's professional deliberations is to risk acting in an inherently *unprofessional* way.

In this regard, we might first note that many recent philosophical explorations of teacher deliberation and judgement have sought to model pedagogical reflection on the Aristotelian notion of *phronesis* or moral wisdom.[8] However, one crucial respect in which the moral wisdom of *phronesis* is distinguished by Aristotle from the productive expertise of *techne* is that the former has a legitimate *affective* as well as cognitive component or dimension.[9] In a nutshell, effective moral judgements cannot be made in the absence of the right kind of sentiments, sensitivities and sensibilities. Hence, insofar as it is appropriate to model the judgements of teachers on *phronesis* rather than *techne*, it is arguable that effective teachers are those whose other-regarding judgements exhibit a more personal concern with or sensitivity to the needs and interests of particular pupils as individuals. Moreover, this idea of the affective character of *phronesis* would appear to sit rather better than the deontic ethics of right and duty with that other familiar Aristotelian claim that there may be (in at least some contexts) as much injustice in treating unequals equally as there is in treating equals unequally.[10] It also fits fairly well with recent psychological critiques of received psychometric conceptions of intelligence to the effect that IQ tests express only one sort of human intelligence, and that there are other valuable forms of social and emotional intelligence that involve significant qualities of human affect.[11] However, it is arguable that any attention to the affective dimension of teacher deliberation and judgement moves us not just away from any ready comparison of teachers with doctors and lawyers, but also towards – insofar as the practice of these occupations also seems to involve legitimate non-cognitive dimensions – possibly closer analogies between teaching and such other occupations as priest, nurse and social worker. But this may also be the moment to recall that education and teaching have not always or even primarily been regarded as professions: that, indeed, there is a time-honoured tradition of regarding teaching, alongside ministry, nursing and perhaps some aspects of social work, as *vocations* more than professions. At all events, although whatever general differences there are between vocation and profession are certainly not clear-cut, they would mostly appear to turn on the sort of considerations we have just aired about the degree to which there may be a legitimate, if not unavoidable, personal or affective dimension to some occupations. These are considerations, moreover, that are perhaps best illustrated by reference to the particular features of diverse vocations.

The affective dimensions of vocation

First and foremost, the notion of vocation is perhaps best exemplified by the ideas of priesthood or ministry as a matter of *calling* (the literal meaning of 'vocation') and by imperatives that compel obedience and service in a rather different way from professional rules and principles. From this viewpoint, a significantly greater degree of continuity would appear to be required between the personal and occupational conduct of priests or ministers than is necessary in the case of professions and other occupations. For example, someone might be a good doctor or lawyer – in respect of upholding the principles and standards of his or her professional practice – without feeling the least incentive to improve as a *person*. There is no very obvious need for the members of such professions to recognise any commitment to the values and virtues of a particular way of life, to exemplify those virtues or values in their own person, or to try to change others for the better in the light of them. Thus (at least in principle), it may be no impediment to being a good doctor or lawyer that one is a liar, sexually promiscuous or even just a spiteful and vindictive person, whereas these short-comings would normally be taken to undermine successful pursuit of the vocations of ministry and priesthood. Above all, of course, obedience to the personal values of one's calling are clearly internally related to any clerical mission to transform the lives of others in specific moral and spiritual respects: it is (at least partly) insofar as the priest is charged with improving the lives of others that he or she needs to exemplify the virtues and values constitutive of such improvement.

However, it is arguable that we also require teachers to be moral exemplars in much the same way as we require priests to be moral exemplars – and for essentially the same reason. On a fairly common view of the role of the teacher, the business of teachers in schools is not only to instruct children in skills or informa-tion, and schools have a proper concern with the development of (as it is sometimes put) the 'whole child', which is usually taken to include affective, moral, social and spiritual development. Again, the duties of teachers are not normally taken to begin and end with the observance of contractually defined obligations, and the good teacher will usually recognise personal responsibilities to pupils that go beyond the call of classroom duty. In this light, it may be reasonable to question the suitability of particular persons for teaching – regard-less of the extent to which they may have met the requirements of knowledge and skill, or of professional obligation in terms of which professions are largely defined – on the grounds that they lack certain crucial qualities or virtues of other-regarding concern and commitment. Indeed, it may be just such consider-ations that underlie a certain disdain for the contemporary discourses of teacher professionalism that is sometimes discernible on the part of educational practi-tioners employed in those more occupationally conservative sectors of traditional grammar and independent schools, where teaching has often been seen as a higher calling to promote the best spiritual and other virtues and values of civili-sation. In the worlds of Mr Chips and Miss Jean Brodie, teaching is a something to be pursued for love rather than money, as a matter of noble aspiration rather than vulgar obligation.

Another occupation that is commonly regarded as a vocation, of course, is nursing – again partly on the grounds that nurses are driven to do what they do more by commitment than financial motives. Moreover, although nursing is usually taken to be the very paradigm of a so-called 'caring profession', it also calls for levels of interpersonal concern and for a range of empathic and sympathetic qualities that are not always apparent in the conduct of standard professions. To be sure, this point needs careful statement. It seems that nurses and (say) lawyers are equally required to balance a real commitment to the needs of clients or patients with a certain disinterested objectivity: in *both* cases it is crucial to walk a fine line between complete personal unconcern and inappropriate emotional involvement with patients or clients. That said, a certain warm fellow-feeling and capacity for emotional support – the proverbial 'bed-side manner' – is clearly more crucial to nursing than advocacy. Moreover, although both nursing and midwifery have evolved into highly skilled and technical enterprises that have aspired to comparable professional status with such other fields of medicine as general practice and surgery, it seems hard to deny that the heart of good nursing lies in a certain legitimate personal engagement with patients, which doctors and surgeons are to a significant degree enjoined to avoid. It seems integral to the role of nurses, for example, to raise the morale of patients and to assist their adjustment to discomforting if not actually terrifying experiences. From this viewpoint, a certain degree of genuine heartfelt care and concern is surely a *sine qua non* of good nursing. On the one hand, of course, such caring invites 'phronetic' construal as a kind of *virtue*: to this extent, such caring is more than mere feeling and requires to be guided by a prudent sense of what is in the best interests, all considered, of the patient. On the other hand, however, insofar as such care includes a proper element of involved affect, it is more than a mere technical skill and cannot – *contra* much (dubious) modern talk of caring skills – be acquired in the manner of a practical technique or procedure: thus, although we might advise a nurse who is poor at bed making to go away and practise her bed-making skills, it would be absurd to require an apparently uncaring nurse to practise her caring skills. At all events, it can hardly be doubted that teaching has often attracted comparison with nursing and other 'caring professions', precisely on the grounds that teachers also need to be the kind of people who can reassure, motivate and boost the confidence of their frequently fragile and vulnerable young clients. Indeed, it may well be that at the pre-school and early primary stages of education, such caring qualities are the key occupational virtues, and we would certainly want to raise questions about the suitability for such work of someone who entirely lacked them, even if that person possessed encyclopaedic knowledge and was a past master of pedagogical method.

One may also doubt whether the professional–client relation as defined on the model of medical or legal practice is entirely appropriate to social work – and, to be sure, personal dealings with social workers have shown me that they do not readily welcome invitations to construe their practice on the model of profession. Once again, the point seems to be that in order to relate effectively to those they serve, social workers need to engage the trust and confidence of these in a way that may well be impeded if not actually undermined by the cold informality and status inequality of the professional–client relationship. Many of the disadvantaged clients with whom social workers have to deal are liable, rightly or wrongly, to feel inferior to or patronised by those doctors, lawyers and other professionals whose social background, class status and very professional discourse set them apart as largely alien beings. To that extent, social workers have to be people who can speak 'the same language' as their clients, and who are ready to cut through the bureaucratic red-tape of professional rules and regulations to secure the rights of those they are employed to help: they need to be people who are clearly 'on the side' of clients (rather than on the official side). But although few latter-day nurses and teachers may have held professional status in quite the same disdain as have social workers, it is notable that there is a well-established tradition of educational anti-professionalism – dating at least from the writings of the so-called 'deschoolers' and other radical educational writers of the 1960s and 1970s – that is quite consistent with such attitudes.[12] Indeed, pre-dating the polemics of deschoolers, progressive educators of various kinds have long been given to such anti-professional sentiments: for example, A.S. Neill of 'Summerhill' explicitly affirmed the importance of the teacher being 'on the side' of pupils.[13] Again, professional dealings with community educators, whose work is to a great extent continuous with that of social workers, have shown that they are also seldom enthusiatic about aspirations to profession and professionalism – for much the same reason that their work requires a special climate of trust and informality between teachers and taught that is liable to be seriously undermined or compromised by the distance and formality of the professional–client relationship. Once more, to be sure, this point requires careful statement: insofar as any teacher will need to exercise a degree of appropriate authority and discipline over pupils, there is to that extent a wrong sort of familiarity between teachers and taught. Still, it seems not just that good teacher–pupil relations are inherently personal in a way that many professional–client relationships are not, but that it is difficult to see how good or affective teaching could take place without personal acquaintance with and attention to 'clients' as individuals, which may be out of place if not actually out of bounds in medicine or law.

The occupational enigma of teaching

Inclinations to include education and teaching among the vocations rather than the professions have doubtless been influenced by all these points. All the same, we also need to observe that the overall territory of education and teaching covers a great deal of ground, and that it may not therefore be appropriate to construe all forms or levels of teaching in such non-professional or vocational terms. For example, any significant construal of teaching as a 'caring profession' seems more appropriate to primary and secondary sectors of education – perhaps most of all to early years – than to further, higher or adult education. Moreover, whereas primary and secondary school teachers might be expected to observe a less strict distinction between the educational development of pupils, and more personal aspects of their welfare and development, college or university teachers would perhaps be expected to draw a rather sharper distinction between the personal and the educational – leaving personal confidences to professional counsellors rather than academic tutors. Nevertheless, there is clearly some case for conceiving any teacher's mission – construed as the pursuit of knowledge and truth – more in vocationally personal than professionally impersonal terms. That said, any such attempt to construe education and teaching in vocational rather than professional terms is also not without its hazards. In the first place, there can be no doubt that regarding teaching as a vocation rather than a profession has often been a pretext for rewarding it poorly in financial terms. Moreover, it is common to find that the caring occupations, not least (early years) teaching and nursing, are often held in rather low regard – as activities that anyone with a whole heart but half a brain might do. In view of this it is hardly surprising that teachers and nurses have often been hard put to show that their work is equal to the demands of the traditional professions, and have struggled to secure appropriate occupational recognition and remuneration. However, difficulties of a rather different sort beset even the 'ministerial' vocationalism of traditional public and grammar school teachers, despite its own 'high church' disdain for the vulgarity of mere professionalism. For on the vocationalist conception of the teacher as a cultural missionary – someone who is charged with defending certain cherished values and virtues – it would be considered pedagogically necessary to exemplify such values and virtues and to transmit them to others. But, although such a conception of the teacher may work well in certain traditional contexts of cultural homogeneity, it fares less well in circumstances of cultural pluralism – where it may well be regarded as a pedagogical vice (of indoctrination) to transmit personally held values. In such circumstances, indeed, the impartiality of professional regulation often seems to have been introduced precisely to ensure teacher neutrality, and to obviate the risk of cultural custodianship crossing the fine line that divides it from unwarranted cultural colonialism.

At all events, we might now ask how precisely we should regard education and teaching – as a trade, a profession, a vocation, or perhaps as something else entirely? In this respect, moreover, there are clearly a number of rather different options. First, it might be argued that teaching does conform to the standard criteria of professionalism, and therefore merits status as full profession alongside medicine and law. Second, it might be held to conform to some of these criteria, but not others: for example, one might suppose that there is a case for regarding teaching as a kind of moral practice, but claim that it lacks the professional organisation characteristic of other professions, or any genuine (scientific) theoretical basis. In view of such partial satisfaction of the general criteria of professionalism, it is common – not least in sociological literature – for such occupations as nursing and social work to be accorded the status of 'semi-professions'.[14] A third possibility, of course, is to regard education and teaching as belonging to an occupational category different from that of profession, but nevertheless not reducible to some kind of trade or blue-collar service: in short we might include teaching along with such other occupations as nursing, social work and the ministry under the heading of *vocation* more than profession. A fourth possibility – possibly reflected in many recent policy initiatives relating to the training of teachers – might be to construe teaching as little more than a 'white-collar' service or trade, and teachers as little more than 'classroom technicians'. Yet a fifth option, however, might be to regard teaching as a uniquely complex activity that combines different characteristics of all these otherwise diverse occupational types.

At the very least, education and teaching would clearly seem to exhibit many of the key characteristics of traditional professions. First, it is hard to deny that they measure well along the important public service dimension. Alongside medicine and law, as we have seen, education might be said to constitute a third crucial condition of civil flourishing, the absence of which might lead us to question the status as civilised of any given human polity: if individual and social flourishing is liable to be undermined by a lack of proper provision of healthcare in the event of medical need, or by the lack of legal defence in the case of unjust imprisonment, it is just as likely to be undermined by ignorance, illiteracy or lack of the skills required to make a decent living. Moreover, whilst the contribution of medicine and law to civilised flourishing is to some extent remedial or compensatory – we seek medical or legal aid mainly in circumstances where there is deficit of health and justice – education and training are more obviously sought for their own inherently life-enhancing benefits. But, regardless of this, insofar as it is clear that education, like medicine and law, is conceivable as a human right or entitlement, it would also seem that it conforms just as well as other so-called 'professions' to the pattern of a moral practice: in this respect, there cannot be much doubt that the same sort of moral questions of justice, equality and respect arise as much for education as for medicine and law. This is also one of the reasons why educational aspirants to professional status have felt the need for teaching to be organised on a professional basis in the manner of other professions: indeed, such organisation has long been a feature of professional practice in Scotland, where a successful General Teaching Council has for many years been responsible for the monitoring, registration and discipline of teachers. However, problems about granting unqualified status as a profession to education and teaching do seem to arise in connection with other criteria of professionalism. First, it is not clear that teaching – subject as it has always been to central and local authority direction and prescription – has ever offered the same scope as other professions for the expression of either individual or professionally collaborative autonomy: in this respect, teachers may indeed appear to be rather closer – in terms of their subjection to the will of others – to such semi-professionals as nurses and social workers than to such full professsionals as doctors and lawyers. Secondly, however, in a socio-economic climate more and more given to calling all professions to public and political account, education and teaching may seem – with increasing central or official prescription of curriculum content and teaching methods – to have suffered more than other would-be professions in terms of the erosion of what little autonomy they may once have had. Moreover, there remains the enduring professional difficulty about the precise role and status of theoretical knowledge in effective educational practice. It is to this problem that we now turn in the next section.

Possible tasks

(1) In the light of the comparisons explored in this chapter between teaching and such other occupations as doctor, minister, nurse, social worker, tradesperson and businessperson (to which one might add others such as police officer, therapist or prison warden), try to identify the key features of teaching that have sustained these comparisons.

(2) Further to these suggested comparisons, try to identify as many respects as you can in which these possible analogies may be in some conflict or tension with one another (for example, identify and explain the respects in which a priestly conception of a teacher might be at odds with a business or managerial conception).

Chapter 4

Educational theory and practice

Profession and theory

It would appear a key implication of recent reflections upon teaching as activity and role that the occupational status of education and teaching – the question of whether it should be regarded as a profession, vocation or trade – turns largely upon the extent and nature of its relationship to some sort of theoretical or principled inquiry. Moreover, given that theory-implicatedness seems a pivotal condition of genuine or full professional status, it would seem that those who seek to claim *both* that teaching *should* be regarded as a profession *and* that theoretical reflection is *irrelevant* to educational practice – as both pre- and in-service teachers sometimes appear to do – are near to cutting off the branch upon which they wish to sit: it is for this reason that those approaches to teacher training that belittle the relevance of theoretical reflection to effective educational practice are invariably regarded as 'deprofessionalising'. That said, there can be little doubt that much public and professional uncertainty persists concerning the nature and place of theoretical or other principled reflection in the education, training and in-service practice of teachers: hence, as lately noticed, positions on this issue range widely and wildly between those who hold that teaching should primarily be conceived as a matter of largely atheoretical 'hands-on' practical apprenticeship in the manner of a trade, and those who incline to a highly theoretical or academic ideal of 'reflective practice' as the goal of professional education. Even among those committed to some ideal of reflective practice, however, there is precious little agreement about the precise character of professional educational deliberation:[1] to that extent, teaching looks more like a profession on some conceptions of reflective practice than on others. At all events, despite the enormous amount of ink that has already been spilt on this question, it is evident that there is still much troubling unclarity concerning the precise epistemic or other conceptual status of educational theory, and about the exact nature of its relationship to practice.

We may perhaps begin by considering a current fashionable political and professional trend towards conceiving the development of professional teacher expertise in terms of the acquisition of so-called 'teaching *competences*'. Although contemporary proponents of competence models of professional preparation are quick to insist that such competences are not to be construed as atheoretical or as entirely neglectful of principled reflection,[2] it would also be somewhat naïve to ignore or overlook the theoretical or intellectual roots of the term 'competence' in a certain tradition of thinking about professional education and training. In short, the contemporary discourse of professional competences is firmly located in a firm tradition of experimental psychology explicitly committed to the reduction of human occupational and other intentional endeavour to behavioural processes of skill or information acquisition. On this so-called 'learning-theoretical' perspective, one might take any (particularly practical) occupation – auto-repair, painting, plumbing, hairdressing or teaching – and *in principle* reduce it to a set of pre-specifiable procedures apt for acquisition via a systematic programme of (broadly conceived) behavioural training. To be sure, it is possible that the main concern of more sophisticated competence models of vocational training is to do proper justice to the inherently practical character of such occupations as teaching, in terms of a primarily practice-focused construal of professional judgement that need not be taken as *entirely* denying any role for principled reflection or deliberation. We might charitably construe such models as claiming – in the spirit of a famous modern philosopher of mind[3] – that while there *is* real reflection and deliberation in the practice of teaching, this needs to be understood less as a kind of theoretical 'cause' of practice, more as a (rational) dimension or modality of practice: in short, rational practice is a special way of proceeding rather than something with peculiar (mental or spiritual) antecedents. Moreover, this would seem to be a fair point in relation to *some* human activities or occupations: whilst there are principled (rule-governed) procedures of auto-repair, cookery or hairdressing – some of which may even be grounded in scientific or other theory – the understanding of a good car-mechanic, cook or hairdresser is surely manifest in the actual *practical* conduct of these activities, rather than in any 'inner' theoretical processes. On this view, there may be no compelling reason to suppose that the principled appreciation of some trades and occupations amounts to much more than acquisition of the practical skills, rules and procedures of such trades.

Still, without denying that teaching is an enterprise to which actual practical experience is presupposed, it also seems less than plausible – for reasons previously touched upon in the second chapter of this work – to regard it as the sort of enterprise in which principles are reducible without remainder to some repertoire of skills or procedures in the manner of auto-repair or hairdressing. Indeed, the principled understanding characteristic of teaching may appear to differ from the expertise of such trades in two key respects. First, good pedagogical practice may appear to be based on or grounded in *academic* theoretical or intellectual reflection of a kind that is not so obviously required of effective hairdressing: although it need not be supposed that good hairdressing is a product of systematic theoretical research or inquiry, some such empirical (notably social scientific) research might seem relevant to the improvement of educational practice. Secondly, however, although auto-repair is clearly grounded in a body of theoretical science, we need not suppose that good car-mechanics would *themselves* require to be acquainted with any such theoretical or intellectual inquiry, whereas we might suppose that the basic principles of their educational practice need to be known by teachers. Thus, while it could be enough that the mechanic simply carries out the correct procedures according to the practical manual, or in accordance with the instructions of others, it might seem more reasonable to require from teachers a principled account of what they are doing, and also of *why* they are doing it. In short, teachers might be expected to have real *ownership* over the theoretical or other principles of their practice of a kind that we would not necessarily require of car-mechanics or other tradespeople. From this viewpoint, it may indeed be objected that professional competence models of teacher education and training appear to involve reduction of pedagogical expertise to mastery of information (empirical theories and official guidelines) and skills (of communication, organisation and management) of a kind that falls short of authentic intellectual and/or critical engagement with the complex principles of professional practice.

The problems of 'applied theory'

However, as also previously noted, the idea that good teaching is a matter of the application to practice of a body of *theoretical* knowledge requiring extended pre-service education and training in the largely academic context of university or college is not without its own difficulties. On the one hand, it is easy to see why those who have aspired to raising teaching to the same professional status as medicine have sought a comparable place for theory in the education and training of teachers. But, on the other hand, although it is hardly reasonable to suppose that someone might effectively practise medicine in the absence of considerable knowledge of such sciences as anatomy and physiology, it is less easy to see what sorts of studies might provide precisely analogous theoretical input to effective educational practice. Indeed, this difficulty seems to have dogged significant postwar attempts to raise teaching to graduate status by replacing the less coherent academic and practical ragbags of former teacher training courses with the more systematic and rigorous studies of academic disciplines purportedly necessary for properly informed professional practice: precisely, to develop a programme of serious academic study comparable to the sort of programmes that underpin professional initiation in other professional fields. Despite this, there cannot be much doubt that some architects of the new postwar professional degrees for teachers did explicitly hold that the academic study of certain educationally applied arts and sciences – history, philosophy, psychology, sociology, and so on – might occupy a more or less comparable role in the education and training of teachers to anatomy and physiology in the education and training of medical doctors or surgeons.[4]

However, insofar as it would not appear that there is much significant analogy between the role of anatomy in medical training and the role of psychology or sociology in teacher education and training, it may be that latter-day emphases on the place of theoretical studies in professional teacher preparation have often served more to compound than erode the time-honoured reservations of many pre- and in-service professionals about the practical relevance of such studies. To begin with, widespread practitioner scepticism about the value of theory is apt to be reinforced by the observation that such theoretical studies do not clearly conduce to the improvement of practical classroom effectiveness. On the one hand, since there are students of teaching whose marked success in academic studies of philosophy, psychology and history is not at all matched by their practical success in teaching, it is doubtful whether such studies can be regarded as *sufficient* for good practice. On the other hand, although it is difficult to see how anyone might be a successful surgeon or general medical practitioner in the absence of some knowledge of anatomy or physiology, it seems perfectly conceivable that someone might be an effective teacher in the absence of any formal knowledge of psychology or sociology whatsoever. In short, insofar as one can encounter impressive classroom practitioners who nevertheless perform poorly on the academic side of their studies, one may doubt whether such studies are professionally *necessary* either. At all events, whatever might be the relationship of such theoretical studies as sociology, philosophy, psychology and history to the professional practice of teachers, it would not appear to resemble that of physiology or anatomy to general medical practice. For one thing, while it is fair to suppose that doctors *apply* their knowledge of anatomy or physiology to practice in some fairly straightforward technical sense, it is not obvious that teachers directly apply psychological or sociological knowledge or hypotheses to educational practice in any such direct technical way. In short, it is not obvious that the study of psychology in the context of professional teacher education should be regarded – like anatomy in the context of medicine – as a professionally *applied science*.

Indeed, any idea that the theoretical disciplines of educational philosophy, sociology of education, empirical psychology, and so on, have something like direct technical application to educational practice – a notion that may nevertheless have been the cornerstone of many modern theoretical conceptions of teacher education – is vulnerable to at least two very general difficulties. The first, upon which we have already touched, is that the empirical or statistical generalisations to which much social scientific research aspires may appear unable to capture or accommodate the fine-grained particularities of real-life pedagogical association and engagement. In fact there are actually different – weaker and stronger – ways of making this point. On the weakest perspective, the trouble with the generalities of much research-based educational theorising is that they stand in urgent need of situational interpretation or contextualisation. On a rather stronger view, the trouble with such generalities is more that they *are* generalisations over matters that cannot be generalised – although it is often taken to be consistent with this complaint that there can be valid forms of research that are more properly addressed to the particularities of educational engagement.[5] However, the strongest version of this complaint (to which the present author is sympathetic) is that the forms of human association characteristic of educational engagement are not really apt for *scientific* or empirical study at all, although they are amenable to other forms of understanding and appreciation: on this view, it might well be said that 'one cannot *study* people, one can only get to know them'.[6]

The second major difficulty for the view that the theoretical educational disciplines have a quasi-technical application to practice is that it is not clear what would *have to* follow for educational policy making from any empirical or statistical educational finding. To take a crude (although not on that account far-fetched) example: if empirical research conclusively demonstrated that rote learning by direct instruction served to promote widespread, quick and efficient mastery of basic arithmetical operations of addition, multiplication, and so on, this finding would surely have some relevance to any political or professional concern to raise standards of numeracy. However, no such finding could *in and of itself* justify any practical conclusion that we *should* introduce rote learning in schools, in the absence of a further evaluative premise or argument to the effect that these are proper means to a worthwhile educational end. But, of course, either the ends or the means could be disputed. To be sure, it is hard to see how sane and sensible educationalists might be actually *opposed* to raising standards of numeracy – but they might well be opposed to raising them in this way. For one thing, it might be argued that while rote learning of this kind produces faster results in terms of certain routine and unreflective calculative powers, it does not readily conduce to the cultivation of a *principled appreciation* of mathematical or numerical concepts and relationships: in short, there may be learning strategies that take rather longer, but produce better mathematical understanding in the long run. But, of course, it could also be argued that the methods of 'eyes-front' formal instruction, including the reduction in levels of classroom interaction that may occur as a consequence of such instruction, also serves to impede the achievement of other valid educational goals concerned with the development of (say) interpersonal and social skills and/or moral virtues.

Taken together, such observations lead us into something of an impasse of conflicting intuitions about the relationship of educational theory to professional practice. On the one hand, we seem to want to say that the practice of education and teaching *does* – more in the manner of surgery or general medical practice than hairdressing – require some theoretical understanding or principled reflection. On the other hand, we may be (rightly) reluctant to admit that theoretical claims or deliberations have quite the same place in education and teaching that they have in surgery. In short, although it seems improper to regard education and teaching as entirely atheoretical or unreflective enterprises, it seems less plausible to regard the theories upon which they draw as licensing any direct or specific practical or technical applications to the actual rough and tumble of professional practice. But if this is not bad enough, there is worse to come. For insofar as it has been regarded as appropriate for professional teacher education to be grounded in an appreciation of those empirical scientific (especially psychological and sociological) theories of human behaviour that have had a discernible technological impact on the development of educational practice, it also seems that many of these social scientific theories (of learning or intelligence), and the policies (of schooling and training) to which they have given rise, are highly questionable, if not downright *wrong*. So, once again, although student teachers and mature practitioners continue to complain that their theoretical education is utterly worthless from a practical perspective, and that any time spent learning about such theories in academic training is completely wasted, teacher educators appear to persist in holding that a thorough initiation into social scientific theories of human nature or learning that are not just practically useless but theoretically *mistaken* is a *sine qua non* of professional education.

Diverse senses of theory

In cases of this sort where our philosophical intuitions seem to pull in two contrary directions, it is often a useful strategy to ask whether some questionable *common* assumption might not underpin *both* of the apparently opposed positions. In the present case, moreover, it would appear that there is at least one such assumption. What seems precisely shared by all too many advocates and critics of theory is a general view of educational theory as a body of empirical scientific knowledge apt for something like technical application to the practice of education and teaching. The key misapprehension – to which not just student teachers but also many educational researchers are prone – consists in casting the principled reflection and deliberation of teachers in an essentially scientific-technical mould. It is insofar as such social scientific theories are unamenable to direct technical application that field professionals readily become disillusioned with any kind of principled reflection, and are strongly disposed to dismiss 'mere theory' as pointless and irrelevant. All the same, such dismissal may itself follow from one or the other (or both) of two mistaken assumptions. First, it is clearly wrong to suppose that if the practical deliberations of teachers are not those of scientific or technical rationality, they are not rational or principled *at all*. But, secondly, even if the speculations of empirical and other educational theory have no direct technical application to educational practice, one should not assume that they have no role at all to play in the principled – even practical – deliberations of teachers. Above all, however, the beginnings of wisdom with respect to these matters may lie in appreciating that our common talk of educational theory is from the outset beset by crucial ambiguity. For we need to recognise that there are at least two significantly *different* senses in which we regard professional or other educational deliberation as theory-implicated.

In the first significant sense of educational theory – the sense it usually has for trainee teachers – 'theory' refers to a set of formal academic studies or disciplines precisely pursued by students in higher education courses of professional education. Such courses of sociology of education, educational history, psychology of education, educational philosophy, curriculum theory, and so on, seek to initiate students into forms of rational inquiry concerned with the discovery of empirical and other sorts of *truth* about the world. It should also be noted that while the rational disciplines of history, philosophy, psychology, and so on, are *genuinely* theoretical – that is to say, they are *inherently* concerned with the discernment of truth or of what *is* – they are only *contingently* concerned with education: more generally, of course, history, philosophy and psychology are concerned with other aspects of human life and experience besides education and teaching. However, when education crops up as a topic of political or public discussion or debate, 'educational theory' invariably means something other than academic discipline: in such contexts, indeed, it is often more or less synonymous with a range of particular educational perspectives, policies or ideologies such as traditionalism, progressivism and child-centred education. In this sense, educational theory is invariably more concerned with the *normative* dimensions of educational policy and practice – with reasonable evaluation and *prescription* more than true or false *descriptions* or explanations of educational conduct and affairs. Roughly, then, whereas educational theory in the first sense of academic discipline is concerned with what we should rationally *believe* (logically or evidentially) about human learning or pedagogical practice, educational theory in the second (more normative) sense is concerned more with what we should rationally *do*. To that extent, moreover, insofar as academic theory is concerned with the discovery of *truth*, it is also genuine theory, whereas normative inquiry or speculation – concerned as it is more with what is *good* or worthwhile rather than true – is less evidently (or strictly speaking) any form of theory at all.

That said, it hardly needs saying that there are and ought to be significant logical connections between rational belief and action: it is only reasonable to suppose that right action is governed by logically coherent and evidentially well-grounded belief. But rational relations between thought and action are rather less than straightforward, and it cannot be too strongly emphasised that confusion between the academic and normative senses of 'educational theory' (confusion that is every bit as evident in professional theorists' talk of 'practical theory'[7] as in politicians' talk of 'barmy theories'[8]) may be a source of mortal educational error. First, as already noticed, it is not safe to assume that even *true* theoretical claims have direct and inevitable consequences for educational practice: hence, any construal of educational argument on the pattern of theoretical or empirical argument is liable to the *naturalistic* fallacy, or the fallacy of deriving *ought* from *is*.[9] On the basis of this reduction, we may wrongly hold that if research says that method Y works for purpose X, and we have purpose X, we should therefore adopt method Y. However, unlike theoretical or empirical argument, practical, moral or evaluative argument is *defeasible*, and conclusions do not follow from premises with anything like the logical necessity of theoretical inference.[10] For one thing, adding premises to a practical argument can radically affect or alter a conclusion. Thus, even though we want X, and Y is a demonstrable means to X, we also want Z, and Z is incompatible with Y: we may therefore judge that we should *not* do Y. In general, wholesale assimilation of normative practical reasoning to theoretical or scientific inference tends towards educational *technicism* or scientism, and to a view of education as a kind of value-neutral social engineering.

On the other hand, however, reverse assimilation of educational theory in the first sense of academic social science to the second sense of principled normative reflection can result in what might be termed *subjectivist* or *relativist* fallacies.[11] Thus, one may be drawn to conclude that since there can be no obvious empirical resolution of certain educational controversies – indeed, we shall in due course be examining some educational issues that do seem to be of empirically irresolvable normative kinds – practical educational perspectives and prescriptions cannot amount to much more than irrational or groundless prejudices or ideologies. Indeed, there is evidence of some contemporary educational theoretical movement in this direction: under the influence of so-called 'non-realist' or 'idealist' moral and social theories, some postmodern and communitarian philosophers have tended to regard educational and other practical perspectives or ideologies as merely expressive of personal or socio-cultural life choice. From this viewpoint, insofar as such diverse perspectives are liable to enshrine different conceptions or justice and (even) rationality, there may be no common conception of reason, logic or evidence to ground a preference for this way of life over that.[12] But any such view is difficult to sustain, and the observation that educational controversies lie in the realm of normative rather than statistical argument does not obviously undermine either the objectivity or validity of much normative argument. For example, corporal punishment was ultimately abolished in Britain (though it is still widely used in other countries) not because it did not technically 'work' (by deterring misbehaviour), but because it was held to be deeply at odds with the educational aims of any reasonably civilised liberal democracy. The key point here is that if any such political and civic order is committed not just to the ideal of resolving problems and disputes by non-violent means, but also to promoting such commitment through education, it would appear practically (morally) inconsistent to promote the sort of school climate in which violent coercion of miscreants was the perceived means of securing order and control. But to point out that a physically violent response to misbehaviour is logically *incompatible* with the overall aims of a liberal education is to offer a moral or *normative* argument against corporal punishment – to which (theoretical) considerations of causal effectiveness are not directly relevant: even if we admitted (what is anyway dubious) that corporal punishment is effective in deterring undesirable behaviour, we can nevertheless insist that it is *wrong* to practise it.

Facts and values

Still, one may be tempted to suppose that these points amount to no more than a deeper evasion of the key question about the rational objectivity or otherwise of human evaluation. For, it will doubtless be said, while we in our liberal-democratic society reject the violent coercion of others, and hence cannot consistently endorse torture or corporal punishment, there are many societies in which people have no such inhibitions or prohibitions – and if there are quarters in which such principles are *not* subscribed to, then it cannot be possible for us to grant such values objective rational status as morally *right*. Hence, our point about the possibility of valid normative argument against violent coercion succeeds only by begging the question in favour of the very liberal-democratic values that eschew such coercion. However, this objection is itself no less question begging. For why should we take the mere fact that a given social group does not object to the use of torture or violent coercion (at least on other people) to cast doubt on the wrongness of such practices (or upon slavery, race hate or the suppression of women)? Indeed, the mistake now seems to be to suppose that because people endorse different prescriptions, and are *entitled* (in a real enough sense) to believe what they like, such entitlement is enough to absolve what they believe from any need for rational evaluation. But surely, and more plausibly, the fact that other people happily cheat on their wives gives me no more reason to doubt that such conduct is wrong than the fact that others believe that the earth is flat gives me reason to doubt that it is round. Moreover, while these issues are large and have been debated by moral philosophers for two millennia, I suspect that the heart of the problem here lies in dubious assimilation of the so-called 'fact–value' distinction to the related but nevertheless *different* distinction between 'is' and 'ought' (or description and prescription). On the one hand, we cannot doubt the logical gap between empirical fact and normative or evaluative prescription: we *cannot* directly derive an ought from an is. On the other hand, however, it is far from obvious that values cannot be derived from facts: indeed, it is difficult to see how our values might be grounded other than in the facts. Thus, for example, it is a hardly disputable empirical fact that some children are more able or intelligent than others. But it does not follow from widespread disagreement at the level of educational policy about what we should do in the light of this fact either that it is somehow problematic to *value* intelligence, or that intelligence is not of general human benefit. After all, our very interest in intelligence – the reason why individual differences of ability and aptitude are of serious concern to us – is that intelligence and ability are of evident and readily appreciable human value: we value intelligence as we value virtue, sociability and nutritious food, and as we detest vice, psychopathy and snakebite. Moreover, we agree in valuing these empirically observable qualities on the basis of other empirically observable facts concerning their connection with human well-being: in short, the relationship between facts about how the world is and human values is clearly brokered by considerations of fundamental human need, weal and woe.[13]

To be sure, we may not agree in our definitions of such values (as we shall see, for example, there is some real disagreement about what intelligence *means*), and we may not prize them above everything thing else we value – which is why there can be no straightforward or uncontroversial derivation of ought from is. There is, to put it mildly, immense normative disagreement about what we should do in the light of observable (albeit not unproblematically measurable) inequalities of human intelligence: should we give more educational opportunities or resources to intellectually more able than less able pupils; should we give them less; should we give them the same? But despite any and all difficulties of non-normative or value-free inference from observable facts or empirical description to prescription, there cannot be much doubt about the value in which intelligence is generally (humanly) held: thus, disagreements between those who would promote sociability over numeracy and those who would do the opposite are not usually disagreements between those who value the one *rather than* the other, but disputes between people who value *both*, but cannot see their way clear to the simultaneous promotion of both. So although there certainly are normative controversies about education that are extemely difficult to resolve, the prospect that they represent different responses to concerns that are more directly linked to the basic facts of human survival and well-being at least leaves open the possibility of better, best or at any rate least worst options. Indeed, insofar as normative moral claims are construable as reasoned arguments for what is most conducive to human flourishing, such arguments would appear answerable or referable to considerations that go beyond mere personal predilection or local custom. Hence, though there are no hard and fast rules here, it is certainly not the case that anything goes in the way of practical moral preference: for example, since any conception of human flourishing will enshrine some idea of justice, and there *might* be reasonable arguments for the infliction of pain or death on others if this might sometimes have more widespread human benefits, it is hard to see how inflicting pain merely for the personal pleasure it afforded might ever be regarded as compatible with *any* humanly intelligible conception of human justice.

All the same, the main point of this distinction between different senses of educational theory, and of the rather different kinds of human inquiry to which they correspond, is to determine more precisely where the logical centre of gravity of teacher reflection and deliberation lies. To this end, in order to avoid the conceptual impasse that leaves us uncertain whether we should construe teaching as a theoretical practice like surgery or as an atheoretical one like hairdressing, we need to appreciate that: (i) while the theoretical disciplines of academic professional study can significantly contribute to effective professional judgement and practice, (ii) they should not be held to occupy either the whole or the centre stage of principled professional reflection, and (iii) they should not (in this light) be regarded as having unproblematic technical application to professional practice. We therefore need a better recognition that responsible teacher deliberation is primarily *neither* theoretical in the manner of the truth-seeking inquiries of physicists or historians, *nor* technical in the manner of the means–end reasoning of good craftspersons, but more a form of *normative* reasoning ultimately concerned with promoting the well-being of others in a wider *moral* sense. In this light, although teachers need to be as informed as possible concerning the nature of human development and learning, and also require some technical competence for the efficient achievement of more immediate instrumental goals and objectives, they also and above all require the intellectual and moral resources and capacities for critical interpretation of information or knowledge claims, and for a principled and/or discriminating deployment of technique. Moreover, the present re-evaluation of received assumptions about the relationship of educational theory to practice has some fairly radical implications for thinking about teaching. For, in general, whereas the prospect of clear theory-based technical solutions to this or that problem is in many enterprises often a good enough reason for adopting such solutions, this may not be so – for already aired considerations concerning the *defeasibility* of moral practical argument – in educational conduct. For example, it is clearly not safe to assume that because rote learning is conducive to teaching multiplication, or because flogging prevents misbehaviour, that it is educationally proper to adopt such practices – even if we endorse those goals to which such practices would be effective means.

Educational theories as moral perspectives

But a deeper reason why so-called 'theory' requires critical normative or moral scrutiny in the context of professional educational reflection and policy making, as we shall shortly see in more detail, is that it is not obvious that (many of) the social scientific accounts that purport to offer us true descriptions of human learning or motivation are theories in at all the same sense as those physical or natural scientific accounts of the universe that underpin a good deal of human technology. Notwithstanding some latter-day (pragmatist and other) philosophical insistence that *all* theories are value-laden, there seems no good reason to deny that the goal of natural scientific theories is nevertheless to tell us how the world *is*: from this viewpoint, even if such theories are not always right, it is still appropriate enough to assess them as right or wrong (rather than as, say, nice or nasty). However, to the extent that social scientific theories of teaching or learning themselves enshrine deeply normative assumptions about how human beings *should* develop, it is not obvious that they can be *true* or *false* in the same sense – and hence also not clear whether such accounts are in anything like the same sense empirically testable *theories* or hypotheses. This does not, as already noted, mean that such accounts are not *rationally evaluable*, but it does signal the need for educationalists and teachers to adopt a rather different intellectual approach to theory from that in which they have often been encouraged. For if the central questions about theories of learning or psychometry are not so much whether they are *true*, and could therefore be *applied* in the classroom, but about whether it is *right* (in some more morally normative sense) to regard intelligence as a capacity for affectively disengaged abstract problem solving, or whether it is conducive to individual, moral and social and flourishing to try to manipulate or control learning by causal techniques, certain familiar concerns about the relevance of educational theory (or principled educational reflection) may no longer seem quite so pressing. For now the key professional questions about learning theory and psychometry are not so much those of whether it would *work* if we tried it, but of whether it would be proper to promote learning or organise schooling in the way such perspectives have sought to *prescribe*.

That said, conceiving matters thus – not least by reference to these precise examples – points to other apparently anomalous consequences of conceiving teacher reflection and deliberation, as well as much of the so-called 'theory' upon which teachers are required to reflect and deliberate, as normative more than scientific in character. For we have maintained that even if theories of learning or psychometry do not qualify for appraisal as true or false in the sense of genuine scientific theories, they may yet be regarded as wrongheaded or unacceptable in others. Hence, whether or not it is possible to brainwash or condition people into certain kinds of behaviour, this is also widely held to be unacceptable in liberal-democratic societies like our own, and the objectionable nature of any such blatant conditioning is also (mostly) reflected in official and/or public educational policy making. But in that case, what could be the point of teaching to student teachers views or theories of learning that are generally regarded as morally or otherwise *unacceptable*, since, by possible analogy, we would not dream of teaching astrology to trainee astronomers or alchemy to trainee chemists? In this connection, however, it may be a helpful alternative to any scientific-technical approach to professional reflection and deliberation to construe the kind of educated reflection and deliberation needed for good peda-gogical practice as essentially 'Socratic'. Indeed, it was very much in the course of an *educational* mission to assist others to live worthwhile lives that the ancient Greek philosopher Socrates sought to examine the ideas of the greatest scholars of his age on human nature and society. By his own admission, however, Socrates embarked upon this task in the grip of a mistaken picture of the kind of knowledge and inquiry needed to yield any understanding of the good life.[14] Having learned from the Oracle at Delphi that he was the wisest of living men, Socrates was convinced that his lack of any real knowledge of anything must prove that the Oracle was mistaken. After a long career of submitting the best and most influential scientific and moral theories of his day to critical philosoph-ical scrutiny, however, he came to realise that the ideas of others were deeply flawed: that, in short, all those he had formerly taken to be more knowledgeable than himself were in fact in the grip of error and delusion. In time, it dawned upon him that the Socratic wisdom of which the Delphic Oracle had spoken lay not in his having more knowledge than others, but in his keener appreciation of the complexity of the issues and of the limits of all received understanding. Hence, on the Socratic view, wisdom (not least perhaps the wisdom of good teachers) is a kind of critical capability or facility, and the truth that wisdom seeks to disclose proceeds largely via the progressive elimination of error. That said, such failure to grasp the Socratic nature of professional inquiry and wisdom may go a long way towards explaining why student teachers often cannot see the point of learning psychological or other theories – not least when these are submitted to (perhaps fatal) criticism by their teachers: they find it hard to appreciate that real gains in our understanding of teaching and learning can hardly be had in the absence of some grasp of mistaken theories, and of *why* they are mistaken.

At all events, the story so far further serves to vindicate previous claims to the effect that education and teaching partake, along with such standard professions as medicine and law, in the basic character of moral practices. Indeed, it is possible that recent exploration of differences between the (non-technical) rela-tionship of psychology to educational practice and the (apparently more instrumental) relationship of anatomy to surgery or general medical practice might somewhat serve to obscure the precise professional character of medicine. As previously maintained, what principally distinguishes medical practice as a profession as distinct from a trade or industry is not so much that medical practice involves the technical application of scientific theories, but that it is unavoidably implicated in complex normative, specifically ethical, considerations and controversies concerning the proper aims of health, and legitimate means to the pursuit of such aims. First and foremost, debates about healthcare – like debates about education – readily give rise to issues about the obligations of professionals with regard to (the rights of) those they are charged with healing. No less significantly, however, medical practice also gives rise to more or less serious – often life-or-death – moral dilemmas requiring hard choices between different and conflicting options. Although some of these issues may ultimately be resolvable in the wake of new medical techniques, we can be just as sure that others are simply consequences of that encounter with tragic choice that is an inevitable part of the human condition. But although the decisions of teachers and/or other educators may seldom have quite the same life-or-death consequences as those of doctors or lawyers, they are just as clearly enmeshed in issues of basic human rights, and in difficult moral choices about education and development, which can have profound implications for the ultimate well-being of young people. From this viewpoint, it is difficult to see how significant initiation into a principled appreciation of questions of educational equity, opportunity and rights – and of how these questions are linked to issues about the organisation of learning, schools and classrooms – should have anything other than the highest priority in the professional education and training of teachers.

Teacher deliberation: generality and particularity again

We might also be tempted to regard such considerations as decisive in relation to the lately considered question about the occupational status of education and teaching – about whether, to be precise, teaching ought properly to be regarded as a profession. For although we observed that education may be regarded – along with such other time-honoured professions as medicine and law – as a morally important public or civil enterprise, we also raised significant doubts about whether teaching is implicated in 'genuine' theory in the same way or to the same extent as (say) surgery or general medical practice. However, having now claimed that the theory (or, perhaps better, principled reflection) into which teachers require academic initiation is not so much applied science, more the kind of normative inquiry that is also centrally implicated in such other moral practices as law and medicine, it might now look as though the way is clear to regarding teaching as a genuine profession alongside others. On this view, what mainly entitles teachers to professional status is not that they require sociological and psychological theories to improve their methods in some technical sense, but that they need such theories (even where these are false) for an educated professional appreciation of the large questions about justice and flourishing in which education is morally implicated. In this light, indeed, education and teaching may appear to be clearer cases of professions than those more routine surgical practices that do not obviously involve their practitioners in significantly autonomous professional judgements and decisions. From this viewpoint, any decisions about the present or future development of pupils that teachers are daily required to make in the rough and tumble of school and classroom life may seem to need quite as much if not more in the way of serious, responsible and principled judgement than anything required of junior medics.

All the same, we have also previously indicated some qualitative differences between the normative deliberations of teachers and other professionals, which might also discourage any over-hasty ranking of education and teaching alongside medicine or law. First, there is the negative point that insofar as teachers and other educationalists are accountable to the political and public policies of particular socio-cultural constituencies, it is not clear that they can ever aspire to quite the full autonomy of other professions. Indeed, I suspect that this point also has a significant epistemic dimension, and rests ultimately upon certain key differences between the knowledge bases of (say) medicine and teaching. For, in the last analysis, the possession by doctors of expert knowledge of the science of human health must mean that lay opinions about medical treatment cannot generally carry the same weight as those of medical practitioners – notwithstanding that patients and/or their nearest and dearest may still be morally entitled to significant consultation over any decision about this or that medical course of action. However, although teachers as citizens have both a right and a duty to contribute to the formation of educational policy through proper democratic process and debate, as well as a professional duty to oppose what they take to be ill-advised or unjust educational policies, the more thoroughgoing normative or moral character of educational deliberation precisely requires teacher reflection and deliberation to be more accountable to the wider public interests of parents, employers and politicians – and therefore places greater limits on professional teacher autonomy. Thus, for example, it is reasonably clear that the opposition of a particular social constituency (say Christian Scientists or Jehovah's Witnesses) to blood transfusion would not normally be taken to undermine professional medical opinion that transfusions are generally good medical practice, even where it is fully appreciated that patients or close relatives have a right to refuse transfusion. However, insofar as the communities served by schools may be taken to have a legitimate say (not least in respect of values) in what is to *count* as good educational practice, a particular social consensus to the effect that a particular school should not offer sex education to its pupils might well be regarded as professionally compelling, even in the face of some principled professional opposition. The key difference is that whereas non-professional consumers of medicine are not in an epistemically authoritative position to decide what is medically appropriate, the non-professional consumers of education have (to a degree) a genuine right to *determine* what is educationally acceptable in a given context of schooling. Hence if, against medical advice, I resist a life-saving blood transfusion for my child, then I may reasonably be held at fault; but if, against a teacher's advice, I resist a certain kind of moral education for my child, I am (within certain limits) less obviously at fault – if the values inherent in the education offered are contrary to what I *desire* for my child.

But secondly, as also previously noted, there seems to be a dimension to the practical or moral aspects of teacher reflection and deliberation that extends beyond the normative interests and concerns of members of such standard professions as medicine and law. To a large extent, the moral concerns of medicine and law are focused more on general or abstract issues of medical or legal rights and duties. It is this concern with rights and duties that gives rise to a familiar professional emphasis on *impartiality*, and which also introduces a certain *impersonality* into professional dealings: by and large, good professionals are those who observe neutral rules of engagement with client or patient, and who steer clinically clear of any kind of personal – not least affective – involvement or engagement with others. This more formal conception of legitimate normative relations between professionals and clients also chimes well, as previously noted, with a distinctly modern emphasis on right and obligation as the key idioms of ethical discourse. Arguably, however, it also enshrines a somewhat attenuated conception of normative practical or moral reasoning (owing much to the eighteenth-century philosophy of Kant, as well as to nineteenth-century political liberals) that does not well reflect the moral deliberations and more interpersonal associations of such 'people professions' or vocations as nursing, ministry and teaching. Moreover, it has been the need to make sense of such more vocational reflection and deliberation that has encouraged recent educational philosophers to return to Aristotle's pioneering analysis of practical wisdom (*phronesis*).[15] As we have already had occasion to notice, it was Aristotle who first appreciated that strict impartiality is not the most salient feature of moral thought, that there may be no less injustice in treating unequals equally than there is in treating equals unequally, and that the kind of deliberation required for genuine interpersonal moral association (rather than, as it were, mere professional–client relations) necessarily involves some affective or empathic sensitivity to the needs of others in their particular circumstances. In short, Aristotle's *phronesis* or practical wisdom is distinguishable from modern *deontic* (rule-based) conceptions of practical reason by virtue of its concern with the particular aspects and circumstances of the individual human case – not least with the feelingful or affective as well as the cognitive aspects of interpersonal association.

Although we shall need to give closer attention to the nature of moral engagement in the next chapter, we may observe for now that any enterprise that involves care and concern for the particularities of personal welfare and development, rather than for justice in some more distributively defined sense, would appear to involve the cultivation of complex normatively indexed sensibilities and sensitivities that go well beyond formal or abstract reasoning about rights and duties. It would also appear that such occupations as nursing, ministry and teaching are barely conceivable apart from such qualities: hence, insofar as any distinction between profession and vocation may seem to turn on these rather different patterns of normative engagement, it may seem wiser to regard teaching as a vocation more than a profession. On the other hand, since questions of rights and duties would seem to be of no less relevance to education than to medicine, and insofar as it is nowadays increasingly recognised that medical practitioners stand no less than teachers in need of the more personal sensibilities of practical wisdom, there might be some case for a rather more thorough revision – with regard to all relevant occupations – of any and all received distinctions between profession and vocation. All the same, it seems clear that insofar as teachers – unlike either doctors or nurses – need qualities of normative or moral reflection and engagement not just to operate well in their professional or vocational practice, but also to assist others to develop such qualities for the purposes of ordinary positive human association, it can hardly be denied that a better appreciation of the nature of moral association and inquiry is a *sine qua non* for educationalists and teachers irrespective of their precise occupational status. It is this topic that awaits us in the next chapter.

Possible tasks

(1) In the light of the two rather different senses of educational theory distinguished in this chapter, consider what forms or modes of knowledge or inquiry a teacher might need to draw upon in order to illuminate or address the following professional issues: (i) the educational value of open-plan schools; (ii) comprehensive versus selective schooling; (iii) the effectiveness of phonic reading methods; (iv) the appropriateness of school league tables; (v) compulsory dance for boys and girls; (vi) compulsory sex education; (vii) separate faith-based schooling.

(2) With regard to each of the seven professional educational issues identified above, construct a specifically *normative* argument to some specific policy conclusion, which also takes account of some likely objections to your argument.

Chapter 5

Wider moral implications of education

Teaching, ethics and moral education

At this point, some readers might be tempted to dismiss the questions we have so far been pursuing about the precise status of teaching as an occupation – about whether teaching is best regarded as a profession, a vocation, a trade or something else – as idle conceptual hair splitting with no serious practical consequences. This, however, would be a mistake: for it should already be clear that rival conceptions of the role of the teacher have potentially quite different implications for how the responsibilities of teachers to pupils, parents, employers and politicians are conceived. Indeed, foremost among these questions is that of whether, in what way, or to what extent education and teaching should be regarded as implicated in the wider moral development and formation of young people. Thus, although it is probably safe to say that education and teaching as pursued in the context of formal schooling have usually been regarded as to *some* extent implicated in moral development and/or the cultivation of positive human values, the nature of that implication would appear to vary according to different conceptions of the role of the teacher. In this regard, we might begin by distinguishing some very broad differences of perspective. First, we may distinguish between those who hold that the knowledge, understanding and skills that educators are concerned to transmit give teachers a privileged status and authority with regard to the cultivation of right moral virtues and values, and those who would claim that teachers are merely the means by which the values of whatever community they are employed to serve are transmitted to the next generation. Secondly, however, we may distinguish between those who share the widespread assumption that schools and teachers have a legitimate role with respect to the formation of the moral and other values of young people, and those who would question the proper involvement of teachers in any such enterprise of wider moral formation.

These distinctions are clearly different – since, for example, one may hold that teachers do have a legitimate role to play with respect to the cultivation of values, whether or not one holds that pedagogues have any special or privileged moral authority – but they also map onto different conceptions of education and teaching in complex and interesting ways. Moreover, these distinctions would also appear to be related to diverse perspectives in ethics and/or the theory of moral value. In the first place, the idea that schools and teachers have no business whatsoever transmitting or cultivating moral values can certainly be linked to the kind of radical, progressive or libertarian conceptions of education and schooling that incline to a social remedial or therapeutic view of education. The lately explored vocational notion that social workers or teachers (perhaps especially community educators) need to be seen as 'on the side' of the client certainly runs counter to any 'paternalist' conception of the teacher as in business to 'indoctrinate' others in a particular way of life or conduct. On this view, individuals are entitled to freedom of choice with respect to moral and other values that may well be construed as deeply *personal* (if not actually *subjective*) matters. In addition, it is also possible to detect some contemporary shift from the rather different vocational conception of the teacher as 'cultural missionary' to a more modern professional conception of education and teaching that is in its own way rather sceptical about the teacher's role as a transmitter of moral or other values. Thus, insofar as teachers have often in past times and (past and present) places been regarded as custodians of the values and beliefs of particular cultural constituencies, they could not be regarded as doing their job properly if they did *not* represent, express and *exemplify* certain fundamental virtues and values. In the process of the latter-day transition to more culturally diverse or pluralist societies that has recently overtaken many developed liberal democracies (such as Britain), however, the idea that schools and teachers *should* act as the guardians of a particular way of life has come to appear more problematic. Indeed, it may be that the general trend towards conceiving education and teaching more in terms of profession than vocation has been one major consequence of sensitivity to this issue, as well as of the perceived need to develop a code of professional ethics based on neutral and impartial respect for educational clients, irrespective of race, colour, creed or other differences.[1] However, the main motive behind any such ethics of impartiality might also be a fundamental liberal suspicion that no-one is entitled to impose his or her own values on other people, since there can be no right or wrong, truth or falsity, with regard to what are ultimately matters of personal opinion and preference. Hence, whereas the transmission of moral and other values was formerly assumed to be part and parcel of good educational practice on at least one time-honoured 'vocational' conception of teaching, the direct or explicit teaching of substantial values turns out to be *unprofessional* on at least some conceptions of teaching as a profession.

There may also be some doubt about the role of schools and teachers in the formation of moral and other values on those more commercial contractual or market-orientated views that regard education and schooling as primarily concerned with the supply of specific commodities – instrumentally conceived information and skills perhaps – to 'clients' or 'consumers'. Indeed, some separation of pedagogical activity from the wider moral and cultural formation of children or young people would appear to be a more or less direct consequence of certain types or approaches to teaching. At one extreme, for example, private coaches or teachers of piano or gymnastics are contracted to provide students or pupils with fairly specific skills according to fairly well-defined and -established criteria: if they teach these skills as required, they have done their job, but that job would also appear to begin and end with the teaching of such skills. In this regard, although the roles of sports coach and music teacher are not entirely devoid of ethical import, and such teachers may certainly fail in *moral* respects – by, for example, physically or sexually abusing their young clients – they are not generally answerable for the wider moral or personal development of their pupils. Although piano teachers may be called to account for failing to teach proper keyboard technique, they can hardly be held accountable if the child goes on to take drugs or fails to learn that stealing is wrong. Again, it may be that some such separation of teaching from education has inspired not only modern radical proposals[2] to restructure educational provision in terms of non-institutional learning networks (providing, in their terms, education rather than *schooling*), but also more recent market-orientated conceptions of educational provision that seem touched with a similar unease about whether schools and teachers (rather than communities and parents) are properly placed to assume responsibility for moral and other personal formation.

Morality, social responsibility and individual liberty

On the other hand, it is doubtful whether such scepticism concerning the moral educational role of schools and teachers is very widespread: generally, indeed, it is not just that (especially state) schools and teachers are commonly credited with this responsibility, but that they are frequently criticised by politicians and the general public whenever and wherever pupils apparently fail to aquire capacities for morally positive interpersonal association.[3] In this respect, however, it has often seemed reasonable to observe some distinction between the 'personal' moral or other values to which people are entitled as individual agents, and more common or 'core' values in default of which, it might be said, civil social order could hardly be sustained. Some such distinction, moreover, is probably clear enough for many practical purposes.[4] On the one hand, even the most pater-nalist of educators is unlikely to require everyone to live by chastity or vegetarianism, even if he, she or others regard these as defensible personal moral principles or virtues. Given the fair range of opinion about such values, it is unlikely that they would be widely shared in contemporary liberal-democratic contexts, and it would therefore be unreasonable to impose such values on others. (That said, one might also foresee a time at which the eating of animals came to be considered as uncivilised as slavery, and in which democratic sanc-tions against meat eating became the order of the day – and one can already see public opinion heading this way with respect to questions about individual liberty and smoking.) On the other hand, however, even the most libertarian educators are unlikely to hold that individuals are free to decide whether public, domestic or sexual violence, theft or child abuse should be regarded as morally acceptable, and would no doubt support legislation to prevent such abuses. In general, then, it may appear appropriate to draw a line between those personal values and commitments that do not obviously entail any infringement of the liberties and/or rights of others, and those forms of interpersonal or social demeanour which are likely have significant implications for general public order. In the tradition of modern (nineteenth century onwards) political liberalism, some such distinction has often been grounded in the so-called 'harm principle', according to which individual agents are entitled to think and behave in any way they wish so long as it does not violently or otherwise intrude upon the rights and liberties of others.[5]

This distinction is useful so far as it goes. In educational terms, for example, it is reasonable to suppose that in at least common schools – those designed to offer public educational provision to those who might not otherwise have access to schooling – educationalists should bear some responsibility for the teaching of those interpersonal rules and principles that underpin much if not most civilised association and legislation. On the face of it, indeed, it is difficult to see not just how any civilised human association whatsoever could continue without some basic recognition that it is wrong to lie, to steal, to bully, to discriminate against others on grounds of gender, race or physical handicap, and so on, but also how any school – as a particular human social institution – could itself proceed effectively in the absence of such basic moral consensus. Indeed, common experience shows us that effective teaching is itself difficult to pursue in the absence of any such basic moral order. From this viewpoint, irrespective of the values and virtues that may be acquired in the home or local community – and it has to be borne in mind that some children may have been taught few if any civilised values – it may be reasonable to regard schooling as a good opportunity to appreciate, acquire and practise the principles of wider civil association. This explains why some modern educationalists, notwithstanding the vaunted moral diversity of contemporary socio-cultural pluralism, have attempted to discover – often via some sort of quasi-empirical or statistical appeal to cross-cultural consensus – a common 'core' of values and virtues for the purposes of moral, social and civic education[6] and as a basis of moral sensibility and order for the common school.

All the same, this conception of the relationship of general education or schooling to moral or social education – as well as the notion of moral understanding or sensibility upon which any such approach seems to be predicated – is prey to some difficulties. First, both the educational approach and the notion of moral association upon which it is based seem rather *instrumentally* conceived: from this perspective, moral formation may seem more a matter of *training* than *education*. In this light, moreover, it would appear that recent global as well as local interest in moral education has been fuelled by overall political and public anxiety at a perceived decline in the behaviour of youth – expressed, for example, in general disrespect for parental, educational and social authority, aggression and violence both inside and outside the school, truancy, vandalism, sexual licence, drug abuse, and so on. Although it has not been entirely unappreciated that such failings cannot be wholly laid at the door of teachers, it also seems to be a common view that firmer social consensus upon what is morally acceptable or otherwise might assist a more resolute stand by schools against this rising tide of apparent moral anarchy. At all events, a prime motive of recent professional interest in moral education and in the moral role of schools and teachers has been a remedial concern with halting the perceived moral rot, and this has equally often seemed to be a matter of reconditioning the conduct of young people in a socially agreed direction.[7] However, although no sane person would wish to belittle these serious contemporary public and political concerns – for, of course, no sensible person could fail to wish for a society in which the young are respectful of the law and others, and are properly equipped to live responsible and flourishing lives – the trouble is that any such efforts at moral rearmament on the basis of socially agreed values threatens to confuse moral education with *social control*.

The conceptual and practical difficulties here are legion. First, it is for many if not most practical purposes simply false to suppose that there is moral consensus in *any* society – not least in liberal democracies of the kind in which many of us find ourselves today. What is deeply misleading about the recent claims of politicians and social theorists to have discovered consensus is that such agreement is usually secured only at the level of vacuous generality at which serious disagreement does not or cannot arise. Do Christians (Catholic, Orthodox and Protestant), Hindus, Buddhists, Muslims, Jews, communists, political conservatives, humanists, atheists or whatever share any moral values? At one level, well yes: they would mostly agree, for example, that honesty, courage, self-control, justice, compassion, responsibility, freedom, and so on, are the sort of positive values that children should be encouraged to appreciate and observe in the home and in the school. At another level, however, they clearly do not share the same moral values at all – for it is, perhaps first and foremost, *moral* differences that *divide* Catholic from Protestant, humanist from religious believer, capitalist from communist, Buddhist from atheist, and so on. What, for example, are we to teach young people in the name of justice? Does justice mean equality? Does equality mean equal regard and treatment of the sexes? But even if Muslims and Christians do construe justice as equal treatment, they may diversely interpret this in ways that have radically different practical implications in the sphere of gender difference. And do responsibility and self-control – especially with regard to issues of sex and drugs (in which young people invariably have some interest) – mean the same thing to religious and non-religious believers? Does even courage mean the same thing to each and every person: does it mean active and dogged loyalty to and/or defence of the interests of one's social group, or can it be expressed in defiance of those interests – when, in recognition of some transcendent moral imperative, one comes to question the priorities of one's own constituency? More generally, is courage best expressed in taking up arms against a sea of troubles, or suffering the slings and arrows of outrageous fortune?

Indeed, the beginnings of wisdom concerning the nature of moral life, inquiry and reflection lie in recognising that disagreement and controversy are of its very *essence*: in this light, one might reasonably suspect that any practical question that turned out to be resolvable by statistical or other quasi-empirical methods would *not* be a genuine moral problem. And although this observation does not in and of itself warrant the over-hasty conclusion (of some subjectivist views of ethics) that there can be no reasonable or rational resolution of moral problems or dilemmas – since it does not obviously follow from disagreement in such other areas of human inquiry as science or aesthetics, for example, that there are no right (or at least no wrong) answers to scientific or aesthetic questions – it does make any uncritical initiation into this or that pattern of approved conduct in the name of 'moral consensus' appear more like moral training or indoctrination than moral education. Moreover, it may also need to be better appreciated that social agreement is neither a *necessary* nor a *sufficient* condition of the positive human value, correctness or truth of a moral claim or judgement. It is clearly not a sufficient condition because there are and have been societies that have subscribed to values and practices – slavery, genocide, the subjection of women, and so on – that we would not nowadays hesitate to regard as quite clearly morally wrong (and that were, more than likely, held to be morally wrong by many right-thinking members of those societies). By the same token, however, since agreement or consensus may be more or less witting collusion in hegemonic or other oppression, it cannot be a necessary condition of moral worth either: some of the greatest of past moral reformers have been lone voices crying in the wilderness against the social concordats of their day that precisely endorsed slavery, sexual oppression and intolerance of minorities. At the very least, moreover, this gives substance to the possibility that moral judgements have some *universal* rational or other objective status or basis that goes beyond mere personal preference or social collusion.

The possibility of moral objectivity

This possibility has, of course, been recognised by philosophers at least since the time of the first great pioneers of moral inquiry, Socrates and Plato. However, although very many distinguished latter-day moral theorists have defended different and diverse non-consensual and objectivist accounts of moral reason and conduct, it nowadays seems that any general idea of moral objectivity that is *not* grounded in social agreement – apart from widely dismissed religious accounts of morality as divine command – is for most citizens of contemporary secular-liberal societies almost beyond comprehension. Indeed, there are notable modern intellectual precedents for the view that if it is no longer acceptable to base public morality on religious revelation – if, as it has also been said, 'God is dead'[8] – then social consensus can be the only serious alternative source or grounding for morality.[9] It is therefore not really surprising to discover that many if not most contemporary educational policy documents endorse moral educational strategies based on what one might call a 'core plus options' view of moral development: on this view, moral formation is regarded as a matter of some accommodation between the voluntary personal adoption of private (religious or other) value commitments, and more compulsory initiation into a largely socially constructed system of interpersonal rules and principles.[10]

To some extent, this approach also confuses the question of whether schools and teachers are morally accountable to society, or vice versa, with that of whether there are different and distinct grounds of moral authority and accountabilty in state-aided religious schools and fully secular state schools. Thus, whereas separate Catholic or Protestant Christian schools will be morally answerable to the community, *both* school and community are ultimately accountable to the moral law of Christian revelation, and a teacher will have moral authority to override parental interests insofar as those interests are at odds with Gospel teaching. On the other hand, if the moral law is a product of secular democratic will, then schools and teachers are merely agents of that will, and it becomes less clear how – or in the name of what – schools and teachers could ever be in a position to offer moral opposition to popular social trends that they take to be morally regressive. At the same time, this may be an additional powerful reason for the state to fudge the issue of the moral authority of education by the marketing and commodification of schooling. If, in a pluralist society, there is no set of common values to which all constituencies might readily subscribe, it might be better for particular schools to be morally answerable to the values of those social or cultural constituences they directly serve. If parents want their children to be schooled in particular sorts of knowl-edge, skills and values, they can send them to schools custom-designed for the provision of such commodities. Moreover, if these religious, secular, selective or other schools offer the customers or clients they serve what they desire for their children, then they will (commercially) flourish, but if they do not, they will fail. At all events, in matters of moral value as in all else, the customer would always be *right*. Hence, on this view, schools and teachers may be regarded as agents of moral formation, but only insofar as they communicate socially or parentally approved values and attitudes.

However, there is something profoundly unsettling about any such line of reasoning. To begin with, a time-honoured way of thinking about education would regard schools and teachers as perhaps the principal agencies of moral formation in society – in a way that goes beyond mere accountability to current social trends or parental predilections. There are surely at least some circum-stances in which we do or should want to say that (good) schools or teachers know better than others what is morally best for young people, and should not merely be pandering to dubious parental aspirations and ambitions – even if parents are footing the bill. For example, it has been my own experience (as a teaching super-visor) to have actually witnessed private school sporting events at which parents could be seen inciting their offspring to unparalleled depths of ruthless competi-tion: indeed, it was fairly clear on such occasions that this was not just harmless fun, but in deadly earnest, and that these were exactly the kinds of attitudes that parents were paying the schools so handsomely to promote. However, one might easily cite other instances of attitudes and behaviour entering the school from the outside community that most teachers would wish to resist as symptoms of moral decline rather than endorse by way of servile obedience to prevailing social trends or (even) political correctness. But if a non-religious teacher is inclined to believe that (for example) the superficial and casual attitudes to human association that some young people import from popular culture – or even from immediate family influence – need to be subverted (rather than, say, cured by the morning-after pill), to what besides divine authority might he or she appeal in a social climate that recognises no moral authority or no ideal of human flourishing beyond individual or social preference?

To begin with, one might well question the idea that if morality can no longer be held to stem from religious revelation, it can only be a matter of social-democratic consensus, or of what the public wants. Indeed, this may well follow from the rather dubious assumption that insofar as morality is a human institution, it is appropriate to ask: *who* determines what counts as moral?[11] On this reckoning, if we deny that either God or the individual decides what is moral right or wrong, 'society' may seem the only remaining source of moral authority.[12] However, it is first worth noticing that we do not assume that something is right or true because *someone* says so in other realms of human inquiry: we do not suppose that any answer to the questions 'Why is 2 the square root of 4?', 'Why do metals expand when heated?' or even 'Why is Shakespeare's *King Lear* regarded as a great (if not the greatest) work of dramatic tragedy?' is to be given by such responses as 'God says so', 'Charlie says so' or 'the British public says so'. On the contrary, we assume in all such cases that the truth or falsity of such claims stands to be determined by reference to *objective* facts, criteria and/or considerations: even in the case of aesthetic inquiry or art criticism we expect to be given objective *reasons* for this claim or that which are precisely *independent* of the mere personal tastes of particular individuals or social constituencies. (For example: 'No, surely Shakespeare's *Othello* or Sophocles' *Oedipus* is superior to *King Lear* in respect of features *x*, *y* and *z*.') But, if this is so, why should we suppose that it is necessary to ask in relation to this or that moral claim who says that this is right or wrong? Indeed, if someone was to ask in relation (for example) to the frightful massacre some years ago of infant school children in the Scottish town of Dunblane, 'Who says this was a (morally) bad or wicked act?', we should surely regard that person as having precisely taken leave of his or her moral senses.

The philosophical search for moral objectivity

To be sure, there may well be occasions on which we are not sure whether a given moral claim is true or false, but this is also true in other realms of human inquiry and does not generally undermine the point that we often know what is right or wrong with some *certainty*. That said, it is one thing to know quite well (in our bones) what is morally right, and another to understand *why* or how it is right: even in mathematics (apparently) there may be propositions that mathematicians regard as certainly true, but that they do not know how to *prove* – and the overriding problem of moral inquiry, and hence for moral education, is therefore that of understanding the *grounds* of moral claims. Indeed, it was more or less in a context of moral educational inquiry that the ancient Greek philosopher Socrates initiated that formal study of moral experience and judgement that we now know as *ethics*. The key question for Socrates was that of how we ought to live – or of what constitutes a flourishing human life. Socrates rightly recognised that this question must lie at the very heart of any worthwhile educational endeavour. Indeed, it is no accident that some of Socrates' crucial dialectical encounters were with professional educationalists and teachers, and that some of the most powerful Socratic critiques are of the educational ideas of his day: from this viewpoint, there has always been a strong case for making the Platonic dialogue *The Gorgias* required reading for all prospective educationalists and teachers.[13] It is in this dialogue that Socrates comes into most conspicuous conflict with the ideas of the so-called 'Sophists', who were really the market- or consumer-orientated educationalists of the day. Essentially, such Sophists as Gorgias and Protagoras were engaged in selling their skills and expertise to the sons (rather than daughters) of well-to-do parents who were ambitious for the worldly success of their offspring. In brief, the Sophists taught that the best possible life was the pursuit of self-interest, and that the key skills they taught – not least 'rhetoric' or the art of persuasion – were especially conducive to securing personal advantage: the privileged young men who were destined for a life of political intrigue in the ancient Greek democratic assemblies would need the skills of artful speech in order to bend others to their will in ruthless pusuit of power and influence (as well as of the material benefits that would inevitably follow from smart deals with well-placed others). At all events, this was the way in which the customers and clients who paid handsomely for the expertise and skills of the Sophists were inclined to conceive the good life. Moreover, as in many contemporary contexts, the ancient customer's view of ultimate value could not be wrong.

Still, it is just this sophistical identification of the good life with the self-interested life that Socrates is at pains to question in *The Gorgias* and other Platonic dialogues. Socrates argues that there is a significant sense – perfectly consistent with ordinary usage – in which the accumulation of power and wealth is certainly not a means to the good life: we can recognise that that there are very many people of great wealth and power – leaders of tyrannical regimes, corrupt politicians and vicious gang bosses – who we should not want to regard as living good lives, and in whose shoes many if not most of us would not wish (for all the tea in China) to stand. Socrates argues, more strongly, that the lives of such people cannot even be regarded as good in their own terms. The tyrant or criminal is also – whether or not he knows it – a deeply wretched and miserable slave to his own greed and lust: his selfish and cruel lack of regard for others is more symptomatic of weakness and dependence than of the self-possession of responsible freedom. To be truly free – indeed, even to enjoy those personal qualities from which real freedom springs – one's conduct requires to be governed by a knowledge of what is right and true: in particular, it would seem that there can be no true *self-interest* apart from respect for *justice*, and no justice without that regard for the common good presupposed to (for example) the four cardinal (Hellenic) virtues of courage, temperance, justice and prudence (or wisdom).[14] Thus, for Socrates, the truly good life is the *virtuous* life, and virtue is a function of, if not actually identical with, *knowledge* of the good. Since it is just this knowledge that it is the business of education in general and moral education in particular to impart, only those with some real insight into that knowledge are well placed to put others on the right track to the good life. Correspondingly, those who have not engaged in serious inquiry into the good life via disciplined pursuit of knowledge and truth are not fit to advise on the proper conduct of education. From the Socratic viewpoint, then, the educational 'customer' (if, indeed, it is appropriate to talk in such a way) is not always right, and politicians, employers and parents may not be best placed to know what is (morally or otherwise) good for their children. Indeed, for Socrates, it is the educators' job not so much to satisfy public or parental desires, but more to *shape* those desires in a properly informed way: in this regard, like Socrates himself, educators might well find themselves deeply at odds with prevailing social attitudes and values.

All the same, the problem that Socrates sets for subsequent philosophers and educationalists is that of determining, if virtue is knowledge, not only what sort of knowledge virtue is, but also the relationship of those who possess such knowledge to those who do not. The view of Socrates' pupil, interpreter and protégé Plato seems to have been that the knowledge needed for virtue was a special kind of formal, abstract or theoretical knowledge – at once more *objective* than scientific knowledge and more *certain* than the truths of mathematics – attainable only by a small minority of intellectually gifted people after a protracted process of formal education and training. On this view, the just society could only be one in which the morally wise minority had (political as well as moral) authority over the ignorant majority – which, Plato notoriously concluded, could *not* mean a democratic society.[15] In the ideal Platonic republic, then, there is a clear sense in which the educator *qua* moral philosopher is also the rightful legislator or *ruler*: no-one could be entitled to lead or teach others who was not a *bona fide* seeker of truth, wisdom and virtue – which would also give the teacher special moral authority over the *hoi polloi* with regard to the matter of how they should live their lives. Clearly, however, few if any of us today live in an ideal Platonic republic – and one key reason for widespread modern preference for political democracy is deep scepticism about any such Socratic–Platonic understanding of knowledge required for the wisdom of moral virue. Although we can appreciate that teachers are sometimes wiser (in a Socratic sense) than parents concerning the true value of education for moral formation and self-understanding (rather than for the pursuit of personal ambition and advantage), we also know that this is by no means always so, and that there will be occasions when precisely the reverse is true. Moreover, this is also surely because it is doubtful whether moral and other *wisdom* is to be measured in terms of what often passes for knowledge in the context of education. Common experience teaches that advanced knowledge of theoretical physics or mathematics does not make someone morally wiser than those who are ignorant about such matters: on the contrary, relatively untutored parents may often have a conspicuously better sense of what is morally best for their children than those with advanced academic or theoretical expertise. Thus, whatever moral knowledge is, it would not appear to be socially, genetically or educationally distributed in the manner Plato supposed: since it is not the sole preserve of the *academically* intelligent, it is arguable that a just society is one that extends some voice on important public issues to all with at least the potential for moral wisdom – which would also seem to mean each and every rationally responsible human person.

The moral authority of teachers

That said, it remains plausible to hold that prospective and practising teachers have an *occupational* or professional duty to aspire to the kind of serious reflection on the nature of the good life that Socrates clearly regarded as a *sine qua non* of good educational practice. Indeed, it is arguable that education and teaching are unique among all other occupations – with the possible exception of ministry – in entailing this requirement. Other professions and vocations have, as we have seen, a clear basis in ethical obligations and considerations: doctors and lawyers are in principle duty-bound to preserve the lives and defend the freedoms of others, nurses are obliged to care for the sick, and social workers have a responsibility to help others in various straitened circumstances; but few occupations besides teaching (and ministry) are so clearly concerned with the actual formation of others in positive values and attitudes. In short, it is hard to deny that education involves improving people in a sense that extends beyond mere coaching or training in information and skills to wider *personal* formation. One possible implication of this is that despite the often unfair targeting of schools for failure to halt the kinds of moral decline for which they could not be held wholly responsible, we do regard it as proper – where pupils appear to be falling short in attitudes and behaviour – to ask what teachers might do to improve matters. Again, it is arguable that there is a legitimate public interest or concern with regard to the personal character and values of teachers that may not apply, or in quite the same way, to doctors, lawyers, nurses and social workers (though again there would be much the same concern about religious ministers). To be sure, this interest can be too intrusive and paternalistic, but it is reasonable to hold that those who are charged with the positive human development of others should not be conspicuously vicious or corrupt persons themselves. In this light, we may observe an *internal* connection between the personal and the professional lives of teachers that there is not in the case of doctors or lawyers: as we have insisted to date, good teachers need to be not only the possessors of certain kinds of skills, but also certain kinds of *people*. It would also appear to be widely held that the promotion of moral values is the concern of all teachers *qua* educators. Thus, even if one held that teaching young people aesthetic taste or values was something best promoted across the curriculum, one might still sympathise with physics teachers who denied that cultivating aesthetic values was either their business or within their expertise. It would be rather harder, however, to sympathise with any claim that teaching moral values was neither the business of nor within the expertise of this or that subject teacher.[16]

Still, this only brings us around again to the all-important question of how this dimension of moral personhood and agency, which we have persistently argued to be part and parcel of the professional demeanour of all good teachers, should be conceived – or even appraised. By what standards may we judge someone to be morally suitable for teaching: to be, more particularly, a fit moral example to others? We have already observed the difficulties of construing moral wisdom on the lines of abstract theoretical knowledge in the manner of Plato: to have moral wisdom or to teach such wisdom to others does not seem to be a matter of acquiring or teaching mere information, or some kind of purely intellectual or behavioural skill. All the same, one significant advance in thinking about the nature of moral life and deliberation – which some[17] have attributed primarily to the genius of Plato's great pupil Aristotle – identifies the reason and deliberation of moral engagement more as a kind of *practical* rather than theoretical reason: thus construed, such reason is concerned less with what to think or believe in some more exclusively intellectual or cognitive sense, more with assisting us to see what to *do* in moral terms (including what to make of ourselves). All the same, although the distinction between theoretical and practical reason has been widely appreciated and debated in modern moral philosophy, there has also been much controversy concerning the proper understanding of practical moral reason. I shall therefore devote the few remaining paragraphs of this part of the book to a brief examination of two very influential, as well as educationally relevant, perspectives on the logical grammar of practical moral deliberation.

Two concepts of practical reason

The first of these accounts of practical moral reason, which derives mainly from the ethical theory of the great eighteenth-century German metaphysician Immanuel Kant, has had an enormous influence not only upon modern conceptions of (liberal) education, but also more generally upon modern social and political theorising. However, Kant's ethical theory is itself more or less a detailed development of ideas to be found in the work of the earlier political theorist Jean-Jacques Rousseau. The basic Rousseauian position, explored in his major political work *The Social Contract*, is that moral and social justice rests fundamentally on a rational principle of practical *impartiality*: 'there is', he says, 'a universal justice emanating from reason alone'[18] that enjoins us to treat others with equal regard unless we can find good (other-regarding) reasons for treating them differently. The key idea, developed in greater detail by Kant, is that there is a kind of rationally self-undermining inconsistency involved in refusing to recognise the claims of others to the basics of a flourishing life – not least if these are the kinds of claim we would want to make on our own behalf as individuals also desiring a flourishing life. Thus, how can any slave-owner, as a rationally *consistent* human agent, deny freedom to others *and* claim it as a right for himself? Rousseau holds that no-one could *reasonably* do so – and, in terms reminiscent of both Socrates and Plato, maintains that 'those who regard themselves as the masters of others are indeed greater slaves than they'.[19]. Rousseau and Kant also remind us of Socrates in arguing that insofar as there can be no real freedom of the kind we associate with human personhood (as a normative construct) apart from such practical consistency, one cannot be a genuine human agent (person) under conditions of practical inconsistency. More specifically, one can be a rational moral agent (person) only insofar as one is faithful to what Kant calls the *categorical imperative*, and the categorical imperative precisely requires us to control our natural inclinations, or the prejudices of our empirical social conditioning, in obedience to rational moral principle. This requires us, for example, to tell the truth and keep our promises as a matter of *general rule*: for if it is presupposed to any *bona fide* participation in the practice of promise keeping that I expect others to honour their promises to me, how could I consistently fail to keep my own promises (whenever, say, they turn out to be personally inconvenient)? Thus, for Kant, personal identity and integrity are more or less functions of moral integrity, and obedience to moral law is the only secure basis of personhood.[20]

Despite the fact that few modern philosophers would endorse Kant's highly metaphysical view of personal agency as rooted in some non-empirical source of rational legislation, it would be hard to exaggerate the influence of his ethics on contemporary social, political and educational theorising. What Kant mainly contributes to contemporary social theory is a moral basis for the kind of political liberalism defended by such nineteenth-century liberals as John Stuart Mill.[21] Insofar as the main emphasis in political liberalism is on maximum (intellectual, practical and economic) individual liberty, it has trouble finding some principled ground of social solidarity or cohesion that might prevent conflicts of individual interest and competition for limited resources dissolving into social anarchy. Although the classical liberal 'harm principle' provides some basis for liberal-democratic legislation by ruling out any pursuit of one's own liberty at the cost of violent or other trespass upon the liberties of others, it does not provide much in the way of a *positive* motive for interest in the common good. Thus, although classical liberals sought to ground such concern in the doctrine of *utilitarianism* – in a rationally self-interested concern for the happiness of the greatest number – many if not most influential modern liberals have regarded Kantian ethics as a more viable basis for any liberal-democratic concern for the common good.[22] On this view, although good liberal democrats will desire the freedom to pursue their own lawful interests and projects, they also need to recognise – on the basis of broadly Kantian considerations about practical consistency – that any such pursuit actually *presupposes* a respect and tolerance for the rights and liberties of others, in the absence of which there may no just or civilised human association. To this end, Kant's metaphysics of moral agency, and his absolute conception of moral law, is converted by modern liberals into a (rather unKantian) moral contractualism for the purposes of liberal-democratic social cohesion: the moral laws of the categorical imperative become the cement of civil society.

It was essentially this medley of Kantian ethics and liberal social and political theory that informed the new liberal educational traditionalism of early postwar analytical philosophy of education. Indeed, the main goal of education on this account was the development of rational *autonomy* conceived as personal development in the light of Kantian principles of respect and tolerance for difference and diversity: the educational aim was to promote maximum personal freedom and independence consistent with responsible citizenship grounded in proper recognition of and respect for the rights of others. However, this went hand in hand with a view of profession in general and educational professionalism in particular that also drew a fairly sharp line between the private and personal and the public and professional. Indeed, we have already seen that the Kantian ethics of reciprocal respect fits very well with any rights-based professional ethics of the kind that might be appropriate to the conduct of law or medicine: on this view, professional relations ought to be impartial and disinterested, and largely insulated from personal values and concerns. But we have also seen that it is rather more difficult to observe any such separation of rights- and duty-based public, civic or professional values from personal values in the sphere of education: since education – as we have argued from the outset – actually concerns *personal* formation, it is hard to see how it can avoid the transmission of values, or of substantial views of the good life, that go beyond mere cultivation of attitudes of disinterested tolerance and respect for others.

Moreover, there can be no doubt that one less than satisfactory consequence of just this liberal conception of educational professionalism was a (briefly) fashionable view that teachers should – on pain of indoctrination – maintain a position of strict value neutrality in any discussions with pupils of substantial moral, religious or political questions in contexts of cultural diversity.[23] Although this position seems inconsistent with any traditional view of education as *inherently* concerned with the cultivation of values, and is now generally held to be untenable, it still deeply infects such sensitive areas of the curriculum as religious education, and it is difficult if not impossible to see how any other position might be squared with the basic tenets of liberal professionalism. However, it may be that an even more worrying downside of the liberal professional separation of the private from the public is a certain avoidance of awkward questions concerning personal suitability for teaching. On the liberal professional view, so long as individual professionals teach efficiently (in some technical competence sense) and observe official rules and prescriptions pertaining to the just and equitable treatment of pupils, they would appear to be fairly free to be or do as they please in their private lives. But the arguments of this part of the book have suggested that it does matter – and that parents may have a legitimate concern with – what kind of *people*, from the point of character and lifestyle, are teaching their children. The persisting (albeit delicate) difficulty is that it is hard to see how teachers – even those who attempt to observe clinical separation of private lifestyle from professional image (and we cannot be sure that all do) – might avoid offering role models to young people in this or that positive or negative respect.

How might this problem be addressed? One prospect here might be to reject any modernist (Kantian) conception of practical reason in favour of an older Aristotelian view, which could also involve abandoning any strictly liberal conception of educational professionalism – at least insofar as any such conception is committed to ideals of strict universal moral impartiality or value neutrality. For Aristotle, as already indicated, it is anyway a mistake to believe that morality and moral objectivity are best exhibited in impartial rule observance – not least if this means ignoring individual differences. We have also seen that any wise educational engagement must also exhibit Aristotelian sensitivity to the different needs and claims of individuals. Hence the task of the good teacher *qua* moral agent and educator is to cultivate the particular personal and interpersonal sensibilities presupposed to Aristotelian *virtues*, not just out of concern for personal perfection, but also in the interests of promoting such practical sensibilities on the part of others. The key to such cultivation and promotion is a grasp of that mode of practical reason that Aristotle distinguished from both theoretical and practical technical reasoning by the term *phronesis* or practical wisdom: such wisdom differs from theoretical reason by virtue of its concern with practical outcomes more than the discovery of truth, but it differs from technical or productive reasoning by virtue of its concern with the pursuit of (morally) worthwhile ends more than efficient or effective means.

Above all, since the moral deliberation of *phronesis* is a matter of reasoning from moral *values* to moral prescriptions, there can be no value-free or neutral resolution of moral dilemmas, controversies and problems. All human agency is morally, socially and culturally situated, the moral education of young people inevitably involves their initiation into particular socio-cultural practices, and the proper role of parents, guardians and teachers is to be exemplars of the highest values and virtues of a given way of life. Indeed, according to a recent rather radical communitarian version of Aristotelian virtue ethics, it follows from this that there can be no common cross-cultural conception of moral education,[24] and that insofar as schools are concerned with broader initiation into qualities of moral character, this must entail separate schooling for different cultural or religious constituences (for example, separate Catholic, Protestant, Jewish, Humanist and other schooling). On the other hand, this counsel of educational apartheid may be far too pessimistic, and it is not clear that an Aristotelian conception of virtue as the cultivation of qualities of moral character (rather than as the initiation of pupils into specific beliefs or principles) is inevitably tied to any such consequence.[25] Indeed, perhaps the supreme virtue of Aristotelian virtue ethics lies in its recognition of the way in which moral principles are essentially regulative of aspects of human nature and association – natural inclinations, needs, sentiments and sensibilities – that render the virtues crucial to human integrity and well-being in *any* cultural context. Thus, to the extent that we do recognise a cross-cultural educational need for pupils to be socialised into honesty, fairness, courage, self-control, compassion, and so forth, one may hardly doubt that teachers who possess such qualites are better fitted to be educators of others than those who do not. Moreover, insofar as it is not clear why I should not learn substantial lessons about honesty, fairness, courage, self-control and compassion from people who do not share my faith or my political values, there seems no reason why children of diverse cultural inheritances might not learn much about such qualities from teachers of character and integrity of any race, culture or creed.

In conclusion, one should also observe the significant role that *affect* plays in Aristotle's account of the practical wisdom of *phronesis*: on the Aristotelian view, practical judgement is not just a matter of the purely 'cognitive' or intellectual inference of valid moral conclusions from true premises, but involves cultivation – partly via proper training – of emotionally grounded dispositions and sensibilities. Although Aristotle shares Plato's view that emotions and feelings need proper ordering in the interests of healthy personal integration, he does not agree with him in regarding them as little more than sources of error and delusion that require strict rational denial or suppression. On the contrary, for Aristotle, rightly ordered feelings and emotions are necessary for sound moral judgement and may themselves be regarded as forms of moral perception: for example, it is indispensable in order to know how to respond properly to the needs of others that one is capable of a certain sympathy or fellow feeling for their plight, and that one also *cares* enough to do something about it.[26] Much the same point, of course, has been made by contemporary educational proponents of the so-called 'ethics of care' who have complained that the moral development theories of such neo-Kantian structuralists and constructivists as Piaget and Kohlberg emphasise the role of cognition in moral judgement to the serious neglect or detriment of the affective dimension.[27] The trouble with ethics of care conceptions, however, is that they often seem to err in the opposite direction of emphasising the moral role of affect to the serious neglect of cognition and principle, and have possibly contributed to the perpetuation of a false dichotomy between reason and feeling in contemporary moral theory. From this viewpoint, it is arguable that Aristotle's analyses of *phronesis* and virtue provide a much better account of the crucial interplay of reason and feeling in moral judgement. It is also, one might add, an account that has much potential for illuminating the 'caring' or vocational aspects of the teacher's role on which we have touched in this part of the book.

Possible tasks

(1) Identify the characteristics or qualities you would associate with a morally developed or well-educated person, and consider different ways in which the (formal or informal) school curriculum might be designed to assist the cultivation of such qualities.

(2) Identify the characteristics or qualities you would associate with an effective moral guide or educator of others, and consider different ways in which the academic or practical curriculum of teacher education and training might be designed to assist the cultivation of such qualities.

Part II

Learning, knowledge and curriculum

Chapter 6

Learning: behaviour, perception and cognition

The philosophy of mind

A key issue over which past and present philosophers have often been divided is that of the relationship of the psychological to the physical, or of mind to body. Generally, one may observe a broad difference between those philosophers who regard the mind and body, or the psychological and the physical, as (in some philosophical or metaphysical sense) *separate* things, and those who regard them as (again in some metaphysical sense) *continuous* if not *identical*. To some extent, this particular philosophical dichotomy relates to another great philosophical distinction between *rationalists* and *empiricists*: many great rationalists, such as Plato, Descartes and (arguably) Kant, have been *dualists* (those who regard mind and matter as in some sense metaphysically distinct or mutually irreducible entities or realities), whereas more naturalistically or empirically minded philosophers, such as Aristotle, Hobbes (and nearer our own time), Bertrand Russell, John Dewey and Gilbert Ryle, have been more inclined to some sort of *monism* (the view that talk of the mental or psychological is in principle susceptible to non-dualistic explanation).[1] On the other hand, there is no exact correspondence between these distinctions, and the picture is more complicated in precise detail: neither Aristotle nor Kant is clearly categorisable by means of these dichotomies, and some major empiricists have subscribed to a view of the mind as conscious apprehension of sense experience (so-called 'phenomenalism'), which is by no means easy to reconcile with any thoroughgoing naturalistic (rather than idealist) opposition to dualism. On the face of it, however, it is reasonable to suppose that any tendency to regard reason, logical analysis and/or inference rather than sensible experience as the most reliable source of knowledge tends to a belief that there is *more* to human understanding than the deliverences of perception or sensation, and that any contrary inclination to regard knowledge as rooted in sense perception rather than rational deliberation encourages attempts to explain mind or psychological experience in the sort of statistical terms by which empirical science mostly seeks to account for the apparent epistemic content of human experience.

At all events, insofar as promoting human knowledge and understanding would appear to be the stock-in-trade of educationalists, time-honoured rationalist and other arguments to the effect that such understanding cannot *itself* be studied or understood as other objects of experience are (scientifically or otherwise) investigated may seem to constitute a serious embarrassment or impediment to any *principled* conception of education and/or its professional status. First, according to many past rationalist *and* empiricist philosophers, much of what human beings have claimed to know as a matter of grounded reason (causal generalisations, moral laws, value judgements, and so on) has no firm evidential basis or unproblematic source in what is actually experienced by human perception: we do not, for example, experience causal connections or the beauty of a painting in the way we (sensorily) experience a patch of red or a high-pitched whine. Secondly, minds appear to possess none of the properties of empirical objects, and one would not expect a thought or feeling to be discovered by dissection of the body in the way that a brain, heart or kidney might be so disclosed and investigated. Thirdly, the idea of bodiless (or at least *human bodiless*) thought is not a logically *incoherent* one (are not computers thinkers without bodies?), and thoughts might even be held to survive complete bodily destruction (so that I can at least *imagine* myself watching my own funeral). Fourthly (worse yet), if thoughts are not empirically investigable in the manner of other objects of experience, then they can only (by definition) be known to those who have them – in which case no-one can ever be in a position to know or comprehend the thoughts of another person. But if this is so, then teachers and educators may seem to be in the impossible position of never knowing either what someone already knows, or whether they have actually learned what they or others have just taught them. It hardly needs saying that many of these claims seem to fly in the face of our ordinary pre-theoretical experience and understanding of the nature of teaching and learning.

But even if we remain sympathetic (as I believe we should) to the rationalist point that the products of mind and thought are not completely explicable in the statistical terms of empirical science, it seems hard to credit the view that thoughts are purely *private* internal objects to which only the subjects of such thoughts have access – and it is precisely against this view that so much modern, particularly twentieth-century, philosophical, scientific and other theoretical work has inveighed.[2] Moreover, there cannot also be much doubt that one of the most powerful and enduring philosophical, scientific and educational sources of opposition to this view has hailed from the direction of what we shall here simply refer to as *behaviourism*. The key philosophical claim of behaviourism is that it is just false to regard many if not most of our attributions of mentality to human agents as referring primarily to private or 'inner' psychological states. Indeed, it would appear that judgements to the effect that someone *knows* how to drive a car or play tennis are normally linked to substantial *public* evidence that the person can perform the tasks in question, and has been reliably observed to do so: we award driving licences on the evidence of public tests rather than on the basis of alleged private experiences. Again, we would usually construe reports to the effect that this or that person desires to get rich quick or intends to sell at a profit as behavioural predictions on the basis of ordinary social or interpersonal acquaintance with previous history (as well as of course on what such persons currently tell us) rather than upon telepathic contact with the agent's private mental experiences. Hence, on a behaviourist view, reports that someone knows, thinks or feels something or other are shorthand ('folk-psychological') ways of referring to what people might be expected to do in such and such circumstances – generally in the light of what they have been prone to do in the past – rather than descriptions of currently occurring 'inner' episodes. From this viewpoint, in having construed reports of mental goings-on as descriptive of the operations of bodily-independent minds or souls, rather than as predictions of the potential or actual behaviour of perfectly public bodies and agencies, rationalist philosophers (such as Plato and Descartes) have simply misconceived the 'logical grammar' of psychological discourse.[3]

Behaviourism as a theoretical or philosophical position undoubtedly derived much support and encouragement from the twentieth-century claims of empirical psychologists to have discovered general statistical laws and principles governing the 'knowledge' acquisition or learning of animals in general and humans in particular: it was, to be sure, the avowed intent of so-called 'learning theorists' to show that knowledge acquisition is no less an empirically discernible *causal* process than any other natural phenomenon. Indeed, from the essentially social scientific standpoint of learning theory, if we can take evolutionary biology to have demonstated the continuity of human nature with the rest of animate nature, and animal learning can be generally understood as adaptive or otherwise to *survival*, it may seem perfectly logical to construe human knowledge, expertise and skill as a complex survival strategy. Those humanoid species who adapted to their environment – via the development of superior technologies of communication or problem solving – survived and transmitted their accumulated expertise as *culture* to the next generation; those who did not, died out. But, on this view, such knowledge and expertise is a purely *contingent* product of trial and error: it is not so much that people first take conscious thought and deliberately put such thought into practice, it is rather that certain practices prove successful (perhaps, for example, the use of a bone as a club to kill prey) and that such practices become entrenched in human behaviour as relatively self-directed or 'principled' dispositions to behave in this or that way. From this viewpoint, although certain forms of highly adaptive behaviour arise as responses to environmental pressure, they are subsequently internalised or registered in the brain or central nervous system as survival conducive habits, traits or dispositions: roughly, environmental stimuli produce responses that are then reinforced and honed by persistent use into what we are accustomed to describe in more 'epistemic' or psychological terminology as 'knowledge' or 'understanding'. Moreover, by means of some such story, twentieth-century behaviourists did much to revitalise a well-entrenched empiricist account of the nature of learning known as *associationism*. According to such leading lights of the empiricist tradition as Hume and Mill,[4] most if not all laws and principles of human understanding – even those that many past rationalists had argued to be logically necessary or *a priori* – are ultimately products of the habitual (causal) association of experientially conjoined events: nothing is to be found in the mind that was not first in empirical experience ('nihil est in intellectu, quod non prius fuerit in sensu').

The empirical investigation of learning

The first hard empirical support for such a story is usually taken to have been provided by the celebrated animal experiments of the Russian biologist Ivan Pavlov. In the course of measuring canine salivation,[5] Pavlov discovered that dogs could be made to salivate in response not only to the natural or 'unconditioned' stimulus of food, but also to any other sensory impression that they might come to associate with the introduction of food. In the now familiar case, the dog's dinner (unconditioned stimulus) – to which the dog invariably (unconditionedly) responded by salivating – was regularly accompanied by the ringing of a bell. In due course, however, it was discovered that the dog, having *associated* the bell with being fed, would (conditionedly) respond to the (conditioned) stimulus of the bell – even when no food was present. On the face of it, the dog's behaviour had undergone change or modification in the light of an apparently 'inner' connection of perceived events. But although Pavlov's work was to have great influence on the development of empirical psychology – not least upon such founding fathers of the American school of learning theorists as J.B. Watson[6] – the so-called *classical conditioning* of Pavlov and other early behaviourists is open to fairly obvious objections as a scientific account or analysis of even non-human animal learning. The key problem, of course, is that although the behaviourally conditioned dog is able to do something that it could not previously do, it runs rather against the grain of ordinary usage to describe it as having *learned* to salivate to the sound of the bell – as we might readily describe even a child who has learned his or her tables by rote as now having learned to multiply by two. For surely what the child has accomplished is a capacity for *voluntary* or witting engagement in (in this case) a *rational* procedure, whereas the newly acquired 'behaviour' of the dog is no more than a neurophysiologically engendered *reflex*. (Pavlov, indeed, took himself to be engaged in *biological* investigation and was not primarily concerned to advance the study of psychological phenomena.) Moreover, this should also alert us to the hopeless generality of the definition of learning, as any 'modification of behaviour', that experimental psychologists have sometimes actually given: if I fall down and twist my ankle, my pedal capacities will be modified to a limp – but it would not seem at all proper to say that I had *learned* to limp.

It is precisely away from any such focus on the 'mechanical' association of physiological reflexes that the *instrumental*, purposive and *operant* conditioning of later learning theorists attempts to move. Subsequent behaviourists sought to show that genuine learning occurs only when behaviour adapts to environmental pressures in the interests of furthering the survival-related *ends* and *goals* of the conditioned life-form. One reason why we may be unwilling to describe Pavlov's dog as having *learned* to salivate to the bell is that such behaviour can hardly be regarded as conducive to the active desire-satisfying behaviour and flourishing of the animal; indeed, it is not hard to see how such Pavlovian behaviour modification might be extremely *unfavourable* to survival. However, if adaptation to the pressures of conditioning can be shown to be consistent with a creature's survival-related needs and interests – with, in short, what the animal would normally be actively disposed to seek – then we may appear to have something a bit more like real learning. Something rather more along these lines would appear to have followed from E.L. Thorndike's pivotal experiments on 'instrumental conditioning' with cats.[7] In these experiments, a cat was placed inside a box – in which, however, the lid could be released by the operation of a internal trigger. In (presumably) a frenzy of panic, the cat beats about the box until it *accidentally* triggers the release mechanism. Upon release from the box, the cat is first rewarded or 'reinforced' with food prior to being re-incarcerated with a view to repeating its initial escapological feat. The perhaps not altogether surprising outcome of this feline manipulation was that the intervals between being replaced in the box and making good its escape lessened with repeated enclosure: the cat seemed to be *learning* – by a more or less intelligent process of trial and error – to solve a problem in the interest of securing certain optimal goals of freedom and food. From this Thorndike deduced two significant principles of learning that he called the 'law of exercise' and the 'law of effect': whereas the first of these emphasises the role of repeated exposure to the stimulus as crucial to the fixing of responses, the second emphasises the role of motivation in learning. On this conception of learning as conditioning, then, responses are not just crucially linked to the desires and goals of a given agency, but also depend for modification and reinforcement on repeated natural or artificial conditioning. Moreover, it is not just that if responses are not reinforced they will not be entrenched in behaviour, but that if the reinforcement is negative (disappointing or punishing) rather than positive (congenial or rewarding), responses are liable to inhibition or extinction.

However, there could hardly be a better known representative of twentieth-century learning-theory than the American experimental psychologist B.F. Skinner, whose work was to have an enormous popular as well as academic influence on postwar theorising about human nature and behaviour. As well as having a considerable theoretical impact – through such works as *Science and Human Behaviour* – on the mainstream pragmatism of such major modern philosophers as W.V.O. Quine,[8] Skinner also came to exercise wider intellectual, socio-cultural and political influence via such more popular productions as *Beyond Freedom and Dignity* and *Walden II*.[9] For present purposes, Skinner's *operant conditioning* may be considered a more elaborate and sophisticated development of Thorndike's instrumental conditioning, but his claims and ambitions for behavioural conditioning undoubtedly outstrip those of any previous advocate of this general approach to learning. Going beyond Thorndike's trial-and-error learning, Skinner appears to have considered it theoretically possible to condition anything in anything, for almost any given pairing (within certain obvious physical limits) of tasks and agents: first, by analysing the task to be learned into its basic behavioural components; secondly, by systematic reinforcement of each of these basic components in proper logical order. From this viewpoint, Skinner's own experimental achievements in the field of behaviour shaping were hardly less bizarre than they were novel. Thus, in one famous experiment, Skinner taught pigeons to play a game of table tennis by reducing the game to a series of molecular skills, and systematically reinforcing each and any movement of the pigeons (picking up bats with beaks, hitting a ball over a net with bat in beak, returning the ball in like fashion, and so on) that resembled or approximated the human execution of this or that table-tennis skill.

Closer to present concerns, indeed, Skinner seems to have held that human learning differs from animal learning not so much in kind, quality or principle, but only by virtue of its greater practical complexity and sophistication. Thus, to whatever extent human reinforcement or motivation may differ from that of other creatures (money or praise, perhaps, having more effect than pellets of food), the kind of conditioning that the experimental psychologist applies to the shaping of animal behaviour is no less applicable to the human case – and the procedures of task-componential analysis and systematic programming of the behavioural components are essentially the same. In this connection, Skinner was an educational pioneer of so-called *programmed learning*, and also – perhaps in some anticipation of the pedagogical innovations of more recent information technology – of *teaching machines* conceived as efficient (and perhaps teacher-proof) engines of programmed instruction. More significantly, in his political and utopian writings, Skinner advocated the wholesale behavioural re-engineering of human nurture in the interests of a rationally ordered vice- and/or error-free society: he offers the prospect of a brave new world in which all behaviour is shaped and controlled by behavioural technologists in accordance with some some vision of human sweetness and light. And while this vision clearly raises more questions than it proposes to solve (including, perhaps, not just the question of whether such a human order might be possible, but also that of whether it is one we should *want*), there can be no doubt that the pedagogical approach of Skinner and other learning theorists – precisely the idea that broader educational aims and goals might be addressed by more detailed and systematic specification and targeting of the elements of learning – has had an enormous influence on contemporary 'behavioural objectives' approaches to curriculum planning.

Behaviourism, agency and meaning

For the moment, we shall confine our attention to the educational status of the basic learning-theoretical views just considered, leaving for a later chapter examination of the more particular difficulties of behavioural objectives models of curriculum planning. In this regard, there would appear to be two separate but related sources of educational unease concerning any such 'scientific' approach to understanding learning, one of which we have already had occasion to notice in the course of moving from the classical conditioning of Pavlov to the instrumental and operant conditioning of Thorndike and Skinner. The problem with the habitual or 'mechanical' connections of classical conditioning is that they seem to be focused on the (no doubt neurophysiologically grounded) re-routing of reflexes over which the subjects of experiment have little or no *voluntary* control. From this viewpoint, classical conditioning blurs a familiar pre-theoretical distinction between *agency*, or what we deliberately and voluntarily *do*, and *passivity*, or what happens to us regardless of our will in the matter – a distinction that is of crucial importance for the ascription of *responsibility* in educational and other (moral, legal, political) contexts. Indeed, it would appear to have been some such distinction that instrumental and operant conditioning sought to preserve in building upon the *voluntary* responses of experimental subjects, and in emphasising the instrumental or goal-orientated nature of their submission to behaviour shaping: the cat, rat or pigeon cooperates with the experimenter – but only so long as the cooperation is in line with the achievement of its own goals. However, although there is undoubtedly some difference between the processes of classical and instrumental conditioning in this respect, the difference seems of little real significance with respect to any distinction between genuine agency and passivity. The fact is that although the rat or pigeon achieves the goal of securing food, and attaining food certainly features here as *its* goal, we can hardly count finding its way about the maze or playing table tennis among its goals – for insofar as these activities are concerned, the animal can have little idea what is happening to it. Similarly, in the would-be human sphere, the behaviour of any citizens of Skinner's Waldenian utopia may well be shaped with their *compliance* – presumably with the aid of this or that incentive – in accordance with some master plan or conception of the good; but it is still not *their* conception of the good, and any role they might play in achieving it could only be as servile *automatons*.

However, this difficulty is closely related to another problematic feature of conceptions of learning as conditioning – that of the apparent inability of such views to account for any *meaningful* grasp of what is learned. We need not doubt that it is the sincere aim of learning theorists to increase or heighten the *intelligibilty* of learning via the adoption of a more logical and/or systematic approach to pedagogy: on the face of it, it seems quite plausible to suppose that insofar as a complex skill is a causally ordered sequence of events, it might be best or most efficiently learned according to some programme of behaviour shaping that faithfully and intelligibly reflects that causal order. The trouble is, however, that to whatever extent this might serve to promote the systematic instruction of an activity, it is not inevitably conducive to the *educational* learning of it – and might, indeed, be actually inimical to any such educational appreciation. In the case of Skinner's pigeons, for example, it seems clear enough that whatever they have learned, they have not learned to play table tennis, and it may even be doubted that they have learned a skill – in any very meaningful sense of this term. Indeed, what may need questioning here is the very assumption that even practical skills are no more than causally ordered sequences of physical movements – for this neglects the vital consideration that skills, as opposed to natural regularities, are forms of *principled* or rule-following behaviour deliberately engaged in for particular *purposes*. The conditioned pigeons are no more performing the skills of table tennis than a spider is exercising weaving skills or a honey bee is dancing. Indeed, this point is of the utmost educational and pedagogical significance – since (from first-hand experience) I have found that teachers of physical and practical activities are often seduced by the idea that a skill is just a sequence of physical movements into distinctly less than meaningful approaches to teaching. It is all too tempting, for example, to suppose that if one's goal is to teach a particular ethnic dance to a class of pupils, and an ethnic dance is just a particular pattern of physical *movements*, then one has successfully taught that dance when the children can physically perform that pattern of movement.[10]

All the same, if a behavioural scientist set out to condition a troop of chimpanzees into the (as far as possible) movement-perfect performance of a Greek folk dance for some pantomimic purpose, we could only have the same doubt about whether the apes were dancing as we had over the table-tennis 'playing' pigeons. From this perspective, learning to dance must be more than simply performing a sequence of movements. But if so, what more: or, to put it another way, what is any true dancer capable of that chimpanzees are not? A partial answer to this question rests on a very important distinction between human and animal agency – namely, that a human agent learning to dance is capable of deliberate observance of rules and conventions, whereas an animal only behaves in accordance with such rules.[11] In short, there is at least this difference between the non-rational brute and the rational school child: that the animal submits to causal conditioning in certain patterns of movement in order to secure the reward of food, whereas the child is capable of recognising and following rules under direct instruction in order to *perform the dance*. In short, the child – but not the animal – is capable of grasping the rules and principles that are constitutive of a *dance* as distinct from some mere random sequence of movements. But this answer may not perhaps go quite far enough, since a human student of dance may be capable of following the rules and conventions in order to perform the dance with hardly more appreciation of what the dance *means* than the brute whose dancing behaviour is (to it) only a means of securing the reward of food. Indeed, one likely cause of poor dance education is that students learn this or that dance only as a system of rules and/or routines – which, though performed in logical order or sequence, are nevertheless executed entirely without regard to what the dance *means*. Just as young children may first approach reading as a mechanical process of rule-following, so pupils can be taught to dance as a matter of mechanical rule-following: but just as no education in literacy could be confined to such reading by rote, so nothing worth calling dance education could be restricted to analogous mechanical moving. In this respect, there can be blind rule-following, just as much as there invariably is blind behaviour in accordance with causal conditioning.

Surely, however, what is required for any educational appreciation of dance, dancing or any other humanly worthwhile activity is that rather wider understanding of what one is doing that depends upon a grasp of its broader human and cultural import and purpose. It should also be clear that any such appreciation must exhibit an order or dimension of semantic complexity that quite transcends the grasp of any simple mechanical procedure. In the case of dance education, for example, it is at the very least likely to entail appreciating that the movements of a given dance are – rather than contingently connected physical events – precisely *intentional* steps and gestures through which a given socio-cultural constituency has sought to celebrate or give ritual expression to such aspects of its communal life as prayer, thanksgiving, connubiality or martial success. But, in this light, it is also crucial to grasp that such appreciation should not be regarded as just so much academic knowledge and information *additional* but inessential to the ability to dance conceived as a mastery of so many physical movements: on the contrary, such appreciation can hardly be less than *constitutive* of what it means *to dance* in any significant *practical* sense. To perform a given dance step or gesture as symbolically expressive of nuptual bliss or bellicose intent is to *dance* in a way that imitating one physical movement after another is *not* – just as appreciating a passage of writing as tragedy or farce is reading in a way that parroting words in sequence, even as an exercise of deliberate rule-following, is not.

Kant and the constructivist turn

Hence, from an *educational* viewpoint, what any account of learning in terms of behavioural conditioning falls short of explaining are the processes by which human students come to *understand* – in other words, to grasp the *sense* or *meaning* – of those activities and forms of knowledge that by and large contribute to educational development. First, then, to whatever proper extent the mastery of an art such as dance, or a science such as physics, may require the causal bonding of stimulus and response – underpinned, perhaps, by the formation of neural networks – it cannot *only* be a causal process, since it requires the ability to observe or follow *rules* which are neither more nor less than *constitutive* of the activities in question. No dance or physical experiment that occurs in the absence of the conscious following of this set of experimental principles or that set of dance rules could even count as dancing or experimenting. But, secondly, even such rule-following may fall short of real *understanding* if those to whom the rules have been taught are not yet wise to the *purposes* that the rules are designed to serve or achieve. In this light, the rules of dance, physics or mathematics make sense only against a background of complex and sophisticated human institutions and practices that can hardly be other than incomprehensible to any creatures lacking the kinds of (human) culture in which such institutions and practices are embedded. In sum, learning theory cannot account for meaning because meaning is a product of *rational purpose*, and such rationality is not reducible without remainder to the causality of stimulus and response. It is this difficulty that so-called 'cognitive psychology' attempts to confront by proposing to account – still, as far as possible, within the explanatory terms of natural scientific inquiry – for the way in which human understanding would appear to be significantly implicated in the active construction of meaningful perspectives on experience. In short, cognitive psychology explicitly recognises that the account of learning as rule-following to which we seem precisely to be drawn by consideration of the human case must demonstrate the effective bankruptcy of any conception of knowledge- or skill-acquisition as mere passive response to the contingencies of environmental stimulation.

The key philosophical influence on cognitivist attempts to explain learning in terms of the active construction and imposition of principles or rules on experi- ence has to be, once again, the eighteenth-century German metaphysician Immanuel Kant – upon whose ethical views we touched in the previous chapter. There we saw that insofar as Kant considers genuine moral judgements to be rationally *self-justifying* (logically incontrovertible) laws or rules of conduct, his moral philosophy is just about as thoroughgoingly *constructivist* as it is possible to be: to the extent that moral judgements constitute a type of prescription that is utterly dissociated from the normal workaday motives, wants or inclinations of agents, they are entirely innocent of empirical content or any necessary connec- tion with sensible experience. For Kant, then, morality requires to be understood in terms of the rational *imposition* of rules or principles of pure practical reason on the rough and tumble of human practical experience. That said, Kant's epis- temology – his view of how we can come to know objective reality – is somewhat less radically constructivist to the extent that it takes our knowledge of the world to be a matter of the crucial *interplay* of rational principle *and* sensory input. This idea is neatly captured in Kant's famous dictum that 'thoughts without content are empty: intuitions without concepts are blind'.[12] With respect to the question of what we can know of the world, Kant agrees broadly with Hume and other empiricists that the limits of our knowledge are set by what we can sensibly expe- rience. In this light, there can be no *rational* demonstration of (say) the existence of God (which must be a matter of faith) or of freedom of the will (which is nevertheless a presuppostion of practical reason) since there is little in the way of sensible experience upon which we might base demonstrable knowledge of such claims: from the viewpoint of (scientific or other) *theoretical* knowledge of the world, then, ideas of God and free will are mostly ('empty' though by no means useless) thoughts without content. But Kant also disagrees with the empiricists that human knowledge is merely habituation to sensory stimuli, holding that to whatever extent sensory input is necessary for human knowledge or under- standing, it cannot be sufficient: many non-human animals have sensory awareness, but one may fairly doubt whether they *know* things – in the sense of theorising or making rational judgements about the world. Hence, insofar as some creatures may be said to have 'intuitions without concepts', they are ratio- nally 'blind' and cannot have knowledge.

Gestalt and cognitive psychology

Some of the earliest twentieth-century attempts to give empirical expression to this key Kantian insight were made by so-called 'Gestalt' psychologists in the course of *empirical* experimental investigation into the nature of perception, involving both human agents and non-human animals.[13] The Gestaltist point was precisely that human perception could not merely be the product of sensory input, since perception is inherently *interpretative*, and interpretation is a matter of the subsumption of sensory experience under meaning-constitutive categories and concepts. At its simplest, the point is that human (*and* some non-human) perceivers see the world not as it is actually *given* in sensory experience, but as structured according to organisational principles that agents appear to bring actively to experience. For example, the psychologist Wertheimer discovered that if the flashing of a light at a particular position was followed by the slightly delayed flashing of a second light in close spatial proximity to the first, perceivers would generally report this as a continuous *movement* of light from one position to another, rather than as an experience of two successive but separate events of illumination. This process of cognitive 'closure' – which Wertheimer termed the 'phi-phenomenon' – is the same as that which enables us to perceive a series of successively illuminated lightbulbs at a fairground as an animated cartoon of Mickey Mouse, rather than as just a succession of flashing lightbulbs. It is the same principle that underlies our inclination or capacity to interpret a drawing on a piece of paper (for example, the ambiguous 'duck–rabbit' figure familiar from contemporary discussions of the complexities of perception) as a duck or a rabbit, rather than just as a meaningless doodle.

But Gestalt psychologists also appear to have regarded the organisational capacities that agents bring to perception as having some sort of basis in the human and animal need to solve practical problems of perhaps survival-related significance. Thus, the Gestalt psychologist Köhler famously claimed to have observed chimpanzees engaging in something like means–end practical reasoning in order to solve a 'problem' deliberately orchestrated by the experimenter. Having placed bananas beyond the reach of caged apes, the experimenter also deposited a set of short connecting rods inside the cage. Although these rods were individually too short to reach the bananas, the apes apparently soon 'worked out' that they could reach the fruit by joining them together to create an extended instrument of banana retrieval. On the Gestaltist view, then, (at least 'higher') animals as well as humans are capable of some degree of meaningful conceptualisation of experience.

At all events, the key Gestalt insights that meaningful perception presupposes organisational principles and capacities, and that such principles and capacities may have their basis in the need of human and other creatures to solve practical survival-related problems, clearly had some influence on the subsequent efforts of such cognitive structuralists as Piaget, Bruner and Ausubel to make sense of human meaning-making as such.[14] In particular, Piaget boldly aspires – ultimately, of course, in the spirit of Kant – to give an empirically grounded account of the development of human theoretical knowledge and understanding from its primitive origins in early infant behaviour. In this connection, however, Piaget seems from the outset to call into question what would appear to be one Kantian obstacle in the way of any naturalistic account of the genesis of human rational capacities – namely, Kant's rather schismatic conception of knowledge as the imposition on sensory experience of concepts and categories that cannot themselves be regarded as abstracted or otherwise derived from experience. On the face of it, it seems hard to deny that Kant's epistemology is bedevilled by a dichotomy of reason and experience that largely recapitulates the mind–body dualism of the founding father of modern philosophy, Descartes. The trouble precisely is that if mind and body are ontologically distinct entities, how might any kind of empirical story about the evolution of human theoretical or rational capacities be possible? However, it seems to be an article of faith for Piaget that some such naturalistic explanation of rationality *must* be possible, and his basic strategy – to be followed in essence, although interpreted differently, by other cognitive psychologists – is to argue that the principles and concepts which mature reason brings to the raw data of sensory experience are not given fully fledged to human agents by virtue of innate endowment, but acquired by them over a long course of *development* through a series of qualitatively distinct phases or stages. In this regard, although modern cognitive developmentalists parted company with their behaviourist colleagues in denying that rational agency is reducible to behavioural habituation or conditioning, they were clearly at one with them in taking such agency to be nevertheless a particular kind of goal-orientated behaviour that does indeed have its roots in early childhood responses to environmental stimuli.

Indeed, for Piaget – again other cognitive developmentalists do not appear to disagree in general principle – the origins of reason lie in the essentially pre-linguistic expressions of infantile curiosity at what he calls the *sensori-motor* stage of development: newborn infants have no power to express themselves or their view of the world through language, but their behaviour is from the very outset goal-orientated – driven by needs for nourishment or affection – and it may be interpreted in terms of essentially (instrumental) rational strategies of survival or self-preservation. All the same, instead of conceiving the development of reason as a matter of mere quantitative enlargement of some such responsive reper-toire, Piaget construes it as more a matter of *qualitative* transformation of or transition from this relatively primitive and unreflective type of (albeit proto-) rational agency to one at which a more principled account of experience is sought by young children.[15] Thus, whereas at the *pre-concrete* or *intuitive* stages that succeed Piaget's sensori-motor stage, the search for meaning via some sort of reflective or principled explanation is more a matter of hunch and intuition than of systematic rational calculation, at the stage of *concrete* operations children are beginning to structure experience in terms of rules that systematically map the causal order of immediate experience. Indeed, the key goal of concrete opera-tion is the internalisation by children of external causal order in the form of mental or 'cognitive' rules and principles: at this stage, in short, learning is primarily a matter of extrapolation or *abstraction* from experience. But concrete learning is still very much tied to the direct deliverences of sensory perception: chidren learn by the identification, description and/or depiction of this or that feature of observable experience. However, the ultimate educational goal of cognitive developmentalism is that children or young people should in due course progress intellectually beyond focus on the present and particular to a stage at which they can reason – mathematically, scientifically or morally – at some remove from experience: Piaget refers to this as the stage of *formal* operations. Indeed, just as the mature mathematician is one who can grasp conceptual relationships apart from their empirical instantiations, so Piaget seems to hold – in the grip of a more or less Kantian moral psychology – that mature moral agency is a matter of the grasp of universal moral principles to which considerations of empirical or practical utility are largely irrelevant. In this respect too, Lawrence Kohlberg's famous theory of moral development – though more empirically grounded than Kant's, and more detailed than Piaget's – aspires to much the same ethical ideal of abstract duty for its own sake as one finds in both Kant and Piaget.[16]

Some difficulties with cognitivist approaches

All the same, with regard to the main educational concerns of this chapter, there can be no doubt that cognitive psychology and allied theoretical attempts to explain how human agents succeed in giving meaning to perceptual and sensory experience represent a significant advance on the stimulus–response analyses of learning theorists. For the most part, such major mid-twentieth-century cognitive structuralists as Piaget and Bruner give a fairly plausible account – to this extent broadly consistent, as we shall see, with the work of such major modern philosophers of knowledge and meaning as Dewey and Wittgenstein – of meaning as *principled* understanding or rule-governed experience, and they also make a good stab at explaining how highly abstract or theoretical understanding might be held to develop from less reflective (if not pre-reflective) procedural and/or instrumental knowledge. However, such accounts of cognitive development are also the source of significant theoretical difficulties and problems, which are at least partly reflected in some uncertainty about the logical or evidential status of such theories. For a start, then, we may ask what reason(s) we have to accept the accounts of cognitive development provided by structuralist and constructivist psychologists. Indeed, there is a clear reason why we could not accept *all* of them, for – as I have argued elsewhere[17] – they are not conspicuously consistent with each other: the epistemic basis of Bruner's developmental view, for example (and other instances can be cited), seems not just different from but also palpably at odds with Piaget's. But, if developmental theories do epistemically or otherwise differ, on what basis might we decide which is true and which is false?

One possible response at this point, of course, is that insofar as such accounts purport to be based upon observation-based research and experiment, they ought to be *empirically* confirmable – or at least refutable – in the same way as other scientific theories. The trouble is that it is not obvious that cognitive developmental claims enjoy anything like the same relationship to statistically describable natural events and processes as the theories and hypotheses of such 'hard' sciences as physics and chemistry – despite the fact that cognitive psychology has sometimes flirted with, or claimed some authority from, the neurophysiological investigations of so-called 'cognitive science'. There are, to be sure, deep difficulties about any such pretensions of cognitive developmental theory to natural scientific credentials – and these soon become apparent in the course of reflection upon some of the early naturalistic speculations of Gestalt psychologists. In general, Gestalt psychologists were disposed to explain the holistic or structured rather than piecemeal or atomistic character of human perception – as exhibited in the phi-phenomenon and/or 'closure' (the interpretation of fragments of figures as wholes) – in terms of the development of 'hard-wired' neural configurations. But whatever plausibility such explanation might have for the human ability to perceive fairground illuminations, it cannot have much for the interpretation of ambiguous figures. For to whatever extent we might be inclined to attribute individual failure to perceive contiguous points of light as a movement of light in terms of the breakdown of a neural mechanism, we are surely less likely to appeal to any such breakdown to explain all, if any, failures of agents to grasp differences of interpretation. The key point is that to be able to perceive the duck–rabbit figure in this way or that is to be able to *read* the figure as a duck or a rabbit – and this is surely more a matter of *education* and training than of physiology. Indeed, since the right physiology certainly cannot be a sufficient condition of being able to see the figure as a duck or a rabbit – for we could imagine agents having the physiology but not the cultural frame of reference in which duck or rabbit identification was possible – it cannot figure prominently in any very illuminating explanation of how such interpretation is possible. Clearly, what is left untouched by any hard scientific or statistical account of the grasp of meaning is the role of human *culture*, not least the contribution to human understanding of that key device for the expression and communication of human culture – namely, language.

Points related to those already made about Gestaltist natural scientific pretensions also apply to the work of mid-twentieth-century cognitive structuralists. Although there is less in the way of explicit neuroscientific speculation in the work of Piaget, Bruner and Kohlberg, their work nevertheless appears to enshrine deeply problematic naturalistic, quasi-scientific and 'acultural' assumptions. Indeed, one of the reasons for the manifest lack of interest in the particular cultural determinants of human understanding and meaning-making on the part of many psychological structuralists is that they took themselves to be tracing – in a basically Kantian spirit – the deep structural or grammatical form of cross-culturally common processes of human intellectual and moral development: as post-Kantian structuralists, Piaget, Bruner, Kohlberg and others sought to uncover developmental trends to which all normal human growth ought to be subject – irrespective of cultural variation. I believe that this is an assumption that so-called 'post-structuralist' and other contemporary cultural theorists have been right (notwithstanding often problematic overstatement) to question. From this viewpoint, for example, the trouble with Kohlberg's theory of moral development may be not so much that it is a *mistaken* description of the culturally invariant process of moral growth upon which any theory of moral instruction requires to be based, but rather that it is not really any kind of *description* at all.[18] Indeed, the more that influential twentieth-century post-Kantian conceptions of morality have come to be criticised from the perspective of neo-Aristotelian virtue ethics, neo-idealist communitarianism and the psychoanalytically grounded ethics of care, the more it appears that Kohlberg's theory is just one rival normative view among others: as such, it is arguably – in form as well as content – more a matter of prescription than description. Above all, it is not clear that there is anything of a naturalistically objective kind – anything beneath the cultural surface – of which it might be said to be descriptive: from this viewpoint, the cognitive processes of structural psychologists may seem to be no more than myths or fictions. It is this possibility that we shall proceed to explore in more detail in the next chapter.

Possible tasks

(1) In the light of what has been said in this chapter about the nature of educational learning, consider what curricular provision one might make to ensure that any learning of dance, sport, musical or other skills is a genuinely educational experience.

(2) Consider under what circumstances it might be regarded as defensible to employ rote learning as a means to the mastery of numeracy or other skills in any contexts of school education or training.

Chapter 7

Learning: meaning, language and culture

The empirical psychological predicament

We have seen that the behavioural experiments of learning theorists are hard put to account for the *semantic* or meaning-implicated aspects of learning: insofar as the kind of learning presupposed to human education entails some *understanding* of what is learned, and understanding is a matter of a grasp of its *meaning*, behavioural psychology seems of questionable utility in accounting for any such educational understanding. Gestaltists and cognitive structuralists argue that human meaning-making cannot be entirely explained in terms of behavioural processes, because understanding (a dance or a picture) is a matter of active imposition of meaning-constitutive rules and principles on the brute data of sensory perception: this is the basic Kantian insight that 'intuitions without concepts are blind'.[1] However, the question now arises of the *source* from which these principles of construction might be derived. It is at this point that cognitivist or related constructivist accounts seem to face something of a dilemma. On the one hand, if they adopt Kant's position of maintaining that the principles by which psychology organises experience are logically *a priori* and/or necessary, they appear vulnerable to some kind of irreconcilable Cartesian or other dualism of mind and body, or reason and sense-experience, which also carries the burden of explaining the origin of such principles. On the other hand, however, there are serious objections to what may seem to be the only alternative of supposing, like Piaget and other modern cognitivists, that such organising principles are abstracted from sensible experience. First, there are well-rehearsed difficulties about understanding concept formation in terms of abstraction, which go back to Plato.[2] For one thing, given that the particulars we are inclined to include under this or that concept are often fairly disparate (consider, even in the case of concepts of direct sense-experience, the wide variety of colour shades to which we apply the term 'red'), it is hard to see how they might be regarded as having some *common* abstractable feature – apart, that is, from being the particulars we have *chosen* to refer to by this or that label (which is basically the philosophical position known as *nominalism*). For another, it is highly implausible to suppose that *some* concepts might be formed by abstraction from *any* feature of sensible experience: consider, for example, the difficulty of abstracting the logical sign for negation ('not') from common experiences of negativity (whatever that might mean).[3]

A related problem about any cognitivist view that the principles of experiential organisation are abstractions from experience is that of how we could *know* this to be so. Much here seems to turn on the cognitivist claim that this might be determined *empirically*: it may appear plausible to suppose from repeated observation that children develop (in perhaps culturally invariant ways) certain principles of experiential organisation. But how could *empirical* inquiry support any such claim? In order to be a strictly empirical generalisation, any such claim must rest on *induction*: repeated experience serves to support a general rule to the effect that learners (here and everywhere) organise their experience according to such and such principles – because all hitherto observed learners have been observed to do so. But such inductive generalisation is always open to *disconfirmation* in the light of further experience, and (as Hume[4] showed) cannot conclusively establish that things will always continue as previous experience has led us to expect. In short, it may be that further research shows that hitherto unobserved learners do not make sense of experience (as, say, organised in terms of cause and effect) in the same way as those previously observed. Thus, on the one hand, if cognitive structuralists argue that organising principles are discovered on the basis of empirical scientific investigation, then the claim that such principles have a key role in the meaningful organisation of human experience cannot be shown to have more than *provisional* or contingent status. On the other hand, if (closer to Kant) they argue that such organisational principles are *necessary* features of any meaningful human experience – that any learners anywhere would *have* to organise their experience in this or that way – it is not clear how any such claim might be grounded in empirical scientific investigation, as distinct from the kind of metaphysical considerations that precisely support an *a priori* rationalist dualism of reason and experience.

To be sure, there is another way in which cognitive and other conceptual structuralists may be inclined to maintain that certain *a priori* principles of rational organisation are necessarily presupposed to making sense of features of human experience. We have already observed that Gestalt psychologists sometimes sought to account for such organisational principles as 'closure' in neurophysiological terms, and such later cognitivists as Chomsky have opposed associationist views of language learning on the grounds that any such learning requires the grasp of a *grammar* that could not itself be acquired through experience, and which we might therefore suppose to be innately encoded or biologically 'hard-wired' into the neurophysiology of potential language users.[5] However, the same general difficulty that we observed in the case of behaviourist theories of learning concerning the potential gap between meaning and (any empirical) process also arises here. Indeed, in criticising behaviourism, we noted a crucial connection between the failure of learning theory to give an account of meaning, and behaviourist blurring of the distinction between the processes we undergo and the actions we undertake. It is precisely insofar as the notion of human agency requires some reference to intention or purpose – to the capacity of human agents to plan their actions and invest them with sense and significance – that human action cannot be reduced to mere sequences of 'colourless' behavioural or physical events. In this light, however, it is not much clearer why the causal operation of hard-wired grammatical programmes would guarantee the meaning of human experience or activity, than it is how such meaning might be generated by the acquisition of environmentally conditioned sequences of behaviour. Moreover, we have lately observed that no scientific story in terms of neural wiring could be sufficient to explain such Gestaltist phenomena of experiential organisation as 'closure' – since it is quite conceivable that someone might possess the hardware apt for the identification of a given ambiguous figure as a rabbit rather than a duck, but yet be unable to recognise the rabbit aspect insofar as they are culturally or environmentally denied (as was once true of Australian Aborigines) any direct access to rabbits. In short, possession of a rabbit concept would appear to require more than just the presence and/or operation of some internal biological mechanism. What, however, might this be?

Recognising the world 'out there': Hume and Kant

The most obvious temptation now, perhaps, is to suppose that some direct personal acquaintance with rabbits would be enough to supply the conceptual deficit: in short, that what the agent would need to acquire a concept of 'rabbit' is some kind of experiential access to rabbits. Surprisingly, however, it is not obvious that this is so – at any rate, if such acquaintance means only the entry of creatures we refer to by this term into our experiential field. The fact is that agents may *not* recognise rabbits – or, at least, those creatures under that name that we (in our culture) give to them – even though they are within their experiential reach. Of course, what agents do not see as rabbits they might well see as something else – as members of a larger, less differentiated category of rodentine creatures, or as a kind of walking foodstuff;[6] but it is also just possible that they might not even see rabbits at all – even though they are (or would appear to us to be) directly under their noses. Moreover, if this possibility seems hard to grasp, it may only be because we are in the grip of a powerful picture of concept-acquisition of long and distinguished philosophical pedigree. This picture is a central feature of the philosophical tradition known as (British) *empiricism* – although it can also be found in non-empiricist philosophical perspectives, and it probably survives vestigially even in Kant's ingenious reconstruction and synthesis of rationalism and empiricism. The basic idea behind this view of concept-formation is that concepts are effects of the unmediated impact of experience on the human senses. According to Locke, the main founding father of British empiricism, any knowledge of the world expressed in true judgements involves the exercise of *ideas* (his term for concepts), such knowledge is acquired via the senses, and therefore the ideas presupposed to such knowledge are best construed as causally engendered mental representations of an external order of things.[7] In short, the concept of rabbit is engendered in us by the causal impact on our senses of a particular object in the world 'out there': without that impact we could not have the idea of rabbit, and given the presence of the source of that impact in our perceptual field, it is difficult (on the face of it) to see how we might *avoid* having that idea. Notoriously, however, the high priest of empiricism, David Hume, was more sceptical about the very existence of any such Lockean external objective order. Hume argued there can be no certain knowledge of anything beyond the flux of fleeting impressions (sounds, textures, colours, and so on) that constitutes our immediate experience – and which, as they pass or subside, leave behind traces in the form of ideas: on this view, concepts or ideas are no more than faded (faintly recollected) sensory impressions, and no idea could have genuine sense unless it can be shown to correspond to some actual (past or present) impression.[8] Hence, for Hume, only two kinds of statement or judgement can have genuine meaning. On the one hand, there are what he calls *statements of fact* – in which the constituent terms of such propositions correspond to impressions: statements such as 'the cat sat on the mat' or 'bachelors are less prone to heart attacks' would fall into this category. On the other hand, there are what he calls *relations of ideas* – which are merely definitions of terms or rules for the uses of words: statements such as 'a bachelor is an unmarried man' and 'a square is an equilateral rectangle' fall into this second category. The empiricist view is essentially that concepts or ideas acquire sense by *referring* to items of experience: in short, in 'the cat sat on the mat', the terms 'cat', 'mat' and 'sat' function logically or grammatically rather like *names* or descriptions of things, properties or relations. Moreover, this basic empiricist view of concept acquisition as a matter of direct reference to experience survives well into twentieth-century philosophy: it resurfaces in one well-known form, for example, in the 'picture theory of meaning' of Wittgenstein's early *Tractatus-Logico-Philosophicus*.[9]

Still, whatever the initial plausibility of this basic theory of concept-formation, it has been the concern of many modern philosophers – particularly of the last two centuries – to call it into question. In this connection, a major source of criticism undoubtedly hails from the direction of what we may call post-Kantian *idealism*. There are different, more and less plausible, forms of idealism. What might be called 'subjective idealism' is just the radical (empiricist) sceptical view that we can have no knowledge of the world beyond our 'inner', mental or subjective impressions of it: for all we know, what we take to be experience of an objective order of things and other people is just a dream or hallucination to which no stable reality actually corresponds. The Irish philosopher George Berkeley[10] seems to have held some such view (expressed in the slogan 'esse est percipi': to be is to be perceived) – and, as we have seen, Hume also sailed perilously close to it. It is doubtful, however, whether subjective idealism is at all coherent. Most notably, Kant criticises the explicit idealism of Berkeley and the more implicit idealism of Hume on the grounds that it only makes sense to claim that all experience is subjective given that very distinction between the subjective and the objective that idealists deny we can make: if all experience is subjective, then we might just as well say that *none* of it is – for we can make sense of the subjective only by contrast with what is objective.[11] How, for example, can Hume draw the distinction between fact and falsehood if all impressions are on the same experiential level, and there is no basis upon which to draw the distinction between veridical (true) and non-veridical (illusory) sense-perceptions? Hence, Kant's attempt to reclaim the distinction between objective reality and subjective experience from subjective idealist scepticism has two main foundations. First, he argues that the objectivity of genuine perception is given precisely by the conformity of our experience of reality to certain rational principles of causal order, identity and difference, and so on: for example, objective things and real events are distinguished by (respectively) their *stability* and *regularity* from the protean nature of subjective dreams, delusions and hallucinations. Hume held that causal laws were rationally contentious or dubious inferences from experience. Kant argues that such Humean doubts about the rational basis of causal order could only be raised by someone who already understands the world as ordered in certain specifiably rational ways: to that extent, rational principles of identity and difference, cause and effect, and so on, are logical preconditions of any intelligible human experience, and if things were as Hume suggests they might be, he would not even be in a position to describe this circumstance. Again, all this is summed up in Kant's famous dictum that 'intuitions without concepts are blind'.

But Kant also held (the other half of the above dictum) that 'thoughts without content are empty'. He agrees essentially with empiricists that experience marks the bounds of what may be intelligibly thought and said: what we can know of the world in any substantial sense of the term 'know' (that is, excluding definitions or other logically true statements) must ultimately be based on experiences we have reason to suppose objectively grounded. Thus, one reason why 'tritons eat mermaids' is hardly intelligible, let alone true, is that it cannot correspond to any objective experience – precisely because there is nothing in sensible experience to which the terms 'triton' and 'mermaid' could correspond. In this regard, despite Kant's insistence that sense-experience needs conceptualisation in order to be meaningful, it is not clear that he greatly questions the empiricist idea that meaningfulness is significantly a function of reference to objective experience. Moreover, Kant is at pains to insist that one principal condition of the truth of our knowledge claims consists in their relationship or correspondence to those objective states, events and particulars that he expresses through the idea of 'things-in-themselves'. Indeed, it is because Kant fails to question the empiricist idea that all perception is of the *appearances* of things – their observable properties of size, shape, colour, odour, texture, and so on – that he feels compelled to say that something 'behind' appearances is needed to secure the complete objectivity of accurate perceptions. On this view, 'things-in-themselves' are not *themselves* sensible or perceivable – for if they were, they would only be further sense-impressions; rather they are the utterly imperceptible and pre-conceptual (and therefore purely hypothetical) objective substrates of such properties and qualities. Thus, for Kant, it seems to be a general condition of the meaningfulness of a knowledge claim – and therefore of our understanding of it – that it refers or corresponds to ordered sense-impressions that are themselves grounded in the objective extra-sensible reality of 'things-in-themselves'.

Conceptual idealism: the social provenance of concepts

Kant's epistemology represents a kind of crossroads in modern philosophy: his work is a necessary reference point for all subsequent philosophical attempts to understand knowledge and concept-acquisition – and, with regard to his educational relevance, we have already observed Kant's decisive influence on modern cognitive psychology. However, the most immediate response and challenge to Kant's work was to come from a new nineteenth-century brand of idealism. Although such post-Kantian idealism[12] is mainly sympathetic to Kant's critique of the subjectivist tendencies of much empiricism – particularly to the idea that unconceptualised sensations or impressions could not in and of themselves give rise to knowledge – it also raises the most obvious difficulty for Kant's account: the role in his epistemology of 'things-in-themselves'. For what possible explanatory role could be played by things or objects about which absolutely nothing can be said because they underlie all appearances – and are, by that token, themselves beyond conceptualisation? The short answer given by post-Kantian idealists to this question is that insofar as it cannot play any intelligible role, we might as well abandon the 'thing-in-itself'. On the new idealist view, Kant is right to claim that there can be no coherent conception of the world on the basis of unconceptualised sensations alone – and that meaning is therefore a function of the imposition of concepts and categories on the impressions of sense – but he is mistaken in holding that the intelligibility of concepts and/or the validity of knowledge claims rests upon their correspondence to an objective reality lying 'out there' beyond or 'behind' our concepts of it. In a nutshell, the world or reality as we experience and understand it is comprised not so much of objects or things as of *ideas*.

It is extremely important to distinguish this kind of idealism – which we shall here call *conceptual idealism* – from the subjective idealism of such empiricists as Berkeley. Unlike subjective idealism, conceptual idealism does not take our knowledge of the world to be just a dubious personal construction from individual sense-impressions, but agrees with Kant that it involves the rational ordering of experience – recognising significant distinctions, for example, between more and less credible or trustworthy experiences. Where it effectively departs from Kant is in denying that what gives meaning, coherence and validity to our best epistemic claims is not any external order of unconceptualised 'things-in-themselves' – for there can be no such external order (or none that we could talk about): in short, the world is made or 'constructed' according to our conceptions, and has no order in and of itself. But if our picture of the world is not determined by the independent order of things as they are in themselves, from whence could it derive, other than from (as subjective idealism maintains) individual personal experience? In a nutshell, conceptual idealism holds that the concepts and categories by means of which human agents seek to make some sort of non-subjective sense of their experience are *interpersonal* or *social* in origin, and are constructed in the course of human cultural evolution. The new idealist insight is that both Kant's epistemology and the empiricism of which it is critical are prey to the common error of supposing that knowledge is a matter of personal confrontation with experience, and that the problem of objectivity is essentially that of accounting for the way in which the individual can break through the veil of appearance to make contact with the hard reality lying 'behind' that appearance. For conceptual idealists there is no such reality, and human meaning-making is less an individual than a *collective* matter: knowledge is in a significant sense conventional – as, indeed, historically changing conceptions of what counts as human knowledge might seem to confirm – and human groups construct their knowledge perpectives in response to evolutionarily encountered problems of survival. Nineteenth-century idealism is therefore a prime source of the widespread contemporary philosophical thesis of the *social character of meaning* – the view that human meaning-making is interpersonal rather than individual, and that human interaction and community are necessarily presupposed to any sort of conceptualisation.

The obvious problem for conceptual idealism, however, is that if our perspectives on the world are not to be judged true or false, credible or incredible, by virtue of their correspondence or otherwise to an objective order of 'things-in-themselves', how might they be validated? Broadly speaking, idealism replaces correspondence (to things-in-themselves) with *coherence* as the key criterion of meaning and truth. Although there can (by definition) be no concept-independent assessment of how things-in-themselves are, there can be evaluation of different conceptual perspectives in terms of logical coherence or consistency: thus, it will be more reasonable to believe some things than others on the grounds that we are well advised to avoid (practical as well as theoretical) inconsistency, and even within the terms of our local conceptual conventions there will be better sense-dependent grounds for some propositions than others. Hence, it would seem sensible from any *rational* point of view to deny the statement 'tritons eat mermaids' on the grounds that this proposition cannot be both true and false, and that there is hardly any empirical evidence for supposing that either tritons (as fish-men) or mermaids (as fish-women) exist. Indeed, on a highly rationalist view of conceptual idealism associated with the great German idealist G.W.F. Hegel, the application of such rational criteria to the plethora of socially constructed human perspectives may be expected (in the literal fullness of time) to lead to a conception of the world that is *absolutely* true rather than just locally credible. Thus, according to what may be called *absolute idealism*, human inquiry advances by the systematic rational sifting of often contradictory human perspectives in the interests of an ultimately incontrovertible 'God's-eye' grasp of ultimate truth – and Hegel seems to have conceived human history as a matter of conceptual or 'spiritual' evolution towards some such absolute vision. On this view, different socio-cultural constituencies have developed different and conflicting conceptions of the world in the course of their evolution, but since these perspectives are often far from logically consistent, they are not simultaneously credible. Thus, since these perspectives are as finite and limited as the human minds that construct them, they stand in need of correction and completion through an historically embedded process of so-called *dialectic*. The dialectical comparison and/or contrast of one perspective with another, of what Hegel calls 'thesis' with 'antithesis', is therefore held (ultimately) to yield an intellectual 'synthesis' that resolves all contradictions in the interests of a more comprehensive error-free vision of reality.

Several educationally significant philosophers of some stature are more or less directly indebted to Hegel and nineteenth-century idealism – and, in later chapters of this work, we shall consider the views of Karl Marx and John Dewey, who may (in their different ways) be regarded as key exponents of the thesis of social character of meaning. Both of these philosophers repudiate empiricist and 'realist' epistemology in favour of a social constructivist conception of meaning-making, and regard human knowledge and inquiry as subject to evolutionary development and change – although Dewey is ultimately unsympathetic to the absolute idealist tendencies of both German philosophers. For the purposes of this chapter, however, it may be more illuminating to explore the implications for understanding learning and concept-acquisition of a body of philosophical work that might seem somewhat remote from either Hegel, Marx or Dewey. All the same, it is arguably in the twentieth-century work of the philosopher Ludwig Wittgenstein that we come nearest to an account of concept-formation that most clearly identifies the difficulties of representational theories of meaning: in particular, Wittgenstein's seminal *Philosophical Investigations*[13] represents perhaps the most sustained modern attack on the idea that concepts are internal mental ideas or inner impressions that take on meaning by referring to aspects of experience. Despite this, Wittgenstein seems more obviously indebted to such pioneers of modern logical analysis as the German mathematician Gottlob Frege and the British logician Bertrand Russell than to any philosophers in the idealist tradition. Indeed, the notorious picture theory of meaning he defended in his early *Tractatus* was deeply influenced by the representationalism of Russell's own empiricist epistemology of 'logical atomism'.[14] All the same, Wittgenstein's later posthumously published work, which is expressly intended to demolish the picture theory of meaning, is arguably more continuous with some of the key anti-representational insights of Frege – as well as with a Deweyan instrumental construal of the nature of ideas and concepts as more like *tools* of public commerce than inner sensible representations. However, it is probably best to introduce Wittgenstein by way of some observations on the work of Frege.

Frege's revolutionary semantic insights

Frege was primarily a mathematical logician, and his pioneering formalisation of an important segment of natural language was largely a by-product of his even more ambitious project to derive mathematics from logic.[15] However, his inquiries into the nature of reason and inference begin with an examination of the basic notion of a thought.[16] From the outset, he clearly distinguishes thoughts as the *content* of psychological states from their conscious experiential or subjective embodiments or expressions: a thought is a *logical* rather than a psychological entity. From this viewpoint, the thought that (say) 'the boss was in a foul mood' is what is common to some such range of psychological states as 'he believed the boss was in a foul mood', 'he expected the boss was in a foul mood', 'he feared the boss was in a foul mood', and so on. This 'de-psychologisation' of thought is a key move in the development of Frege's logical grammar: whatever empiricists and others may have believed, Frege argues that thoughts are *not* empirical impressions, sensations, conscious states or other 'internal' psychological events. In support of this insight, he introduces a range of other important distinctions between concept and object, function and concept, and sense and reference.[17] Frege's logical distinction between concept and object reflects (roughly) the ordinary grammatical distinction between subject and predicate, and is primarily concerned to distinguish between terms that *refer* to objects in the world and terms which do not: thus, in 'the boss was in a foul mood', the subject term functions like a *name* and refers (presumably) to an objectively existing person, whereas Frege regards the predicate ' – was in a foul mood' as a concept expression that does not refer (ignoring the rather technical sense in which Frege held that concepts rather than objects are the referents of predicates[18]) in the sense of picking out experienced particulars. We might be tempted to judge otherwise, since we could at least feel drawn to say that in the sentence 'the bus is red', ' – is red' refers to a colour. But it may help here to distinguish reference from *description*: insofar as ' – is red' and ' – was in a foul mood' are *adjectives*, they describe things, but as adjectives they are grammatically incomplete apart from the objects they describe and should not therefore be held to refer as names do. Indeed, perhaps Frege's key insight rests on his recognition of an analogy between grammatical predicates and algebraic functions. In algebraic expressions of the form '$2 (x)^2 + (x)$' mathematicians distinguish between what they call the *argument* 'x' and the *function* '$2 ( )^2 + ( )$' – which is what remains after the removal of 'x': whereas the argument – whatever 'x' refers to or stands for – has significance apart from the function, functions are 'unsaturated' expressions having no determinate sense apart from arguments. For Frege, in 'the boss was in a foul mood', 'the boss' functions (with other name-like expressions) like a mathematical argument, whereas the concept expression ' – was in a foul mood' behaves logically like an algebraic function.

However, the distinction of concept from object and the analysis of concept in terms of function interlock with another key Fregean distinction between sense and reference. Irrespective of their referential functions, according to Frege, all linguistic signs have a *sense*. Crucially, indeed, it is the possession of a sense by both concept expressions and the sentences to which they contribute that enables us to understand – grasp the *meaning* of – such false statements as 'Tony Blair is the king of Siam': contrary to those empiricist theories according to which any sentences that do not correspond to facts or definitions must be *meaningless*, we can clearly *understand* 'Tony Blair is the king of Siam' (for example, we can imagine what it would be like for it to be true) even though there is no experience to which it corresponds. Thus, although such 'unsaturated' concept expressions as ' – is the king of Siam' do not have reference, they have a sense. But it is also clear from the analogy with mathematical functions that we cannot be sure precisely what the sense of a predicate expression is in advance of its application to a subject term: just as a mathematical operation such as 'the square root of …' has no clear meaning in advance of its application to particular arguments – and, of course, such application is liable to give rather different values for different arguments – so it cannot be very clear what ' – is the king of Siam' means in advance of its true or false predication of some object term. In the case of many predicates, indeed, it would seem that we could hardly know what is being said of an object until we know just what object it is being said of.[19] Consider, for example, what it means to predicate the most general term of evaluation ' – is good' of something. If we ask what this *means*, it soon becomes clear that it means nothing *in general*. Rules or criteria for the application of ' – is good' to 'this knife' will be quite different from those we utilise in applying it to 'this doctor' or 'this woman': in short, a knife is good in quite a *different* sense from a professional role or a human being – and it is crucial for proper understanding to distinguish between these diverse senses of goodness. But just as predicates need subject terms in order to make determinate sense, so objects can be definitely identified only in terms of the properties expressed in predicates: I can know who Tony Blair is only via a set of descriptions that are presumably logically exclusive of his being the king of Siam. At all events, meaning appears to be a function of the grammatical cooperation or interplay of reference and predication: the one cannot make much sense without the other. Frege expresses all of this in his well-known aphorism that we should 'never ask for the meaning of a word in isolation, but only in the context of a proposition'.[20]

Wittgenstein's development of Frege

Wittgenstein's influential exploration of meaning and understanding in his *Philosophical Investigations* and other posthumously published works can be taken (in contrast with his earlier, more Russellian *Tractatus*) as an extension or ampification of these key insights of Frege. By way of ground-clearing, however, Wittgenstein sets out to show – via what has come to be known as the *private-language* argument[21] – that any empiricist or other account which takes concept-formation to be a matter of individual abstraction from the deliverances of sense-experience is bound to be incoherent. Just as Frege's work on the foundations of arithmetic had shown that one could not possibly derive simple or complex mathematical concepts of '2', 'minus 9', 'the square root of', and so on, from empirical experience, Wittgenstein sets out to show that concepts (Fregean 'senses') could not *generally* be derived via individual discrimination of aspects of inner or outer sense. Indeed, both Frege's anti-empiricist conception of number and Wittgenstein's private-language argument belong to a time-honoured tradition of philosophical concern about the nature of concept-formation reaching at least as far back as (and most obviously to) Plato. Plato's notorious theory of forms – the idea that since sense-experience cannot be considered a reliable source of genuine knowledge of the world, the concepts that guarantee such knowledge must hail from an intelligible realm of pure ideas that lie outside any sensible order – is clearly driven by a very real concern about how the concepts through which we understand the world of experience might have causal or other origins in that experience.[22] In philosophical contemplation of a cricket ball, for example, we might ask how we acquire the concepts of round and red – and the empiricist's reply is essentially that we derive them from repeated experiences of red and round things. Plato's point, however, is that since our concepts of red and round are ideal types to which nothing in particular experience corresponds, this hardly seems possible: the cricket ball is not perfectly (mathematically) round and is only one of the shades of red (which may be significantly *different* from other shades) to which we regularly apply the term 'red'. From this viewpoint, we may seem compelled to say (in the manner of one well-known contemporary judgement on this precise issue) that concepts are *mind-made*, and *applied* to human experience rather than abstracted from it.[23]

Wittgenstein's arguments against empiricist ideas of concept-formation are not at all far removed from such Platonic considerations. If the grasp of meaning is modelled on the idea of confrontation between the individual and *unconceptualised* sense-experience, how indeed might the individual succeed in abstracting the concept of 'red' from any such experience? Could this perhaps be achieved by some kind of inner *pointing* (ostension) to the items of experience to which he or she wished to draw attention? But how would the subject know what to point to, or which features of a given experience to identify as salient: how should he or she decide that these impressions count as red, whereas those are orange or purple? Even in the case of public rather than 'inner' experiential pointing there would need to be some grasp on the part of those for whom the pointing is intended that it is this rather than that feature that is in question – something, in short, to give meaningful contextualisation to such pointing. All the same, someone might say, there would have to be at least some cases of concept-formation by 'inner pointing'. For example, insofar as psychological experiences are *private* more or less *by definition* – just as I can only experience my pain, so you can experience only yours – how could I acquire concepts of such essentially 'private' experiences as being anxious or in pain other than by inner or 'private' ostension. Wittgenstein's repudiation of the empiricist account of concept-formation, however, is best appreciated in relation to his more surprising claim that even our concepts of psychological experience could not be acquired by any process of private reference to intrinsically internal states.

For one thing, Wittgenstein denies that it does follow from my inability to experience other people's pain that I cannot *know* that they are in pain – for such a conclusion would only follow from the assumption that the concept of pain, and any knowledge of the other's pain, is primarily a matter of 'inner' or private experience. Without denying that such experiences do enter into our avowals and ascriptions of pain, Wittgenstein holds that even insofar as the concept of pain is descriptive, it is not descriptive of an (indicated) experience. Certainly, in teaching children the concept of pain, parents will use the term descriptively in connection with people falling into nettles, fracturing limbs, receiving first aid, and so on. But, according to Wittgenstein, when people give vent to the first-person utterances 'I'm hurting' or 'it's painful', they are not at all describing or referring to experiences, but *expressing* how they feel: first-person pain utterances are *themselves* forms of pain behaviour. (This is the point behind Wittgenstein's rather paradoxical claim that it does not make sense to say 'I know that I'm in pain': knowledge claims are normally made on the basis of evidence – but I do not need *evidence* that I am in pain.) Thus, far from resting on private reference and/or abstraction, acquiring the concept of pain (as just one case of 'inner' experience) is as public a matter as acquiring any other concept: the descriptive content of the concept is taught by parents to children in relation to perfectly observable (and verifiable) circumstances of hurt and injury, and the expressive uses are encouraged in circumstances where parents want and need to know if their children are unwell. A central concern of Wittgenstein's here, again very much in the spirit of Frege's important insights into the nature of concepts and predication, is to dislodge the (empiricist and other philosophical) assumption or prejudice that the concepts expressed by grammatical predicates are invariably *descriptive* of (sensory or other) experience: thus, although we may also teach children that an adjective is a describing word, it appears that this need not always be so. If, for example, I observe that 'Helen is a beautiful girl' or 'the sorbet is delicious', it may not be that I am here *describing* Helen or the dessert, but rather that I am *evaluating* them as more pleasing or attractive (to my taste) than other girls or desserts. Likewise, if I say 'I'm over the moon', I am not obviously describing anything (not least my spatial position), but expressing how I feel.

Indeed, Wittgenstein argues that the surface grammar of linguistic usage is often quite misleading – so that, for example, what might seem to function like an adjective may not actually do so. We have already indicated that even with respect to genuine adjectival uses of the tricky term 'good', we may need to apply different criteria or rules of evaluation in relation to 'good girl' from those we utilise with respect to 'good knife': indeed, some philosophers of meaning-as-use have (contentiously) argued that to call persons 'good' in a moral sense is not to describe them at all, but to *commend* or express personal admiration for them.[24] Be that as it may, if someone says 'Good morning' on a very rainy day, one would clearly have got hold of the wrong end of the stick to say: 'No it isn't, stop telling lies.' Here, it is a plain error to construe the term 'good' as functioning *either* descriptively *or* adjectivally: what someone clearly intends by saying 'Good morning' is not to describe the weather, but to *wish* me well in my business of the day. (In this respect the American idiom 'have a nice day', though more irritating, is less grammatically misleading.) Wittgenstein insists that such mistakes are endemic in past philosophical treatments of the problems of knowledge, mind, morality, religion, aesthetics, and so on, and that a great many philosophical puzzles rest ultimately on a failure to appreciate that language has many practical uses other than to describe or report on the world. Wittgenstein is fond of an analogy between language and a box of tools: just as the tool box contains diverse implements for different uses, so language contains the resources for promising, complaining, commending, approving, commanding, questioning, explaining, and so on, as well as for describing. In this connection, Wittgenstein is also sceptical of the received philosophical method of trying to *define* the meanings of words in terms of *necessary* and *sufficient* conditions – holding that this also encourages the idea that a term like 'good' has a fixed or once-and-for-always sense, which might be determined by ascertaining what or how it describes. Wittgenstein therefore insists that we should look not for the meaning of a term but to its *use* – by which, of course, he means to say that a grasp of the use is the key to a proper appreciation of the meaning.

However, if understanding or the grasp of meaning is not a function of reference to aspects of inner experience, but a matter of mastery of the grammar of usage in different contexts of human agency, endeavour and association, it cannot be an *individual* or 'private' psychological achievement. As we have seen, even the conceptualisation of aspects of personal experience is something to which contexts of interpersonal and public communication are presupposed: a pre-linguistic Robinson Crusoe raised by animals on a desert island could certainly feel and suffer pain, but he could not meaningfully be said to have a *concept* of pain in the absence of a language in which the term 'pain' could acquire a determinate context of use. For Wittgenstein, then, concept possession is essentially a function of the capacity to grasp the complexities of linguistic usage, and the grasp of such complexities depends in turn upon initiation into the inevitably cooperative and interpersonal practices that give point to such usage: hence meaning and understanding are quite incompatible with the idea of a 'private language'. It is in this connection that Wittgenstein insists – again somewhat perplexingly – that 'understanding is not a mental process'. The common temptation here – which too many past philosophers have not resisted – is to suppose that understanding is a *psychological* phenomenon, and that it must therefore go on 'in the head'. Wittgenstein's rather surprising claim is that understanding goes on not in the head, but in perfectly public contexts of teaching and learning. In fact, on this view, what 'goes on in the head' – the inner experiences that a learner has in the course of learning something – may be quite irrelevant to the business of learning this or that. It may help here to bear in mind that we speak of people understanding things even when they are asleep or unconscious: a person who is unconscious will have no experiences, and someone who is asleep may be dreaming, but neither of these circumstances is of relevance to the fact that he or she (right now) understands quantum theory or knows how to play 'Tiger Rag' on the clarinet. Understanding is not a mental experience but a capacity or a *disposition*: a person understands when he or she has now grasped 'how to go on' with respect to some public procedure or (mental or physical) skill. We need to get into our heads the point that, as a later philosopher has put it, 'meanings ain't in the head'.[25]

Concepts as social, interpersonal and practical rules

For Wittgenstein, in sum, a concept is not an inner experience, but a kind of *rule* that has a primarily practical (though not necessarily instrumental) use within some context of human life. It is also a rule that requires public criteria for its correct application: a learner has understood or grasped a concept when he or she can execute a procedure or follow a rule according to standard practice or common convention. From this viewpoint, concept-acquisition could never be a matter of the private labelling of internal impressions, for how could we know from this that we had got something right? But this shows that the rule-following presupposed to concept-acquisition is more a *socio-cultural* matter than a natural-developmental process: meaning and understanding are essentially products of active participation and engagement in interpersonal and cooperative human institutions and practices. Moreover, the distinctive character of human meaning and understanding is given primarily through that form of public communication familiar to us as language: language-acquisition is thus the most potent – if not the only – source of human concepts and conceptualisation. All of this, if true, has immense implications for understanding human conceptual development, and for issues about the contribution of scientific or experimental psychology to our understanding of such development. For example, we have already noted the general tendency of some empirical psychologists to construe the conceptual development of children in terms of the quasi-biological development of age-related cognitive structures. In this respect, there can be no doubt that cognitive psychologists have made rather heavy weather of explaining the conceptual transitions that are said to occur from pre-concrete to concrete learning on the basis of Piaget's conservation experiments. What, psychologists have asked, can explain how a child moves from a mistaken judgement that the same amount of water is more in the tall thin beaker than it is in the short fat one, to saying that the amount is the same? Whereas some notable cognitivists have offered some rather far-fetched epistemological explanations to explain such transitions, they are in fact quite inexplicable in empiricist terms, but very much less mysterious on a normative Wittgensteinian view of concept-formation. For, on a Wittgensteinian view, we have only to recognise that an infant's mastery of language is less advanced than a primary child's: that whereas the younger child may use a term like 'more' to mean either 'heavier' or 'taller', the older child may more easily discriminate. In short, although conceptual growth is a matter of the progress of principled understanding, such progress follows not from the biological development of cognitive *processes*, but from enhanced grasp of practice and usage.[26]

There can also be little doubt that the language of 'process' has come to play a very suspect role in modern theorising about learning and the curriculum – probably under the direct influence of modern cognitive pychology. Indeed, it would appear that a certain preference for the expression of educational objectives in terms of the cultivation of *processes*, rather than the production of so-called 'products' or 'outcomes', seems to have gone hand in hand with the cognitive psychological rejection of behavioural objectives analyses of learning and curriculum. The fair complaint of cognitive psychologists against such analyses is that such objectives can often be achieved in the absence of real understanding: indeed, it has been the time-honoured complaint of progressive educationalists that the rote and mechanical learning of skills and information of bygone schooling has all too often been meaningless, and has made little or no lasting or significant impact on young minds or lives. So it is not hard to agree that there is more to learning and education than the promotion of blind behavioural outcomes. But latter-day educational sloganising to the effect that the process is more important than the product, or worse, that we should seek to promote processes *rather than* products, is liable to serious and debilitating educational ambiguity and confusion.[27] On the one hand, it precisely suggests a dualistic conception of processes as entirely separate from, or only contingently related to, products or behavioural outcomes. For whilst in the course of learning children may well experience valuable psychological states or processes – of, say, enjoyment, satisfaction, and so on – that are only contingently related to learning outcomes, it is not at all clear how these might constitute *educational* aims of teaching. Athough we may well agree that it is a good thing for children to experience confidence, satisfaction and enjoyment in the course of their learning, and recognise that good teachers are those who try to ensure this, we should also recognise that this could not possibly be an *intended* aim of teaching: that, indeed, parents would have cause to complain about any teacher who had made his or her pupils happy or confident without teaching them anything. It would appear, all the same, that careless talk about the importance of process over product has encouraged some recent tendency to regard the promotion of such inner states of well-being as actual aims of education – which (however desirable they may be) they are not.[28]

On the other hand, however, if processes are construed as the operations of thought or understanding, or the grasp of principles and reasons, it should by now be clear that they cannot be conceptually separated from so-called 'products' or 'behavioural outcomes'. In short, if the slogan that the process is more important than the product comes down to the claim that there can be no real knowledge without *understanding*, then – insofar as understanding is the mastery of public and interpersonal rules, practices and procedures – it can make little real sense to say that process matters *more than* product. Indeed, any idea that one might have understanding of an activity or skill apart from the procedures and practices that embody such understanding could only rest on the dualist mistake about mind that seeks to account for meaning in terms of private experience. Thus, Wittgenstein's observation in *Philosophical Investigations* that understanding is *not* a mental process gets straight to the heart of what is wrong with empirical psychological analyses of conceptual learning in terms of the growth of cognitive processes or structures – and, hence, to a proper appreciation of the confusion inherent in any educational talk of process rather than product. Indeed, Wittgenstein went so far as to question the value of modern experimental psychology as a coherent theoretical enterprise. At the very end of the *Investigations*, he declares that the problems of empirical psychology are not to be excused on the grounds that it is a young science in need of further refinement: the trouble is, he said, that psychology is all 'experimental methods and conceptual confusion'.[29] In view of the enormous and often less than helpful influence

of empirical psychology on educational theory from the beginning of the twentieth century to the present day, educationalists might often have done well to
take these very famous philosophical sentiments more closely to their hearts[30].

Possible tasks

(1) Bearing in mind the potentially misleading nature of simple definitions,
consider how you would set about teaching a young person to appreciate
what is meant by the words 'tragic', absurd' or 'ironic' as applied to this or
that human situation or work of art.

(2) Consider how you might go about assisting a child to appreciate the
metaphorical or analogical character of a passage of poetry.

Chapter 8

Knowledge, explanation and understanding

Epistemology and the problem of objectivity

In this part of the book so far, we have been critical of a widespread naturalistic dogma to the effect that understanding and/or explaining human learning is primarily a matter for empirical *psychology*. As we have seen, it seems nowadays widely assumed that human learning, construed as a natural process like any other, is apt for scientific description and explanation in the manner of other natural processes, that human learning could hardly be other than evolutionarily continuous with non-human animal learning, and that the modern experimental (behaviourist, cognitivist or other) methods that have provided some insight into non-human learning processes might be expected to assist our understanding of any and all human learning. In the previous chapter, however, we explored some of the difficulties faced by various psychological approaches in explaining what is distinctive about human learning – not least certain problems about accounting for meaning and understanding – which might well serve to shake too great a confidence in any such enterprise. From this viewpoint, indeed, it would appear that what stands most in need of questioning is the apparently innocuous social scientific assumption that it is proper to regard the objects and goals of teaching – learning, understanding and knowledge – as kinds of *empirical* process. But we have also observed that much modern cognitive theory and cognitive science is infected with dualist tendencies reflecting the difficulties of the two great intellectual traditions of modern philosophy – rationalism and empiricism – as well as those additional problems created by Kant's heroic attempt to combine or synthesise these traditions. Modern psychology therefore generally confronts us with an uncomfortable dilemma. If one thinks as a *rationalist* (in a tradition from Descartes to Kant and some modern cognitive structuralists) that sense-experience cannot be the sole source of knowledge and understanding, one is prey to the problem of tracing the source of explanatory principles (of thought or cognition) and of showing how these relate to the external (material) world they purport to explain. If, on the other hand, one thinks as an *empiricist* (in a tradition from Locke and Hume to modern experimental psychology), then one faces the difficulty of accounting for the way in which the knowledge or explanatory principles through which we comprehend the world are derived from the brute data of sensory input. Either way, these perspectives raise the awkward question: how can there be *objective* knowledge of the world of human experience that might support any claim that it is *rationally justified* to think in this way rather than that? The present relevance of this question, of course, is that unless we can have grounds for supposing that some ways of conceiving the world are more rationally defensible than others, then *education* – as distinct from this or that form of training, habituation or even indoctrination – is barely conceivable.

This question, of course, is fundamental to the philosophical discipline of *epistemology*, and the best point of entry into this particular philosophical field is also clearly provided by the work of the great founding fathers of the western philosophical academy, Socrates, Plato and Aristotle. Moreover, despite their early pioneering role in the development of ideas about knowledge and learning, the ancient philosophers do not seem to have been at all unaware of the sort of problems we have already examined in relation to modern learning theory: indeed, since they were arguably at least as privy to them as any modern social and behavioural scientists, it would be a serious mistake to dismiss such intellectual giants as no longer relevant to contemporary discussions of knowledge or education. In particular, both Plato and Aristotle seem acutely appreciative of the fundamental difficulties and shortcomings of reductive materialist or physicalist accounts of human knowledge.[1] From this perspective, the materialist accounts of mind and soul of such ancient philosophers as Anaxagoras, which were so trenchantly criticised by Socrates, are not logically far removed from the speculations of modern cognitive scientists. It was very probably under the spell of Socratic scepticism about such theories that Plato proceeded to develop his own metaphysically dualist epistemology – in turn criticised by Aristotle – which effectively denies any basis for genuine knowledge of reality in sensory or empirical experience. Thus, as we have seen, whereas a long tradition of philosophy and social science extending from such classical empiricists as John Locke to such modern empirical psychologists as Piaget has largely assumed that the concepts through which we order and classify the data of sensory experience are somehow mental abstractions from the particulars of sensory experience, Plato utterly rejects any such account of concept-formation on the grounds that such abstraction must *already* presuppose possession of the concepts in question. In opposition to any such view, Platonic *idealism* (usually called, in relation to the problem of acquiring mathematical concepts, Platonic *realism*) asserts that concepts are non-empirical idealisations deriving from an *intelligible* rather than *sensible* realm of experience – though for Plato, of course, such intelligible forms are precisely what are *really* real and enduring, whereas what is experienced by the senses in the sensible (empirical) realm is little more than subjective and fleeting illusion.

The Platonic conditions of knowledge

Despite the fact that Plato's theory of forms raises still unresolved problems of immense epistemological, psychological and educational significance, his uncompromising metaphysical dualism – as Plato's own great philosophical pupil Aristotle is quick to point out – is generally hard to sustain. Still, in the course of developing this theory, Plato offers a philosophical analysis of the nature of knowledge, which – despite some modern reservations – is nowadays largely held to have identified the principal *necessary* (if not sufficient) conditions for theoretical cognition. Moreover, Plato's account is a direct response to an ancient brand of epistemological subjectivism or scepticism not too far removed from certain modern and postmodern forms of (moral and other) solipsism and idealism. His primary target is the apparent psychologising about knowledge of Socrates' great contemporary (the sophist) Protagoras, who is credited – by virtue of an identification of knowledge with perception – with having held that 'man is the measure of all things'.[2] Plato's Socrates ascribes to Protagoras the view that since knowledge is a function of individual perception – what I experience as hot or red, you (for all I know) may experience as cold or blue – what is true for me is not so for you: in that case, knowledge must be relative to personal or individual opinion. If this was Protagoras' view, Plato rightly rejects it as falling foul of a common ambiguity in our perceptual usage: for, of course, whereas what we sometimes mean in claiming to have perceived that something is so is that it *is* so, all we mean at other times is that we *take it* to be so. In the first case, perceptual claims are tantamount to knowledge claims; in the second – the case in which what I take to be hot you take to be cold – they are little more than subjective (psychological) expressions of opinion or belief. Hence, although Plato agrees that knowledge does (at least in the human case) seem to involve some (psychological) state of apprehension or cognition – so that it would be conceptually odd to say that I know that it is raining, but I do not believe it – it is clear that such psychological claims may fall well short of knowledge. Indeed, although I can *believe* largely what I like (that, for example, the moon is made of green cheese, or that the Forth Bridge crosses the Clyde), such beliefs do not in the least amount to knowledge – since, of course, they are *false*, and one can have *knowledge* only of what is *true*.

Hence, although Protagoras rightly recognises that there is a psychological dimension to knowing, he fails to appreciate that knowledge differs from such psychological states as belief and opinion by virtue of an internal relation to *truth*: to that extent, Plato's account of knowledge as true belief already represents an important advance on Protagoras' view of knowledge as little more than a conviction that things are no more than we take them to be. But does this mean that knowledge is equivalent to true belief? Some such idea might well be suggested by widespread educational and other use of the term 'knowledge' to signify little more than *fact* or information: from this viewpoint, a 'knowledgeable person' is someone who has memorised or can call to mind as many facts as possible – and tests of general knowledge on media quiz shows are usually mainly focused upon such feats of recall. However, such facts are also sometimes referred to as 'useless', and such feats of recall may be of little more than passing entertainment value: more recently, indeed, the useful epithet 'inert' has been used to refer to the rather educationally sterile status of such information or facts considered in themselves.[3] Furthermore, it seems to have been a regular complaint of past and present educational philosophers that education has all too often been focused upon the transmission of such useless or inert facts to young people in schools. Thus, not only has such fact-communication been memorably satirised in the character of the Victorian schoolmaster Gradgrind in Charles Dickens' novel *Hard Times*, but it has been the standard objection (rightly or wrongly) of progressive or liberal-minded educationalists to the more technicist 'behavioural objectives' orthodoxies of modern state educational policy that they also largely – albeit in the name of knowledge – trade in the promotion of much meaningless, 'inert' or useless information.

But there is also a common sense of what it is to know something, in which one might feel driven to *deny* that someone who believes what is true has genuine *knowledge* of that truth. Suppose that I am haunted by the conviction that a long-lost friend is presently thinking about me – and it is also (by coincidence) the case that she *is* so thinking of me. It would clearly be stretching matters to grant the status of knowledge to any such vague intuition, even though it would be proper to call it a true opinion or conviction. Again, I might be convinced as a lifelong UFO spotter that there is intelligent life on some planet of Arcturus – and, as it happens, there *is* intelligent life on this world. Once more, I have a true belief, but not one that clearly counts as *knowledge*. So what is it, then, that such true beliefs lack that prevents us from regarding them as cases of knowledge? The trouble seems to be that although such claims are true, they are related only *contingently* to the truth, and the believer appears to have no discernible rational *grounds* or *evidence* for the truth of such claims. It is perhaps Plato's greatest epistemological insight to have recognised that some such consideration sharply distinguishes knowledge from facts, information or mere true beliefs. In this connection, he introduces a *third* crucial condition of knowledge in the form of what he calls a *logos* or account. However, although the term *logos* is invariably translated by the English 'word', it should be clear that the Greek term is richer than the English one – as, indeed, we may be led to suspect when we read at the beginning of St John's gospel that: 'In the beginning was the Word, and the Word was with God and the Word was God.' Here, to be sure, it is fairly evident that 'word', as a direct translation of *logos*, refers less (as in English) to some grammatical sign, and more to some general *principle* of intelligibility or meaning: God as 'Word' is no mere linguistic entity, but That which gives meaning and purpose to anything or everything that might count as intelligible. (From a theological viewpoint, indeed, any 'beginning' in which God as 'Word' stands to the world is probably better interpreted constitutively – more in manner of Aristotelian 'formal cause' – than temporally in the more modern sense of efficient cause.[4]) Hence, in the context of Plato's analysis of knowledge, the meaning of *logos* would seem to be located somewhere in the semantic range of 'justification', 'account', 'rationale', 'proof', 'explanation' or 'ground'.

At all events, Plato's enduring epistemological legacy is a basic analysis of knowledge as subject to three key constraints. First, there is what we may call the *psychological* constraint: one could hardly consistently claim to know that *p* (where '*p*' stands for any sentence, statement or proposition), but not believe it. Secondly, there is the *truth* constraint: whereas I can believe that the moon is made of green cheese, I could hardly be said to *know* that this is so – since, of course, the moon is not so made. But, thirdly, there is also what we might call (a little misleadingly, given a widespread modern empirical construal of this term) the *evidence* constraint: I might truly believe that there is no monster in Loch Ness, but I could hardly claim to *know* this in the absence of (empirical or other) grounds or evidence. As already noted, despite some latter-day reservations about the joint sufficiency of these conditions of knowledge,[5] this general Platonic account of the logical contours of knowledge has survived relatively unscathed into contemporary epistemology. This idea of knowledge as essentially *justified true belief* has clearly also informed the progressive and liberal-traditional conceptions of education and educational development of very many past and present educational philosophers.[6] Indeed, it may be hard to see how any educational philosopher worth his or her salt could ever have regarded the educational enterprise as other than directed towards the cultivation of psychological capacities for the rational pursuit of what is true and right rather than false or confused. Thus, on the general authority of a broad educational church, the educated person is he or she who has achieved a significant degree of liberation from the grip of ignorance and confusion via the development of such epistemic capacities – and it is more or less this conception of the relationship between knowledge and education that links Plato's famous analogy of the cave[7] to R.S. Peters' more recent characterisation of the (rationally uninitiated) child as 'the barbarian at the gates of civilization'.[8]

The Platonic account: problems for education

In the light of such widespread consensus about the general character of knowledge and understanding and its central educational value and significance, what possible philosophical controversy or disagreement might still remain about education as the promotion of knowledge? Modern educational philosophers are, of course, divided by several sources of controversy about education and knowledge. First, they disagree over the question (especially in the light of the so-called contemporary 'knowledge explosion') of what sorts of knowledge should be transmitted by schools and other educational institutions, and this is an issue we shall explore further in the next chapter. Secondly, there is a not unrelated issue about whether the rational pursuit of knowledge is a suitable educational goal for all learners. Here, although Plato certainly thought that the pursuit of justified true belief was a proper goal for some members of society (the guardians and auxiliaries of his ideal state), he was notoriously reluctant to regard such pursuit as appropriate for the intellectually inferior or less able: in this regard, moreover, he has been widely followed by modern educational theorists and policy makers – and we shall need to look more closely at this question in part III. Thirdly, however, there is a further related question concerning whether the pursuit of knowledge is the *only* proper goal of education, and about whether exclusive focus on the rational or cognitive (or upon an exclusively cognitive interpretation of the rational) may not be neglectful or distortive of such other key aspects of human development as the social, the emotional and the physical – and something is also said about such questions elsewhere in this work. For now, however, there is some need to address a logically prior question about the relationship of justification to truth, which has significantly divided those who would otherwise agree that education is the pursuit of knowledge (broadly defined as justified true belief), and which continues to bedevil modern, contemporary and so-called 'postmodern' educational philosophy.

The basic difficulty is already fermenting in Plato's philosophy. For although Plato's epistemology is, as we have seen, largely prompted by a desire to demonstrate that knowledge claims are grounded in objective truth rather than subjective perception, the distinction he draws between the intelligible world of absolute ideas and the sensible world of mere appearances in the interests of such objectivity drives a wedge between thought and world that pulls in rather the opposite direction. The main problem turns upon the nature of the internal or inferential connection that Plato – or any theorist of knowledge as justified true belief – is apt to recognise between justification and truth. Like most philosophers who equate objective knowledge with *certainty*, Plato regards mathematical truth as the very essence of objectivity. On the Platonic view, mathematical truths such as '2 + 2 = 4' are true *necessarily* – or, as some modern logicians would put it: 'true in all possible worlds'.[9] On the face of it, that is, it is reasonable to hold that if such statements are true, they are not just true here and false there, or true today and false tomorrow, but *once and for always* true. '2 + 2 = 4' would be true on any world in any part of the universe, or even if there had been no universe – and not even God could render such truths false.[10] However, Plato also appreciates that such mathematical objectivity is precisely connected to the logical *certainty* or *necessity* of mathematical proof or justification: this is the precise point of importing the notion of proof or justification into the very idea of knowledge. But that is effectively to admit that mathematical truths are not true in and of themselves, quite irrespective of any other considerations: on the contrary, they are true by virtue of their place in a system of mathematical rules and principles that are *constitutive* of their truth. Thus, although such mathematical truths are in a real sense *absolutely* true within a given rational ordering of numbers – and even if there could be *no* such rational ordering in which '2 + 2 = 4' turned out to be false – it is none the less the case that such statements are truths *only* relative to a particular system of rules.

Moreover, it is not entirely clear that mathematical truths are true in all possible worlds, as some past rationalist philosophers seem to have supposed. Kant, like Plato, regarded mathematical truths as necessarily true, and held that geometrical definitions precisely exemplified such necessity; but modern geometricians have demonstrated that geometrical principles and proofs are highly *conventional*, and that there are (for example) geometrical systems in which the angles of a triangle do not add up to 180 degrees. Likewise, although some notable modern philosophers of mathematics (including Frege) have been Platonic realists about number – holding that numerals do actually refer to numbers conceived as non-empirical objects – many more have subscribed to a view of mathematics as the human construction of inferential systems for purely conventional purposes (of measurement or whatever).[11] Moreover, such considerations concerning the rational conventionality, even arbitrariness, of mathematics have been applied in modern and postmodern times to almost every sphere of human endeavour. To begin with, it is not entirely implausible to regard various expressions of human value – the substance of human moral and artistic endeavour – as purely conventional. Thus, although Plato sought to defend an absolute or universal moral objectivity against the ancient Greek Sophists, who regarded moral judgements as essentially expressive of local culture and social convention, more recent communitarian social and moral theorists have insisted on the historically conditioned character of human value judgements in a spirit much closer to the Sophist Protagoras than Plato – and, on the face of it, diversity and disagreement may appear to be more obvious features of moral life than universal rational consensus. Indeed, it is worth noting that it is not so much that people do not have justificatory reasons for their moral beliefs, but that their beliefs are likely to be justified in terms of diverse and rival normative sytems that validate different, often contradictorily opposed, moral conclusions.[12] The same would seem to apply to our judgements about what is good or bad art. The judgements of artistic quality of our society are not necessarily shared by different cultures with different standards – and such judgements are increasingly questioned from within our own society by those (such as feminists, immigrants from other cultures, young people, and so on) who regard inherited standards as merely the legacies of past hegemony and prejudice.

But the idea that truth is only relative to a system – the consequence of a strong construal of the internal relation between truth and justification – has exercised an even more alarming influence in the sphere of science. It is tempting to regard natural science as the last bastion of objective reality against which our best knowledge claims might be assessed as correct or incorrect, true or false: surely, after all, such scientific generalisations as 'metals expand when heated' would have to be true, if they are true at all, by virtue of describing how things are 'out there' in a reality that obtains independently of any statements we make about it? In the previous chapter, however, we noted the emergence of a nineteenth-century post-Kantian idealism that stresses the evolutionary and historically conditioned nature of all human ideas and practices, and affirms the socially constructed character of all reality. In turn, such idealism has greatly shaped a non-realist *pragmatist* conception of science[13] that rejects as quite unintelligible any conception of perspective independent reality – and has exercised great influence over modern and postmodern theorising about knowledge and learning. According to pragmatists, insofar as there is no conception-free reality awaiting human description and explanation, it is not helpful to regard scientific theories as *descriptive* of anything at all, and better to regard them as technical devices for the solution of survival-related problems linked to all too human interests and purposes. Of course, some purposes – such as the search for a cure for cancer – will be of *general* rather than merely local human interest; but scientific activity is nevertheless driven by human interests, needs and *values*, rather than by any pursuit of disinterested truth – for there is no such truth. To be sure, the mainstream of non-realist and pragmatist philosophy of science is far from sceptical or relativist about the potential for substantial betterment of the human condition of scientific progress: precisely it regards natural and social scientific knowledge as offering the best possible route to the evolutionary advance and survival of the human species. But while wholeheartedly endorsing the general historicism about knowledge and inquiry of pragmatism, more recent postmodern thinking about science has been more ready to call its claims to human betterment into question.[14] Indeed, since it is not obvious that science and technology have always been on the side of human or environmental improvement – on the contrary, they have often (particularly in the twentieth century) served human destruction and environmental degradation – science is to be regarded as just one value-laden, hence questionable, perspective among others. But, from this viewpoint, the claims of science to serve general human interest are also bogus because it hardly makes sense to speak of *universal* human value: in the words of a leading spokesman of postmodernism 'there are no overarching metanarratives'.[15] At all events, since epistemic claims are not liable for evaluation as true or false in relation to some mind-independent reality, the main criterion of validity cannot be correspondence, but only *coherence* or *utility*.

Idealism, pragmatism and John Dewey

The general relevance to social and educational theory of these neo-idealist observations about knowledge, reality and value is two-fold. First, they engender a certain suspicion that since human knowledge cannot be based on objective value-free truth, what counts in most places as knowledge is simply expressive of the ambition of one social group to wield exploitative power and control over another. In part III, we shall look more closely at this notion in relation to the views of Karl Marx and others. Secondly, however, they give rise to a conception of learning according to which knowledge is more a matter of active 'meaning-making' than of passive reporting on some ready-made reality – and it is now time to look more closely at this idea in relation to the specifically more educationally focused ideas of the American pragmatist philosopher John Dewey. Like other pragmatists, Dewey was deeply influenced by the nineteenth-century European idealism of Hegel and others. He therefore largely agrees with idealists: first, in rejecting the empiricist conception of understanding as a matter of the causal impact of an 'external' world on an 'internal' mind or soul that registers that impact in the form of sense-impressions; secondly, in his endorsement of a social constructivist account of meaning. Like idealists, pragmatists reject the dualism of subjective mind and objective world inherent in the 'passive spectator' account of knowledge-acquisition, and construe understanding or meaning-making as a function of active engagement with historically and economically determined problems of human flourishing and survival. Relatedly, pragmatists endorse the idealist view of any such engagement with human practical or other problems as essentially social or communal, and hence reject the distinction between the individual and society also implicit in empiricist epistemology: human agents could not *single-handedly* come to any coherent understanding of the world, and therefore the conceptualisations through which agents do make sense of things have a significantly *external* origin – not, of course, in any Kantian realm of unconceptualised objects, but in a socially or culturally generated and inherited body of meaning-constitutive principles. In short, there is at least this much general agreement between pragmatists and idealists: that (contrary to the claims of empiricism) rather than having meaning individually thrust upon us by the causal impact of an objective order of external things that is itself meaningless, we find meaning by virtue of active initiation into and engagement with the inherently *social* and interpersonal institutions and practices of this or that cultural inheritance.

Dewey's own personal brand of pragmatism – which he called *Instrumentalism* – goes along with most of this. However, although he was initially drawn to Hegel's absolute idealism, Dewey's own liberal-democratic inclinations eventually led him to reject the monolithic notion of truth entailed by that idealism – not least Hegel's totalitarian and paternalist conception of the state as the political embodiment of that truth. In this respect, Dewey also differs significantly from Marx, who – despite his own materialist or economic revision of Hegelian dialectic – did seem to hold that the contradictions inherent in any and all class-based economic exploitation must eventually yield to an absolute conception of the good based on an (at least initially) imposed redistribution of wealth: for Marx, any final eradication of the injustice of inequality would be rooted in an impersonal conception of what is right and true from which there could be no real rational dissent. To Dewey, this is anathema insofar as he believes that the very progress of human inquiry, to which the business of human meaning-making is presupposed, turns on freedom to engender new intellectual perspectives, theories and hypotheses – which any 'absolute' view of the truth must preclude: from the Deweyan standpoint, knowledge is always provisional, and 'absolute' idealism therefore threatens to undermine that very freedom to make or remake the world of human experience precisely promised by conceptual idealist rejection of external objective constraints on human thought. All the same, Dewey is clearly hostile to all of the dualisms – between mind and body, knowledge and world, individual and society – rejected by idealists, as well as to any and all dualisms in general.[16] Above all, however, Dewey is probably the greatest ever critic of the so-called 'passive spectator' view of knowledge-acquisition, which he took to be a consequence of classical empiricism, and which he regarded as in turn exemplified by a traditional or conventional fact-transmission conception of schooling and education. Essentially, then, Dewey deploys a sustained critique of the empiricist conception of knowledge-acquisition in the service of a distinctive and influential philosophy of education, and his social constructivist conceptions of knowledge-acquisition and school curriculum have had a enormous influence on the development of non-traditional, progressive or child-centred modes of education and pedagogy (despite Dewey's own repudiation of libertarian or 'anything goes' progressive education).

Basically, Dewey's view of knowledge-acquisition is non-realist, but naturalistic and evolutionary, in the manner of much post-Kantian idealism. On such a view, one should conceive human knowledge not as an extended report on a fixed objective world that learners register by passive individual observation, but as the ever-evolving product of active engagement with the survival-related problems of historically conditioned human communities. According to instrumentalist pragmatism, it is better to regard knowledge as a kind of tool or technology for manipulating or controlling experience (just as primitive humans used their stone axes or bone clubs as a kind of survival-conducive technology) than as a body of information or objectively true fact: in short, scientific theories are operational strategies – instruments apt for further refinement – not descriptions of reality. On this view, moreover, knowledge evolves in adaptation to *changing* human needs, just as technologies evolve, and any knowledge (as fixed fact) without such evolutionary potential would be humanly useless. Consequently Dewey generally construes useful and effective school learning in terms more of the active mastery of skills or procedures than of the absorption of information, and utterly rejects the 'Gradgrindian' model of education as fact-learning satirised by Dickens. For Dewey, good science education is less a matter of memorising tables of elements than of mastering empirical investigative and experimental methods or procedures in the manner of novitiate scientific researchers; good geography is less a matter of learning facts about the Amazonian basin than of acquiring cartographical skills; good mathematical education is better conceived as the acquisition of practical techniques for measurement than as the rote learning of tables, and so on. Moreover, in much the same breath as he repudiates the passive-reception conception of education, Dewey also rejects the correlative empiricist conception of knowledge as a matter of logically discrete subjects or bodies of information. If modes of knowledge are more like skills, then there is no obvious reason why their application should be confined to particular realms of experience: just as we may use a hammer in sculpture as well as carpentry, we can use mathematics in art and woodwork as well as in science. Hence, Dewey subscribed to an *holistic* conception of knowledge in which different techniques of human inquiry are brought together or integrated for the investigation of this or that aspect of experience precisely in the interests of more vital and meaningful learning. Dewey was thus also dismissive of traditional *subject-centred* schooling, and instead advocated an integrated curriculum focused on practical problem-solving. In the hands of W.H. Kilpatrick and other followers of Dewey, this led to the explicit development of a topic-centred curriculum (the so-called 'project method') that was to have widespread educational impact.[17] In Britain, for example, ideas of integrated curricula exercised a formative influence on the new progressive post-Plowden (in Scotland, 'Primary Memorandum') primary curriculum, which also placed explicit Deweyan emphasis on collaborative, experimental, discovery and practical problem-centred learning.[18] At least since this time, it has been not unusual to encounter in both professional *and* official contexts of educational theory and policy a certain constructivist conception of pedagogy which invites us to regard primary children as 'little scientists' engaged in authentic exploration of the world in a spirit of uncoerced personal 'meaning-making'.[19]

The virtues and vices of pragmatist pedagogy

To be sure, it would be all too easy to overstate the influence of such constructivism: there are more and less plausible versions of pragmatist pedagogy on offer, and they would each need to be evaluated on their particular merits. All the same, something should here be said about the general virtues and shortcomings of such constructivist discourse, and about the epistemic assumptions upon which it appears mainly to depend. Indeed, in view of the greater heat than light that seems to have been generated by some local debates about Dewey's educational influence,[20] it might be fair to begin by appreciating the more positive educational aspects of the pragmatist approach. Thus, we may readily agree with pragmatists in rejecting any conception of human inquiry that takes the learning of physics, history or geography to be no more than the passive absorption of so many bodies of inert fact. Likewise, one may also endorse the pragmatist emphasis on the educational importance of the learner's *active* appreciation of the logical 'grammar' of forms of human knowledge and inquiry – precisely, of the groundedness of conclusions in evidence and proof, of the complex interconnectedness or interplay of different forms of knowledge and understanding, and so on. On the other hand, however, there seems to be little here that is markedly at odds with any *realist* epistemology as such: *critical* realists would certainly agree that the various traditions of natural and social scientific (and other) inquiry through which human agents have tried to conceive their world are subject to revision and development and cannot ever be taken to provide fixed and final accounts of how things are. The difference between critical realists and non-realists or pragmatists, however, clearly turns on the former's acceptance and the latter's rejection of the idea that there is nevertheless a world to be understood that is significantly and substantially independent of our human conceptions, inclinations and interests. But with respect to this question, idealism and pragmatism may seem on the face of it rather less plausible than realism. Although the ways in which we conceptualise the world may indeed follow human values and interests, it also seems reasonable to suppose that whether our conceptualisations are right or wrong, true or false, must depend more upon the way things are in the world than upon how we are prone to conceive them. Thus, for example, as a human agent in search of life-sustaining food, I might be driven to observe a distinction between mushrooms and toadstools on the grounds that the former are edible and the latter are poisonous; but that I can so distinguish must depend on a non-subjective scientifically ascertainable difference between natural kinds of fungus.

Clearly, much here hangs upon what is meant by the pragmatist or non-realist rejection of the idea of value-free facts. On a weaker interpretation, the idea that facts are not value-free might merely mean that our conceptualisations follow human interests; but, as we have just seen, this hardly seems inconsistent with the idea that our theories stand or fall by the test of how things actually *are* in a world independent of our conceptualisations. However, on a stronger non-realist interpretation of the kind implied by some influential postmodern educational philosophies, as well as by some more radical constructivist policy documentation, it would seem that any and all distinctions between fact and value are to be abandoned in favour of effective assimilation of the former to the latter. On views of this sort, any and all inquiry becomes a matter of personal 'meaning-making', by virtue of which learners are free to conceptualise the world as they wish. But any such extreme constructivist or progressive rhetoric of discovery learning and/or meaning-making only needs stating in order to appear utterly implausible. To be sure, any effective instruction in the knowledge that plants gain nutrition by photosynthesis, or that caterpillars metamorphose into butterflies, will attempt to assist the child to understand why this is so, to acquaint him or her with techniques of investigation and inquiry, and to leave open the possibility of rival scientific explanations of why such things are so. But it must border on autistic delusion to suggest that the factual content of such instruction is no more than the product of some individual or collective process of conceptual construction or meaning-making: that, to echo the Prince of Denmark, nothing either is or is not, but thinking makes it so.[21] Indeed, bearing in mind the extent to which the idea of active inquiry or meaning-making has often been valorised in constructivist theorising about pedagogy, we should be alert to the educational hazards of any idea that it is the first if not also the last task of teachers of history or science to equip children with the skills or techniques of historical or scientific inquiry. Although I certainly think that equipping learners with such skills should be regarded as a significant part of good education in these subjects, it is far from obvious that it is either the only or the most important part – and, at all events, it clearly cannot be the educational point of departure.

It cannot be the point of departure, of course, because in order for learners to make sense of investigative skills, they clearly need to acquire a grasp of the point, object or *raison d'être* of such investigation. Indeed, acquiring some such grasp would appear to lie at the heart of the education of both those learners who will proceed to be serious academic scholars of a given science or art, and those who will not. For it is surely the *educational* point of teaching science or history that whether or not young people are to proceed to be scientists or historians, they *all* need to acquire some grasp of how the world actually *is*, as well as of who they themselves are by virtue of some appreciation of the cultural traditions and *events* that have made them who they are. From this viewpoint, although there may be significant debates between biologists about how photosynthesis or metamorphosis should be explained or understood, it is clearly a *sine qua non* of any natural scientific education for learners to appreciate that these are not mere questionable hypotheses, but features of the world to be explained. Again, although professional historians may wrangle about the causes and/or proper interpretation of the Reformation or the Jacobite rebellion, what *all* children first need to acquire by way of historical education is a grasp of these as events that actually *happened*, as well as something of their serious implications for contemporary intercultural associations and conflict. To be sure, for any of these events to be meaningful to children they may need to be linked to their human and/or socio-cultural experiences and interests; but it is still necessary to distinguish and separate any such pedagogical task from the vocational enterprise of assisting individuals to acquire the skills of a professional scientist or historian. Indeed, an appreciation that good history and science are not merely the unbridled products of constructivist imagination, but matters of (as far as possible) impartial accountability to facts and evidence, is surely integral to becoming a responsible professional scientist or historian. From this viewpoint, it may not matter greatly whether children 'discover' these facts for themselves by their own reading in the school library, or whether they are actually instructed in them by an inspired teacher – as, more than likely, the culturally uninitiated were once acquainted with the history and traditions of their race or tribe by the songs and stories of bards and balladeers. However, the general point is plain enough. If the message of radical constructivists and meaning-makers is that education cannot be reduced to simple (rote) instruction in disconnected or meaningless facts, we need have no quarrel with it – though the point is also fairly banal, and it is not at all at odds with realist epistemology. But, on the other hand, if the constructivist verdict is that there *are* no plain facts of the matter with regard to any inquiry, then the point totters on the edge of absurdity.

The varieties of objectivity

In so putting matters, however, we should avoid taking too lightly one of the most pressing issues of contemporary educational philosophy and theory. For it seems likely that present-day theorising about the educational role of knowledge is widely bedevilled by largely uncritical acceptance of a fashionable epistemological and ethical non-realism or idealism, which is nevertheless (despite its often enlightened appearance and progressive credentials) a potential source of serious theoretical and practical educational damage. Such idealism has exercised most influence on education from the directions of moral, social and political philosophy, where – irrespective of important educational implications of the communitarian insight that human moral, spiritual and religious identities have significant cultural and historical origins – there is also much evident error regarding the relationship of theory and value to practice. However, non-realist or idealist infection of educational epistemology from pragmatist and other sources is just as if not more problematic, given the tangle of fairly elementary confusions in the philosophies of mind and knowledge that underpins the non-realism of much constructivist theory of learning. First, as already observed, much idealism is almost certainly driven by a quasi-Platonic anxiety to achieve something like a tight formal or analytical connection between truth and justification: since mathematics exhibits such a connection, it is tempting for idealists to seek it in other realms of human life as well. Thus, insofar as the moral conclusions of a community may be held to follow from principled moral premises, it is tempting to suppose that the premises must serve to justify or validate the conclusions in accordance with some logically demonstrable pattern of theoretical or practical inference. But as Aristotle perfectly well shows in his critique of Plato,[22] any such general patterning of human inquiry on the model of mathematical reasoning is hopelessly procrustean. Moral reasoning is not like mathematical reasoning – and both of these are probably different again from scientific, technical and/or aesthetic reasoning: each of these forms of reasoning or inquiry bears on experience in its own particular way – and, as Aristotle surely rightly insists: 'we should not expect more precision than the nature of the subject matter admits'.[23]

For Aristotle, indeed, moral reason is more a matter of a descent into particular experience than of Platonic ascent to abstract principle – a fact ironically neglected by the idealist communitarians who pay lip service to Aristotelian particularism whilst nevertheless attempting to bind the diverse moral deliverances of conflicting cultural perspectives in the shackles of rival traditions of reason or inference. Indeed, it seems to be the very same idealists who emphasise the historical emergence of ideas from practices who are also most anxious to insulate moral and other principles from any and all tests of practical experience.[24] But in Aristotelian terms, it is also crucial – notwithstanding the fact that Aristotle regarded both mathematics and science as theoretical rather than practical inquiries – to distinguish the *a priori*, abstract or non-experiential character of mathematics from the evidentially and empirically grounded natural sciences. It is surely at this point, above all, that idealism turns the general logic of explanation topsy-turvy. For however plausible it might be to claim that we have the mathematical facts we have because of the mathematical proofs we have, it is no more plausible to claim that scientific facts are a consequence only of our scientific explanations than it is to suggest (as moral constructivists and prescriptivists have claimed) that we only regard as good what we are disposed to commend.[25] The relationship of fit of our scientific theories is from theory to the world, and if the world is not as our theories take it to be, then it is not the world but our theories that are mistaken. At this point, indeed, there is evidence of much idealist and pragmatist confusion between the two rather different senses of knowledge on which we have already touched – namely the *factual* sense of knowledge, on the one hand, and the theoretical or *explanatory* sense, on the other. If one interprets all references to knowledge in the strong idealist sense of explanation, then one risks binding what is to be explained in the straitjacket of this or that theory – which precisely separates thought from the world, and makes it difficult to see how there might be any apprehension of experience that is not simultaneously explanatory of it. But there clearly is a familiar more attenuated sense of knowledge by which I can know that things are so, even though I do not know what makes them either how or what they are

– and without the former knowledge, I could hardly come to have the latter. It is in this sense that I know that Britain is an island, that spiders have eight legs, and that Tony Blair is the current British prime minister: these are contingent facts (products of circumstances which might not have been), and they would not therefore have passed Platonic or other idealistic tests of genuine knowledge. All the same, I know that such facts are true, and I cannot think of any good idealist (or non-psychotic) reason which might tempt me to call them into question.

At all events, there can be no serious doubt about the concern of education with the transmission of knowledge, and no less doubt about the philosophically vexed nature of knowledge. Much epistemology has certainly floundered on the rock of the so-called 'search for certainty', which has itself been compromised by serious ambiguities in the very notion of certainty. Plato was the first philosopher to point out that knowledge is not equivalent to any subjective sense of strong opinion, since there can be knowledge of only what is objectively *true*, and two millennia later Wittgenstein takes up much the same theme in denying that knowledge can be identified with any subjective feeling of certainty, since epistemic claims are conceptually linked to evidence and proof.[26] However, the shift from psychology to logic in the search for certainty has been equally fraught with hazard: some rationalist and empiricist philosophers have argued, for example, that since the only statements we can know with certainty are such logically analytic or *necessary* propositions as 'a square is an equilateral rectangle', I can have no real knowledge of the *contingent* fact that the piano in my front room has one broken key – which seems at least counter-intuitive, if not absurd. But such problems are yet further compounded by a new idealist or pragmatist identification of knowledge with certainty in the wake of Kant's insight that there can be no unconceptualised experience (intuitions without concepts) and therefore no knowledge of a world as it is in itself prior to human perception. On this view, there can be no testing of the truth of statements in terms of their *correspondence* to the world because we can have no conception of things as they exist independently of our statements about them: in that case, truth can only be a matter of the *coherence* or *utility* of our statements and is assimilated to consistent judgement as 'warranted assertability'.[27]

But, of course, any such blurring of the distinction between truth and judgement is as fallacious as it is epistemically and educationally disastrous. For, although Kant was right to insist that there is no unconceptualised experience, and (consequently) wrong to hold that any idea of things-in-themselves could be meaningful, nothing here serves to undermine the dependency of true statements upon how things are in the world: the fact is that the truth of any statement that the piano in my front room has one broken key depends primarily upon how things are in my front room, rather than upon its logical coherence with other statements (notwithstanding any other epistemic significance of such coherence). In this light, the key point of idealists and coherentists against any realist understanding of truth in terms of correspondence – that it is simply incoherent to suppose that we might measure this or that conceptualised perspective against an unconceptualised reality to see whether the former is true

– is merely a red herring. All that is needed to sustain the important distinction between judgement and truth is the minimal correspondence theory of truth defended in Aristotle's *Metaphysics*, which maintains that 'to speak truly is to say of what is that it is, and of what is not that it is not'.[28] It should hardly need emphasising, however, that in default of some such non-epistemic notion of truth, we may (in the worst possible sense) end up thinking that we can think what we like – and the consequences of this for education could hardly be other than fatal. Moreover, it is something of an irony that contemporary neo-idealist epistemologies have often been inclined to attack the so-called 'foundationalism' of (some) realist conceptions of truth on the grounds that they foster dogmatic illusions of certainty, and discourage proper habits of open inquiry.[29] In fact, it is arguable that the reverse is the case, and that a good sense that our theories and explanations stand to be judged – and perhaps found wanting – against an obdurate but (probably unimaginably) complex reality provides a much better safeguard against our worst intellectual pretensions and delusions than any view that the world is essentially of our own epistemic making. The latter, indeed, may fail to distinguish not only truth from judgement, but also fact from fantasy, and science from sorcery. In the next chapter, however, we may turn to some basic educational philosophical questions concerning the place of knowledge in the school curriculum.

Possible tasks

(1) In view of the Platonic analysis of knowledge as justified true belief, consider how you would set about assisting a child's meaningful knowledge of the fact of Elizabeth I's imprisonment of Mary Queen of Scots.

(2) In light of a (postmodern?) claim that the Old Testament Book of Genesis, Darwin's theory of evolution and Charles Dickens' *David Copperfield* are all narratives, consider how you might go about assisting a clear appreciation of the epistemic differences between such texts.

Chapter 9

Curriculum: purpose, form and content

Knowledge and education

In the first two chapters of this part of the book, we argued that it is mistaken to construe human conceptual learning, or knowledge-acquisition, as a quasi-naturalistic process (of behaviour modification or 'cognitive development') apt for investigation via some kind of empirical science: on the contrary, any meaningful (human) educational learning (rather than animal training) is a matter of *normative* initiation into socially constructed and/or constituted rules, principles and values that no statistically conceived processes could even begin to explain. However, we also noted that this emphasis on the social character of meaning, and any corresponding denial of the possibility of a pre-conceptual appreciation of how things are, has often been held to have problematic consequences for the very idea of *objective* knowledge, and hence for any notion of education as initiation into rationally justified forms of knowledge and understanding: if what we teach children and young people in schools amounts to no more than the socially inherited or culturally conditioned perspectives of this or that social group – locally but not universally valid values, virtues and practices – it may seem impossible to observe any significant or substantial distinction between education and socialisation or indoctrination. In the previous chapter, however, we argued that this conclusion would appear to rest on certain fundamental errors about the relationship of knowledge to truth. First, proper observance of a familiar distinction between the epistemic character of judgement and the non-epistemic nature of truth[1] may help to free us from an excessively formal or analytical conception of the relationship of knowledge to the world – and certainly from any idea that any given knowledge claim would have to be formally or necessarily true: although my claim to know what I had for breakfast this morning does not express a *necessary* truth (since it is only a contingent fact that I had breakfast at all), it is, for all that, something I may properly be said to *know*. Secondly, we need to avoid a common non-realist and/or pragmatist confusion between senses of knowledge as fact and explanation that leads to an implausible assimiliation of what is to be explained to that which purports to explain – and hence to any unacceptable suggestion that the observation that plants obtain nourishment by photosynthesis is provisional in the same way as this or that current physical hypothesis concerning the precise mechanics of this process. In short, the thesis of the social provenance of meaning and knowledge does not require us to deny that there are facts that are objectively true, that we can *know* things on the basis of non-subjective proof, evidence or just plain observation, and that such objective knowledge – rather than subjective local or other opinion – should form the basis of school or other education.

In that case, there is also little reason to doubt or deny that the central philosophical issue of the school curriculum – which we shall be exploring briefly in this and the final chapters of this part of the book – is that of determining which potentially objective kinds or forms of knowledge and understanding (broadly construed to include social and personal capacities and practical skills, as well as academic knowledge) are appropriate for inclusion in any formal programme of school-based education. That said, this way of putting matters might also be regarded – not least in the present climate of educational reflection – as rather less than sensitive to the kind of issues about the social context of education that communitarian and other educational philosophers have recently been concerned to raise. For although there is clearly a powerful case for arguing that the educational value of knowledge rests more upon whether it is objectively true than upon whether it is socially or culturally approved, it need not be that the same objectively grounded educational content is equally valuable or appropriate to the requirements of each and every social constituency. Indeed, more controversially, there may even be some sociocultural and/or economic reasons for supposing that what is most immediately appropriate to the needs and concerns of a given social group, or at least to particular individuals within that group, may *not* be what is objectively (or, at any rate, provably) true.[2] Still, before we proceed (more generally in this chapter, and in more detail in part III) to examine the educational implications of individual and cultural difference, it may be useful – in the interests of greater clarity about the respects in which individuals might need to be equipped for rational and responsible agency in a modern civilised polity – to develop some of the more basic considerations about the role of education in the promotion of personhood explored in chapter 1. Indeed, I think that this has been largely the point of departure (rightly or wrongly) of much modern liberal-democratic educational planning – especially in planning that reflects an increasing contemporary trend towards central or national curricula. We shall therefore focus mainly in this chapter on those fairly general features of the form and content of the school curriculum widely regarded as fundamental to rational curriculum planning in developed liberal democracies such as our own. In the next and final chapter of this part of the book, however, we shall proceed to some critical appreciation of the principal contemporary approaches to the organisation and appraisal of the school curriculum conceived as the main social institutional vehicle of formal educational delivery. Significant questions concerning the appropriateness or otherwise of adopting more pluralist or particularistic approaches to curriculum planning – specifically in respect of cultural or individual differences – will be considered more closely in part III.

Curriculum, education and schooling

First, as argued in chapter 1, it is advisable in any initial thinking about the content of the school curriculum to bear in mind not just the wide diversity of objective forms of knowledge and understanding of potential relevance to individual or personal flourishing, but also the rather *different* respects in which these may serve to promote such flourishing. In this connection, the distinction between schooling and education we observed in chapter 1 suggests that it is mistaken to regard the school curriculum as *exclusively* concerned with education in the purest (or purist) sense of promoting an understanding of the world for (as it is said) its own sake: thus, there are clearly many qualities human agents need for effective functioning and well-being that are worthy of curriculum space, despite having quite straightforward instrumental or extrinsic utility. For example, although it would be unreasonable to expect any basic school curriculum to accommodate or cater for the advanced levels of vocational skill that would equip someone to be an architect, a business executive or a garage mechanic, we readily recognise a proper curricular place for the cultivation of technical, economic and design skills relevant to such occupations. Likewise, there is clearly also a valid place in the curriculum for the cultivation of self-help technical and domestic skills – of cookery, woodwork, electrical engineering, horticulture, wordprocessing, and so on – which, irrespective of their small widespread vocational benefit, would seem to be of considerable potential value for the independent practical, economic and other functioning of individuals. Again, despite the controversies surrounding moral education, parents and society in general are surely right to expect teachers to try to foster and reinforce those basic moral and social rules and/or dispositions of honesty, fairness, courtesy, tolerance and respect for others presupposed to civilised interpersonal association – irrespective of the particularities of personal belief. Such basic training would, to be sure, lie more in the realm of what Aristotle regarded as moral habituation than of moral education; but it is difficult to see how, in the absence of such training, there might be anything worth calling moral education at all. Likewise, it would be hard to deny a rightful curricular place to a wide range of physical and other recreational activities – of athletics, gymnastics, dance, outdoor pursuits, games, and so on – precisely in view of their aesthetic value and/or general health- or leisure-related human benefits.

In short, at the risk of parroting the conventional platitudes of official policy documents and school mission statements about the aims of education, we are more or less bound to admit that socially institutionalised schooling could hardly other than be concerned with the promotion of informed rational agents who also possess capacities for responsible interpersonal association, and the basic knowledge and skills required for a useful economic contribution to society, as well as for independent and healthy personal functioning. Hence, insofar as schools are concerned with the promotion of general personal and social flourishing, and such flourishing is hardly conceivable apart from certain qualities of rational understanding, the possession of interpersonal and vocational skills and a physically healthy lifestyle, it cannot be a great mystery why the subjects and activities we actually encounter in most school curricula have in fact come to be there. In this regard, indeed, those philosophical issues that have sometimes arisen concerning the legitimacy or otherwise of including this or that subject in the curriculum – about whether, for example, there is a proper place for hockey or Latin – would often seem to have been generated by the sort of procrustean curriculum theories which have held that subjects ought to be excluded if they are *either* not economically useful (instrumentalism) *or* not intrinsically worthwhile forms of knowledge (non-instrumentalism). However, it is not just that there are *many* reasons for including activities in the curriculum, but that individual activities will often find a place for rather different reasons: there are, for example, many different reasons for including physical education – even though it is *neither* (for most people) economically useful *nor* an intrinsically worthwhile form of knowledge (in any significant educational sense). This, of course, is not inconsistent with recognising that there is a perennial professional need for discussion and reassessment of the place of particular subjects or activities in the school curriculum: after all, individual and social priorities are liable to alter over time, and what was once relevant and valuable may well be overtaken by subsequent events. For example, the value of secretarial skills of shorthand may no longer be quite so clear in an age of advanced information technology, and the sporting skills of boxing once taught in some schools may now be subject to wider moral and/or health-related debate. Moreover, one overwhelming reason why such discussion might be considered professionally indispensable is that better appreciation of the curricular place and contribution of a subject is part and parcel of understanding its contribution to human development – which is also a key condition of teaching it effectively and well. Indeed, long experience as a teaching supervisor has taught me that unsatisfactory practical teaching in the classroom or gymnasium is at least as often the result of teachers' poor conceptions of why they are teaching what they are teaching, as of poor presentation, communication or organisation.

At all events, with these considerations in mind, it may now be useful to examine some of the basic principles of curriculum design that have governed the attempts of recent educational theorists and policy makers to address problems of the content and organisation of the school curriculum. At this point, indeed, it seems sensible as well as convenient to organise this chapter around discussion of those five common criteria of recent official and professional curriculum design and development of balance, breadth, coherence, continuity and progression – not least since these criteria would appear between them to identify the key conceptual, normative and practical questions about the character and content of any reasonable or rational school curriculum. In the course of examining these criteria, however, we shall need to ask a number of awkward questions about the precise theoretical and/or practical role of these principles in curriculum design. One such question is that of whether it is possible to arrive at interpretations of these criteria which are sufficiently clear and unambiguous to serve the main purpose for which they often seem to be invoked – namely the construction of a rationally objective (and perhaps consensually acceptable) school curriculum for a liberal-democratic polity. Perhaps an even more pressing question, however, is that of whether these criteria may even be considered mutually consistent under some of their most common or obvious interpretations.

Curriculum balance

First, let us consider the idea of educational *balance* and the standard view that a good or acceptable curriculum ought above all to be a balanced curriculum. On the face of it, the concern with balance is the perfectly proper one of ensuring that a school curriculum is not over-concentrated on some aspects of children's development at the expense of others. Thus, we have already been at pains to emphasise here and elsewhere that the school curriculum has a legitimate concern with the social, moral, domestic, vocational and health- and leisure-related as well as 'purer' educational aspects of individual flourishing. In a related vein, postwar progressive educational developments in Britain and elsewhere have often been pursued in the spirit of a slogan that 'education should concern the whole child'.[3] Notwithstanding the reservation that it might be rather less misleading to hold that 'the school curriculum is not just about education', one may nevertheless agree with a broad concern here about the excessively intellectual or cognitive emphasis of much traditional primary schooling, and its concomitant neglect of more social, emotional, physical and creative aspects of human development. That said, it is not entirely clear that we would all agree on the question of what a more balanced curriculum should be balanced between, or about how any items in the balance might be weighted with respect to each other. Indeed, it should be equally clear that any employment of the term 'balance' in this context is little more than an uncashed metaphor, and probably acquires what little sense it has from its slightly more perspicuous application in other professional contexts. Thus, for example, we can have some idea of what might constitute a balanced diet on the grounds that there are reasonable natural scientific criteria of physical health: without regular intake of a certain specifiable range of minerals, proteins, liquids, vitamins, and so on, a person's physical flourishing is liable to observable and fairly well measurable decline. The obvious difficulty for any more analogical curricular application, however, is that of determining what might count as plausible educational or personal developmental equivalents of vitamins and minerals – or, worse yet, the appropriate intakes or dosages of any such curricular ingredients.

Hence, even if we distinguish as we have between schooling and education, and recognise that – insofar as education is simply one of the functions of schooling – any school curriculum has a responsibility to equip young people with knowledge, capacities, qualities, skills and dispositions that reach beyond the purely intellectual or the cognitive to the social, moral, emotional and practical, it is still far from entirely clear what one should include and what one could or should leave out. To take one obvious example – though it is also one with wider implications for the status and place in the school curriculum of such other subjects and activities as moral, physical and sex education – there is little general agreement about the place and status of religious experience in human development, about how or whether religious education is possible, and even about whether there is a place in the schools for any sort of encounter with religion.[4] For some, religious experience is a vital and indispensable aspect of human development, so that there may be no 'whole' development of the child in the absence of some religious education or initiation; for others, however, religion is simply a source of dangerous human delusion of a kind that education should primarily be concerned to oppose or eradicate. In short, one person's key aspect of educational development is another person's indoctrination. Here, of course, those who feel strongly in one or the other of these ways might be tempted to say that there must be a *correct* view of the epistemological or semantic status of religious understanding and experience, and that if we can just find the right rational arguments (say, for or against the existence of God), then we should have a conclusive reason for the curricular inclusion or exclusion of religious instruction. The trouble with any such conclusion, however, is that it follows precisely from ignoring the evaluative or normative dimension of religious and other sorts of education. Insofar as religions have their source at least as much in commitments to certain practical precepts – to *live* in this or that way – as in the truth of any epistemic claims, it is simply a mistake to suppose that even if such 'theoretical' proofs were available, they would settle the question of the right to receive or be protected from religious education. To take a secular analogy, one might as a socialist consider conservative views to be demonstrably wrong, but this would hardly license trying to prevent others living according to conservative beliefs or principles, or justify the dissemination of socialist principles in the school curriculum. Insofar as such matters are of no less *practical* interest and concern than they are of theoretically demonstrable truth, they cannot be decided upon purely intellectually or politically disinterested grounds. Indeed, it is arguably some such attempt to decide the question of religious education that has led to the present unsatisfactory compromise in schools which mostly conceives RE in terms of teaching about world religions.[5] On the face of it, this approach might be held to reconcile any and all opposed interests: it satisfies the atheist by avoiding any explicit inititaion into religion, but also satisfies the believer by at least making knowledge of religion available to children. From another viewpoint, however, it may well be that it satisfies neither, since, to the believer, this is not religious education at all, and to the atheist, it is merely wasting valuable curriculum time on so much meaningless nonsense.

But even if we could agree what the proper ingredients of a well-balanced educational curriculum should be – in terms of educationally worthwhile forms of knowledge and understanding, virtues, vocational or personal skills, and so on – there is still the question of what relative weighting these might be given in the schooling of children. In short, we are clearly faced with significant evaluative problems about balance even in relation to those areas of curriculum content where there is large agreement about what we should on no account exclude. To be sure, it is difficult to envisage any curriculum model or proposal excluding native language studies (especially the skills of literacy), mathematics and arithmetic (especially the skills of numeracy), history, geography, some science (nature study, physics, chemistry, biology), some literary and other arts (novels, drama, poetry, visual arts, music and possibly dance) and some physical education (sports, games, gymnastics and athletics). But it is clearly less easy to determine how much curricular space might reasonably be allocated to these different areas of the curriculum. Thus, as educational history amply demonstrates, whereas more traditional curricula incline towards greater emphasis on the basic skills of literary and numeracy, and the more (allegedly) hard 'factual' disciplines of history, geography and science, more progressive curricular dispensations are apt to place greater stress on such more creative and practical areas of the curriculum as imaginative writing, drama and art and craft. However, such curriculum decisions follow not from any value-neutral calculation, but from deep evaluative choices and commitments. Hence, although this is also not so say that any and all such choices are bound to be subjective or irrational – since there is clearly much genuine scope for rational debate about curriculum design – it is likely to be at least misleading and at worst misguided to attempt to quantify over educational provision by means of precise time or percentage allocations to curriculum content in the manner of some recent curriculum initiatives.[6] Here, moreover, it is not just that such quantification suggests a degree of precise rational calculation that the nature of the problem scarcely admits, but that it seems generally unwise to think of a school curriculum as something that can or should be conceived in quite this quasi-statistical way.

Curriculum breadth (and depth)

The problems of the so-called *breadth* criterion of curriculum provision are related to, and to some degree an extension of, those of balance. On a fairly naïve view of the matter, it might be held that the knowledge, understanding and/or skill of an educated person is just more *extensive* than that of the uneducated person: that, indeed, the more widely a person's knowledge and understanding ranges, the better educated he or she is. Moreover, the point here need not be the crudely quantificational one that educated persons are better *informed* than uneducated ones (though this may well be so): it could be rather that the educated have a better rational grasp of the logical diversity of forms of human knowledge and understanding than the less well educated. One such fairly sophisticated conception of the epistemology of curriculum planning – the so-called 'forms of knowledge thesis'[7] – was, of course, widely influential in the heyday of postwar analytical philosophy of education. On this view, someone could hardly count as educated in the absence of *some* initiation into each token of a specified range of types of (scientific, mathematical, socio-cultural, religious, moral, artistic/aesthetic, philosophical) knowledge and understanding regarded as definitive or constitutive of human rationality: indeed, educatedness might here be held to be significantly manifest in an agent's capacity to distinguish between diffent forms of human inquiry, and between the different sorts of questions to which they give rise. Hence, to take either side of the familiar debate in North America and elsewhere between (biological) evolutionists and (religious) creationists would be largely symptomatic of a defective education: the trouble with both creationists and evolutionists is that they are both mistakenly inclined to construe the essentially poetic or mythopoeic language of Genesis as a purportedly scientific explanation of the origins of the world. On a forms of knowledge view, then, it would be a significant mark of educated sensibility that one is able to tell epistemic chalk from cheese. But while there is much to be said for this observation, it also gives rise to awkward questions about how widely the knowledge of the educated person should range, and over precisely what sorts of curriculum content. To begin with, the forms of knowledge thesis was primarily concerned to identify an indispensable range of strictly *educational* content – defined by reference to the seven or eight intrinsically worthwhile forms of human rationality; but once we have appreciated that this would be likely to occupy more curriculum space than could ever be available, we should also bear in mind our perennial point that the school curriculum is answerable to a wider range of social, personal, practical and other needs and purposes than would seem to be addressed by forms of knowledge.

To some extent, the idea of constructing the school curriculum around forms of knowledge seems to have been precisely designed to address the potential problem of too many subjects in the curriculum. In this respect, of course, it is important not to confuse *forms of knowledge* with school *subjects*: thus, whereas geography is one subject, it would be regarded as involving different forms of knowledge (natural science, humanities, moral inquiry), and although physics, chemistry and biology are different subjects, they might be held to be but different modes or aspects of one (natural scientific) form of knowledge. One obvious advantage of this idea, as actual curriculum planners were not slow to realise,[8] was that it might precisely afford opportunities for real economies in curriculum planning. Thus, for example, the trouble with the claim that no-one could count as educated without some significant appreciation of the arts is that it may seem to commit us to a rather extravagant programme of initiation into literature, drama, art and craft, music and dance for each and every child. On a forms of knowledge thesis, however, all that might be required to cover the artistic dimension of education is an initiation into some *one* of the arts as typical of the general logical grammar of artistic activities as such. Again, much the same strategy could be applied in the case of empirical science: instead of initiating children into physics and chemistry and biology and psychology, one might simply introduce them to one of these subjects construed as a token of the general type of scientific inquiry. However, these very examples also point to the profound implausibilty of the view – and this aspect of forms of knowledge thinking has been subject to much general and particular criticism (especially with respect to the arts) by educational philosophers. In relation to the sciences, for example, it has been forcibly argued that the grammars of inquiry, conceptual vocabularies and experimental procedures of physics, chemistry and biology differ so much from one another that it is difficult to see how there might be much meaningful conceptual transfer from one discipline to another – and, of course, it is not at all clear (as we have already observed) that an enterprise like scientific psychology counts as an empirical science in anything like the same sense as these other disciplines.[9] However, when we turn to the arts, it seems even more unlikely that understanding poetry might afford much insight into painting pictures or composing music, and clearly people who are quite proficient in one sphere may be utterly clueless in another.[10]

But if all this is so, and each of these intrisically worthwhile forms of knowledge and understanding, skill or practice has its own peculiar and unique features, then the emphasis on educational breadth faces formidable problems of selection from the enormous potential range of educationally relevant human interests and inquiries: if archaeology, entomology, astronomy, palaeontology and other more specialised sciences foster understandings unavailable through the study of physics, chemistry and biology, what compelling reasons could there be for preferring the latter for curriculum inclusion over the former? However, when we now take into account all the subjects, activities and practices that are not intrinsically worthwhile forms of knowledge in the above sense, but still have vocational, social or health- and leisure-related claims to be included in the school curriculum, the problems of curriculum planning are massively compounded. For how are we now to weigh the claims of forms-of-knowledge-grounded subjects against those of the many less academic, more instrumental or more vocational subjects and activities that might also seem to have some right to a place in the curricular sun? How, for example, should we balance the potential contribution to human development of an arguably mind-enhancing but relatively impractical form of knowledge such as astronomy against a very useful but relatively educationally limited practical skill such as auto-repair? We need not doubt that both such forms of understanding and activity are humanly valuable, or that there might well be a place (if not perhaps a large place) for either of these enterprises in the school curriculum. Indeed, I have also no wish for now to quarrel with those who might want to dispute my characterisation of auto-repair as of more limited 'educational' significance than astronomy. The point of present concern is only that such activities are surely educationally or otherwise significant in very *different* senses – and that, given these different senses, it becomes hard without extreme evaluative prejudice to decide in favour of the one rather than the other, if there is not sufficient room in an overcrowded curriculum for both.

But perhaps the major problem raised by any large emphasis on curricular breadth arises from the potential conflict or tension of this idea with an equally proper aspiration towards educational *depth*. Basically, curriculum conceptions of a forms of knowledge variety turn on a particular conception of education as a matter of a wide-ranging acquaintance with the greatest possible *extent* of rational human understanding. However, it is possible to question not just how far any such initiation can and should go, but also whether this conception of education is a very reasonable or practicable one. First, if one refused to regard as educated any person who had not been successfully initiated into all the human enterprises we might consider to be educationally worthwhile, surely hardly anyone would so count – since, to be sure, individual differences of talent and interest will preclude much if any success in some activities for most if not all of us. Indeed, in the light of previously aired arguments to the effect that the distinctness and particularity of humanly worthwhile forms of knowledge and practice precludes their simple classification into a pre-specifiable number of logical types, it may be that any attempt to account for education or educated-ness in terms of initiation into a set range of disciplines or activities is a complete non-starter. Moreover, insofar as we do clearly regard quite variously informed and talented people as educated, it may be that education is more like what Wittgenstein was inclined to call a 'family resemblance' notion:[11] like members of a family, those we regard as educated certainly share some features in common, but this would not have to be some common repertoire of forms of knowledge or expertise. In a rather less Wittgensteinian vein, indeed, it might be argued that what is mistaken here is not any search for necessary conditions or general criteria of education, but rather the direction of the search: it might be better, for example, to look in the direction of the motivational or other attitudes of those we consider educated than to the precise content of their under-standing. In this connection, it has been explicitly argued that focus on curricular breadth has often wrongly emphasised coverage of content at the expense of the development on the part of young people of a real passion for, or commitment to, *some* worthwhile form of human engagement. More particularly, it has been urged – not least in relation to those less able pupils whose capacity to cope with the acacdemic rigours of a forms of knowledge curriculum is often held to be limited – that it is better for children to leave school with 'one genuine enthu-siasm' than with a superficial smattering or aquaintance with many subjects.[12] This is, of course, a controversial point of view – which also raises significant questions of justice and equity of a kind we shall need to examine in part III. But there may nevertheless be some real truth in the idea that a preoccupation with content sometimes usurp an arguably more legitimate educational concern to engage children more deeply and meaningfully with what they are required to learn. This point, moreover, leads us naturally enough to the next key curriculum principle.

Curriculum coherence

Again, on the face of it, there cannot be much general quarrel with any insis-tence that the content of the curriculum should be *coherent*: at all events, one could hardly wish it to be incoherent. The trouble here, however, seems to be that any call for curriculum coherence is either requring something so general as to be trivial – in which case it may hardly seem worth emphasising – or it is claiming something very much more radical and *controversial*. First, indeed, it is necessary to determine precisely what any alleged relations of coherence are supposed to hold between – as well as, perhaps, exactly how such relations are supposed to hold. On the one hand, if coherence is required only between the parts of particular subjects or lessons, then – irrespective of any difficulties involved in achieving this – such coherence could hardly be other than an intrinsic goal of any and all good teaching: how, we might ask, could teachers regard their task as involving anything other than some attempt to make what they teach clear and intelligible to others? That said, as we noted in our discussion of teaching, such intelligibility may be achieved in a variety of ways, and it is not obvious that any set of 'top-down' or external prescriptions would guarantee or ensure such intelligibilty. On the other hand, however, it could be that the demand for coherence is meant to apply rather more widely to the curriculum: to the programme in general, perhaps, rather than to this or that subject in particular. Indeed, in the light of the postwar progressive emphasis on the education of the 'whole child', this could be taken as an invitation to embrace ideas of curriculum *integration* of the sort that have certainly influenced the recent theory and practice of the primary curriculum in Britain and other parts of the world, and which in the previous chapter we traced back to the radical curriculum ideas of John Dewey and W.H. Kilpatrick.[13] This more radical but controversial conception of curriculum coherence would maintain that if the general programme of study that children are required to undergo in schools is to be of any real educational worth, then it should be experienced more as a meaningfully interrelated whole than as a meaningless array of discrete or fragmented bodies of information or activity. In short, the more general demand for coherence may seem to be better met by a progressive or integrated than by a traditional or subject-centred curriculum.

Indeed, despite powerful arguments to the effect that a subject-centred curriculum affords a rather more systematic and focused approach to the study of specific scientific or artistic disciplines – especially at secondary stages of schooling – there is certainly also a real case for linking areas of the curriculum in the interests of greater educational intelligibility. A case in point is that of the teaching of ethnic dance, which we considered in chapter 6. At that point, in the course of discussing the problems of a behaviourist approach to dance teaching, we complained that too great a focus on the promotion of practical skills or techniques may lead to a neglect of the artistic and cultural considerations that give meaning to dance as a socio-culturally constituted form of purposeful human endeavour. If we now ask where we might turn for the ideas that would give relevant sense to such dance, it seems reasonable to suggest that some sort of collaboration between physical education teachers and teachers of geography, history, religion, music or art might be helpful in this regard – to the ultimate reciprocal benefit, indeed, of all parties to such collaboration. From this viewpoint, we need not doubt that the systematic attempts that have been made in modern primary schools to forge cross-curricular links between traditionally discrete subjects – for example, the creation of 'environmental studies'[14] from science (or 'nature study'), history, geography, economics, and so on – have often led to rather more meaningful contextualisation of traditional subject knowledge, and to more lively and attractive learning. Indeed, it is likely that the scope – especially in early years teaching – for imaginative integration of scientific, artistic, religious, moral, lingusitic and mathematical learning is generally greater than many teachers have to date appreciated

On the other hand, it would appear that there is some need for caution and restraint with respect to any such more general idea of curriculum integration. First, the already noted point about the need for better defined and more focused study at secondary levels of education, together with the more evident possibilities for integration in early years, seems to indicate the greater general suitability of such approaches to elementary or primary stages of education. Although it may greatly assist the motivation and understanding of small children to learn history in the context of drama, or mathematics through practical measurement of samples in nature study, it may be hard to regard any analogous learning strategies as more than mere distractions in the context of serious high school learning of the politics of the Reformation or quadratic equations. Indeed, as we shall shortly observe, there is a politically powerful body of educational opinion which is inclined to see such inter-curricular contextualisation as a frivolous distraction even at the primary level.[15] But even if we do not dismiss all such integrative approaches in the secondary school – as I think we should not (and as I think the case of dance teaching serves to reinforce) – it is still crucially important to appreciate the proper limits of integration: that, in short, it would be folly to attempt any wholesale integration of the school curriculum, since any curriculum will contain much that is not readily integrable. Hence, while there may be quite plausible cases for combining aspects of history with drama, cookery with geography, or even moral education with cricket, it is easy to to see how the search for integration could become strained and artificial, resulting in some very much less meaningful constellations of learning. In sum, whereas the general complaint is that without closer specification than is usually given of what is meant by coherence, it may be difficult if not impossible to understand exactly what this particular curriculum prescription is asking for, the more particular reservation is that if it is addressed towards any radical reorganisation of the curriculum along integrated rather than subject-centred lines, it could hardly be other than a deeply controversial educational imperative.

Continuity and progression

In one form, the problem of curricular *continuity* may be regarded as a product of the postwar development of rather different patterns of primary and secondary schooling in Britain and elsewhere. Of course, there have always been some significant differences between primary and secondary schooling, reflecting a rough-and-ready distinction between the more general concerns of primary education and the more specialist and vocational needs of secondary schooling. In this connection, it has often been that whereas state education pupils would be under the supervision of a single class teacher for each of their primary years, they would then move on to experience different specialist teachers in the course of their secondary education. Prior to the advent of pragmatic progressive conceptions of knowledge and curriculum and cognitive developmental approaches to thinking about learning and pedagogy, however, there was often not much difference between primary and secondary schooling with respect to overall content, organisation and methods. Indeed, primary and secondary curricula tended for the most part to be subject-centred, and pedagogy – if not actually focused on the rote learning of skills and/or the retention and recall of facts and information – mostly inclined towards formal styles of whole-class instruction. It was the gradual influence on professional educational theorising of the cognitive psychological idea that the understanding of children develops through qualitatively different stages, rather than just quantitatively or incrementally, reinforced by holistic and integrative pragmatist conceptions of knowledge and curriculum, that was to open up something of a theoretical and practical gap between much contemporary primary and secondary schooling. However, although some contexts of primary education were quite dramatically overtaken, for good or ill, by integrative and developmental curricular innovations of broadly progressive intent, and probably few have been entirely untouched by the newer psychological and curricular ideas, the traditional secondary educational bastions of more specialist teaching remained largely free from such non-traditional pedagogical and curricular innovations. In consequence, the rite of passage from what might be called primary progressivism to secondary tradtionalism has become a source of not just cognitive but also social and emotional difficulty and trauma for pupils in many contemporary contexts of schooling.

There can also be little doubt that much contemporary official and other educational policy making and curriculum planning has been much exercised by this issue of primary–secondary continuity – with little evident success in generating any satisfactory resolution of the problem.[16] Indeed, some approaches to the difficulty – for example, those that have looked to the creation of such intermediate stages of schooling as 'middle schools' – may seem only to have exacerbated the difficulties of primary–secondary transition: whatever the administrative, pedagogical and social advantages of such intermediate stages of schooling – and it is possible to recognise some – it is not clear how the introduction of *two* discontinuities between stages of schooling would satisfactorily address the problems generated by the existence of a single such gap. From one perspective, of course, it may be that such discontinuities are just an inevitable part of any human progress to maturity that no institutional arrangement could eradicate entirely. All good parents are familiar with that sense of anxiety that so often accompanies their child's first day at school – a feeling that may re-occur just as intensely when their sons or daughters eventually leave home for college or university. Thus, although it is natural enough to take whatever measures one can to reduce any pupil or parental trauma on such occasions, it is difficult to see how human experience might be purged completely of such discomfort, and by no means clear that it should be. That said, it is arguable that there are more educationally significant problems of transition or continuity from a primary 'progressive' to a secondary 'traditional' curriculum, and it is not at all easy to see how these might be resolved given a widespread assumption that different curriculum structures enshrining different modes of learning are indeed appropriate to primary and secondary levels.[17]

There can also be little doubt that in those contexts of schooling where the gap between primary progressivism and secondary traditionalism is most marked, the curriculum has become something of a ideological battle-ground between opposed political and educational perspectives.[18] In this regard, the two common strategies for bridging the gap, or smoothing the transition between primary and secondary education – namely of making the upper years of primary more like secondary education (perhaps by the introduction of subjects), or the lower years of secondary more like primary education (perhaps by the introduction of integrated topics or projects) – may appear neither theoretically nor practically satisfactory. First, from a practical perspective, insofar as they really only relocate the curricular discontinuity up or down the school, they do relatively little to eliminate any actual educational shortfall between primary progressivism and secondary traditionalism. Secondly, however, in the absence of a sound theoretical or principled reason for making upper primary more like secondary, or lower secondary more like primary, any movement one way or the other is unlikely to reflect more than a political or ideological preference for the 'hard' discipline of direct instruction over the 'soft' creative and/or socially cooperative benefits of primary progressive learning, or vice versa. But as we shall see in part III, although it is arguable that there are genuinely irresolvable differences of ideology here, it is also possible to hold – in line with previous observations in this part of the book about the possible conceptual confusions of much cognitive developmentalism – that what really needs questioning is any false and dogmatic opposition between subject-centred secondary education and project-centred primary education. From this viewpoint, perhaps what is rather required is a more intelligent and fine-grained appreciation of the value and uses of both of these curricular strategies across all stages of education and schooling.

At all events, such considerations lead us fairly naturally to the fifth and final curriculum principle of *progression*. The demand for curricular progression is usually intended to reduce a frequently deplored incidence of 'vertical' repetition (for example, covering the coal-mine as a project in upper primary, and then again in early secondary geography) and of 'horizontal' overlap (for example, simultaneous covering of aspects of ancient Greek culture in both history and drama) of areas of school study. The key pedagogical assumption here, of course, is that systematic progress to new curricular pastures – the covering of as much ground as possible in the available time – is an unqualified educational good. Once again, however, although it is possible to appreciate the dangers of unecessary duplication of curriculum content – especially if the associated teaching is also stale or uninspired – it is not at all obvious that any reworking of familiar curricular territory has to be educationally redundant, or that relentless progress to ever new content is of inevitable educational benefit. In this connection, it should be clear that a great deal depends on how a subject or a topic is taught, and that two different teachers may approach the very same content in very different ways. It is also clear that this issue relates back to questions of curriculum breadth versus depth upon which we have already touched in this chapter. It may be too readily assumed by curriculum planners – perhaps given an over-hasty equation of education with knowledgeability – that good education is precisely a function of wide content coverage. However, it is also possible that the more widely such content ranges, the more shallow and superficial any educational consequences will turn out to be. We have also observed that any philosophy of education that models educational development on the pattern of uniform initiation into a pre-specified range of forms of knowledge and understanding may be dangerously procrustean, given the actual diversity and unequal distribution of individual pupil talents, aptitudes and interests. In this regard, it may be unreasonable to look for a common measure of educational success, and a disastrously counter-educational policy to try to run all children through one and the same educational gauntlet after the manner of many contemporary national curriculum initiatives. At all events, it can often be of mutually reinforcing educational benefit for different perspectives on the same issues to be adopted simultaneously in different subject areas, or for topics to be revisited at a deeper level further on up the school. Indeed, the influential cognitive psychologist and curriculum theorist Jerome Bruner has famously championed the idea of a 'spiral curriculum', which precisely turns on the idea of increasingly deeper return to much the same topics in the interests of enhanced conceptual development.[19] In general, however, such points may serve to remind us that just as some perfectly reasonable interpretations of breadth or balance may be at odds with this or that interpretation of curriculum coherence, so certain breadth-related emphases on progression may be at variance with efforts to promote depth and significance of learning.

From this perspective, it would appear that none of the lately considered five principles of curriculum design are fit for straightforward and/or joint employment or application in the absence of close and critical scrutiny. Indeed, in the simplest possible terms, it would appear that under certain familiar interpretations of these key curriculum ideas, it is far from clear that a balanced, broad, coherent, continuous and progressive curriculum *would* constitute the best possible educational experience for children. In this respect, it would seem that such principles are better regarded as labels for curriculum *problems* – as occasions for critical discussion – than as solutions to such problems. At the very least, it could not be other than a mistake to suppose that such principles, as they often appear in official and semi-official curriculum initiatives, might be utilised in curriculum design in the manner of quasi-scientific solutions to technical problems. Hence, perhaps the biggest danger to which deployment of such notions is prone – a danger against which we have continuously warned in this work – is that of mistaking what are essentially moral or normative concepts, issues and concerns for something more like hard objective indications, measures or standards of successful educational engagement. The hazards inherent in such confusion, moreover, will continue to exercise us in the next and final chapter of this part of the book.

Possible tasks

(1) A contrast has been observed in this chapter between a conception of education as a matter of broad acquaintance with a range of knowledge forms and an idea of education as initiation into 'one genuine enthusiasm'. Consider the limits of these extreme positions with a view to the possibility of some accommodation between them.

(2) Another contrast has been observed in this chapter between a broadly traditional subject-centred approach to secondary curriculum planning and a more 'progressive' integrated model of primary education. Consider some of the difficulties to which such thinking might give rise and examine possible alternative approaches.

Chapter 10

Curriculum: process, product and appraisal

Education, schooling and accountability

To date, we have upheld a significant distinction between the processes of training or enculturation by which the young are prepared for adult civil and economic life and the institutional means by which these are promoted: although, to be sure, this contrast may be marked in a variety of ways, it is certainly reflected in the difference between education and schooling. It may well be, of course, that this distinction has not always been either well marked or of equal significance in all societies: in pre-civil or economically less developed cultures the processes and/or agencies by which the young are initiated into adult ways may often be more or less integrated into the day-to-day habits and practices of the tribe. Hence, insofar as schooling in such societies is provided by the community, and almost any member of that community may be involved in teaching, the rite of passage from child to adult that modern societies mark by the distinction between school and *both* home *and* work – as well as by a corresponding division of labour between teaching and other professions – may not have had the same status and implications as it has in modern developed polities (though we may again note that these distinctions have also been attacked by contemporary radical and progressive educationalists as inappropriate even for developed economies[1]). With regard to societies like ours, however, we have argued that confusion between schooling and what goes on in schools – between the tax-funded institutions of child-minding and their educational and other purposes – may well engender significant confusions about the precise ways in which such institutions are accountable to the communities that support and fund them.

Thus, as we have seen, some cross-purposes concerning educational accountability may have followed from a failure to distinguish the educational from other goals of schooling: in this respect, the non-instrumentalism of those who insist that the main purpose of schooling is to transmit intrinsically worthwhile educational knowledge and understanding seems no less mistaken than the apparently opposed instrumentalist or utilitarian assumption that its only purpose (worse yet, the only purpose of *education*) is mainly or solely to promote vocational or other socio-economically useful skills and benefits. What neither of the parties to such debates seems to appreciate is that schooling exists for a diversity of benefits and purposes – including, to be sure, not just education and vocational training, but also (arguably) child-minding and basic health care. In this light, although utilitarians and other instrumentalists may properly insist that schooling is a means to an end, this does not prevent our regarding education as an end in itself as *one* function of schooling – something that may, perhaps indeed should, be pursued without primary regard to economic or other social benefit. Likewise, although liberal traditionalists and other non-instrumentalists are right to insist that education is primarily answerable to the higher demands of truth and justice, they are also in error if they proceed to deny that schools have more basic concerns with physical health and socio-economic benefit – from which perspective, of course, the school curriculum must be accountable to parents, employers and politicians as well as to professional interests. Thus, although this consideration also raises – as we have previously seen – some very awkward normative, political and practical questions concerning the proper curricular balance of these diverse purposes and concerns, it is beyond serious question that there should be some such balance of content: schooling could be no more exclusively concerned with knowledge for its own sake, or just with training for adult work, than it could be just for child-minding or providing free lunches.

The all-important question of how such balance is to be achieved, of course, takes us into the realms of curriculum *evaluation* – which is also a mine-field of normative questions of the sort we started to explore in the previous chapter. Moreover, we might still want to ask whether it is reasonable to look for any definite answer to such questions – or, at least, for some kind of rational or objective basis for determining the general form and content of the school curriculum. Indeed, in the light of arguments to date, the prospects for any widespread agreement on such issues may seem really rather dim. To emphasise, as we have, the social and cultural character of meaning is to acknowledge that the school curriculum is a 'a selection from the culture' in the fairly radical sense that it reflects particular cultural values that may admit of no impartial or disinterested rational appraisal. As part III will show more clearly, insofar as diverse cultures and sub-cultures celebrate different goals and ideals, different values and virtues may be enshrined in curricular provision in locally divergent if not actually conflicting ways: in that case, problems of curriculum design and planning are invariably prime sites of moral or ethical controversy – which, it may also be feared, are also unsusceptible of neutral or disinterested rational resolution. Consider, by way of obvious example, the different status likely to be accorded in Roman Catholic and secular humanist schools to religious and scientific education – not to mention the rather diverse curricular forms that such studies are likely to take in these different contexts. That said, any such conception of education and the school curriculum as essentially moral (and hence ethically contentious) enterprises may seem rather at odds with a previously explored and nowadays influential technicist account of education as an essentially scientific project ultimately answerable to empirical research into value-neutral processes of teaching and learning. Hence, for numerous modern advocates of school improvement and effectiveness, the problems of curriculum design have seemed to be largely those of constructing an experimentally grounded technology of pedagogy for the 'delivery' of schedules of human learning – in accordance perhaps with such rationally 'self-evident' criteria of breadth, balance, coherence, continuity and progression. In this light, with the assistance of science – notably that science of learning and pedagogy developed and refined in the course of the lately departed century – it may indeed seem reasonable to aspire to a rational ideal of objective evidence-based curriculum planning. To be sure, any such conception would need to accommodate the possibility that diverse local circumstances and values will require school pupils to be taught different things in various places, but it might nevertheless provide the basic form of any and all rational curriculum planning – as well as, perhaps, grounds for rational professional criticism of some traditional educational practices.

The curriculum and educational assessment

Some of the difficulties to which any such purported science of pedagogy is prone have already been explored in this part of the book, and in part III we shall need to engage in a more detailed examination of the implications of construing education and curriculum as moral and evaluative rather than technical projects or enterprises. However, in the interests of a slightly better grasp of these issues, it will be the main concern of this chapter to raise some critical questions about one of the widely claimed benefits of a scientific approach to learning and the curriculum – namely its alleged conduciveness to the systematic and rigorous *assessment* of pupil learning. On this topic, moreover, although one need not doubt the time-honoured interest of professional educational philosophers and theorists in issues of policy and accountability, it would appear that there has until recently been a relative dearth of searching philosophical inquiry into questions of educational assessment. This may seem all the more surprising given the extraordinarily powerful contemporary impact of technicist notions of assessment and accountabilty on the general enterprise of official and professional curriculum design and implementation. In this regard, it is hardly possible to ignore the way in which a not altogether prepossessing instrumentalist discourse of behavioural outcomes, attainment targets and performance indicators, of levels and grades of achievement, and so on, has lately come to play a key structural role in the design of centrally devised curricular programmes and initiatives in many educational systems across the world. Moreover, the development of such educational newspeak would seem to have been directed to something like total overhaul of the content and direction of education, teaching and training in the service of procrustean accommodation to latter-day political emphases on the more economically productive aspects of schooling.

Indeed, as it has sometimes been colourfully put, the assessment tail may now in many places have come to wag the curriculum dog. Of course, interest in the assessment of learning as such is nothing new to educational theorists and policy makers in general, or to educational philosophers in particular: in a socio-political as well as epistemological form, such interest clearly goes back at least as far as Plato.[2] The rather different turn that such interest seems to have taken in more recent times, however, has been in the direction of systematic empirical-psychological technical measurement of performance, and – in the light of late twentieth-century neo-liberal preoccupation with global market competitiveness – towards a vision of education and learning as essentially subservient to the achievement of measurable economic objectives. On this view, in short, education and schooling are conceivable primarily as means to pre-specified socio-economic ends. Moreover, whatever we may think of the way in which the modern world has gone, there can be no doubt that accepting the distinction between education and schooling, and the commitment (in part) of schools to goals of vocational and other training which that distinction implies, also means accepting that schools must play their part in helping to prepare and assess the fitness of pupils for adult occupational and other responsibilities. On this view, although there is no absolutely necessary connection between *education* and that complex apparatus of examination for certification that has blighted the lives of so many young people – since there is no reason why, as progressive and radical educationalists have continued to insist, the education of young people could not be freed from such evils at least in their present anxiety-generating forms – the connection between *schooling* and *some* species of formal assessment seems less questionable. In short, schools *are* partly accountable to society for equipping children and young people with the skills – not least the basic skills of literacy and numeracy – that enable responsible post-school contribution to the common good. In a related vein, Plato was in the *Republic* clearly very interested in the possibility of sorting and grading pupils according to ability, and in the training of them for ability-related vocational roles – and, as we shall see more clearly in the next part of the book, an already significant Platonic influence on the development of modern schooling was to be further reinforced by an early to mid-twentieth-century empirical-psychological preoccupation with the development of intelligence testing.[3]

Still, the Platonic (or perhaps Socratic) interest in the testing, monitoring or assessment of pupil learning does not begin with the socio-economic or political concerns of the *Republic*. In fact, it has a deeper source in Plato's more general metaphysical and epistemological inquiries into the relations between experience and truth, knowledge and opinion, meaning and understanding, and so on. We have already seen that the relatively advanced Platonic epistemology of the *Theaetetus*[4] gives rise to a basic definition of knowledge as justified true belief. However, Plato's more general appreciation that assisting someone to *know* something is crucially a matter of bringing him or her to understand the rules and principles that lead of *logical necessity* to a given conclusion is already well illustrated by the remarkable pedagogical narrative of Socrates and the slave boy in his earlier dialogue, the *Meno*.[5] Although the *Meno* is ostensibly concerned to demonstrate the rather implausible Platonic doctrine that all knowledge is recollection, it is more often regarded as a profound early analysis of the art of the teacher. In this dialogue, Socrates succeeds in enabling an untutored slave boy to construct (in diagrammatical form) a square twice the area of a first square, by using the diagonal of the first as base. Socrates undertakes this via the employment of a sequence of open questions to which the youth initially returns mistaken answers. Each mistaken answer, however, is utilised by Socrates as a point of departure for new questions that gradually point the boy towards the correct solution. However, the key Platonic (and/or Socratic) point is that effectively assisting someone to *know* that a square constructed on the diagonal of a first square is twice the area of the first square is a matter not of *telling* him or her that this is so – a fact that, if not understood, is unlikely to be retained – but of ensuring that the learner has grasped the geometrical principles that ensure that this is so. This, moreover, involves monitoring each step of the learner's understanding – a process that may also entail leading the learner into 'virtuous' or constructive errors to the purpose of stimulating further, more principled reflection.

At all events, this perspective locates good teaching very much in the teacher's own thorough and clearly articulated grasp of what is to be taught: thus, if the topic is to be an episode of history, the teacher will need not only accurate knowledge of the key events of that historical period, but also some grasp of the overall historical context of those events – including something of the previous historical trends that gave rise to them, as well as of their subsequent historical significance and implications. Generally, however, the Socratic art of pedagogy consists in guiding the learner clearly through a logically coherent narrative with constant, continuous and close monitoring of key stages of understanding: the good teacher is he or she who can accurately track the pupil's grasp of the logical order of a given content over the course of a learning sequence. From this viewpoint, assessment is not just a pedagogical extra or luxury that might be dropped from any programme of education – as examination and certification might be jettisoned in the interests of reduced pupil stress and anxiety – it is an indispensable feature of good teaching. Thus, whereas bad teaching is teaching in which teachers have themselves a poor grasp of the meaning or significance of what is taught, and in which the pupil's own grasp is poorly monitored, good teaching is that in which teachers themselves have a clear and thorough understanding of what is to be learned, and utilise all available means and methods to ensure that the learner's experience precisely maps that understanding. It is also arguable, by the way, that this picture of the difference between good and bad teaching cuts across any distinction between so-called 'traditional' and 'progressive' approaches to education (which, as I shall try to show in due course, is not anyway primarily a distinction of pedagogical method). From this perspective, there is some reason to doubt a common reading of the Socratic pedagogy of the *Meno* as a kind of anticipation of specifically *progressive* methods – especially as Plato is not, after all, a conspicuously progressive educational theorist. Hence, irrespective of the traditional–progressive dichotomy, one may hold that the slave boy narrative is principally concerned to identify some basic logical features of *any* good teaching.

In search of a science of assessment

At all events, the discussion so far appears to have identified two common purposes of assessment in the contexts of education and schooling: first, for the intrinsic pedagogical purpose of keeping tabs on the progress of pupil knowledge and understanding; secondly, for the more questionable 'external' purpose of sorting learners into different categories of ability for socio-economic more than strictly educational purposes. It may also be that this distinction corresponds – although by no means exactly – to another distinction of contemporary assessment theory, between *formative* and *summative* assessment.[6] Whereas formative assessment is largely concerned with that more informal monitoring that all good teachers employ in order to track the moment-to-moment progress of pupils' learning, summative assessment is the more formal kind of testing by which educationalists attempt to ascertain – often at the end-point of a course of study – whether and to what extent young people have achieved the basic learning objectives and outcomes of this or that formal curricular programme. The latter sort of assessment has, of course, often been used to provide the hard evidence upon which children can be sorted, graded or streamed for diverse educational, social or vocational purposes. Moreover, although the official architects of those centrally prescribed assessment-driven curricula that have recently spread throughout the modern world are usually at pains to deny that any regular appraisal of children is meant to serve such elitist or Platonic sorting and grading, it would certainly seem that testing at putative key stages of development has given summative assessment pride of place over formative assessment in the context of public, professional and political debates and concerns about comparative quality of educational provision between particular schools. Of course, policy makers will insist that formative assessment has also an indispensable place in the teacher's armoury of professional skills – indeed, such assessment skills have usually a central place in competence models of professional expertise – but such official curriculum mongers may also be given to the suspicion that formative assessment is liable to the subjective vagaries of individual professional judgement, and cannot therefore have hard scientific objectivity. From this perspective, to be sure, it may be not just the learning of learners that is held to require strict monitoring, but also the professional judgements of teachers.

Without questioning all or any of the purposes for which formal tests and measures of attainment have been employed in the history of assessment, we have already in this part of the book raised some awkward philosophical questions about the idea that educationally significant learning can be measured and quantified in quasi-scientific terms. All the same, no-one with the least familiarity with twentieth-century developments in experimental psychology could fail to appreciate the direct intellectual heritage of the contemporary instrumental curriculum and assessment jargon of behavioural outcomes, attainment targets and performance indicators from the early equally instrumental and mechanistic learning-theoretical terminology of stimulus, response and reinforcement. Indeed, a significant link in the evolution of modern curriculum theory and policy from initial scientific-psychological analyses of learning seems to have been forged in the course of an early twentieth-century application of broadly associationist learning principles to the management of automated production known as Taylorism.[7] Although Taylorism was primarily an attempt to apply behaviourist principles to skill-acquisition to the purposes of mechanically efficient factory production, the principles and procedures upon which it rested are not too far removed from those that underpin contemporary managerial efforts to rationalise professional teacher and other expertise in the form of competence models of training. However, it is also a relatively short step from any such reductive analyses of vocational expertise to latter-day educational attempts to express goals of pupil learning in terms of behavioural objectives and attainment targets. The basic idea in all these cases is that it ought to be possible to construe the learning of any subject or skill as a more or less complex episode of human behaviour analysable in principle as a sequence of empirically observable events. On such a view, of course, the events in question will also have significant causal links with the environment: there will be other events which have caused them, as well as events that they in turn cause. But if the behaviour of learners is interpreted in this way as a closed causal system, it is also deterministic and predictable. In that case, the whole process would seem to be at least in principle causally manipulable via a technology of pedagogy grounded in an empirical science of learning. If education is a matter of the acquisition of knowledge and skills understood as events in a causal chain of actual or potential behaviour, then human agents may – via a technology of teaching – be systematically programmed in whatever knowledge and skills we might wish them to learn.

Is this a generally feasible view of educationally significant learning? First, we have already in this part of the book noticed considerable problems about behaviourist analyses of learning *per se*. That said, although behavioural objectives models of learning and assessment clearly have origins in reflex or stimulus–response psychology, it is less plausible to regard all modern proponents of curriculum targets and objectives as necessarily committed to crude causal theories of learning. We have already seen, to be sure, that (metaphysical) forms of behaviourism are deeply problematic insofar as attempts to reduce learning to causal processes fail to leave much room for genuine human agency, and/or to account for meaning as a precondition of such agency: to the extent that such theories regard learners as little more than causal systems to be programmed, they blur crucial distinctions between education and conditioning or indoctrination in a quite unacceptable way. But it would clearly be a mistake to identify completely any such blatant pseudo-scientific behaviourist reduction of the mental to the physical with the kind of logical analysis of skills and subject matter that learning theorists have also regarded as a means to effective causal conditioning in such knowledge and skills. Hence, although *traditionalist* or subject-centred pedagogies are commonly characterised as committed to clear pedagogical analysis of the principles of a given subject matter, in a manner that is certainly consistent with an objectives-focused approach to teaching, it is hardly plausible – especially given the liberal educational aspirations of much modern traditionalism – to regard such tendencies as behaviourist on such grounds alone. Indeed, there would seem to be some theoretical danger at this point of confusing *analysis* with *reduction*. For, of course, although any behaviourist reduction will require analysis, not all such analysis is reductive in this (or any other) sense. In fact, behaviourist approaches to learning and education require analysis just and only insofar as all coherent education and learning requires it. On the face of it, good teachers (whatever their metaphysical views) will want to ensure that their teaching is as coherent and intelligible as possible, and this can only mean some attempt to present a given subject matter in the most logically accessible way.

Arguments against objectives-based assessment

But does it mean this? To be sure, the above point serves as a welcome corrective to any implausible suggestion that the objectives approach must reduce learning to no more than the meaningless rote learning of routines and facts:[8] after all, the very *point* of the adoption of an objectives approach for its proponents is that it conduces to the sort of lesson planning that would enable learners to make the best possible *sense* of what is taught. Still, any such corrective remains open to the objection that such logical ordering of subject matter may not be the best possible way of rendering a given subject matter intelligible to pupils. Once again, however, there are weaker and stronger versions of this objection – neither of which seems clearly decisive against objectives or target-orientated approaches to assessment of the kind that appear to underpin contemporary key stage educational testing. Indeed, the weaker point – which we might call the *pedagogical* objection – is more about teaching strategy than about the logical structure or content of what is to be taught. In this regard, we have already observed in earlier discussion of teaching that strict or routine observance of the logical structure or order of a given subject matter may not be the best or most attractive way to teach it. From this viewpoint, good teachers may need to employ a variety of imaginative devices to attract the jaded attention of pupils to potentially dry or 'unsexy' school subjects. These may involve some 'lateral' use of striking images, analogies and metaphors – perhaps the reinterpretation of historical or mythical themes in more popular-cultural terms of greater apparent relevance to pupils – which might also appear to veer momentarily from the straight and narrow path of obvious subject coherence. One may here recall the enchanting ways in which Lewis Carroll managed to air so many educationally significant mathematical and logical issues and problems in the course of his otherwise not especially coherent Alice stories. However, the fact that mathematics teachers may begin their lessons by playing the banjo or singing funny songs about numbers has little real bearing on the question of whether we need to teach mathematics in a way that has to respect the logical systematicity of the discipline. The significance of songs and banjos is only that teachers have sometimes to resort to indirect or roundabout methods in order to ease the entry of learners into what may otherwise be the dry and difficult logic of this or that subject.

In our earlier discussion of teaching, however, we indicated a stronger possible point against approaches to learning and assessment that stress order, coherence and systematicity: for, of course, it is worth recognising that not all of the subjects, skills and activities into which we aim to initiate pupils aspire to anything like the same logical order as mathematics. As Aristotle argued with respect to understanding moral discourse, 'we should not expect more precision, than the nature of the subject matter admits',[9] and from this viewpoint there are clearly forms of knowledge, understanding and skill that do not aim primarily, if at all, at strictly deductive systematicity or coherence in the manner of mathematical and other sciences. Indeed, perhaps the best examples of disciplines or activities of this nature are to be met in artistic and aesthetic educational fields, where it is the perfectly proper task of teachers to assist pupils to appreciations, interpretations and creative achievements that are not at all strict logical consequences of precise axioms or principles. From this perspective, what we might call the *creativity* objection to an objectives approach to curricular planning would take issue with the idea – which may indeed link causal theories of learning to behavioural objectives conceptions of pedagogy – that meaningful learning primarily concerns the achievement of *predetermined* ends, and that assessment is therefore mainly a matter of *measuring* outcomes against such pre-specifications. Indeed, although it would seem to be a feature of successful mathematics or science teaching that pupils are able to follow the reasoning they have been given to the *same* logical or scientific conclusions, it is not clear that this would be a general condition of good art teaching.

I recall visiting, many years ago, an end-of-term art school exhibition in a northern English gallery, and being impressed by a series of paintings I took to be the work of a highly original new talent. In seeking to note the name for future reference, however, I discovered that the paintings were the work of not one but *several* different young painters from the same school. In view of this, I felt compelled to revise an initial judgement to the effect that these paintings were all the work of a single original pupil in favour of the verdict that these were artistic products of the not-so-original pupils of a very powerful teacher. This example, however, raises the tricky question of whether we should consider the pedagogue in question to be a *good* art teacher – as we might of course regard a mathematics teacher whose pupils all reasoned to the same (correct) conclusions as a good teacher (leaving aside the issue of the educational value of such results if they were merely rote learned). On the one hand, of course, art teachers clearly share with mathematics and other teachers the responsibility of teaching *something* to their pupils in the way of particular subject-specific concepts, skills and techniques. But insofar as good art or poetry teaching is also concerned to foster a degree of originality or individuality of expression on the part of pupils, any teacher who seriously restricted such scope for personal expressive manoeuvre might be taken to have *failed* in a fairly key respect. In this light, it would seem that the formidable challenge of good teaching in arts subjects is to walk a fine line between equipping pupils with the knowledge, understanding and skills that are the technical prerequisites of successful artistic expression and production, and suppressing that singularity of personal expressive vision which is also a *sine qua non* of authentic artistic engagement.

Still, notwithstanding any such difference between 'logical' and 'expressive' activities and disciplines, there is clearly much scope for the mastery of objectively measurable knowledge, understanding and skills in the arts: the effective teaching of painting, poetry, music or creative dance is bound to involve the grasp of artistic traditions, knowledge of media and the acquisition of specific techniques and skills that are legitimate objects of both informal and formal assessment.[10] Indeed, unless one takes a less than plausible subjective or 'anything-goes' view of artistic and/or aesthetic knowledge and understanding, it is difficult to ignore the fact that the artistic traditions of different cultures enshrine standards, canons and criteria of significant appreciation and productivity that are ignored only at the gravest artistic peril. Hence, although arts may trade more in the ambiguities of trope and metaphor than in the literal truths of science or the formal truths of mathematics, there would nevertheless seem to be logical limits to meaningful diversity of even artistic interpretation – and the gap between good and bad art is often measured in terms of such limits. Where any 'objective' assessment of art seems to depart from mathematical assessment, of course, is that there may be no 'universally' right answers to artistic questions or problems in the sense that there might be to mathematical (or, at any rate, arithmetical) questions. Whereas it is in principle possible to appreciate – for anyone who takes the trouble to grasp the relevant procedures – why mathematical conclusions follow with something like logical necessity from a given set of axioms, it is usually held that such criteria of strict correctness do not apply to the arts, especially in the light of their 'relative' cultural, moral and other evaluative associations. Despite this, however, there is clearly *qualitative judgement* in the arts, and such a thing as genuine *informed* expertise and opinion about what counts as better or worse painting, music or poetry. Hence, although it would be philistine to suppose that arts are taught only so that learners can distinguish good from bad art, it is certainly true that they are taught with a view to meaningful appreciation – which inevitably involves the cultivation or training of discrimination and discernment. In short, the fact that there is space for creativity and diversity of interpretation in the arts – that they are not exclusively concerned with the achievement of precisely predetermined objectives – does not mean that there can be no *objective* assessment of artistic quality.

Thus far, then, it would appear that the 'pedagogical' and 'creativity' objections to objectives approaches to curriculum planning and assessment are far from decisive, and it is not at all easy to see what real alternative there might actually be to some such view. In particular, it is rather hard to see to what the vaunted alternative of the so-called 'process' model of curriculum – which often seems to be predicated upon 'pedagogical' and 'creativity' objections to objectives models – actually amounts as a coherent model of curriculum planning.[11] As we have already seen, 'process' pedagogy – under the dual impact of pragmatist epistemology and cognitive psychology – inclines to a *constructivist* account of learning which strongly favours topic-centred and integrative approaches to curriculum organisation. But although the generally antipathetic attitude of 'process' learning theorists to subject-centred curricula might appear to support a genuine 'process' alternative to objectives-based curriculum thinking, there are two strong reasons for doubting whether this is really so. First, as already indicated, there is no compelling reason to suppose that integrated conceptions of curriculum organisation are in and of themselves inimical to any objectives approach to lesson planning: indeed, it seems no more difficult to plan topics in terms of objectives than it is to plan the teaching of subjects in this fashion. Secondly, however, although we have argued that objectives approaches to curriculum design are significantly separable from any empiricist metaphysics of behaviourism, it is likely that 'process' models of learning are more deeply implicated in that dubious dualist metaphysics of cognitive psychology that regards the growth of understanding as an 'inner' developmental occurence. But the conjunction of these two points places the very idea of a 'process' model of curriculum planning in something of a dilemma. On the one hand, if we interpret the process curriculum as a form of radical *progressivism* wholeheartedly committed to a view of learning as entirely subjective child-centred discovery – a putative 'in-the-head' development into which there can be no legitimate pedagogical intervention – it is impossible to see what *pedagogically* coherent sense we might make of the idea of curriculum *planning* at all. On the other hand, if the process model does allow for the possibility of (albeit more progressively *covert*) teacher direction towards this or that pedagogical goal, it is hard to see why it would have to depart radically from any general objectives conception of planning. In this light, it is probably safe to say that insofar as it is hard to see how teaching as a systematic attempt to promote learning could really avoid the deliberate adoption of particular pedagogical means or strategies to more or less specified educational ends, it may be no more than a *formal* point that curriculum planning involves the adoption and employment of objectives. Indeed, this point seems to have been conceded by those who, whilst appreciative of the creativity objection to the use of objectives in arts education, have nevertheless sought to address the problem of assessing artistic development via appeal to a language of *expressive* objectives.[12]

Understanding and the assessment of 'rich knowledge'

We should not conclude this part of the book, however, without some attention to an educational philosophical controversy that has recently surrounded the idea of *summative* objectives-based assessment – or the kind of formal educational assessment characteristic of key stage testing in standard national curriculum initiatives.[13] The case against the assessment of formal tests and examinations, it should be clear, does not question either the appropriateness or otherwise of planning by objectives, or that it is in any way inappropriate to aspire to objective *knowledge* of what learners have learned at the end of a programme of study. The main complaint seems to be rather that the instruments adopted by educational professionals for the testing of knowledge – namely the formal tests and examinations upon which so much academic certification is based – are practically inadequate to measure genuine or worthwhile pupil understanding. It is also crucial to appreciate that the debate turns principally upon the difficulty of assessing and testing for what has been called 'rich knowledge', and that the difference between more and less rich knowledge to some extent reflects the distinction we explored in chapter 8 between knowledge in the strong Platonic sense of understanding the whys and wherefores of things, and knowledge in some weaker more informational sense. The basic objection is that although the time-honoured forms of formal educational assessment that underpin much certification are adequate for the testing of basic information and skills – and it is not denied that the acquisition and mastery of basic information and skills represents an important if not indispensable aspect of educational development – such methods cannot even begin to measure the quality of *understanding* of deeper learning. We should also recognise that this is not merely a *practical* or technical objection to such methods of assessment: the point is not that currently available instruments of educational measurement are simply too blunt but that with further research and development they could be made rather more precise; on the contrary, the complaint is a *conceptual* or philosophical one to the effect that such methods could never in *principle*, regardless of further practical refinement, be expected to achieve the educational purposes for which they are apparently deployed.

To begin to see what is at issue here, let us recall the example earlier used to illustrate the shortcomings of a behaviourist or causal account of knowledge-acquisition. Suppose, then, that we are faced with the task of ascertaining whether a given class of pupils has learned or come to 'know how' to perform a given ethnic or folk dance. As we have seen, it may be tempting to suppose – especially under the influence of a not wholly implausible empiricist conception of skill-acquisition – that to learn the dance is to master a sequence of component movements: on this view, assessment is a simple matter of checking whether the pupils have learned the movements in the right order. But we have seen that pupils may learn this in a way that would hardly warrant much of a claim that they know how to dance – and this is arguably because some understanding of the purpose of the dance or of its human meaning would seem presupposed to any real ('rich') dance knowledge. We should also see that it would be missing the point to say that what pupils lack in this respect is some information about (the social context) of the dance in addition to the dance movements – for if the dance is not just movements, it is not movements plus information either. Indeed, dance is not obviously either *movements* or *information* at all. For one thing, any proper practical assessment of the dance would focus not upon physical movements as such but upon the terpsichorical *performance* of ritualised *actions*; for another, the knowledge that the dancer requires is not so much knowledge *about* culture and values but culturally nuanced *performance* knowledge – or 'knowledge how' – of *dance*. In short, it seems unlikely that if the complex cognitive, practical and evaluative sensibilities presupposed to an educated practitioner appreciation and mastery of a dance could not be acquired via the mastery of 'blind' physical movements, or by the learning of factual information, they might be acquired by some combination of these.

But there are obvious objections both to this example and to any point about formal assessment it might seem to be making. First, the dance example may appear to complicate the issue quite unnecessarily by focusing on the sort of practical knowledge that may involve an experiential dimension, or even some degree of natural ability, which we could not expect to be assessable as taught knowledge or skills: if I have some special natural ability – say, to wiggle my ears – then it is difficult to see how this might be subject to external assessment (since, for one thing, it would be difficult to see how anyone other than myself could be an authority on how to do it well). But, secondly, it may seem rather simple-minded to suggest that knowledge of dance or anything else is resistant to formal assessment because it is not reducible to *facts* or movements – for, of course, forms of formal assessment can test much more than fact retention. Indeed, much of the current debate about the impotence of formal assessment to measure 'rich knowledge' has focused upon the notion of 'connected under-standing' – precisely the sort of grasp of inferential or explanatory relations between facts or information that characterises Plato's conception of knowledge as 'justified true belief'. But it should also be clear enough that even tests of basic arithmetic purport to tell whether pupils have gained some such connected understanding. Thus, for example, a worksheet of multiplication problems is designed to detect whether pupils have an adequate grasp of the (albeit mechanical) rules of a basic arithmetical operation, not simply whether a series of disconnected facts have been retained. To be sure, even if children have merely rote learned their tables, any application of such learning to multi-plication questions will require the acquisition of a mental *ability* that goes beyond mere memorisation: there is a difference, for example, between solving multiplication problems via the application of arithmetical operations, and solving them by the more or less inspired guesswork often associated with multiple-choice examinations. Moreover, insofar as meaningful learning has been observed in this part of the book to be largely a matter of mastering the essentially *public* (inferential, explanatory and other) rules and principles appar-ently presupposed to any human understanding, it is difficult to see how anything that could *not* be tested might count as genuine knowledge at all: indeed, this point, that there cannot really be any such thing as 'private' or untestable knowledge, would appear to lie at the heart of the philosophy of both Kant and the later Wittgenstein.[14]

The limits of assessment reconsidered

If this is generally the case, however, it may be hard to see how any academic or practical subject or activity under the curricular sun might be unamenable in principle to objective testing by this or that form of summative or other assess-ment. If the key to rich knowledge or connected understanding of a human discipline is a grasp of the public rules that govern the successful conduct of that activity, then there is no reason why valid and reliable assessment procedures could not be constructed to measure the extent of a pupil's understanding of that activity. Let us repeat that it is not our concern here to discuss the practical or technical limitations of current assessment procedures and instruments: that would be the business of experts on psychometry not a matter for educational philosophers. All we need for now is to know whether such testing is a feasible enterprise, and we seem to have a quite strong epistemological argument in favour of this possibility: on this view, it would not much matter whether it was dance or basic multiplication that we needed to test, because either way it would seem that if we are really prepared go to enough trouble, there are ways in which we might fairly accurately assess the extent of someone's knowledge of *anything* we might want to assess. Of course, there are potential *practical* and/or technical pitfalls here – which seem fairly evident in relation to the teaching of dance. Indeed, the most general problem would seem to be that the measuring device might fall well short of proper assessment of the activity in question, so that procrustean accommodation of the activity to the measuring device actually inclines to *distort* its precise character. Thus, in the specific case of dance, it is easy to see how any reductive understanding of dance in terms of physical movements and some more informational grasp of aspects of cultural context might fall short of that educated dance knowledge (theoretical and/or practical) inherent in expressive *performance* and artistic *appreciation*: from this viewpoint, certain methods of summative assessment might be based on not just a superficial but also a quite distorted conception of the enterprise that the methods are concerned to assess. But even in the case of the subtle culturally conditioned practical knowledge of dance, it must be possible to assess objectively whether it is being learned *properly*: insofar as the learning of it is a matter of the mastery of public conventions, rules and procedures, such conventions and procedures could not be learned other than by teaching, and any successful teaching of these must be answerable to certain objectively identifiable standards.

Indeed, leaving aside the complex and complicating practical aspects of learning to dance, dance as an art form is clearly a source of great satisfaction and significance to many people more from a *spectator* than a performance perspective: from this viewpoint, dance enthusiasts and dance critics may well have a better or more articulate appreciation of what constitutes quality of dance performance, or of what is or is not great dance, than many dance practitioners – and this is something that (*ex hypothesi*) they will have learned in a fairly conventional academic rather than practical way. Thus, is it not fairly obvious that teaching appreciation of dance, like teaching any other aesthetic or artistic appreciation, must be largely a matter of looking at a great deal of dance, studying and comparing different traditions, conventions and styles of dance and coming to an objective grasp of its meaning and significance through much the same sort of rule-governed 'connected' understanding that characterises meaningful comprehension in mathematics, science or history? In that case, although there are clearly ways in which such knowledge and appreciation might be inadequately measured, we might still expect it to be fairly accurately or reliably measured by good teachers through good tests (at one extreme, for example, via PhD theses and vivas) in a not markedly controversial way.

All the same, there is remaining room for suspicion that it is not ultimately plausible to conceive the knowledge and appreciation that even a dance expert might claim as having been acquired in any such straightforward fashion. The obvious persisting difficulty is that dance, like other arts, is a site of serious debate and controversy, and that expertise in dance is more commonly characterised by reference to disagreement than otherwise. Indeed, to the extent that understanding and appreciating dance seems to be deeply implicated in evaluatively sensitive judgement, interpretation and appreciation, the difficulty here would seem to be the idea that the connected understanding presupposed to rich knowledge consists in the rather crude application of established meaning-constitutive rules to a given realm of human experience. The problem is that to whatever extent meaning is rule-constituted, it is not necessarily constituted by universally *agreed* rules: from this viewpoint, it is not just that dance theorists do not agree about what constitutes good or bad dance, but that they often do not even agree about what constitutes *dance* (as distinct from, say, meaningless gestures).

It would be all too easy to dismiss this point as merely a restatement of the earlier so-called 'creativity' objection to behavioural objectives models of assessment: is the point here not merely that there is an inherent subjectivity or open-endedness about artistic endeavour, and therefore some inevitable uncertainty about how to evaluate productive outcomes that are not obviously answerable to pre-specified criteria? However, insofar as the deep disagreements about what constitutes dance (whether, for example, dance is about the expression of emotion or about the construction of formal movement patterns) appear to be reflected into all other curriculum disciplines and activities, the point cannot be just this. Moreover, although it is likely that the difficulties here are probably most evident with respect to the equally evaluatively vexed area of moral education, it should be clear that the conceptual issue (upon which we have previously touched in this work) about whether the moral use of 'good' is a matter of description, prescription or emotional expression is not at all on the same level as any normative debate about whether this or that course of action is morally right – even if any satisfactory answer to the second sort of question should depend upon settling the first. The heart of this difficulty is best appreciated in relation to the insights of Frege and Wittgenstein concerning the nature of concept-acquisition and the relationship between language and the world considered in chapter 7. According to Frege and Wittgenstein, as we have seen, concept expressions are not exclusively concerned to pick out features of experience in a descriptive way, and understanding non-descriptive (prescriptive, evaluative, appreciative, celebratory) discourse is a matter of grasping the complex convention-governed terms of familiar usage. But even if we are not bewitched by common usage into thinking that a non-referential term is descriptive (that, for example, 'pain' refers to some inner thing), it is an open question whether received linguistic conventions actually identify philosophically meaningful or defensible senses of a given term. Insofar as this is so, however, there is potentially as much of an issue about whether mathematics is a matter of invention or discovery, whether history is the learning of fact or interpretation, and whether physics offers descriptions of the universe or practically convenient models as there is about whether morality is the grasp of universal principles or the formation of personal commitments, or whether dance is emotional expression or the construction of formal movement patterns. From this viewpoint, there may be as much uncertainty over the logical status of '2 + 2 = 4', 'nothing can exceed the speed of light' or 'Columbus discovered America', as there is about whether this act of mercy is (morally) good, or this picture is pretty.

There can be no doubt, moreover, of the implications for educational assessment of these apparently recherché semantic considerations – and concerns such as these may well lie at the heart of recent claims that the formal assessment of much contemporary educational testing must fail to measure the connected understanding of so-called 'rich' knowledge. Any such failure is likely to be most evident, to be sure, at the higher or more advanced levels of human inquiry. Thus, during the examination of his PhD thesis (later to be published as the *Tractatus-Logico-Philosophicus*), Wittgenstein is famously supposed to have told his examiners Bertrand Russell and G.E. Moore that they could not possibly understand it.[15] Whether or not this episode occurred (which it may well have done), it was certainly the case that many distinguished philosophers of the day (including Russell) had some trouble understanding the new philosophical directions opened up by Wittegenstein in *Philosophical Investigations* and other posthumously published works. The same is clearly true of other great innovators in a variety of fields of human endeavour: the physicist Albert Einstein and the jazz musician Charlie Parker are two random examples of pioneers whose work was too far ahead of the time to be widely appreciated in their time. And, to be sure, although few teachers are destined to encounter innovators of the stature of Wittgenstein, Einstein or Parker in their day-to-day practice, it not unreasonable to suppose that many may teach pupils whose potential or actual grasp of some subject is greater than their own, and that the understanding of such pupils may well be beyond the power of any received educational schedules of assessment to measure. Thus, although there is surely some danger in any esoteric assumption that there are forms of knowledge and understanding that are inherently resistant to objective educational assessment, teachers and educational assessors also need to avoid the equal and opposite danger of assuming that existing assessment measures are adequate to capture all there might be to human understanding of this or that endeavour. To go down that road would be to succumb to an educational dogmatism, which – although it is also deeply alien to that true spirit of Socratic inquiry upon which we have so often touched in this work – may all too often and all too fatally have infected past practitioners of the pedagogical art.

Possible tasks

(1) Identify a range of possible instances in which forms of formal assessment might be held to have a distortive effect on the learner's educational appreciation of some subject, activity or skill.

(2) Consider the circumstances and/or the sort of evidence that might lead a teacher of some art, science or practical skill to suspect that the learner's appreciation, mastery or understanding had outstripped his or her own.

Part III

Schooling, society and culture

Chapter 11

Liberalism, impartiality and liberal education

Modern developments in educational philosophy

The postwar reconstruction of Anglo-American educational philosophy sought to bring philosophy of education in line with important developments of twentieth-century analytical philosophy. In the United States, this perhaps largely involved further consolidation of an already well established relationship between American educational philosophy and theory, and the 'home-grown' pragmatist mainstream: John Dewey, a key figure in the development of modern pragmatism, was also widely recognised as the principal patriarch of American philosophy of education. However, in consequence of the relative lack of philosophical interest in educational theory of the Oxbridge pioneers of logical analysis (Bertrand Russell and A.J. Ayer[1]) and 'ordinary language' philosophy (Ludwig Wittgenstein, Gilbert Ryle and John Austin[2]), and a largely historical and uncritical approach to educational ideas in the professional training of teachers, the new analytical approach to philosophy of education in Britain was bound to appear more revolutionary. All the same, what both American and British approaches to a large extent shared – despite that erosion or narrowing of the gap between conceptual and empirical questions characteristic of modern pragmatist thought[3] – was a certain claim to academic or 'scientific' *neutrality* with regard to normative issues and questions of particular human (moral, political, religious) belief and value. For much of the twentieth century it was common for broadly analytical English-speaking philosophers to hold that their main task was to engage in impartial analyses of concepts, and none of their business – even in such practice- and policy-related fields as ethics, political and social philosophy and philosophy of education – to advocate particular social, moral or other perspectives and policies.

In this respect, however, an important late twentieth-century development in analytical philosophy consisted in the appreciation that any such distinction between conceptual analysis and normative commitment was difficult if not impossible to sustain, and the key episode in this paradigm shift is usually taken to be the 1971 publication of John Rawls' seminal work of moral, social and political philosophy, *A Theory of Justice*.[4] In this work, Rawls undertook the rational defence of a particular normative order – essentially an egalitarian version of liberal democracy influenced heavily by Kant and classical liberal theory – in a manner previously declared out of bounds by modern conceptual analysts. By the time Rawls' work appeared, however, postwar analytical philosophy of education was also having trouble observing any purported distinction between conceptual analysis and normative commitment – not least in persuading other educational theorists and policy makers to accept the premises, arguments and conclusions of educational philosophers as the 'value-neutral' deliverences of completely impartial analysis. Indeed, the ideological roots of much if not most Anglophone educational philosophy (as, indeed, of much analytical philosophy of the time) in the moral and political perspectives of the high enlightenment – especially, again, in the ideas of Kant and Mill – were already fairly evident from the outset. In addition, as already noted, many postwar analytical educational philosophers drew heavily upon the (broadly conservative) educational ideas of such nineteenth-century liberal educationalists as Matthew Arnold who regarded education as a matter of the preservation and maintainance of (high) culture via the promotion of open and critical liberal-democratic inquiry. Hence, the new analytical philosophy of education was for the most part a liberalised form of educational traditionalism that regarded the development of individual rational autonomy – the promotion of a responsibly critical stance to received traditions and values – as the principal goal of education. But although there can be little doubt that this conception of education was at the time propounded with a degree of breezy confidence that disinterested conceptual analysis had shown it to be the *only* rationally defensible educational position, the basic ideological presuppositions of the view were not slow to attract criticism.

In some respects, I do not believe that early radical criticisms to the effect that liberal traditionalism was *elitist* – that, for example, the forms of knowledge thesis was little more than a justification of the traditional grammar school curriculum – entirely hit the mark.[5] If anything, postwar analytical philosophers of schooling and curriculum inclined to a fairly *egalitarian* view of educational provision: the new liberal traditionalism departed significantly from previous class-based forms of traditionalism – and was, at least in principle, not inconsistent with the aims of comprehensive or non-selective schooling for all.[6] That said, it was soon evident that analytical educational philosophers were significantly divided among themselves concerning the proper direction of educational policy – and that any differences of view here were the consequences not merely of philosophical disputes about the meaning of concepts, but of diverse evaluative or *normative* preferences: just like ordinary people, philosophers of education subscribed to particular *values* as conservatives, socialists, liberals, Marxists, Roman Catholics, Protestants, Jews, atheists, humanists, feminists, Freudians, Darwinians, and so on. From this viewpoint, drawing on different cultural and intellectual traditions, it was clear that they could disagree profoundly about the *justice* or effectiveness of comprehensive schooling, the appropriateness or otherwise of teaching on homosexuality in schools, or the rights and wrongs of mixed-gender classes in football without necessarily disagreeing significantly about the *meaning* of any of the key terms in normative debates.

All the same, the value-implicated nature of such disagreements were to become much clearer in the wake of Rawls' philosophical reinstatement of normative inquiry in 1971. The most immediate criticisms of Rawls hailed from other analytical philosophers who shared his commitment to liberalism but rejected the egalitarian (Kantian) dimensions of his concept of justice.[7] But rather more radical criticisms – in the name of a *communitarianism* that questioned some of the key assumptions of liberalism itself – emerged largely from the 1981 publication of Alasdair MacIntyre's *After Virtue*.[8] In this work, MacIntyre (soon to be followed by many other influential philosophers) appeared to question – in a way that strikingly recapitulated the criticisms of Kant of nineteenth-century idealists – the very possibility of discerning culture-free conceptions of justice and rationality of the kind upon which much liberal theory appeared to rest. Indeed, it was MacIntyre's work that largely initiated the long-running modern moral, social and political debate between liberals and communitarians, which is only now showing signs of running out of steam.[9] However, since the impact upon contemporary educational philosophy of this debate has been as considerable as its significance for moral, social and political philosophy in general, we shall devote the present chapter: first, to an examination of the liberal–communitarian dichotomy as such; secondly, to a brief account of the basic form and structure of liberal and liberal educational theory. We shall then proceed, in the following chapter, to a closer analysis of the communitarian response to the liberal perspective, and to some exploration of its educational implications.

Varieties of liberalism and communitarianism

After many years of heated controversy, it would appear that any distinction between liberalism and communitarianism is not just complex, but also a potential source of serious confusions: indeed, I suspect that this contrast or dichotomy is implicated in two rather different philosophical distinctions. The first of these is a (perhaps metaphysical) distinction between different conceptions of the relationship of the individual to society. One time-honoured way of conceiving this relationship – most typical perhaps of the atomistic analyses of empiricism – is to explain (or explain away) society in terms of individual membership: in short, to regard society as neither more nor less than a collection of individuals. This is basically the analysis of society offered by the great English political theorist Thomas Hobbes in his pioneering work of social contract theory, *Leviathan*,[10] but it would also appear to be the view of society implicit in the famous (or infamous) observation of the British neo-liberal Prime Minister Margaret Thatcher that 'there is no such thing as society' (as distinct from, we were presumably meant to infer, individuals and individual interests). However, the equally time-honoured alternative to any such view is to hold that it is hardly possible to make sense of individual human personhood apart from its socio-cultural associations: on this view, since the very idea of individual personality is normatively weighted – to be a person is to be a particular bearer of shared and inherited social values, virtues, beliefs and interests – there can be no real personal identity apart from society. In this respect, those reared apart from society or otherwise deprived of the knowledge and values enshrined in a particular socially constituted language and culture may be (biologically) human, but they hardly qualify as *persons* in the normatively implicated sense of that term that we outlined in the first chapter of this work. This position has also been upheld in one form or another by some distinguished past philosophers. Some such view seems to have been held by Aristotle (among perhaps other ancient Greek philosophers) and – as we have seen – it was to find a powerful voice in the nineteenth-century idealist reaction to Kantian rational universalism of such otherwise diverse philosophers as Hegel and Marx. Both Hegel and Marx appear to have thought that human ideas and values are the products of gradual social or cultural evolution, and that individual agents are best understood as participants in, contributors to and bearers of such socially constituted ideas and values. As Marx pointedly put it: '[I]t is not the consciousness of men that determines their being, but, on the contrary, their social being that determines their consciousness.'[11]

Another contrast between liberalism and communitarianism, however, seems to reflect more of a *normative* distinction between different conceptions of the sources and legitimacy of moral and political authority. The basic difference here is between views that take the collective to have moral and/or political authority over the individual, or which put the individual at the service of the state, and those that assert the authority of the individual over the collective, or which regard the state as essentially in the service of the individual. Above all, however, it is important to be clear that these two distinctions are not co-extensive. To be sure, it would appear that some who have held individuality to be socially constructed have also been political collectivists: both Hegel and Marx, for example, held (in different ways) that individuality is socio-culturally constituted, and that individuals *should* be subject to the authority of the collective. Likewise, some political champions of individual rights and freedoms over state control and interference have also exhibited marked tendencies towards 'metaphysical' or explanatory individualism: largely true to its empiricist origins, for example, the political individualism of classical liberal theory often seems to have assumed the metaphysical priority of the individual over the collective – and, as we have seen, Thatcherite neo-liberals have insisted that society is essentially a metaphysical fiction. But there is also ample evidence from past social and political theory that these different distinctions between liberalism and communitarianism do not always coincide in this fashion. To begin with, as a clear enough metaphysical individualist, Hobbes was nevertheless a believer in the authority of the state over the individual: so, although he could hardly be regarded as a metaphysical or political communitarian – since moral and political power was also for him to be invested in an absolute sovereign whose authority was supposed to extend over individual and community alike – he was just as certainly no liberal either.

More significantly, however, Aristotle seems the best case of a philosopher who subscribes to the metaphysical priority of society and culture over the individual, but, on the other hand (apparently unlike Plato), regarded the state as essentially in the service of individuals rather than vice versa – offering an (albeit limited) defence of individual freedom over imposed authority.[12] To be sure, given the immense inequalities and unfreedoms (of class, wealth, gender, and so on) he was prepared to tolerate, it would be hard to regard Aristotle as a liberal in any contemporary sense of this term, but his work makes it reasonably clear that any political assertion of individual rights and autonomy over state or collective control is not *inherently* at odds with endorsement of a socio-culturally conditioned conception of individual personhood. Moreover, it would seem that separating these two rather different ways of thinking about the relationship of the individual to the collective may help to expose some possible confusions in latter-day accounts of the liberal–communitarian issue. For liberalism seems above all to be an essentially *political* perspective that is as such mainly concerned to uphold the rights and freedoms of individuals against undue state interference and control – and although it has to some extent been historically associated with atomist or metaphysically reductive analyses of society, there seem to be no necessary grounds for any such association. On the other hand, it would seem to be the main concern of communitarian perspectives to identify a particular view of the *formation* of human identity and values, and – although some such view has often been associated with extreme collectivist politics of Hegelian, Marxist and Platonic kinds (although it is also uncertain where Plato stood on the question of the priority or otherwise of society and culture over human individuality) – it is not at all clear that communitarianism would have to be committed to *any* specific, either totalitarian or liberal-democratic, set of political principles or procedures.

That said, the communitarian idea that human motives, beliefs and values are products of specific socio-cultural inheritances and traditions would appear to raise significant difficulties for liberal democracy in the predominantly diverse cultural contexts of modern developed economies. On the face of it, there would appear to be less of a problem reconciling the idea of individual liberty with that of cultural conditioning in circumstances of Aristotelian polity, where different members of the democratic assembly might nevertheless be expected to share a common set of social aims and values: in such circumstances, political disagreement is more likely to be about the appropriate means to achieve a given end (of wealth production or martial success) than over the moral status of a given aim or value – and, indeed, this observation sits fairly comfortably with Aristotle's own explicit claim in the *Nicomachean Ethics* that moral deliberation is primarily about *means* to the proper achievement of generally agreed goals.[13] To be sure, ancient Athenian democracy with its characteristic emphasis on individual liberty (over, for example, equality) was forged in the fires of a struggle for independence (in company with other Greek city states) against the oriental despotism of its powerful Persian neighbour. In this regard, Aeschylus' poetic masterpiece on the Promethean theme[14] – dealing, as it does, with the defiance of Zeus by the titan Prometheus – is at once a potent symbol of collective national resistance to external (colonial) domination, and a celebration of

(Athenian) democratic liberty over any internal (state) despotism. But the first stirrings of liberal democracy in modern western Europe – under the influence of such early to mid-enlightenment philosophers as Locke and Rousseau – are addressed to a rather different set of social pressures and challenges. Indeed, enlightenment champions of liberal democracy seem concerned more with the internal threat of social breakdown in the face of deep divisions of belief and value within the same nations or communities than with any external threat of cultural or socio-political colonialism. The widespread religious and political strife that followed in the wake of the second great Christian religious schism of the European Reformation was to shake the foundations of social order in many leading western centres of civilisation in a way that called for profound reassessment of the rational basis of civil order.

The origins of liberalism

Indeed, it was just one such post-Reformation civil upheaval that led the English political philosopher Thomas Hobbes to argue that imposed state control in the form of an absolute sovereign was the only way to guarantee social order, and resolve the deep differences of value and interest that could only be expected to arise between individuals or particular social constituences in the essentially artificial human condition of civil society. For Hobbes, the natural state of human existence – what he calls the 'state of nature' – is a state of complete individual liberty in which men are pitted against one another in ruthless competition for scarce survival-enhancing resources: life in a state of nature is thus 'a war of all against all' and human prospects are generally 'solitary, poor, nasty, brutish and short'.[15] Hence, in the interests of social harmony and security, it came to seem advantageous for men to agree to give up certain of their 'natural' entitlements to liberty and freedom of expression (which Hobbes mostly considered to be inherently divisive and anti-social), and submit to the protection of coercively controlling laws: civil security could only be purchased at the price of freedom – a freedom that, however, Hobbes considered to be little more than a recipe for anarchy. Moreover, for Hobbes, insofar as even tyranny and despotism could never be worse than anarchy, it could never be reasonable or rational to rebel against or overthrow the sovereign source and guarantor of civil law and order.

However, as the first great modern advocate of liberalism, John Locke is concerned – precisely in the name of individual liberty and freedom of belief and conscience – to oppose just this view: indeed, he seems much concerned to find rational ground for final revolutionary disposal of what he took to be the royal tyranny of his day.[16] To this end, he attacks the theory of the divine (ecclesiologically sanctioned) right of kings beneath which such tyranny often appeared to take refuge. From a liberal viewpoint, indeed, the dubious alliance of state with church (either Protestant of Catholic) all too often served as a pretext for the official persecution, by followers of the current state orthodoxy, of so-called 'religious heretics' on the 'wrong' side of the confessional fence. Above all, however, in the spirit of an older tradition of English parliamentary democracy, Locke argues that government can only be considered legitimate insofar as it has popular consent, that a condition of such consent is respect for individual freedom, and that among the most important liberties that the state should be concerned to protect is that of (religious and other) faith and conscience. In short, unlike Hobbes, who believes that the principal role of absolute sovereignty is to curtail individual freedom, Locke holds that it is the task of the state to enable freedom of thought and expression, and to constrain only those expressions of (religious or other) bigotry that would seek to deny freedom of belief to others. On this view, liberal democracy may largely be conceived as a political mechanism for the peaceful negotiation of value diversity and conflict.

But such a view also raises large questions about the rational or other basis of any such negotiation. In this respect, Hobbes seems close enough to the mark in holding that civil order rests upon the rule of law, and that any such law must depend upon a degree of rational consensus about what is and is not legally permissible. But what could be the basis of any such rational consensus in circumstances in which people are deeply divided – perhaps to the point of mutual *opposition* – in their values? It appears that Locke located such consensus in the idea that there are natural human *rights* that: (i) stem from the idea of common humanity; (ii) cut across any and all human differences; and (iii) must therefore command the attention and respect of any rational legislation. Indeed, as one of the great intellectual influences on the American revolution, Locke's views are clearly reflected in the American constitutional asseveration that all citizens have the right to life, liberty and the pursuit of happiness. But conceptual difficulties about talk of human rights notwithstanding (the nineteenth-century English jusrisprudent Jeremy Bentham referred to rights as 'nonsense on stilts'[17]), there is the obvious difficulty that proposed rights can conflict. As well as hearing of the right to life of the unborn child, one may also hear of a mother's right to pursue happiness unencumbered by an unwanted pregnancy – rights to which it is practically impossible to accord simultaneous respect in many actual circumstances. Moreover, most culturally plural contexts will contain not just religious (and other) believers in the priority of the child's right to life over (if it comes to a choice of one or the other) the mother's right to pursue her own well-being and happiness, but also those (champions of the so-called 'right to choice') who hold quite the opposite view. How might such conflicts possibly be legally settled or negotiated in a way that would satisfy these conflicting interests? Indeed, the trouble with any and all general claims to human rights of life, liberty and happiness is that such entitlements would appear to be based upon contingent and far from self-evident or self-justifying features or characteristics of human nature. In addition, it seems less than clear where any list of such rights might be supposed to begin or end: in addition to the right to liberty, are there also rights to a minimum wage, nursery education or a sexual partner? Hence, in default of more substantial normative grounding, it is difficult to see how any such rights-based claims might cut much ice with respect to the framing of public policy and legislation.

Rights and duties

However, it has been also been common for moral and social theorists to regard rights as correlative to or interdefinable with *duties* (a duty may be formally defined as no right not to do so and so, and a right as no duty to prevent this or that[18]): on this view, it is possible to claim entitlement only to those benefits that also incur corresponding responsibilities or obligations. Some theorists, of course, have (like Locke) regarded rights as the more basic and have sought to ground duties in the recognition of these: hence, if there is a right to human freedom, then others have a duty to respect it, and there is a *prima facie* case for legal protection of such a right. But it is also possible (and perhaps more plausible) to reverse the order of derivation here, precisely by regarding rights as consequent upon duties. This is the approach of so-called *deontology*, and the strategy adopted by both Rousseau and Kant.[19] The key insight of Rousseau, as previously seen, is that the very notion of human (practical) reason is predicated upon that of a universal moral law. According to this view, any rational or consistent exercise of practical deliberation requires that we regard others (with respect, say, to some social policy) as equal to ourselves, unless there is some morally appropriate reason for treating them differently (in which case the onus is upon those who would discriminate to justify any suggested differential treatment – presumably on the grounds that such treatment conduces, if not to the actual benefit of those prone to such discrimination, then at least to the greater good of the community as a whole). At all events, the key point here is that equal respect is not to be regarded as a right in view of some contingent feature of human nature: human agents are not equal as a matter of *fact*, but only in virtue of some formal recognition of a practical *obligation* to treat others equally.

But upon what might any such obligation be based? The deontological view would appear to be that it rests upon recognising: (i) that I cannot *consistently* deny to others any benefits that I would expect them to extend to me; and (ii) that it is therefore (correspondingly) reasonable to extend to others any benefits that they would rationally extend to me. Of course, this does not apply to all desires, expectations or benefits – for there are many personal tastes and interests that I would not expect others to share. The key test here, as Kant makes clear, lies in the extent to which particular wants, expectations and benefits are susceptible of rational generalisation or *universalisation*. From this viewpoint, there are clearly goods I desire – for example, liberty and freedom from (sexual, racial or religious) discrimination or harassment – that I cannot reasonably or *rationally* expect to be respected by others without also incurring some reciprocal obligation to respect their own interest in such benefits. Thus, although it is proper in this light for me to speak of a *right* to freedom or equal treatment, any claim to such a right is entirely dependent upon my recognition of a corresponding *duty* to respect the right of others to such freedom – and, apart from such recognition, any and all such claims to rights must be void. Rousseau's ethics of universal moral duty can also be regarded – like the more natural rights of Locke and others – as basically a response to Hobbes' claim that freedom undermines security: since, for Rousseau, any just polity depends upon the free recognition of its citizens of a duty to respect the freedom and equality of others, there may be no legitimate civil legislation in the absence of either the individual self-rule of autonomy or the rule by popular consent of democracy. At the same time, however, Rousseau's deontology may appear to license a much more interventionist conception of the role of the state than one finds in Locke. Whereas, for Locke, the state exists to perform the largely negative function of promoting individual liberty, the state for Rousseau has a much more positive duty – as the voice of genuine democratic will – to promote justice as equality and reduce differences of wealth and status. Hence, whereas Locke's ideas find expression in the more laissez-faire, enterprise and not notably egalitarian culture of post-revolutionary America, Rousseau's philosophy was to yield more bitter harvest in the bloody levelling aftermath of post-revolutionary France.

All the same, it is not implausible to construe modern liberal democracy as an attempt to combine the minimalist and non-interventionist Lockian notion of the state as the custodian of human freedom with a more Rousseauian conception of human rights or liberties as grounded in or legitimated by more general or formal rational principles concerned as much with common as with individual benefit. In this light, any feasible conception of human autonomy or citizenship would need to embody some appreciation of the social duties and responsibilities upon which any and all individual rights and entitlements depend. To this end, indeed, more recent liberalism has usually been a cocktail of the central ideas of the great nineteenth-century heirs to Locke's liberal empiricism – notably those of the high priest of liberalism, John Stuart Mill – and (some version of) that ethics of deontology distilled by Kant from the social, political and educational philosophy of Rousseau. The key liberal ingredient is, of course, the pivotal idea of Mill's essay *On Liberty*, that respect for individual liberty is the only reasonable basis of democratic polity: that the only legitimate reason for denying freedom of thought or action to anyone is potential harm to others – and, of course, Mill's liberalism is also underpinned by a *utilitarian* ethics which makes promotion of happiness and prevention of harm to others the cornerstone of morality.[20] All the same, many modern liberals have regarded utilitarianism – which bases morality mainly on the idea of universal human benevolence – as an excessively austere and demanding ethics, which is also a source of deeply intractable moral dilemmas and paradoxes.[21] For this reason, more recent social and political theorists in the modern liberal mainstream have often turned to some version of (Kantian) deontology in the search for a principled basis for political liberalism.

On the face of it, however, there are reasons why Kant's ethics may seem to provide unpromising support for a liberal social and political theory – and it is easy to see why Mill was himself far from sympathetic to it.[22] First, as a radical empiricist, Mill was bound to find the rationalist metaphysics of Kant's account deeply uncongenial. As already seen, Kant's moral (categorical) imperatives are held to be logically grounded in or derived from certain formal features of moral reasoning alone, and do not depend for their truth or validity on any contingent features of human experience – either upon natural human motives (since it is not feeling that makes my actions good), or upon the consequences of actions for the weal or woe of others (since it is not how things turn out that makes my action good). Hence, Mill's utilitarian attempt to define moral action squarely in terms of *empirical* consequences stands in marked opposition to any such account. But secondly, although a philosopher as mild-mannered as Kant could hardly be accused of fomenting bloody revolution – and he did explicitly part company from some radical features of Rousseau's social, political and educational philosophy[23] – there are egalitarian tendencies in Kant's ethics that might well license rather illiberal and interventionist public policies with respect to welfare and education. Modern liberals are not notably well disposed to politically interventionist attempts to reduce wealth and status – especially if this involves undue constraint or inhibition of the (perhaps wealth-producing) activities of more able and talented members of society: thus, for example, if any overarching Kantian principle of respect for persons demanded strict equality of opportunity for all children in a non-selective system, many modern liberals might object to this on the grounds: (i) that it involves a denial of the right of parents to educate their children as they please; and (ii) that the educational levelling involved in any such procedure might well impede or disadvantage more able children. Arguably, then, any appropriation of Kant for the purposes of liberal theory would appear to require its adjustment in two fundamental respects: first, it must be purged of its deeply metaphysical and non-empirical character; secondly, the more problematic egalitarian features of deontology may need modification or dilution in a more conspicuously liberal direction.

Liberalism, morality and objectivity

By far the most impressive attempt to square liberal theory with a Kantian ethics – one whose influence, indeed, would be hard to exaggerate – is that of John Rawls in his widely influential 1971 work *A Theory of Justice*. Rawls' attempt to deal with the rationalist metaphysics of Kant's ethics is not in itself notably innovative – drawing as it does on one of two common strategies for non-metaphysical or empiricist interpretation of Kant's ethical ideas. The main trouble is that Kant, not unlike Plato, aspires to an *absolute* conception of moral judgement as characterised by complete objectivity and certainty. Since moral agency needs as a matter of practical fact to be *motivated*, but no unsullied moral objectivity can be found in the empirical realm of allegedly self-interested human motives, Kant locates the source of moral imperatives in a non-empirical metaphysical self (the *noumenal* self) that is essentially a construct of pure (practical) reason: moral objectivity is thus for Kant a matter of *non-empirical* recognition of the compelling force of certain exceptionless rules or principles. However, like Plato's similarly motivated theory of forms, such moral certainty and objectivity is purchased only at the high price of metaphysical implausibility and practical inutility: in the last analysis, there is no reason to believe that any such metaphysical self exists, and it could have little human interest or value in the inherently practical rough and tumble of moral experience even if it did. In this light, the best prospects for Kant's theory would seem to lie in reinterpreting it in more empirically plausible terms. In this connection, it seems possible to construe the key idea – that morality involves rules that are *universalisable* – in one or the other of two principal ways. The first of these recognises that moral agents characteristically act on the basis of principles to which they are *committed*. But if one repudiates the Kantian metaphysical self of principles that are *as such* universalisable, one is forced to recognise that different empirical experiences may lead equally committed moral agents to universalise diverse and often mutually contradictory principles. This is largely the view of morality of so-called *prescriptivists* (or 'non-cognitivists') – as well as of basic Kohlbergian moral developmental theory:[24] on this perspective, as a matter of consistent self-legislation, morality is (for the agent) *universal*, but it is not in any substantial sense *objective*, since it rests ultimately on personal (if not subjective) preference and inclination.

As we saw in chapter 5, however, the other common move is to abandon any unqualified Kantian universalisability of moral principles in the interests of a certain (limited) *objectivity*. In effect, this involves construing Kantian universals not as principled personal commitments, but as *social* laws and rules: this is essentially the time-honoured approach of *contractualism*. The idea is not especially new to modern analytical moral, social and political theory: in fact, one of the earliest attempts to offer an explicitly contractualist interpretation of Kant's ethics is to be found in a pioneering work on moral education by the great French sociologist Émile Durkheim.[25] Indeed, Durkheim argued in a very anti-metaphysical way that the job of educationalists in secular societies should be to foster the same reverence for the contractually conceived social rules – the democratically determined laws and principles of social order and cohesion – that teachers in traditional religious social contexts had formerly encouraged towards God: critical obedience to the rules of social contract was to be the main aim of moral education. But, of course, although any such contractualist reconstrual of Kant secures a certain *objectivity* for categorical or other interpersonal imperatives, it gains this at the price of absolute universalisability. If I live in a society which legislates that drivers should keep to the right side of the road, it is *objectively* rational (in the interests of everyone's safety) for me to comply; but, of course, insofar as I may at some point move to a society where I am required to drive on the left, there is also a certain social *relativity* to the rules. At all events, a key strategy of Rawls' project would appear to involve the reinterpretation of Kantian universals in something like contractualist terms: from the perspective of overall social and political justice the basic rules we need to establish are those that enable us to live together in relative peace, harmony and cooperation – despite the differences of personal value and particular interest that all too often threaten to divide us.

However, since the citizens of modern culturally plural liberal democracies do differ in the potentially divisive respects of religion, class, race, gender, sexuality, and so on, the key problem for a contractarian ethics is to devise a set of generally compelling social rules – rules that can command universal or at least majority allegiance in a given social context – that, on the one hand, are substantive enough to secure civil order and security, and that, on the other, avoid illiberal restrictions of individual freedom: whereas too much legislation and regulation heralds the injustice of state tyranny, the absence of common rules threatens the injustice of dog-eat-dog anarchy. Utilitarian legislation seems an unpromising strategy in this regard, since it is difficult – in the face of plural and competing conceptions of human worth and flourishing – to sum human benefit in anything more than a majoritarian way. Can a Kantian ethics do any better? For Rawls and other deontologists, the prime ethical significance of the Kantian routing of objectivity through the idea of universalisability lies in the appeal to *impartiality*: the point of deontological universalisation is that it seems to provide a way of regarding each and every person without fear or favour. On the other hand, treating everyone impartially in the real world – irrespective of different means, status and needs – does all too often seem to involve treating some unjustly. In view of this, can Kantian universality of impartiality be interpreted in such a way as to avoid insensitive generalisation? It is very much in response to this problem that Rawls introduces his ideas of the original position and the veil of ignorance.[26] He asks us to suppose ourselves in the position of not yet knowing what the circumstances of our birth and life are likely to be – whether we are going to be intelligent or stupid, rich or poor, black or white, male or female. In such conditions, what would it be *rational* to legislate for in terms of just social and public policy? The key claim here is that it would make best sense to aim for a set of policies that strike a balance between further disadvantaging or undermining the well-being and security of the least advantaged without curtailing the freedom and prospects for further development of the advantaged. If I am to be born rich and intelligent, I may expect to make some contribution (through taxes and so on) to helping the less well off – so long as this does not unduly undermine just those liberties and prospects upon which my effective contribution to the common good depends. On the other hand, however, if I am to be a poor person of few talents I would hope to be safeguarded from further disadvantage and/or oppression – not least that which might follow in the wake of further advantaging the already privileged. In short, as both Rousseau and Kant essentially argued, the best possible social order is that which promotes individual autonomy to pursue the *common good* to the best of natural personal endowment: such a social order would also be an essentially liberal-democratic polity constructed upon the legislative deliverences of impartial moral deliberation.

Liberalism and liberal education

In retrospect, it is clear that the new philosophy of education of the early postwar period – whether it hailed from American pragmatist or British 'ordinary language' sources – promoted a view of education for all that was broadly committed to a liberal-democratic social theory along some such lines. The key aim of such education was an enlightenment notion of self-government strongly patterned on Kant's conception of moral autonomy – though by no means exclusively concentrated upon moral agency. It seems to have been generally held that via a fairly traditional initiation into the various modes of human inquiry of (for example) forms of knowledge epistemology, individuals might be equipped with the rational capacities for judicious post-school roles and choices as citizens, workers, friends, spouses and parents. In this respect, many new liberal traditionalists could be regarded as heirs to that nineteenth-century conception of liberal education to be found in the work of Arnold, Newman and others. The basic goal of education, on this view, was the production of a community of rationally emancipated individuals, possessed not only of the self-knowledge required for sensible personal choices in the interests of individual flourishing, but also of the capacity for civilised cooperation with others towards the common good. Although such an ideal would not have to be secular, for it would certainly be possible for rational individuals to be religious believers, a feature of *rational* religious commitment would be a clear appreciation not only of the non-scientific expressive or aesthetic status of religious belief, but also of the impropriety of basing public policies upon the more particular (cultural and/or personal) religious values, commitments and preferences of this or that community of faith. In this respect, a good religious education would enable believers to distinguish the chalk of personal or collective religious faith from the cheese of provable scientific fact. To this end, a clear (Kantian) distinction would need to be observed between the claims of personal faith and those more general requirements of practical (moral) reason upon which wider public policy might be based.

However, on this new enlightenment view, such secularised morality comes down to little more than one or the other (or some unstable combination) of the two modern reinterpretations of Kant lately considered: in short, morality is a matter either of observance of rational democratic consensus, or of consistent commitment to self-accepted principles. Moreover, these two modern recon-struals of Kant would appear to be combined in the most influential postwar theory of moral education. On the Kohlbergian view, moral maturity is basically a question of consistent obedience to self-legislated principles, but (presumably) in those circumstances in which my personal commitments conflict with those of others, the gap between my interests or commitments and those of others is subject to a process of democratic negotiation in which the overall good of the community is decided by rational consensus. Thus, for Kohlberg, deciding what is morally appropriate on a given occasion is a matter of largely Rawlsian reflec-tive equilibrium between personal principled commitment and the consensus of the 'community of justice'; but it would also appear to be a matter in which the consensual outcomes of democratic process have, in the interests of civil law and order, very much the casting vote. At all events, Kohlberg's view was in its heyday widely endorsed by educational philosophers as well as by social scien-tists, and one may also discern the general form of a rather similar liberalised Kantianism in the moral educational accounts of leading postwar educational philosophers. For example, despite his significant sympathies with an Aristotelian moral psychology and pedagogy, the principal pioneer of British analytical educational philosophy, R.S. Peters, was evidently disposed to a fairly unrecon-structed form of Kantian deontology in his writings on moral education, and the same ethics of duty and right is also apparent in his work on liberal democratic principles and polity.[27] Again, it is plausible to interpret the moral 'form of knowledge' of forms of knowledge epistemology as a form of of post-Kantian prescriptivism, and some related work on secular morality was clearly motivated by a concern to decouple morality from religion in view of the wider uses to which such a secular consensual rather than religious morality might be put for liberal-democratic purposes.[28] On the whole, then, the new liberal educational vision is one of (at least potential) neo-enlightenment sweetness and light: the world of liberal educational traditionalism is one in which the lion of social divi-sion shall lay down with the lamb of toleration, the swords of intercultural conflict will be beaten into the ploughshares of common social purpose, and we shall study sectarian strife no more.

All the same, the great – for many the *divine* – founder of Christianity is also source of the highly illiberal claim that He came to bring not peace but a sword.[29] Behind this unsettling pronouncement lies the idea of a divine truth and judgement that is not at all a matter of rational democratic *consensus*. Indeed, if there is any such thing as moral truth – as, of course, Kant was not the only great enlightenment philosopher (in his own way) to hold – then why should we suppose it to be established by consensus? Why, more particularly, should we hold that if there is conflict between our consistent commitments and majority will, it is the court of general consensus that has the casting vote? Indeed, it seems a particular difficulty for a view such as Kohlberg's – which appears to hold that legitimate moral verdicts are available on the basis of *both* personal universalisation *and* democratic consensus – that it offers us no plausible rational procedure for preferring one verdict to another in the event of conflict.[30] Suppose, for example, that from the premises that murder is wrong and abortion is murder I universalise to a strong pro-life position on abortion – but that it is nevertheless the majority opinion in my social context that abortion should be available on demand: it would surely be extraordinary for me to accept this judgement as decisive merely on majoritarian grounds – and, if I do not accept it as decisive, it is just as surely not inappropriate for me to reject the authority of my community and to campaign against pro-abortion legislation. Indeed, are we not nowadays largely sympathetic to the civil rights workers who protested on the basis of personal conscience against the consensually established racist legis-lation of American southern states?

The point here, of course, is not that it would ever be appropriate to engage in unlawful violent or non-democratic methods of protest against public policies with which we disagree – though it is also clear that individuals and groups have formerly had to resort to such methods of overcoming serious injustice when more rational means of persuasion proved to no avail. Political and civil legisla-tion is inevitably a matter of hard compromise: hence, since it is impossible to please all of the people all of the time, it may be necessary in contexts of serious value conflict to accept that democratic consensus must prevail in the greater interests of social harmony and security – and it will almost always be preferable to seek to reform public policy by non-violent and democratic rather than violent or coercive means. From this viewpoint, the politics of consensus may be regarded as the pragmatic best of a bad job. That said, a key issue of present concern is whether it is proper to model *education* in moral or other aspects of human development on any such approach to the resolution of value conflicts. What is of most value about liberal-democratic consensus is that it rightly holds that individuals are entitled not only to their own opinions, and to the proper political expression of such opinions through democratic procedures, but also to proper protection of this right from the persecution of others who may not share them – even if (perhaps especially if) those others form a significant majority. From an educational viewpoint, however, it is arguable that liberal-democratic thinking courts confusion between the moral legitimacy of a given view, on the one hand, and (either or both of) individual entitlement to hold that view or its apparent social consensual warrant, on the other. The fact that I know something to be right does not mean (as Plato and some theocratic and other societies seem to have held) that I am justified in requiring that others hold it too; but nor does the fact that I adopt a belief as a matter of consistent rational principle, or that it is held by most of the members of my society, mean that it is *true*. There is massive confusion about this issue in contemporary educational theorising – as well as much evidence that this confusion has spilled over into official policy making with regard to moral, social and citizenship education.[31] Hence, although almost everything remains to be understood about the proper nature and direction of moral education – and we shall continue to pursue this vexed issue in later chapters – we should at least be clear that modern liberal notions of individual entitlement and democratic consensus provide far from sure grounds for moral knowledge and truth.

Possible tasks

(1) Try to identify what might constitute a reasonable set of aims for a broadly liberal education in a culturally pluralist democratic society. Consider which school subjects or forms of study you would regard as appropriate for inclusion in a liberal curriculum, and which kinds of study you would not regard as appropriate.

(2) Consider some of the possible difficulties or drawbacks inherent in any attempt to conceive individual education or formation as a matter of initiation into fundamentally liberal-democratic principles of human association.

Chapter 12

Community, identity and cultural inheritance

Problems with liberal traditionalism

At the outset of the previous chapter, we acknowledged some difficulties about any strict conception of educational philosophy as 'conceptual analysis'. Indeed, a general problem with much early postwar analytical philosophy of education may be reflected in the titles of many essays of the period that proposed to undertake analyses of 'the' concept of education (or autonomy or indoctrination or whatever). In the light of already noted instabilities of sense to which familiar concepts of education and teaching are prone, one might well question whether it is at all reasonable to look for a single unitary or uncontestable account of this or that educational notion. On the other hand, any such point needs handling with caution. It would be clearly absurd to maintain (as sometimes nevertheless seems to have been held) that there is *nothing* of general interest to be said about concepts of education, teaching and learning as such – and, indeed, we have sought to identify interesting generalities of this kind in this work. For one thing, it could not make much sense to claim that concepts of education and teaching are utterly disparate, or entirely devoid of *any* common features: if this were so, we could have little reason for regarding diverse accounts of education *as* nevertheless conceptions *of* education. Secondly, as we have elsewhere tried to show, it is important to appreciate that social scientists have proposed some highly revisionary causal accounts of education and learning that need to be exposed as distortive of such notions *per se*.

That said, beyond a certain level of formal generality, it is clear there are substantially different conceptions of learning and education. Hence, for example, although professional educational theorists and policy makers may need to appreciate that *any* meaningful conception of *education* – as opposed to habituation, indoctrination or whatever – should aspire to the promotion of *understanding* as well as behavioural competence, they also have to decide what to include in and what to exclude from the curriculum on the basis of evaluative judgements and preferences that would seem to transcend any formal analysis of 'the' concept of education. It is at just this point that we may feel forced to conclude that we cannot sensibly continue to talk of 'the' – only of 'which', or perhaps 'whose' – concept of education. In this light, what the new liberal traditionalism of analytical educational philosophers of education may have seemed unable to address is a large question about the relationship of education to culture and tradition, which had long been pressing in such other culturally plural liberal democracies as the United States, but which was also coming more to the fore in an increasingly multi-cultural Britain. One significant practical dimension of this problem is that of how a host culture should receive or attempt to accommodate – in educational and other socio-political respects – the different and sometimes conflicting cultural traditions of immigrants and refugees from different parts of the world. In this respect, it is something of a problem that although the educational significance of cultural heritage appears to loom large in the evident emphasis on tradition of liberal traditionalism, the idea of 'tradition' inherent in this notion is nevertheless more formal than substantive. Indeed, although the high priest of modern educational traditionalism, Matthew Arnold, actually defined education as the *transmission of culture*, he also made it quite clear that this should not be taken to mean the transmission of any *actual* culture – the knowledge, beliefs, values and virtues of a particular social group – but rather, as has been noted, the promotion of some (Platonic) educational ideal of 'the best that has been thought and said in the world'.

But this precisely raises the question of the rational grounds for any estimate of this or that curricular content as 'best'. At all events, whether it regards 'the best that has been thought and said' as the scientific, moral, religious and artistic products of western civilisation *as such*, or as simply the most appropriate educational content for (some or other) economically developed western liberal democracy, liberal traditionalism runs into problems. To be sure, it is likely that liberal traditionalism has most often inclined to the first and stronger of these positions: it has all too often been *western* white Anglo-Saxon Protestant science and technology, fine art and liberal-democratic politics that have been upheld as the highest achievements of humanity, and therefore as the most appropriate basis for education – so that if colonials really want a decent education, they would be best advised to apply to Oxbridge. But it should be clear that both the stronger and the weaker construals of liberal traditionalism court a dangerously illiberal cultural colonialism. On the one hand (the stronger position), if the flower of achievement of western culture is the 'best that has been thought and said' *tout court*, then (on the broadly egalitarian educational aspirations of such liberalism) there cannot be much question that it would be unjust to deny its educational benefits, irrespective of other cultural heritage, to any who are intellectually capable of benefiting from it. On the other hand (the weaker position), if the 'best that has been thought and said' is indexed to a particular cultural inheritance, there is no less a presumption in favour of basing education upon such inheritance in any given social context. In that case, if a *liberal* traditionalism is committed to anything, it must surely be to upholding the practices and institutions – of freedom of speech and conscience – of a liberal-democratic society; but how could this be done by teaching the political or religious values and virtues of strict subservience or obedience to authority of some theocratic or otherwise authoritarian cultures? Thus, even if some 'multi-cultural' lip service is paid to the music or art forms of immigrant cultures, a liberal traditionalism cannot be what it is without upholding certain concepts of autonomy and freedom of expression that are deeply subverted in the cultural expressions (even the art and music) of other less liberal or democratic societies. In short, if the liberal-democratic way of life upheld in the liberal traditionalist curriculum is taken to be the only one worth living *as such*, then it may appear to claim in a potentially offensive way that those who live their lives according to other values and principles are living inferior lives. On the other hand, if it claims that it is only *one* kind of life, and that the liberal curriculum is appropriate only to those who want to live that life, then it faces the problem of justifying the provision of that curriculum for general consumption in a culturally plural society where some consumers may have different values.

New philosophical horizons

However, some four decades after the postwar analytical revival of educational philosophy, the world has moved on, and the theoretical perspectives and practical challenges faced by educationalists have inevitably had to move with them. In particular, the rapidly advancing globalisation of economic, intellectual and other human endeavour – accompanied and facilitated by exponential growth in commercial and other human movement around the world and major developments in information technology – has inevitably had some impact upon the intellectual horizons of academic philosophers across the world. In this regard, it may be reasonable to complain of both the main analytical traditions of American pragmatism and British 'ordinary language' philosophy of half a century ago that they were given to a certain high-handed philosophical insularity with respect to philosophical and/or intellectual traditions in other parts of the world: the Atlantic Ocean and English Channel constituted not just geographical but effective intellectual barriers between Anglo-American 'linguistic philosophy' and the apparently different philosophical traditions of continental Europe, Asia and Africa. But many of these European and other philosophical and/or intellectual movements owed much to a nineteenth-century tradition of post-Kantian critique associated with such diverse thinkers as Hegel, Schopenhauer, Marx, Nietzsche and Kierkegaard – most of whom exhibited a broadly 'idealist' concern with questions of the social or *cultural* genesis of human knowledge and understanding. Perhaps first and foremost, as well as directly influencing an important European current of post-Marxist philosophy, Marx also had a profound influence on such influential Frankfurt School 'critical theorists' as Habermas, Adorno and Marcuse.[1] However, Nietzsche and Kierkegaard were to have formative influence on the *phenomenology* and *existentialism*[2] of such philosophers as Heidegger, Sartre, Merleau-Ponty and Gadamer, and on the *post-structuralism* of Derrida, Foucault and Levinas – as well as, beyond these, upon the so-called 'postmodernism' of Lyotard, Baudrillard and others. In addition, some continental philosophers showed strong Freudian attachments and influences,[3] and the work of such European psychological and anthropological structuralists as Piaget and Lévi-Strauss continued to draw inspiration directly from the Kantian tradition.[4]

Despite this, for many Anglo-American analytical philosophers, the main weaknesses of such philosophical traditions lay in their philosophically 'impure' or methodologically eclectic – Marxian, Freudian or other – influences: precisely, they failed to observe crucial distinctions between the *empirical* questions of sociology, psychology, anthropology, and so on, and the *conceptual* questions – questions about the *meaning* of key concepts – that many analytical philosophers took to be the sacred ground of philosophy. To be sure, although radical empiricists as well as pragmatist philosophers in the tradition of Dewey had insisted upon some methodological continuity between philosophical and empirical inquiries, it was still largely a 'dogma' of much Anglo-American lingusitic philosophy – not least of the Oxbridge 'ordinary language' or 'use-theoretical' approaches which had directly informed British and other analytical educational philosophy – that questions of *contingent* fact were essentially distinct from or irrelevant to *analytical* issues about the *meaning* of terms. On this view, no facts about the different ways in which cultures thought or spoke of (say) education and training could be expected in and of themselves to provide any clear appreciation of any *conceptual* distinction between these notions. Hence, while some cultures might run these terms together, either speaking indifferently of the same developmental processes as training or education, or refusing to recognise any distinct concept of education as knowledge-acquisition for its own sake, this would not show that there was *no* intrinsic conceptual distinction between education and training. So, although socially constructed natural language might seem to be the proper place to commence any search for significant semantic distinctions (where else, after all, might one begin?), it could still be held that such distinctions were *discovered* rather than *created* by usage: that, in short, they had a certain inherent quasi-Platonic status which insulated them from the contingencies and idiosyncracies of actual culturally conditioned idiom.

Although, as previously noted, pragmatists had ever been ever inclined to reject this view in one way[5] – attacking the time-honoured empiricist (Humean) distinction between 'necessarily' true definitions ('bachelors are unmarried men') and contingently true factual statements ('bachelors spend less on child-care') – this general perspective was to be even more strongly repudiated by the continental school of philosophy known as 'post-structuralism' or *deconstructionism*. As the name implies, deconstruction involves basic rejection of the Kantian universalism of those linguistic, anthropological and psychological *structuralists* who hold that the apparently diverse culturally conditioned concepts and categories by virtue of which different social constituencies attempt to bring meaning and order to their experience nevertheless have a common and universal basis which reflects the way that *any* coherent understanding *must* go. For example, as already seen, although psychological structuralists such as Piaget and Kohlberg do not deny that different individuals and cultures exalt and celebrate diverse (even contradictorily opposed) values and virtues, they insist that there is nevertheless a common and invariant *form* of moral development, and that the proper goal of moral maturity is in all cases (whether or not a given society recognises this) the achievement of moral *autonomy* defined as the capacity to act impartially on the basis of self-legislated moral principles. In other words, like Kant, they hold that although there is a sense in which our understanding of the world is a mental *construct* – human reason *makes* meaning from the contingent flux of sensory data – the rules (of cause and effect and so on) by which reason finds experience intelligible could not be otherwise than they are if experience is to *be* intelligible at all. This is exactly what post-structuralists, pursuing the method of deconstruction, *deny*. Under the influence of Nietzsche and standing ultimately in an idealist tradition going back to Hegel, such philosophers as Derrida and Foucault have argued that there are no such conceptually necessary conditions of coherent understanding: on the contrary, all human ideas and values are culturally conditioned and have a traceable social history or *genealogy*.[6] Even within a given cultural tradtion, the most basic human notions of person, agency, sexuality, sanity, criminal responsibility, are liable to evolution and re-evaluation, so that we can no longer be sure that these ideas signify for us what they did for our forebears – and, by the same token, we also cannot be sure that these terms will have the same meaning for those who come after us as they have for us. Thus, like pragmatists, post-structuralists – and the so-called 'postmodernists' who have largely ploughed further in these philosophical furrows – appear to deny that there are any conceptual universals or necessities for philosophical analysis to discover.

Now although such views have not been received with unbounded enthusiasm in all contemporary philosophical quarters, it is not hard to see why notions of a generally idealist bent have had no small impact in the spheres of moral, social, political and *educational* theory. For however hard it might be to believe that the conclusions of mathematics or physical science are mere products of social or cultural convention – to hold, for example, that there are no necessities in mathematics, or that scientific explanation might dispense with any notion of causal generality – it may seem plausible to suspect that human conceptions of moral virtue and value might exhibit no such invariance or universality. Indeed, this suspicion would appear to be supported by three interrelated insights upon which we have already drawn in this work. The first of these notions, aired in the first chapter, is that education is best conceived as the development of *persons*, and that the idea of a person stands to be distinguished from that of a human being as a *normative* rather than a biological construct: our understanding of a person is thus essentially that of a human or other agent who is implicated in a complex network of more or less rational institutions and practices. The second idea, extensively aired in part II, is that the epistemic and semantic dispositions or capacities of rational human agency are themselves a function of that rational agency: in short, mind is not *logically* prior to agency, and human persons could not have the mental capacities they have without benefit of practical engagement in interpersonal projects and practices. The third idea, also aired in part II, is that such epistemic and semantic capacities are in some sense (to be clarified) *socially constructed*, and that any human understanding of experience is crucially indexed to socio-culturally determined or conditioned goals and purposes. Moreover, a significant implication of this point is that insofar as such goals and purposes can and do vary with the economic conditions of diverse socio-cultural constituencies, it is possible for human agents to differ – possibly to the point of mutual contradiction – in their conceptions of what is good, worthwhile or true.

The communitarian conception of person and agency

At one level, of course, all of this may seem to revive a perennial complaint – of centuries-old pedigree – against any dualistic (Platonic or Cartesian) conception of mind or reason. In our own day, indeed, this complaint is probably most evident in the persistent objections of contemporary communitarians to the so-called 'view from nowhere'[7] inherent in Rawls' idea of a Kantian practical deliberator concealed behind the veil of ignorance of the 'original position'. Communitarian critics of Rawls and related liberal views reject the very idea that the socially dislocated or disinherited rational choosers apparently presupposed to much liberal theory might be the source of authentic moral values. On the communitarian view, values are identity-constitutive, and one acquires them via social initiation and formation in a particular community of shared belief and practice: we do not choose who we are, and we are never in a position to speculate who we might be as disinterested sources of rational choice. Indeed, it might be said that only a social theory already deeply corrupted by the instrumentalism of rational-economic liberalism could conceive the relationship between value and identity in any such dissociated (more or less Cartesian) way. But such criticisms themselves merely echo the nineteenth-century idealist response to the autonomous rational servant of the moral law of Kantian construction – from which, of course, they also derive direct inspiration. As we saw in part II, Kant's epistemology maintained that if the subjective experiences of agents were to be sources of genuine knowledge, such knowledge claims would need to correspond to an objective reality lying beyond experience which he called the *noumenon* or thing-in-itself. In part I, however, we also explored Kant's claim that for moral judgements to be objective they would have to be grounded in rational principles quite untainted by ordinary empirical human motives and inclinations. But this, for Kant, could only be possible given an 'other-worldly' metaphysical source of such principles – a noumenal *self* – which also belonged to a non-empirical realm.

However, we also saw that nineteenth-century conceptual idealists shrewdly discerned the epistemological redundancy of the idea of the thing-in-itself: after all, what explanatory work might usefully be done in the theory of knowledge by a hypothetical object by definition beyond the reach of experience? But, by the same token, the noumenal self of Kant's ethics – the alleged rational autonomous self underlying empirical character and personality – may seem no less redundant or illusory than the noumenon of his epistemology: there may seem no less reason to doubt that genuine moral agency is grounded in some unobservable metaphysical source of moral spontaneity underlying the self of personal and interpersonal experience. In short, idealists reject a residual strand of Cartesianism in Kant – the idea that the 'real' personality or self is something behind, beyond or above apparently embodied human personality. But, in that event, the real moral experiences of human agents are to be discovered precisely in the empirical rough and tumble of interpersonal relationships and association – and, indeed, we can only make sense of what it *is* to be a moral agent in particular, or a person in general, by reference to immersion in the knowledge, beliefs, values and dispositions of a given community: in short, community needs to be conceived as prior to individuality, rather than as – on Cartesian, empiricist or Kantian views – artificially constructed from relations between metaphysically discrete centres of consciousness, reason or sense.

This is also more or less the Aristotelian position – forged in the fires of reaction to Plato's own rational or metaphysical dualism[8]. Like Kant, Plato sought to secure a certainty, impartiality and purity for moral notions of virtue and justice that he did not regard empirical experience as adequate to ground: since there are no more instances of unsullied virtue and justice in the world of human experience than there are empirical instances of pure redness or circularity, he supposed that our ideas of such things cannot be abstracted from experience and must be derived from some purely rational source of *intelligible* forms. Without denying the appropriateness of any such search for pure Platonic precision in the non-empirical realm of mathematical reasoning, Aristotle held that Plato utterly misconstrued moral life and experience. According to Aristotle, indeed, Plato's main mistake was to conceive moral inquiry on the quite inappropriate model of mathematical reasoning. Unlike the purely intellectual or theoretical world of mathematical precision, the moral realm is concerned with the untidy particularity of human practical affairs. Above all, for Aristotle, moral deliberation should be conceived as a form of essentially *practical* rather than theoretical inquiry, and there are for him several significant consequences of this recognition. First, the primary goal of moral reasoning is not discovery of any sort of *truth* – of, for example, Plato's form or definition of the good – it is rather with the pursuit of moral goodness, specifically with the cultivation of those qualities of character commonly called *virtues*. These, moreover, are practical *dispositions* rather than intellectual capacities, and we recognise virtue in what people *do* rather than in what they know. Secondly, although moral conduct involves a kind of principled reasoning (which Aristotle calls *phronesis*), such reasoning involves proportioning action and judgement to the particular circumstances and demands of a situation, rather than following general rules: thus, as already noted, Aristotle observes (again by way of implicit criticism of Plato's rather indiscriminate theory of justice) that there is potentially as much injustice in treating unequals equally as there is in treating equals unequally. Thirdly, the particularity of moral judgement entails a certain inevitable imprecision or 'more-or-lessness': as noted above, Aristotle also says, 'we should not expect more precision than the nature of the subject matter admits' – since one cannot expect to get things unqualifiably right in the untidy realm of moral response (where, of course, whatever we do is likely to have its practical or moral downside).

In line with such observations, moreover, Aristotle is a (metaphysical) *communitarian* in much the same sense as idealist critics of Kant: that is, he conceives human individuality and personhood as essentially derivative of human association and social engagement. Humans are inherently social animals, and many if not most significant human virtues – such as justice, liberality and courage – are social in character and orientation. It is therefore hardly surprising that despite other significant philosophical differences between Aristotle and modern post-Kantian idealists (Aristotle is not, to be sure, *any* sort of idealist), modern communitarians should have drawn upon both Aristotelian virtue theory and non-realist cultural perspectivalism for inspiration. Indeed, what is sometimes called the 'post-analytical' moral and social philosophy of contemporary communitarians is essentially an attempt to combine Aristotelian ethics and nineteenth-century idealism in the interests of a rather different appreciation from liberal theory of the relationship between individual identity, morality, culture and civil polity. In this connection, the 1981 publication of Alasdair MacIntyre's *After Virtue* – together with the subsequent appearance of *Whose Justice, Which Rationality?* (1987) and *Three Rival Versions of Moral Enquiry* (1992) – constitutes a landmark in postwar moral and social philosophy. Moreover, as a philosopher explicitly interested in educational questions – and who has also written several significant essays on the educational implications of his own brand of non-realist communitarianism[9] – MacIntyre has exercised enormous influence over recent educational philosophy and theory. However, other educationally relevant works along the same broadly Aristotelian and/or idealist communitarian lines have included Charles Taylor's magisterial *Sources of the Self* (1989) and *Multiculturalism* (1992), and (in a more Aristotelian direction) numerous works of Martha Nussbaum, including *The Fragility of Goodness* (1986).[10]

Educational implications of communitarianism

As already indicated, there are significant differences of philosophical view and emphasis between all these writers – which I shall not, in what follows, attempt to explore or pursue. What is needed for present purposes is some idea of the main respects in which this broad current of Aristotelian and idealist communitarian thought is at variance with much of the modernist liberal and liberal educational theorising of the immediate postwar period. To begin with, recalling a theme of the sixth chapter of this work, the claim that there is no pre-social or cultural self of the kind entertained (in albeit rather different senses) by Descartes, Kant and some modern liberals points to the dubiety of any culture-free conception of human learning, knowledge-acquisition or development of the kind for which much modern empirical psychology has apparently sought. If human personal identity is largely a product of initiation into culturally diverse – even, according to the findings of anthropology and sociology, logically *inconsistent* – patterns of knowledge, belief, value and conduct, then certain well-entrenched ideas about education are directly called into question. First, for example, the idea that education might be construed as some kind of technology of pedagogy constructed upon a statistical science of learning and development – an attractive notion to many educational social scientists and policy makers – loses something of its evident appeal: there is no longer, for example, any very pressing reason to hold that educational development – the growth of knowledge, understanding and values – follows some invariant quasi-biological course of development. Secondly, the idea that education is inevitably a matter of initiation into rival traditions of inquiry, value and virtue raises moral and political problems for any common and/or state-regulated conception of education in a multi-cultural or pluralist liberal democracy.

It is this last problem, indeed, that is brought into sharp focus in the educational writings of Alasdair MacIntyre.[11] We saw at the close of part II that most if not all forms of knowledge, understanding or inquiry – mathematical, scientific, artistic or moral – are liable to different logical, semantic or epistemic construals: there are different and competing ways of conceiving criteria of artistic worth or scientific credibility – and, to be sure, it is arguable that some critical philosophical appreciation of such competing versions of inquiry ought to be part and parcel of any adequate educational initiation into them.[12] Of course, it might also be said that this is as it should be, and that it is only proper for students of art, science or mathematics to be at some stage alerted to alternative (formalist or expressive) views of art, competing (realist and non-realist) conceptions of science or rival (realist or constructivist) conceptions of mathematics. For one thing, in a free country, there is no reason why works of art should not be produced according to different and diverse aesthetic criteria in the light of different artistic tastes. For another, if (as seems likely) there is something to the idea that science and mathematics at least aspire to describe an objective world of reality that is neutral between competing conceptions of human flourishing, then it would seem proper to educate would-be scientists in the climate of free and open inquiry that conduces to the unfettered pursuit of truth. But aside from any doubts one might have about any such purported value-neutral conception of science,[13] the idea that forms of human knowledge and inquiry are liable to different logical construals has surely more problematic social and political consequences in other human spheres. For although the value-neutral pursuit of biological science may show us that (say) cloning is possible, we are still faced with the problem of moral choice in the light of such a possibility. But how might we educate for such choice in the face of competing and contested conceptions of moral life and reason?

Alasdair MacIntyre's educational essay 'How to appear virtuous without really being so' addresses this issue in ways that connect with other areas of his work – particularly his *Three Rival Versions of Moral Enquiry*. He observes that much modern popular thinking about the nature of morality seems to be infected by a moral *non-cognitivism* that effectively denies any objective basis to moral judgement. There are also two basic forms of such non-cognitivism: first, an *expressivist* form (emotivism) according to which moral judgements are non-rational expressions of feeling or emotions; secondly, a rational *constructivist* form (prescriptivism) according to which moral judgements are consistent commitments to individually self-legislated imperatives. Kohlberg's influential stage theory of moral development and education is grounded mainly in the second, constructivist perspective. It is no accident that such views have gained modern ascendancy, because both are consistent with that enlightenment mainstream of liberal-democratic thought which is concerned, on the one hand, to defend individual freedom of conscience, and, on the other, to promote liberal democracy as a way of resolving potential conflicts of conscience. There will be individual disagreements about the human potential of cloning; however, these might in principle be resolvable on the basis of interpersonal democratic consensus. On the face of it, this sounds like a highly plausible, even 'correct', account of moral value: although such value is essentially a matter of variable personal taste or individual prescription, it is possible to achieve a certain rational resolution of most if not all particular value conflicts on the basis of social compromise. Indeed, it has seemed that some Kohlbergian combination of individual moral development theory with the idea of a community of justice – precisely dedicated to such social negotiation of interpersonal differences – might be educationally deployed for the successful democratic resolution of such potential liberal disagreement.

On a communitarian view such as MacIntyre's, however, the key moral question is begged in favour of this general liberal picture only at the cost of a considerably skewed understanding of the nature of moral value and its relationship to human identity and culture. The liberal picture appears plausible only by supposing that moral rationality and reasons are quite independent of or separable from their origins in this or that general social or cultural tradition or perspective. To be sure, it is not clear that all liberals have consistently held such a view, and it would seem that a genuine appreciation of the role of culture in human moral formation was a driving force of early liberal theory. However, the idea of the culturally 'unencumbered' self does seem to have been a feature of the modern neo-Kantian liberalism of Rawls and others. But, according to communitarians, any such idea is objectionable on several counts. For one thing, modern emotivist and prescriptivist ethics have prospered in a general social and political climate owing much to the influence of such philosophers as Hume and Kant, and insofar as young people are educated to be ahistorical autonomous moral choosers, they are merely the unwitting products of a cultural perspective that is no less socially constituted and culturally encumbered than others. But consequently, in failing to acknowledge the cultural and other associations and presuppositions of much alleged autonomous moral choice, some liberal approaches to moral education are self-deceived at best and incoherent at worst. On the one hand, it requires little thought to see that any statistically significant responses to Kohlbergian dilemmas[14] about the relative weighting of honesty and respect for life are likely to be determined no less by culturally conditioned moral priorities than by any alleged movement between naturalistically construed developmental stages. On the other, despite having personally observed purported lessons on morality in which children were invited to decide current moral concerns on the liberal understanding that such issues could not possibly admit of right or wrong answers, it should be clear that such denial of rationally accountable *reasons* for moral choice must also preclude any possibility of meaningful moral education.

By contrast, recent communitarians construe moral education less as initiation into some quasi-Kohlbergian rational decision procedure, and more in terms of induction into culturally rooted visions of human good or flourishing – what Charles Taylor has called 'horizons of significance'[15] – that are as much matters of affective sensibility as of cognition. Indeed, it is striking that among those who have recently come to appreciate the role of feeling and emotion in moral response are those so-called 'ethics of care' critics of Kohlberg who note that female responses to moral dilemmas do not always conform to the norms of moral stage theory – precisely because women are inclined to base moral judgement on *feeling* rather than rational principle.[16] In a not unrelated vein, communitarians often follow Aristotle in taking the complex idea of moral *virtue* – rather than the simpler notion of ethical principle – to be definitive of moral life and identity. On this view, the key to moral agency lies in the cultivation of traits of *character* – conceived as dispositional expressions of affectively grounded judgement – rather than in obedience to universalisable rules. Indeed, mindful of the time-honoured educational role of *received* wisdom – as well as of the artificiality of moral cognitivist construals of moral agency as the acquisition of rational moral problem-solving procedures – communitarians also regard moral virtue as best exemplified and taught in the form of myths, fables, epics and other humanly significant narratives. To be sure, it must be a test of the ultimate value of the narratives which inform human cultural traditions that they make coherent sense as visions of the good – MacIntyre speaks of cultural and moral traditions as 'arguments extended through time'[17] – but we are moved to identify with the ideals and aspirations which such narratives celebrate and enjoin largely to the extent that they inspire us towards specific (and arguably objective) standards of self-improvement.

Problems with the communitarian perspective

However, perhaps the most troubling feature of communitarianism is precisely the suggestion that particular socio-cultural perspectives are internally self-validating. If there is no 'view from nowhere' and no pre-social essence of human nature, then there might also seem to be no 'external' or extra-cultural criteria by reference to which the value perspectives of particular social constituences might be judged good or bad, right or wrong. The particular moral values and standards according to which a given social group lives would arguably be immune from criticism by anyone who does not share those values. This would seem to have at least two troubling implications for theorising about human moral values and education: first, the apparently *social relativist* consequence that since particular value perspectives are impervious to criticism from the outside, local social consensus would seem to be the sole guarantee of the moral validity of any value perspective; secondly, the deeply *conservative* corollary that since communities are trapped within the circle of their own self-validating moral ideas, it is not clear how there might be moral advance or progress. In his earlier, more clearly idealist work, Alasdair MacIntyre tried to address this problem in something like Hegelian terms by arguing that although there may be no external 'asocial' conception of value or flourishing, the rational dialogue that arises out of contact and conflict between rival (even contradictorily opposed) value perspectives nevertheless ensures the possibility of some sort of higher or more refined *synthesis* of conflicting views.[18] The trouble is, of course, that any such neo-idealist strategy is far from convincing. First, if there are no independent external standards by reference to which opposed perspectives might be mediated, then it is not clear what the rational basis of any such higher synthesis could be. Indeed, it is not obvious that any such synthesis has histori-cally emerged from dialogue between different world religions and theologies: that, for example, Roman Catholic doctrines have significantly changed in the course of conversations with Muslims or Buddhists (or vice versa) – even if they are nowadays more inclined to live harmoniously together with their differences (and even this is not obvious). Secondly, of course, it is equally unclear from a logical point of view why any such 'higher' synthesis should be regarded as a satisfactory resolution of value conflicts: it is far from obvious that some sort of compromise or harmonisation of opposed views would be *better* than either of the views it mediates between, simply because it does so mediate. Indeed, given the alleged absence of external criteria of mediation, it is unclear how such compromise would constitute a rational resolution rather than simply a third *alternative* controversial view.

An alternative move for anyone who endorses this general neo-idealist or non-realist perspective on moral and other social values, of course, is to fill the gap left by the effective expulsion of neutral reason as an arbitrator of moral diver-sity and conflict with an account of human relations as almost exclusively governed by struggles for ascendancy between different social groups or classes. As the enlightenment rational moral agent concerned with the common good departs the scene, the Machiavellian self-interested power-seeker moves to centre-stage. There can also be no doubt that such a major shift in perspective (although the shift is not at all novel and resurfaces periodically in theorising about these issues) has occured in recent times at least partly under the influence of neo-idealist or perspectivalist communitarian critiques of the new moral rationalism (itself not untouched by a view of human nature as self-interested) of contemporary liberal theorists. Indeed, the main difference between new communitarian social and political theory and so-called 'postmodern' perspec-tives on culture and values is that the essentially ethical focus of the former on issues of human flourishing and common good is almost completely usurped by the latter's emphasis on the hegemonic aspects of human association. According to many post-structuralists and postmodernists, since there is no objective reality beyond our socially constructed conceptions of it, we can hardly regard any claims to objective knowledge and values on the part of past or present philosophers, religious faiths or even scientific communities as other than attempts by this or that social constituency to wield power and control over others to their own advantage: in short, the knowledge and values in terms of which human affairs are here or there organised can hardly be explained in other than *hegemonic* terms. It is likely that the most radical versions of this view have entered contemporary social theory via the influence of the nineteenth-century German philosopher Friedrich Nietzsche on such post-structuralists as Michel Foucault. In the present context, however, it may be more appropriate to examine the no less influential perspective on such matters of an even better known theorist of knowledge as power, Karl Marx – not just because of the considerable consistency of Marx's thought with many contemporary communitarian ideas, but also on account of his considerable latter-day educational influence.

Marx and the hegemonic account of education

As the intellectual inspiration for some of the most cataclysmic events of modern times, of course, Marx should be one of the more familiar figures we have so far considered in this work. Marx is also closely associated with the German idealist tradition, and was directly influenced by Hegel. However, Marx's Hegelian idealism is moderated by the German theologian Ludwig Feuerbach's materialist critique of Hegel.[19] Feuerbach argued that Hegel's interpretation of historical development as a spiritual evolution of ideas was itself but a theological fantasy that could only serve to impede any true understanding of the human condition, and hence ultimately conduce to human delusion and enslavement. He held that God, in the form of Hegel's 'Absolute' or whatever, is merely the projection of human insecurities, made by fearful men in their own image. In basic agreement with Feuerbach's essentially materialist critique of Hegel, especially the idea that it is primarily false *ideas* which prevent people from realising freedom, Marx went further than Feuerbach in arguing that the ultimate determinants of people's weal or woe are neither purely mental nor physical, but *economic*. Marx's hegemonic reworking into an economically conditioned dialectic of class interest of Hegel's conception of historical progess as spiritual evolution has come to be known as *dialectical materialism*. Nevertheless, Marx's Hegelian point of departure inclines him to a profoundly *communitarian* or social constructivist conception of the way in which human agents acquire a meaningful understanding of the world: this is neatly expressed in his already noted communitarian observation that 'it is not the consciousness of men that determines their being, but, on the contrary their social being that determines their consciousness.'

However, Marx also sees such social construction of meaning as deeply conditioned by economic interests which – given the division of labour that has characterised most evolved human societies – are the inevitable source of class conflict: hence, at the beginning of the *Communist Manifesto*, Marx and Engels also famously claimed that 'the history of all hitherto existing societies is a history of class struggles'.[20] For Marx, class membership is itself defined in terms of an individual's relationship to the means of production, and class conflict and antagonism have their basis in the economic inequalities that have in different ages divided master from slave, feudal lord from serf, and bourgeois from proletarian. However, Marx held that the industrial modes of production of his day gave rise to hitherto unprecedented forms of human exploitation Indeed, according to Marx, because there can be no expansion of industrial production without successful market competition, and no such success without the accumulation of capital for investment, such capital growth can only be achieved by a progressive maximisation of profits and lowering of productive costs – in short by ever-increasing reduction of the wages and living conditions of the available workforce. Moreover, Marx clearly thought that such subjection to the profit imperative was degrading and dehumanising to both exploited *and* exploiters. On his view, capitalist owners of production are no less enslaved to the generation of capital than are the wage slaves they employ: both are prey to what Marx calls an alienation (*Entfremdung*) – though this is most obviously true for the industrial worker, whose labour is now no longer even intrinsically fulfilling, but only a means to the barest economic survival.

In the spirit of both Hegel and Feuerbach, however, Marx's key idea is that the economically conditioned cultural consciousness of any social stratum is but a partial and distorted effect of class interest – and hence a form of ideology or 'false consciousness'. Furthermore, it is this false consciousness by which classes both deceive themselves and seek to exercise exploitative dominion and control over other classes. In this respect, moreover, 'the dominant ideas of any society are always those of its ruling class'[21] – and it is this idea that gives rise to the major *educational* implications of Marxism. From the Marxist viewpoint, since dominant classes wield power over subordinate classes mainly through the propagation of ideologies that assert the superiority of some (the rulers) over others (the ruled), schools as social institutions play a key role in maintaining the status quo. Indeed, Marxists hold that the major role of institutionalized schooling in capitalist societies is to manufacture the educational *failure* of working-class children in the interests of maintaining a significant economically exploited workforce for profitable industrial production. This is accomplished by making educational success turn upon a grasp of theoretical or conceptual perspectives to which economic underclasses – since their restricted experience is different from and perhaps more practical than that of dominant classes – have no ready access. On the Marxian view, institutionalized schooling is therefore a principal tool of socio-economic oppression and exploitation. In this light, the proper task of education is not to acquaint children with knowledge of an empirically grounded objective order of things as they actually are – since for Marx, no less than Hegel, there is no such conception-independent order – but to equip individuals with the critical capacities required to question the ideologies into which they have been effectively *indoctrinated* by socialisation (including schooling). Marxist thought has therefore had not only a powerful intellectual and theoretical influence, upon the modern 'critical theory' of Habermas, Adorno, Marcuse and others, and upon the epistemological constructivism of so-called 'sociologists of knowledge' (as well as upon much structuralism, post-structuralism and post-modernism), but also an enormous practical political influence on radical and emancipatory theological and educational movements throughout the modern world.[22]

Such influences, of course, have pulled in different directions. On the one hand, it may be doubted whether Marx consistently subscribed to a thorough-going idealist or non-realist view of human knowledge as such, and he seems to have been inclined to exempt natural science from his general social constructivist interpretation of human values as ideology. Indeed, Marx's view that human liberation rests ultimately on discerning the brute economic realities behind class-based ideological construction – as well as the position of his critical theorist heirs that improvement of the collective human condition, and any associated reduction of injustice, turns upon a more rational-critical appreciation of the hegemonic character of many social practices and institutions – would ultimately appear to depend upon faith in some such scientific or other objective rationality. On the other hand, however, Marx's influence on the sociology of knowledge and post-structuralism has issued in more radical, not to say pessimistic, views of the social construction of meaning, which incline to discern ulterior motives behind all human claims to knowledge and value, and to interpret all human reason and argument as mere self-serving rhetoric. In some ways, the contemporary continental debate between critical theory and post-structuralism (or postmodernism) seems to be a more uncompromising re-run of the argument between communitarianism and liberalism, but with rather less apparent scope (since liberals and communitarians at least share a common commitment to some form of rational reflection) for negotiation. But the key issues are clearly of major social and educational significance in both of these intellectual encounters. It seems educationally crucial, for example, to know whether Catholic or Muslim conceptions of the place of women in society, or of sexual morality, reflect alternative visions of justice or human flourishing into which it might be proper to initiate children as part of their moral and spiritual heritage, or whether such conceptions enshrine deeply unjust power structures into which young people could only be *indoctrinated* rather than educated. Beyond this, indeed, it is crucial to know whether there can indeed be such a thing as education on the basis of reason and argument, as distinct from a kind of counter-indoctrination in rival hegemonic perspectives that cannot but themselves entail the colonial control of some people by others.

All of this gives rise to significant theoretical questions – which, needless to say, cannot be addressed in more detail here. For now, we must rest content with the general observation that there is something paradoxical and self-defeating about any alleged *argument* to the effect that there can be no rational argument. If all argument is ultimately a rhetorical Machiavellian device for securing and wielding power, then we might just as well abandon it in favour of cruder and more directly coercive means of political control. (Indeed, rather than educating the working classes in coercive ideologies, it might make better sense not to educate them at all.) However, we shall postpone discussion of the problems of any indiscriminate hegemonic construal of all argument as political or rhetorical until the final chapter of this work. On the more reasonable assumption that not all argument can be reduced to self-serving rhetoric, and that much moral argument has often been driven by a disinterested concern with the promotion of justice and common good, we may now turn in the next chapter to examine the all-important educational question of how justice as equal respect for all may best be served in the face of significant individual and social diversities of ability, interest, gender and culture: to the issue of precisely how, in Aristotelian terms, we might avoid the injustice of treating unequals equally, as well as that of treating equals unequally.

Possible tasks

(1) Consider how the aims and content of a broadly communitarian curriculum (conceived perhaps with respect to some particular socio-cultural constituency) might differ from those of a culturally pluralist liberal-democratic education.

(2) Consider some of the possible difficulties or drawbacks inherent in any attempt to conceive individual education or personal formation along communitarian rather than liberal-democratic lines.

Chapter 13

Justice, equality and difference

Identity, difference and justice

In the previous chapter, we explored the communitarian perspective on the socio-cultural origins and determinants of human difference, and touched upon some of the possible implications for separate education and schooling of a broadly social-constructivist view of the provenance of human knowledge and values. On the communitarian view, insofar as local socio-cultural heritages may be held to enshrine mutually rival or contradictory conceptions of human flourishing, the moral and other claims and values of any given society will be expressive more of a particular cultural perspective than of disinterested universal truth or principle, and it may not therefore be reasonable to accord a common educational experience to future citizens regardless of their specific cultural or intellectual inheritances. Hence, with particular respect to contemporary problems of moral education, Alasdair MacIntyre has explicitly argued that since contemporary conceptions of virtue or moral conduct reflect culturally diverse moral legacies, there can be no 'shared public morality of commonplace usage' for common educational consumption in contexts of public schooling.[1]

All the same, the moral emphasis in communitarianism is still very much upon the promotion of *justice*. The main concern of communitarians and advocates of multi-cultural or inclusive education is ultimately that certain culturally inherited features or constituents of the identity of some human beings should not be ignored or denied because they do not obviously accord with this or that liberal ideal of rational self-determination. Indeed, if any such liberal ideal is defined more austerely – as a matter of total freedom to choose one's commitments – it may be at odds with a conception of identity that celebrates the importance of obedience to religious authority: hence, Catholic Christians, Jews, Muslims or Hindus may deplore certain kinds of secular liberal inquiry into the basis of faith on the gounds that it reflects an improper or impious hubris. On the other hand, if the liberal ideal is more substantially construed – as a definite commitment to certain western enlightenment virtues and values of (say) unfettered enterprise – it may be held to involve a certain hegemonic denial of the voices and identities of such hitherto culturally, racially or economically marginalised or subordinated groups as women, the labouring or proletarian classes, or those groaning under colonial oppression. Hence, the communitarian concern with justice is very much in conformity with Aristotle's dictum that it may be no less unjust to treat unequals equally than to treat equals unequally. From this viewpoint, communitarian attention to difference often embodies a concern about the rights and entitlement to recognition of individuals who do not define themselves according to the ideals and aspirations of the dominant (upper- or middle-class, highly educated, literate and skilled, white, male, secular or Protestant, heterosexual, and so on) members of the liberal-democratic polity.[2] On the other hand, since it should also be clear that such concerns have hardly been absent from liberal social theorising either, contemporary liberals and liberal educationalists may also be seen to share with communitarians and multi-culturalists a common commitment to an educational ideal of *inclusion* rather than exclusion.

Indeed, despite the fact that there are significant differences between communitarian and liberal approaches to problems of social exclusion and inequality of educational access, there cannot be much doubt that the term 'inclusion' has become one of the major buzzwords of recent educational theory and policy: only the most politically insensitive or attention-seeking of educational theorists and/or policy makers could claim to be against inclusion as an overarching moral principle. Moreover, the grounds of such widespread enthusiasm for inclusion and open educational access at the beginning of the twenty-first century seem clear enough. On the one hand, such aspirations are consistent with a globally growing awareness, not least in the wake of the postwar demise of extreme collectivist social and economic experiments (communist states that have not already collapsed are increasingly inclining to free enterprise), of some (albeit loose) connection between market success and liberal-democratic forms of political and economic organisation – to which some degree of equal regard for all citizens is also clearly presupposed. On the face of it, then, a *strong* economy is tantamount to a *free* economy, which may also seem to presuppose significant educational access, political liberty and economic choice for each and every potential producer and consumer. To be sure, free enterprise is also consistent with existence of those wide differences of wealth and status that command economies aspired or purported to eliminate or reduce; but it is also in the interests of liberal democracies to ensure as far as possible that such differentials are subject to some political and economic constraints, and that they do not lead to the self-undermining creation of radically disenfranchised and/or marginalised non-productive or consuming under-classes. But it would also be excessively cynical to suppose that any liberal-democratic emphasis on inclusion is driven only by economic or instrumental considerations. When all is said and done, liberal democracy is also committed to a moral ideal of equal individual opportunity, and to the freedom of agents – regardless of class, creed, gender, colour or sexuality – to realise their personal potential by all available educational means. That said, however, it would also appear that the most conspicuous feature of institutionalised education from its most ancient origins to modern times has been its manifest inequality and exclusivity.

Indeed, there hardly seems to have been any aspect of past institutionalised education or schooling in which some such degree of inequality has not also been manifest. First and foremost, before the fairly recent advent of popular schooling in developed countries, education was a luxury that relatively few people – only the well-to-do – could afford. For the greater part of human history, then, education has been linked with wealth – not just with regard to the wealth-producing potential of education, but also with respect to the frequent need for wealth in order to secure access to education. Hence, in considering the views on education for democracy of a Rousseau, it has to borne in mind that the progressive education in self-determination that Rousseau recommends for Émile would at that time have been available only to a few youngsters of middle- or upper-class social status and means. But it should also be appreciated that Rousseau did not consider the education he advocated for Émile to be also suitable for the other young subject of his educational reflections, Sophie: for Rousseau, indeed, girls were better suited to a less reflective training in domestic skills, not least in the kind of wifely obedience that male masters of households were entitled to expect.[3] Indeed, well into modern times, it has been possible to discern distinct gender biases in the curricula of many state secondary schools – home economics and dance being mainly the fare of girls and woodwork and football the prerogative of boys. In this respect, to be sure, it is of no small interest that Plato, writing some two millennia before Rousseau, held markedly more enlightened views on the abilities of women – regarding gifted women, alongside able men, as potential Guardians of his ideal state.[4]

All the same, if there is one true father of educational apartheid it would have to be Plato. After all, Plato seems to be the first recorded educational philosopher to have regarded potential or actual inequalities of intelligence and ability as a proper point of departure for rational educational policy making – explicitly recommending that different sorts of (academic) education and (vocational) training should be matched to different (gold, silver and bronze) levels of (natural) ability. It is in this respect (more than his views on gender equality) that Plato's educational legacy was to persist down the centuries to reappear in (amongst other conspicuous modern forms) the British 1944 Education Act.[5] But to these manifestations of unequal educational access and treatment, we may also add those to which we have already alluded concerning race, culture and religion: generations of children of immigrants to such western liberal-democracies as the United Kingdom have had to submit to school curricula which gave exclusive religious recognition to Christianity, and/or which characterised non-western cultures as inferior, primitive or uncivilised. Finally, there is an increasingly vociferous educational lobby which deplores the long suppression and marginalisation of those of so-called 'alternative' sexuality and that takes exception to the social and cultural priority traditionally accorded to heterosexual institutions and lifestyles.[6] Although it will not be possible in this brief chapter to attend to all of these issues of actual or alleged injustice, I hope that the following exploration of some key themes might nevertheless provide some insight into their overall logical character.

Differences of intelligence and ability

Some consideration of the familiar Platonic agenda of proportioning educational provision to allegedly discernible differences of individual intelligence and ability may also afford the best entry point into such issues. Basically, Plato advocated a hierarchical system of education or training ranging from shorter spells of elementary (mainly practical and vocational) training for the less able, to protracted higher (theoretical or academic) education for the more able – with, of course, a range of provision in between.[7] In short, Plato proposed a pattern of selective education by continuous assessment, which was to be followed in practice by generations of later educational policy makers. Such education would involve gradual elimination from the educational process of those judged unfit to proceed further: only those who could keep up with increasingly raised educational hurdles would be allowed to advance to the highest educational stages, and those who were unable to keep up would be systematically weeded out for less mentally demanding employment. That said, the Platonic educational system is essentially meritocratic and has therefore no application in conditions of political oligarchy or plutocracy where educational access is primarily determined by birth, status or wealth (indeed, it was precisely such inequalities that Plato deplored). From this perspective, Platonic meritocracy begins to have real bite in the sort of post-industrial economic climate in which ability precisely assumes more significance than birth or inheritance: somewhat ironically, it has most appeal in the kind of liberal-democratic political climate to which Plato would not otherwise have been very sympathetic. But if any such system of schooling is to achieve a fair matching of educational provision to different levels of ability, it would also appear to require tools for the accurate discernment or assessment of such differences. To this extent, any effective implementation of ability-indexed Platonic meritocracy not only assumes real significance in a more democratic post-industrial climate of educational access for all, but also arguably requires the development of modern empirically grounded social scientific techniques for the appraisal and measurement of human aptitude.

Such techniques – which meshed very well with early behaviourist attempts to construct a natural science of human learning – were developed by late nineteenth- and early twentieth-century pioneers of the psychometric movement in the form of intelligence quotient (IQ) tests.[8] In the course of the twentieth century such tests came to exercise an enormous – and probably baleful – influence on educational theorising and policy making in many parts of the world. Again, one can hardly find a better example of this influence than the selective system of secondary education (in itself a deeply *egalitarian* development in its concern to secure secondary education for all) that followed in the wake of the British 1944 Education Act. According to this development, all children were required at the end of a common elementary or primary education to submit to a pen-and-paper examination – the so-called '11+' – on the basis of which their intellectual and/or other abilities and future vocational potential might be predicted. On the results of this test, children were (initially) to be allocated – according to 'aptitude or ability'

– to grammar, technical or secondary schools: the academic grammar schools were largely hot-houses of administrative, managerial and professional talent (Platonic citizens of gold); the technical schools were intended to train skilled but non-professional workers (citizens of silver?); and the secondary schools were designed to give basic further education and training to those destined for semi- or unskilled blue-collar toil – the proverbial hewers of wood and carriers of water (citizens of bronze). In the event, the technical school largely failed to materialise, and the awesome fate faced by most children was between successful promotion to grammar schools and relegation as educational failures to secondary schools. Although there can be little doubt that this system of selection based on 11+ examination was sincerely designed to proportion educational provision to individual difference – in short, to point young people in the educational and vocational directions best suited to their abilities, needs and interests – there can be much doubt about the deep social divisions (sometimes virtually tearing apart whole communities) such educational apartheid was to create, or about the deep sense of failure it engendered in large numbers of the population. To be sent to secondary school virtually meant the end of schooling at age 15, with little or no prospect of proceeding to higher (particularly university) education.

In a rapidly changing postwar British climate of educational politics and ideology, however, widespread disquiet about the individual, social and economic effects of selective schooling based on psychometric methods eventually came to a head in a left-of-centre-inspired attempt (never fully realised) to replace the divided state system of grammar and secondary schools (Scottish senior and junior secondaries) with a uniform system of *comprehensive* education. The comprehensive ideal was undoubtedly driven by a number of *different* (and probably separable) considerations and imperatives.[9] One was certainly *economic*: large comprehensive schools (often created by the merger of grammar and secondary schools) were less resource-intensive than the smaller grammars and secondaries, they could offer a richer and more extensive range of technical and other substantial provision, and did not impose such heavy financial burdens on already stretched local authorities. A second reason, however, was *social*: a divided system of schooling did appear to separate for once and always the different socio-economic strata of British society in a conspicuously class-based way. On leaving primary school, many entrants to grammar schools would be unlikely ever to mix socially with their secondary-destined playmates again, and this was held to create social class divisions of a kind deeply inimical to the formation of healthy civil democracy. But a key third reason undoubtedly related to the observed weaknesses of IQ and other psychometric devices as predictors of individual ability and potential. It was not just that some children who proceeded to grammar schools on the basis of 11+ success subsequently failed to live up to such early promise, but that a significant number of those who proceeded to secondaries on the basis of 11+ failure proved in due course to have considerable late-flowering abilities. However, having been consigned to schools ill equipped to provide higher academic study, or opportunities to undertake advanced qualifications, it was often difficult if not impossible for such late developers to embark on programmes suited to realising their true potential. Any injustice to individuals aside, politicians and employers were not slow to appreciate the significant and serious implications for the social and economic prosperity of the nation of such early educational and vocational misdiagnosis.

The hazards of psychometry

So what, one might ask, was wrong with the kind of psychometric testing that underpinned 11+ examination? Without rehearsing all that has already been said on this question, it is likely that psychometric testing falls into the same basic error we have already met in this work of assuming that there are invariant features of human development – which, since they are (allegedly) *biologically* rather than *environmentally* or culturally conditioned, are susceptible of essentially empirical scientific appraisal and measurement. At this point, empirical psychological discussions of the problem of psychometric testing have inclined to focus on the difficulty of separating *nature* from *nurture*: they have doubted whether any such tests can ever identify and measure the 'real' genetic component underlying the multiplicity of environmental or external infuences that contribute to the formation of individual personalities.[10] But it is arguable that this way of putting things fails to get quite to the heart of the matter by begging certain deeper questions. For it also needs to be asked here whether it is anyway coherent to suppose that there is any general innate or genetically determined ability or intelligence lying behind social, cultural and other influences on individuals. To be sure, it would be foolish to deny that some individuals are brighter or more quick off the mark than others – and we readily consider these to be more intelligent than others. It may indeed be that there are clearly limiting cases of greater and less intelligence: there may be people who are good at everything and others who are unable (perhaps by dint of unfortunate physical or mental afflictions) to acquire any useful accomplishment. But the truth is that most of us belong to a variable in-between category of individuals who are – by virtue of *inclination* no less than ability – better at some things than others. In this domain, there is greater or less intelligence and ability, but only with regard to this or that form of human inquiry or activity: Janet is good at art and history, but not so good at science and football, whereas the converse is true for John. But insofar as this is so, there seems to be little point in speaking of intelligence as a unitary genetic characteristic that underpins everything that we do: it is surely safer to conceive, identify and evaluate human intelligence, aptitude and ability more in terms of particular domain-specific capacities to perform some tasks and activities better than others.[11]

All the same, might we not still continue to think of these capacities in terms of genetic endowment? In that case, would it still not be true that some individuals are better than others at this or that by virtue of a certain *given* ability? Moreover, do we not commonly hold that some of these (allegedly) given abilities – mathematical and scientific rather than artistic and sporting abilities perhaps – are rather more relevant to determining overall intelligence than others? Again, however, such points seem merely question-begging. First, having abandoned the idea of *general* intelligence in favour of multiple domain-specific capacities, it seems educationally irrelevant whether the capacities are genetically endowed or not: all we need for purposes of instruction is a grasp of who is naturally good at this and who has difficulty with that, and this seems best addressed by attention to the particular responses of individuals in partic-ular learning circumstances, not by prediction on the basis of some all-purpose disposition – for (*ex hypothesi*) there is no such disposition. Secondly, we should also appreciate the grounds upon which some capacities – such as the scientific and the mathematical – have as a matter of fact been valued more than others in this or other past and present societies. First, it would seem that such prefer-ences could hardly be derived from genetic research. It is not that science discovers a gene that is self-evidently superior to other genes, and therefore makes the dispositions it engenders more valuable than others. On the contrary, any preference for some capacities over others is surely a matter of *cultural* (perhaps, more to the point, *economic*) preference – and, of course, such predilections can vary considerably between cultures: in this respect, it may well be that the sort of abstract intellectual capacities that have come to be valued in many developed societies would *not* be rated especially highly in others. In this connection, indeed, it is noteworthy that some psychologists of education have recently argued that the psychometric tradition of IQ testing has tended to elevate and educationally promote precisely the *wrong* sorts of ability and intelligence.

Hence, taking to heart the idea that intelligence is a domain-specific rather than unitary general power, recent champions of *multiple* intelligence have attempted to identify different types of human ability or capacity.[12] Further to this, they have been inclined to compare the abstract reasoning valorised by IQ tests quite *unfavourably* with the kind of intelligent capacities or sensibilities that equip human beings for positive interpersonal association and emotional equi-librium.[13] Advocates of both multiple and emotional intelligence are inclined to point out that it is not uncommon for people who are widely regarded as intelli-gent on the basis of abstract mathematical skills or scientific theorising to be quite unintelligent with regard (say) to the management of their ordinary personal lives and relationships: many hailed as great intellectual or artistic geniuses have led the most disordered personal lives and done untold damage to themselves as well as to others around them. Indeed, proponents of alternative intelligence have argued that there is something deeply distortive about any conception of human intellect which attempts to divorce cognitive ability from human social and affective capacities in the manner of IQ tests. On the one hand, this serves to reinforce the point that concepts of intelligence are far from value-free; on the other, it emphasises the extent to which certain influential conceptions of intelligence have been based upon a rather *unintelligent* separation of so-called 'cognition' from its affective and sensible roots (in a way, moreover, that also reflects that similarly affectively and socially disconnected and disinherited enlightenment view of moral rationality elsewhere criticised in this work). But these points also go some way towards exposing another problem with any assumption that intelligence is a unitary genetic predisposition which gives some individuals more ability *as such* than others. For if intelligence is as much a matter of affect as cognition, then it becomes even harder to see how this might be construed as exclusively genetic – since few if any feelings, interests and motives seem definable in other than social, interpersonal and/or externally referenced terms. Many of our ordinary estimates of intelligence – whether the abilities and capacities in question are socially, artistically or academically construed – take for granted the considerable element of commitment or interest that those regarded as intelligent bring with them to this or that activity: many, in short, are better (sharper, more sensitive, and so on) than others at this or that because they have applied themselves more intently, conscientiously and enthusiastically to the objects of their endeavour (hence the familiar point that genius is one per cent inspiration and ninety-nine per cent perspiration).

Moreover, it is not at all obvious that positive attitudes and inclinations towards personal projects, other-regarding association or whatever are innate more than acquired characteristics. It would be rash, of course, to deny – and as much brain research into feeling and emotion actually claims to demonstrate – that there is some neurophysiological basis to affective life; but without in the least ignoring this, proponents of multiple and affective intelligence also point to research which suggests that neural networks associated with positive affect may be *formed* under the influence of experience rather than already given.[14] In other words, the right sort of upbringing involving cultivation of the right sort of attitudes is a precondition of the relevant hard wiring – rather than vice versa. But related considerations apply even to the purely cognitive or academic goals of IQ testing. First, it has long been recognised that IQ tests are not actually value-neutral tests of pure intelligence, but exhibit fairly marked cultural biases of (middle-)class and (white, western) ethnocentric kinds. From this viewpoint, a significant proportion of 11+ failure reflected not just that many working-class and immigrant children were poorly socialised in the habits of thought and speech conducive to 11+ success,[15] but also that such lack of familiarity with formal modes of learning engendered low levels of confidence and expectation of success with regard to such examinations. It is nowadays well recognised that just as one can coach or train children in attitudes of positive social and emotional openness to others, so one can also coach and train children for success in the IQ tests of psychometric provenance. Moreover, it is fairly clear that this is more or less what traditional preparatory schools have been doing for generations of variously endowed children of well-to-do parents concerned that their offspring should beat the system irrespective of natural talent. At all events, although some of the children allocated to secondary schools on the basis of 11+ failure may have been simply late developers, others were just as certainly the unfortunate victims of serious under-confidence or examination nerves on the day.

Class, culture and difference

But these observations to the effect that children of parents hailing from non-dominant social classes or sub-cultures may encounter difficulty with the more formal forms of discourse they meet in their schooling – not because of poor genetic endowment but because they have been differently socialised – are also useful for avoiding potential and actual confusion of the innatist (IQ) case with a quite different argument for differentiation. For, according to a significant tradition of social and cultural criticism harking back to at least the nineteenth century (one that arguably includes Matthew Arnold, for example), social class and culture may constitute quite legitimate grounds for alternative educational provision for children of different backgrounds. Two widely known twentieth-century proponents of such class-based education – a view that might be termed *conservative traditionalism* – were the poet T.S. Eliot and the novelist D.H. Lawrence.[16] Basically, although conservative traditionalists are advocates of a view of education as cultural initiation, they subscribe to a more generous (sociological) conception of culture as comprehending a wide range of theoretical and practical customs, endeavours and and practices, not all of which are formally academic or literary. On this view, although education plays a key role in the preservation and continued flourishing of high culture, not all individuals may be well fitted to the burdens and benefits of cooperation in this enterprise, and it may well be better to prepare the less academically orientated offspring of working classes for more practical, domestic and technical destinies. Such views are perhaps best exemplified in both the fiction and social criticism of D.H. Lawrence, who persistently argues that there are basically two kinds of people who engage with experience and the world in quite different and even incommensurable ways.

Indeed, irrespective of other reasons for its popularity or notoriety, Lawrence's widely known novel *Lady Chatterley's Lover* is precisely concerned with the uneasy encounter between these two allegedly different experiential worlds. On the one hand, Lady Chatterley is a woman of well-educated sensibilities for whom literature is the key to apprehending and interpreting experience; on the other hand, Mellors the gamekeeper is a man whose relationship with the world is direct and unmediated – one who calls a spade a spade, or by some other down-to-earth term. On the face of it, it seems that Lawrence is concerned to give due respect to *each* of these worlds – although there is, if anything, more than a hint of Lawrencian preference for the authenticity of Mellors' world over the apparent preciosity or artifice of Chatterley's, as well as some explicit affirmation of the value of 'handwork over mindwork'.[17] But as a writer and contributor to high culture himself, Lawrence is far from unappreciative of the literary and other achievements of Chatterley's world, and – as a product of the working class – he is not sentimentally or romantically blind to the shortcomings of working-class life and experience. Moreover, despite his occasional existentialist celebration of working-class existence over middle-class essence, there is no final ignoring of the rather elitist if not authoritarian flavour of Lawrence's educational policy proposals in such works of cultural criticism as 'The

Education of the People'.[18] In such work, Lawrence argues not at all unlike Plato for a highly hierarchical and selective system of schooling that will educate the children of administrative and professional classes in high culture, and train the children of artisans and tradespeople for fairly menial domestic and vocational tasks. Such domestic and vocational training for the masses, it should also be noted, is clearly indexed to gender-specific roles: whereas boys will learn wood-work and mechanics, girls will be trained in the domestic skills of good home-making.

That said, despite the often stridently authoritarian terms in which Lawrence puts this case, it is not clear that he believed the lower orders to be *genetically* inferior: it is just that by virtue of their more practical acculturation and inter-ests, they relate to experience in a different way from those of higher classes – and he would still appear to have held that there is much for the socially elevated to learn about life from their social inferiors. All the same, significant confusion between ideas of genetic and cultural difference, and regarding the educational implications of such differences, is to be found in the work of some conservative educational disciples of both Lawrence and Eliot. Thus, in opposition to the 1960s British trend towards a common comprehensive curriculum, some British conservative traditionalists argued explicitly in favour of an alternative practical 'aesthetic', sporting and vocational curriculum for a general category of children who were apparently regarded as *at once* working class *and* as less intellectually able.[19] The problem that such educational theorists sought to address, of course, was or is that of the frequently observed disaffec-tion of many mainly lower-class youngsters from the conventional academic school curriculum, and their proposals reflected the common assumption or claim that such young people are generally better motivated towards the acquisi-tion of useful technical, domestic, vocational and leisure skills. In short, whereas (allegedly) such children dislike studying science and geography, they may gain considerable fulfilment from mending old cars, cooking three-course dinners or rock drumming. However, such new cultural conservatism also held that such young people are *both* genetically *and* culturally conditioned to prefer such prac-tical over theoretical activities, and it drew upon the innate endowment arguments of the psychometricians, as well as the cultural insights of Eliot and Lawrence, to underpin proposals for an alternative practical and 'aesthetic' curriculum for the academically challenged.

Following Lawrence, however, such new advocates of alternative curricula were inclined to deny the primacy of the academic over the non-academic curriculum, or that some children were merely to receive a second-rate education: the alternative curriculum was to be regarded as only a *different* sort of educational provision better suited to the needs of a particular kind of child or young person. But although, as repeatedly noticed in this work, there is signifi-cant evidence in contemporary educational theorising and policy making of the present-day persistence of broadly separatist (Platonic) approaches to educa-tional provision, any such 'alternative curriculum' thinking would now be generally regarded as both theoretically and politically objectionable. First, from a theoretical viewpoint – aside from the widely (though not entirely) discredited and unfashionable educational reputation of intelligence testing – it should be evident that far from being mutually supportive, arguments from genetic predisposition and cultural formation only serve to neutralise each other. On the one hand, if children are suited to a particular sort of educational provision by virtue of hailing from a particular class or culture, then they are so *irrespective* of their innate intellectual endowment (which would mean that a working-class Einstein should not be allowed to study physics); on the other hand, if young people are suited to a particular curriculum by virtue of innate endowment, then they are so irrespective of class and culture (which would mean that innately gifted working-class children should study academic subjects, and the genetically inferior offspring of kings and dukes should pursue woodwork and games). In short, such alternative curriculum proposals combine diverse arguments for differentiation in a patently incoherent way. That said, we should also note a number of further dubious evaluative assumptions that seem to underlie such arguments.

The education of Sharon and Tracy

To begin with, there is the suspect idea that those whose social backgrounds have hitherto given them access only to popular or low culture should be denied any access to higher culture on the grounds that they must must inevitably find the latter unfamiliar and difficult: on the face of it, this seems akin to the naturalistic fallacy committed by progressive educational writers who argue that since children are naturally inclined to enjoy playing, playing is what they *ought* in formal educational contexts to be doing. Whatever may be said for the educational value of play, any such move from *is* to *ought* is (without extra premises) suspect. But, secondly, there is the not unrelated assumption, not only that intelligence is a unitary genetic disposition which disposes some people to be cleverer *as such* than others, but that it is a capacity which actually *precludes* some from doing what others can do: this time the suspect argument consists in the movement from Sharon is cleverer *as such* than Tracy, to (therefore) Sharon can do mathematics and Latin, but Tracy cannot. Again, however, this does not even begin to follow. First, as previously seen, the very particularity of the things that people are good at, and the fact that forms of expertise may combine in an endless variety of ways – you are better at piano, cooking and history and I am better at science, chess and volleyball – casts serious doubt on the idea of any unitary form of intelligence. But even if some such characteristic did make Sharon *generally* cleverer than Tracy, it would still be implausible to argue to the conclusion that Sharon can understand history and geography but Tracy cannot, and more plausible perhaps to suppose that Tracy does not learn history as well or as quickly as Sharon. Indeed if, as we have also noted, effective learning is as much a function of motivation and interest as innate ability, then it need not even follow from any observation that Sharon is generally cleverer than Tracy that Tracy learns history less well than Sharon – since Tracy may apply her more modest abilities to history with far greater will and enthusiasm than Sharon.

But we should also notice that it would not either follow from Sharon's being generally cleverer than Tracy that Sharon should be invited, encouraged or constrained to pursue mathematics, science and history, whereas Tracy should be persuaded to do home economics, netball and art and craft – for, of course, if Sharon is generally cleverer than Tracy, it is reasonable to suppose that she is likely to be better at these subjects as well. But then the suppressed premise that inclines us to point Sharon down the academic rather than practical curriculum route seems to betray an essentially *evaluative* inclination to accord higher status to academic over practical subjects. For since no such conclusion could be based on natural scientific observations alone, it could surely only follow from a social or *cultural* inclination to give some subjects and activities greater significance or importance than others. In this connection, of course, we have already observed that one reason why educational traditionalists – conservative or liberal – are inclined to rate academic over practical subjects is that they equate (rightly or wrongly) the former with personal development, and the latter with mere vocational training: whereas technical drawing and secretarial skills are only likely to be of much use to those who are going to be draughtsmen or secretaries, knowledge of basic science, history and geography would appear crucially constitutive of well-formed civil and moral personhood and agency. But if that is the case, to deny Tracy access to such subjects on the grounds that she cannot learn them as easily as Sharon (remember she allegedly cannot learn *anything* as well as Sharon) is to deny her what she, alongside Sharon, surely has a right to be – a well-formed and informed person. From this viewpoint, indeed, there would appear to be far less injustice to Tracy in denying her (but not Sharon) home economics and volleyball, since these are skills she might lack without being a well-formed self-determining agent. But, above all else, we should note the crowning error of assuming that it follows from any observation that A is better/cleverer than B at X, that A should be encouraged to pursue further or do more of X than B: for insofar as it does not follow without further argument from any claim that A is cleverer than B that A should do either more, less or just as much as B, this is just another more sweeping instance of the *naturalistic* fallacy. If anything, indeed, the moral implication would appear to lie in the direction of more learning for the less well endowed. After all, if Tracy had less food or money than Sharon, the moral presumption would seem to be in favour of giving Tracy *more* of what she needs. Thus, if education may be regarded as some sort of right or entitlement, it might well appear fairest to offer more of a given educational experience to those who find it difficult rather than easy.[20] Moreover, some such argument might also be adapted to the case of those who are less well motivated to academic study than others – for considerations of educational need could here be held to outweigh or override those of individual preference.

Hence, although we need not doubt that young people have greater and lesser abilities, inclinations and interests, and are more than likely destined for different socio-cultural and vocational futures, there is continued reason to be sceptical about those traditions of educational theorising which propose to base educational policy on naturalistically defined or identified differences of intelligence and ability. It is not just that the idea of natural ability is too hard to define or disentangle from other socially conditioned qualities of interest, taste and application, but that even if it were not, there are genuine moral objections to using any purportedly inferior abilities as grounds for denying this or that group of young people educational access to the kinds of knowledge and understanding essentially constitutive of personal, moral and civic identity. Clearly, however, this does leave us with large and pressing practical questions about how to address the inevitable differences of ability and application that teachers cannot fail to observe in the course of their day-to-day professional monitoring and assessment of children's progress. In this respect, although the fundamental difficulties of developing accurate diagnostic tools for the prediction of ability – not to mention the case against social division – argue more strongly in favour of common comprehensive rather than selective schooling, there would also seem to be a strong educational case for streaming and setting children according to their own learning pace. Indeed, it may be that some such differentiation is no more than part and parcel anyway of the business of good professional practice. There may also, of course, be more or less sympathetic ways of doing this, and a good school should not make slower learners feel inferior. But it is clearly of little educational help to those who most need it to pretend (as some past radical educational egalitarians may have been so inclined) that genuine remedial or other differences of ability and motivation do not exist.

However, just as there are serious problems with the idea of innate intelligence, there must be related objections to any educational policy that attempts to allocate children to different sorts of educational provision on the basis of their alleged more lowly socio-economic position. Here, although there may be a plausible case – along the communitarian lines aired in the previous chapter – for maintaining that the children of some cultures might be exposed to different experiences from children of other cultures, one would need to be sure that the arguments brought to support any such strategy did not conceal darker hegemonic purposes. In this respect, for example, it is necessary to look hard at the arguments of those radical sociologists of knowledge who argued in the 1960s and 1970s that working-class children should be given an education that reflected the practices and values of their own class – including, for example, so-called 'restricted' (informal and demotic) rather than 'elaborated' (formal and academic) speech codes – rather than a schooling in allegedly 'bourgeois' or middle-class knowledge and values.[21] For what may then have looked like a radical, anti-elitist, emancipatory and egalitarian approach to education may now appear with hindsight to have been little more than a recipe for the perpetuation of a vicious cycle of cultural oppression and deprivation: to have been little better, indeed, than the alternative curriculum proposals of conservative traditionalists. At all events, there cannot be much doubt that a modern liberal commitment to treating everyone educationally equally insofar as there are no educationally pertinent reasons for doing otherwise has usually been driven by a deep antipathy to the injustices of much past conservative traditionalism, and (whether or not such liberal strategies have always been well judged) it would appear strained if not question-begging to suggest that any such approach is little more than than a wolf of bourgeois hegemony in sheep's clothing.

The grounds of legitimate educational differentiation

All the same, there may indeed be injustice in treating unequals equally, and there clearly are respects in which individual or cultural difference might be used to ground differential educational treatment based upon proper recognition of diversity. Insofar as education is concerned with the promotion of qualities of personhood, and personal formation is only conceivable in terms of initiation into some set of invariably contested cultural values or commitments, it is difficult to see how all aspects of personal development might be addressed in a completely general or impartial way. There are, for example, awkward questions about educational provision with respect to the highly identity-constitutive matter of language. Setting aside issues of the actual political suppression of minority languages in some parts of the globe, there are clearly many children in such western liberal democracies as Britain and the USA who are required by formal education to acquire knowledge and understanding in languages other than those of native origin. In the course of such learning, however, it cannot be doubted not just that the values and forms of thinking of the second language are significantly different from those of the first language, but also that these differences are likely to put learners at odds with the values and perspectives of biological parents and cultural community. But, of course, perhaps the most conspicuous identity-constitutive respects in which the linguisitic or other practices of a culture are likely to divide it from other cultures are religious and moral. Whatever one's view of religion, there can be no doubt that it serves to define the highest values and aspirations – the precise 'horizons of significance' – of many human communities, and that for many such communities some sort of religious initiation will therefore constitute the very core of anything worth regarding as a proper education. For one thing, it is hard to override in the name of some common liberal education the profound concerns of many religious parents from many faith communities that such an education – especially if it fights shy, in the interests of impartiality, of substantial religious initiation – must fail to respect their deepest aspirations for the formation of their children in their most cherished religious and moral values. So, for example, many religious (and secular) parents deeply deplore what they take to be the too tolerant and shallow attitudes to sexual and other human relationships – perhaps exemplified by the non-marital cohabitation or 'alternative' sexuality of practising teachers – that they are able to observe in a liberalised state sector of education. Thus, whereas past pressure (from British Roman Catholics) for separate religious education turned upon a concern for the preservation of a minority religious faith and culture in a different religiously affiliated national educational system, more recent calls for separate faith schools have come from those who reject the essentially 'valueless' secularism of an essentially liberalised state system.

Moreover, without entering debates about who is right or wrong on the precise questions of sexual or other morality that divide advocates of separate religious schooling from secular liberal advocates of common schooling, it should be clear that the most pressing problems of educational justice arise precisely at this point. Those who believe (not necessarily or always, it should be said, on religious grounds) that homosexuality and cohabitation are wrong, and that they should not be exemplified in the lives and persons of teachers or even tolerantly entertained as possible potential 'lifestyles', are clearly entitled to their view – and it is not obvious that such views or their rivals can be *wrong* in the way that believing that the moon is made of green cheese is obviously wrong. Thus, unless particular groups intend the violent suppression of those they regarded as wrong or deviant (which religious believers probably in general do not), it may be the height of illiberality to deny that they should have their progeny initiated into the beliefs and practices they hold to be right. But the trouble now is that the beliefs of many religious and other tradition-ally defined groups may well seem inherently discriminatory to secular (and even some religious) liberal eyes. For example, both Catholic Christianity and Islam have often been accused by liberals of an oppressive if not demeaning attitude to women that regards them as second-class citizens at best, and as at worst no more than the property of men. On the other hand, of course, the same religious views that have been regarded as a pernicious expression of unjust religious hegemony by secular liberals have also been defended by educated and intelligent Catholic and Muslim men *and* women as a proper appreciation of the rather different contributions that different sexes have to make to human flourishing, and to the earthly realisation of divine purpose. Indeed, it has been argued that, far from being demeaning, Christianity and Islam show the highest possible regard for women – a regard that some precisely find to be lacking in strained liberal political and educational attempts to offer precisely equal opportunity to males and females: why should it obviously show more respect to women to encourage them to play football at school, or to allow them to fight on the front line in wartime? All that we can say for now on these questions, of course, is that they are enormously difficult to settle. However, such issues do serve to indicate the ineradicable place of human preference and choice in the determination and pursuit of educational goals – a preference or choice that may also seem (perhaps some-what ironically) to be better reflected or honoured in a communitarian politics of recognition than in liberal omnitolerance. It may also be that these consid-erations of preference and choice are educationally reflected nowhere more clearly than in the disputes about educational authority and discipline, to which we now turn.

Possible tasks

(1) Consider what differences of curricular provision it might be reason-able to try to make for individual pupils or groups of children in respect of diversities of (i) class, (ii) culture, (iii) language, (iv) religion, (v) gender, (vi) mathematical ability, (vii) sexuality.

(2) Consider some of the individual and cultural differences you might not want to accommodate in the school curriculum in the interests of equality of educational access, individual emancipation and/or social cohesion.

Chapter 14

Freedom, authority and discipline

A persisting dichotomy

In this chapter, we shall examine some fundamental issues of educational authority, freedom and discipline via exploration of the time-honoured distinction between traditionalist or subject-centred education and progressive or child-centred education. In this regard, it may be as well to begin by acknowledging the rather dismissive attitude of many contemporary educationalists to this rather hackneyed distinction. Nowadays, indeed, it seems to be widely held by educational philosophers, theorists and policy makers that any such traditional–progressive distinction is an entirely spurious or redundant one: that if this dichotomy has not already been seriously overtaken by recent educational developments and policies, it is at least in principle resolvable in favour of some sane educational compromise between what may otherwise only be regarded as quite unacceptable extremes. Despite this attitude, it will be one concern of this chapter to show that the dualism is a real and persisting one, and that claims to the effect that it is resolvable rest mainly upon serious misconstrual of the precise logical status of the distinction. It seems likely, for example, that much misunderstanding of the traditional–progressive distinction is implicated in the sort of errors about the relationship of educational theory to practice that we explored in part I of this work. That said, even the most politically insensitive could hardly fail to notice that the traditional–progressive dichotomy is alive and well in almost every contemporary public debate about educational policy: it is not in the least difficult to find hot-off-the-press commentary on key issues of educational philosophy, theory and policy – such as falling or rising educational standards, teacher accountability or the (allegedly) declining morals of the young – in which the dichotomy looms as large as ever. It is therefore of crucial importance to understand why, like the poor, this particular bone of educational contention is always among us, and this above all requires a proper appreciation of what is precisely at conceptual or normative stake between so-called educational 'traditionalists' and 'progressives'.

First, then, what might be meant by describing an educational perspective as traditionalist or progressive? A key obstacle to answering this question is that it is not clear that these terms serve to mark any *single* distinction. Indeed, since the opposition in question has been subject to some rather crude philosophical and/or popular caricature and simplification, it may be instructive to engage in some criticism of received views in the interest of a clearer appreciation of what the traditional–progressive dichotomy is *not* about. In this connection, one widespread reading of the distinction is already apparent in the association of traditionalism with the teaching of subjects (not children), and progressivism with the teaching of children (not subjects). As I have elsewhere argued,[1] such interpretations of traditionalism and progressivism are to some extent encouraged by a certain loose construal of ordinary reports of teaching as two-term relations: it is tempting to suggest that for any given statement of the form 'Mr Smith teaches X', traditionalists would be people who replace X with 'mathematics' or 'woodwork', whereas progressives would be more inclined to substitute 'Sarah' or '4B'. But aside from the fact that any such putative two-term relation seems (grammatically speaking) to be no more than a contraction of the three-term construction 'Mr Smith teaches X to Y' – in short, teachers would be more precisely said to teach subjects *to* children – one may be hard put to identify examples of traditionalists who did not think that they were also teaching children, or progressives who have set out to teach only children and nothing else. By the way, according to a refined version of this interpretation – proposed by the distinguished co-authors of an influential postwar introduction to philosophy of education[2] – traditionalism is a doctrine about educational *content* and progressivism is a doctrine about *methods*: indeed, it was alleged to be a key advantage of this interpretation that it might enable easy accommodation of apparently irreconcilable differences between educational traditionalists and progressives. All the same, this account fares no better than the above subject-versus child-centred version of the distinction. Indeed, aside from the plain fact that traditionalist educators have often been extremely interested in methods (one need look no further than to behavioural objectives approaches to learning and curriculum), it is more than a little ironic that perhaps the most famous or infamous progressive school of modern times – A.S. Neill's Summerhill – was roundly criticised by Her Majesty's (UK) Schools Inspectorate for its complete lack of interest in pedagogical innovation, and for its naked and unashamed use of quite didactive 'chalk and talk' methods.[3]

However, related problems also beset a widespread contemporary interpretation of the traditional–progressive dichotomy as a distinction between different kinds of teaching skills or strategies.[4] On this view, traditionalism is just an approach to teaching that deploys largely formal (didactic or rote) methods of instruction, and progressivism is an approach that eschews formal instruction in the interests of more open, exploratory and collaborative methods of learning of an interdisciplinary or integrative kind. Again, an apparent advantage of construing the traditional–progressive dichotomy in this way is that if the two perspectives are held to be primarily *methodological*, it might seem possible to determine by something like empirical research which teaching methods are precisely most technically effective for this or that classroom use. It is tempting, in short, to suppose that the weary centuries-old debates between traditionalists and progressivists might once and for all be settled by value-neutral scientific method. Indeed, such a perspective has been adopted by several latter-day British educational theorists and researchers of some academic repute. Thus, one researcher – also given to frequent and strenuous denials that the traditional–progressive distinction has any present-day relevance – has precisely sought to submit the effectiveness of alleged traditional and progressive methods to empirical test.[5] More recently, however, another very (politically as well as professionally) influential British researcher into primary education has claimed, in rather more temperate if no less forceful terms, that the source of much poor primary education can be traced to the dogmatic adoption by teachers of a one-sided diet of (allegedly child-centred) teaching *methods* – suggesting, once more, that age-old disputes between traditionalists and progressives may be rendered irrelevant by more professional adoption of a mixed economy of research-based *teaching skills*.[6] According to such views, to persist in regarding differences of educational policy and practice in terms of allegiance to this or that partisan repertoire of teaching strategies is to be held captive by outdated educational ideologies that can have no place in a modern climate of objective scientific thinking about professional educational practice.

The attractions of such attempts to resolve the traditional–progressive issue are plain enough, and it might be a fine thing if some such strategy was successful. Unfortunately, however, such manoeuvres completely miss the point. To begin with, one cannot help wondering where precisely are the educational bunkers into which some recent teaching researchers claim to have stumbled. If anything, it would appear (in the light of the author's own regular observance of primary teaching) that it is any alleged polarised (formal versus informal) employment of teaching methods that has long been overtaken by events. Indeed, quite explicit introduction to a mixed economy of teaching styles and strategies – comprehending direct exposition and instruction, explanation, questioning, discussion, inquiry, activity, and so on – has long been standard fare in most institutional courses of professional training, and the pedagogy of pre- and in-service teachers nowadays routinely embraces a balance of formal (directly instuctional) and less formal (exploratory and collaborative) teaching. Such mixed teaching approaches may be more or less successfully tried, but if they are unsuccessfully executed, the fault is likely to be more a function of inept *implementation* than methodological bias. But it is above all unclear what implications any such one-sided diet of educational method might have for the issue between educational traditionalism and progressivism. As we have already seen, Neill's educational method was criticised on the grounds that it followed a largely formal programme of formal 'chalk and talk' instruction; but if progressive ideology *just* is the use of informal methods, how could Neill's universally acknowledged radical or progressive approach be criticised on the grounds that it used formal or *traditional* methods? There is clearly much confusion here, and it almost certainly follows from the rather superficial assumption or *dogma* that the traditional–progressive distinction is primarily conceivable by reference to differences of pedagogical method. To be sure, whatever there is to the idea (upon which we shall shortly touch) that there is some *general* traditionalist inclination towards more formal pedagogy, or of progressivism towards more 'open' teaching methods, it may still be that there is no *necessary* connection between these larger educational ideologies and particular pedagogical styles.

The normative basis of the traditional–progressive distinction

The root confusion here is more evident when we turn to a related problem concerning any attempt to submit traditionalism and progressivism to the test of empirical effectiveness. The trouble is that the viability of any such strategy surely depends upon being able to test and compare the methodologies of the allegedly opposed perspectives against *common* criteria of educational success. But it is not hard to see that this must amount to something of a methodological stumbling-block. For let us suppose, to take a crude but effective example, that the test of an effective educational method is that it is more conducive to success in formal examinations. In this case, of course, we *might* not be surprised to find that 'traditional' methods of formal instruction and rote learning are better for this purpose than 'progressive' methods of discovery learning. Does this then prove the educational superiority of progressive over traditional methods? Clearly not: for the 'progressive' is quite free to reject the achievement of formal certification – or even *any* academic objectives – as proper aims of education. In fact, this is precisely what progressives of the A.S. Neill variety seem at pains to maintain: they reject examination-orientated academic learning as largely inimical to the promotion of confident, well-balanced and socially mature individuals. Moreover, in case anyone finds this an extreme or overdrawn instance, there are clearly other homelier but nevertheless related ones. Hence, as we have previously indicated, there have been serious recent proposals to return to methods of rote learning in state schools in view of their alleged effectiveness for the promotion of numeracy skills.[7] Clearly, however, one would not need to belong to some lunatic progressive educational fringe to contest such proposals on the grounds that rote learning may fail to produce the kind of numeracy we want, or that such methods are not obviously conducive – and may even be quite inimical – to the promotion of other worthwhile educational aims. Moreover, the key issue here is less that of which of these various positions is justified, more that of what would *count* as appropriate educational justification. From this viewpoint, it would seem to be a mistake – the mistake of the educational technicist – to suppose that these are issues that could even *in principle* be resolved by empirical methods. For, to the extent that such questions are questions of *value* more than empirical fact, it would appear that any such resolution of them – if they are held to be rationally resolvable at all – would have to turn more on serious normative, evaluative or moral argument and debate than upon neutral empirical research and inquiry.

How then ought we to understand the traditional–progressive dichotomy? As already noted, one difficulty in the way of any straightforward answer to this question is that there are almost certainly different distinctions at work here – or, at any rate, diverse forms of traditionalism which seem to contrast in different ways with diverse forms of progressivism. That said, any such observation could itself hardly make much sense in the absence of some *broad* grasp of the traditional–progressive distinction, and I believe that there is indeed a more general but still useful way of characterising the difference between these positions. Moreover, insofar as progressive theories have generally developed as radical responses or reactions to more orthodox, conventional or 'traditional' educational perspectives, we might first seek a rough grasp of the distinction by attention to the basic features of a traditional conception of education. Here, as previously noted, educational traditionalism was given a fairly precise definition by the nineteenth-century poet and social critic Matthew Arnold, who regarded education as the transmission of culture, and culture as 'the best that has been thought and said in the world'. On this view, educational traditionalists regards education as the chief means or instrument by which a given human community ensures the continuity of its way of life – or, at any rate, all that is considered most worth preserving about that form of life – from one generation to another: in short, education is one key process or mechanism – alongside family and workplace – by which individuals are prepared for responsible, cooperative and productive social living. Educational traditionalists have also invariably held that such cultural initiation into 'the best that has been thought and said in the world' is a positive or *beneficial* process, and that individuals would be much impoverished in the absence of such initiation: in this vein, as we have seen, the modern educational philosopher R.S. Peters – without question a latter-day (albeit liberal) traditionalist – famously described the small as yet educationally uninitiated child as 'the barbarian at the gates of civilization'.

Traditionalism and anti-democratic arguments

On this view, education has a distinct social purpose, and it is not therefore surprising that something akin to a culture transmission view of education has been defended by many social theorists – not least by so-called 'sociological consensus' theorists or structural functionalists.[8] Moreover, given the fairly common-sense appeal of the idea that education has a civilising effect on people, it may seem difficult to see how such a view of education might be denied, or – in the event that it is so – what could possibly constitute a viable alternative to it. All the same, this fundamentally traditionalist view of education was to be called into question, precisely in the name of a radical alternative, by the great founding father of educational progressivism, Jean Jacques Rousseau. In this connection, we should appreciate that Rousseau's educational ideas were also a product of sophisticated social-theoretical reflection upon the role of education in adapting the individual to civilised interpersonal association.[9] Rousseau's main concern as a social and political philosopher was to identify the conditions under which a particular sort of polity – civil democracy – might be possible:

hence, his educational philosophy is concerned to specify the individual capacities and qualities that would enable effective democratic participation. From this viewpoint, despite Rousseau's evident respect for Plato as an educational philosopher, it should be recalled that the educational ideal Plato propounds in his *Republic* (described by Rousseau as the finest treatise on education ever written[10]) is both traditionalist and deeply undemocratic. As already seen, since Plato regarded intelligence as the largely innate possession of a small social minority, and held that only the intelligent could be educated in the qualities of wisdom required for effective political rule, he concluded that a just society could only be one in which the wise minority ruled the ignorant majority. Since the intellectually inferior and less well-educated citizenry could not possess the wisdom to know what was in their own best interests, they could make no significant contribution to deliberation on matters of social and public policy, and a just society could not therefore be a democratic society.

What is therefore particularly distinctive about Plato's traditionalism – unlike, it should be said, the mainstream of contemporary traditional and other educational thought – is that it is profoundly anti-democratic. The Platonic educational system is consequently one in which there are two basic forms of schooling: on the one hand, a kind of training in social conformity and vocational skills for the great unwashed masses; on the other, a 'real' education in (what we would now call) rational autonomy for the ruling elite. Plato here clearly advocates the matching of specific kinds of *education* and training to the execution of particular socio-economic functions and responsibilities. All the same, even in Platonic terms, it seems clear not only that one needs a certain sort of education *in addition* to innate ability in order to be capable of responsible public policy making, but that any *exclusive* training as a hewer of wood or carrier of water is liable to render one unfit for political participation. But if that is so, it may be that there is some sleight-of-hand in Plato's anti-democratic argument. For the Platonic sorting of people into two kinds, one of which is unfit for rule by virtue of lower *educational* attainment, as well as the dubious claim (roundly criticised by Aristotle) that reflection upon public policy issues requires the exercise of abstract rational capacities, lends more plausibility than there might otherwise be to the claim that the majority are unfit for political participation on grounds of inferior *intelligence*. Indeed, although Plato seems to employ the idea of educational difference, based on alleged diversity of intelligence, as an argument *against* democracy, one might well turn the inference on its head and argue for common or undifferentiated education on the basis of a commitment *to* democracy. Moreover, bearing in mind the large class, gender and other inequalities of his own day – some of which he seems to have been fairly content to tolerate – this is generally the way that Rousseau's own thought goes. But before Rousseau can give rein to any such argument in favour of general or popular education for democracy, he needs to address another key complaint against any idea of popular government – namely the argument that ordinary citizens are unfit to rule themselves, not so much because they are stupid, more because they are morally *corrupt*.

In this connection, Rousseau's work needs to be understood primarily as a response to the influential claims of the English political philosopher Thomas Hobbes – the first of the classic modern social contract theorists – who had argued much along these lines less than a century before him. Hobbes' social and political philosophy may be considered the first great modern attempt to provide a social theoretical explanation of human civil, moral and political order after the fashion of natural scientific accounts of the order of nature. Just as early modern empirical scientists sought a statistical or mechanistic explanation of the movement of celestial or other natural phenomena in terms of the control by natural forces of otherwise independent material objects, so Hobbes sought to explain society in terms of the compulsive power or force of social law over otherwise socially independent individuals. Hence, just as we might seek to understand the physical universe as a collection of stars, planets and other astral bodies ordered and controlled by gravity, so Hobbes sought to conceive society as a collection of independent biological entities controlled by civil laws, rules and sanctions. Moreover, as previously noted, Hobbes clearly held that in the interests of avoiding total social breakdown, it was imperative that individual human agents, as sites of unreconstructed self-interest and selfishness, should be kept in check by civil laws. The state of nature that Hobbes supposed to have preceded civil society is – in a world of constant competition for limited resources – a 'war of all against all', and a state in which 'life is solitary, poor, nasty, brutish and short'. On this view, without powerful social constraints and legal sanctions, inherently anti-social individuals would tear each other apart in competition for coveted goods and advantages. For this reason, Hobbes held that social security could not be secured by anything less than the complete surrender of individual freedom to imposed authority. This is also why, as previously noted, Hobbes defended a doctrine of *absolute* sovereignty, according to which – since the only altenative to tyranny would be anarchy – there could never be any political justification for the overthrow of even despotic civil authority.

We have already observed that Locke, second of the classical contract theorists, regarded such defence of absolute sovereignty as objectionable on grounds of the threat it presents to individual liberty: for Locke, it is the business of the state not to coerce or restrain individuals but to enable them to pursue their personal projects – so long as these do not interfere with the liberties of others. However, by virtue of his rejection of Hobbes' entire analysis of the relationship of the state of nature to civil society, Rousseau's criticisms would seem to cut deeper than Locke's. Indeed, in the light of contemporary anthropological reflections on the pre-civil societies in the Americas and elsewhere, Rousseau argues that the state of human nature as Hobbes conceived it is hardly credible. In the spirit of Aristotle and much communitarianism, Rousseau holds that human nature is inherently social, and that there could never have been a time at which human beings lived the solitary and predatory lives of some non-human species. Indeed, Rousseau held that the available evidence from native America and elsewhere showed the lives of (comparatively) primitive nomads to be characterised less by anti-social aggression and more by a high degree of cooperative behaviour: insofar as primitive tribespeople regarded themselves principally as members of communities and as contributors to the common good, they could not even be said to possess any strong sense of individual self. So from whence could have come the high level of individual self-awareness and self-interest assumed by Hobbes to be an essential feature of the human condition? Rousseau maintains that it did not so much *precede* entry into civil society, but was more a *consequence* of it. Rousseau persuasively argues that the strong modern sense of individuality arises with the division of labour entrained by transition from primitive nomadic hunter-gatherer cultures to the socio-economically more complex urban centres of civil society.

In the first place, the more economically sophisticated modes of subsistence of civil societies encourage pursuit of individual professional and other specialisms, and the accumulation of private property – the latter constituting for Locke an important condition of individual identity formation and personal expression. Thus, whereas land was common property to nomadic native American hunter-gatherers, and it made little sense to think of it in terms of individual ownership, the specialist herders and gardeners of settled cultures become proprieters or *owners* of land – having 'mixed it with their labour'.[11] In the light of such observations, Rousseau shrewdly observes that 'the first man who, having enclosed a piece of ground , bethought himself of saying "this is mine", and found people simple enough to believe him, was the real founder of civil society'.[12] More crucially, however, Rousseau held that it is just such accumulation of personal and private property which encourages some individuals to regard themselves as superior to others. Thus, compounding the (arguable) dishonesty of claiming ownership of what by rights belongs to no-one, possessive individuals are prone to the hubris that Rousseau famously referred to as *amour propre*: he regarded such vanity or false pride as precisely the source of all the ills, injustices and internecine strife of civil society. This general explanation of the evils of society is also the basis of the celebrated Rousseauian doctrine that people are by nature *good*. By this, however, Rousseau does not mean that human nature exhibits no tendency to evil action or corruption, or that even in a state of nature people will always behave like angels: he means only that the self-interestedness of humans that Hobbes takes to be part of their natural condition or constitution is actually something *acquired* in the course of certain processes of socio-economic development. According to Rousseau, the pre-civil state of nature is conducive to altruism and cooperation, whereas the post-natural state of civil society engenders social division, rivalry and mutual antagonism. But it can now be seen that Rousseau has quite dramatically reversed Hobbes' analysis of the relationship of the individual to society: whereas for Hobbes people are by nature aggressive and anti-social and their only hope of salvation lies in forced submission to the order and constraints of civil society, for Rousseau the inherent social nature of people – which inclines them to the cooperation and altruism of the pre-civil state – is actually prone to distortion under the corrupting pressures of more advanced levels of socio-economic evolution.

Progressive goodness and democracy

It also needs to be appreciated that, contrary to some caricatures of his position, Rousseau did not believe that there was any reasonable prospect of halting the inevitable process of human socio-economic evolution in the interests of a return to the state of nature. Rather, he held that what was needed was progress, in the light of a disinterested concern for the common good, to a higher level of conscious individual commitment to the freedom and equality of all citizens. He also held that such concern for the common good was possible only via rational appreciation of that universal moral law to which we have already referred in previous mention of Rousseau and Kant. The problem as perceived by Rousseau was that the corruption engendered by transition from the innocent state of nature to the fallen civil state made it difficult for individual human agents to recognise the authority of any such absolute moral imperative. Moreover, Rousseau also held that much of the corruption to which individuals are prone in the civil state could be laid at the door of the socialisation and/or education which children and young people received at the hands of parents and teachers: it was in the home and school that children were educated in the false beliefs about themselves and others which perverted natural moral reason. It was in such contexts that some young people – particularly the children of the well-to-do educated classes – would come to think of themselves as superior to the lower orders and to learn to despise and exploit them. Hence, Rousseau argues in his key educational work *Émile* for a primarily prophylactic conception of education largely concerned to protect the child from the venal influences of society and to promote an unbiased appreciation of the rights and freedoms of others. It is also, in *Émile*, a significant feature of such unprejudiced development that the learner should learn more by direct *practical* experience of the world – by discovery and experiment – than by direct instruction in received 'wisdom': the lessons of nature are for Rousseau inevitably more universally valid than the lessons of local convention. At all events, he regarded the development of such practical reason as basic to the promotion and production of responsible democratic citizens capable of concern more for the common good than for self-interest.

Although the extent and significance of Rousseau's philosophical and educational legacy is a matter of ongoing controversy, there can be little doubt that his work sets the general pattern of subsequent 'progressive' educational thinking from his own to the present time. This is so despite the fact that many modern brands of progressivism have neither acknowledged nor honoured Rousseau's influence, and that different strands of the general pattern of Rousseauian educational thinking have to some extent unravelled in diverse latter-day traditions of progressivism. Thus, among the many different forms that progressivism has taken in modern times, it seems possible to discern two main types that reflect rather different educational emphases. The first of these, as we have previously observed, is mainly associated with the work of the American pragmatist philosopher John Dewey, and such disciples of Dewey as W.H. Kilpatrick. Although Dewey rejected the label 'progressive' and was quite hostile to the asocial aspects of Rousseau's educational theory, his pioneering educational methodology of topic-based inquiry, discovery and experiment – which has been also been regarded as the root of the alleged progressive ills of much primary education in Britain and elsewhere – is nevertheless close to the spirit of Rousseau's own pedagogical suggestions. The second main type of progressivism, however, is widely associated with the British founder of Summerhill, A.S. Neill – although it is probably more justly attributed to Neill's own friend and mentor, the American psychologist and teacher Homer Lane, whose own Little Commonwealth was the inspiration and blueprint for Neill's school.[13] Although there is not much evidence of direct Rousseauian influence on Lane and Neill either, and while (unlike Dewey) these educationalists had relatively little interest in questions of pedagogy or educational methodology, their own psychoanalytically inspired work well reflects the Rousseauian idea that the allegedly indoctrinatory climate of conventional schooling is largely uncongenial to healthy development of the authentic freedom of human rational autonomy. Like Rousseau, Lane and Neill held that conventional schooling mainly serves to undermine the confidence and self-determination of children and to turn them into slaves of current prejudice – and, going arguably further than Rousseau, they held that responsible freedom can only be acquired in the free and uncoercive conditions of self-governing schools .

As these divergent trends indicate, however, although a progressive ideology of liberation and a progressive pedagogy of discovery and experiment do not *need* to be conjoined in a Rousseauian way, these two basic ideas nevertheless serve to define the principal ways in which educational progressivism is liable to depart from traditionalism. First, there is the idea that, far from being wicked or corrupt, and only redeemable by forced initiation into the received wisdom and values of a given society or culture, human nature is at least potentially if not actually good, and therefore best flourishes in conditions of freedom. Secondly, there is the idea that it is at least dubious if not downright mistaken to hold that the received wisdom of a given cultural tradition does represent the best that has been thought and said, and that therefore good educational practice should be regarded as an initiation into such wisdom: on the progressive view, education should therefore be more concerned to promote the habits of critical thought and reflection needed to question current knowledge and values. The first of these ideas is strongly emphasised by such psychoanalytic progressives as Lane and Neill, who – although not greatly exercised by pedagogical considerations – clearly take attitudes of critical questioning to be part and parcel of any education in freedom. The second idea receives most emphasis in the work of such pragmatic progressives as Dewey and Kilpatrick, who – though not greatly exercised by the psychotherapeutic dimensions of self-determination (as well as being not at all sympathetic to the anti-social aspects of some progressive thought) – also insist that the heart of education should be the cultivation of habits of criticism and free inquiry. In general, then, progressives hold that nothing is to be taken on the basis of authority alone, or as beyond the pale of reasonable questioning and debate.

Given that all this is so, the traditional–progressive debate is not essentially or primarily – even in the case of the pedagogical progressivism of modern pragmatists – a debate about the relative merits of teaching methods, or concerning the priority or otherwise of content over the needs and interests of the child. To be sure, there may be some very general pedagogical tendencies here. In the interests of promoting such aspects of psychological well-being as confidence and self-esteem, progressives are more likely to give the individual pursuit of personal interest priority over instruction in prescribed content: it is in the light of such emphasis that a current ideology of nursery education is widely characterised by practitioners as a 'child-centred' or 'progressive' one.[14] Again, it is likely that if one is committed to progressive questioning of authority or authoritative sources, then one is also likely to give pride of place to questioning, inquiry and discovery over more overtly didactive pedagogies. However, as we saw in the case of Neill's blending of non-coercive education with old-fashioned didactic pedagogy, this *need* not be so – and, indeed, one may miss the educational point entirely by too hasty assimilation of the broader ideological distinction between traditionalism and progressivism to narrower methodological or pedagogical concerns. Above all, the traditional–progressive divide expresses or represents a *normative* distinction between two rather different conceptions of the role of education in preparing individuals for social membership, and of the proper balance of authority, discipline and freedom in any such preparation. Insofar as traditionalists and progressives incline to radically different – more and less optimistic – views of human nature, they are disposed to rather different estimates of the extent to which pupils need firm discipline or may be trusted with freedom. Like Hobbes, traditionalists are inclined to regard human nature as in thrall to deeply ingrained anti-social and self-interested tendencies: thus, left to themselves and without external authority and discipline, human beings would be incapable of civilised cooperation and self-restraint. Like Rousseau (on most days), however, progressives are more inclined to regard human nature as fundamentally benevolent, and to view the more sociopathic aspects of human association as a function of various kinds of post civil-societal injustice and inequality.[15]

Authority, discipline and punishment

In this connection, the difference between traditionalists and (at least some) progressives on the question of punishment in schools is instructive. It is clear that punishments of this or that kind have been part of the fabric of discipline of much conventional institutionalised schooling. Thus, although the once customary canings and beating are largely a thing of the past in most (though not all) civilised countries, less physical modes of discipline and punishment – in the form of detentions, punishment excercises, withdrawal of privileges, and so on – are a fairly routine part of the coercive apparatus of most state schools. Traditionalists will insist that without such deterrents general anarchy would prevail. But thoroughgoing progressives would argue that this simply confuses authority with simple obedience to imposed rules: although they do not deny the need for social and other rules – not least in a complex social situation like a school – they are inclined to question the idea that sane and civilised rule-following best follows from the coercion of unwilling subjects. In particular, such modern psychoanalytic progressives as Lane and Neill have wished to tell a fairly complex psychological story about the deeply debilitating effects of such coercion on human development. Thus, although they would not disagree with Rousseau that the ills of society are often to be traced to the development of socially divisive false pride or hubris, they would view even such apparently superior attitudes as largely symptomatic of individual insecurity, anxiety and inferiority (and Rousseau himself explicitly maintained that those who regard themselves as the masters of others are even greater slaves than they[16]). Moreover, though the pivotal psychoanalytic idea of repression plays a key role in the educational and therapeutic accounts of Lane and Neill, they seem at one in rejecting Freud's essentially pessimistic or traditionalist view of human nature. Thus, whereas Freud appears to have held that repression is an inevitable consequence of human forward development if the dark forces of the Id (non-rational or irrational desires) are to be brought under the control of the Ego (the rational 'reality' principle), Lane and Neill held that insofar as there is nothing inherently negative about the basic human instincts and inclinations, any such artificial control can have only disastrous effects on the development of stable, mature and responsible human beings.[17]

Thus, whereas many traditionalists seem to have held that the controls of externally imposed discipline offered the most promising solution to difficulties raised by indiscipline and deviance, Lane and Neill held – very much in the spirit of Rousseau's identification of society as the problem rather the solution – that such controls were themselves often the cause of such difficulties. Indeed, dealing from the outset – as both Lane and Neill did – with problem or delinquent children, they regarded punitive or coercive discipline as the traceable psychological cause of the anti-social behaviour of such children. The trouble seemed to be that many such children had been deprived of the freedom of responsibility and trust precisely conducive to a sense of real human potency and worth: having had the very will to freedom crushed out of them, they were now capable only of self-loathing and of a correspondingly defensive hostility and resentment towards others. The way forward for such children, according to Lane and Neill, could only lie in freedom rather than coercion. All the same, they were careful to insist that real freedom means rational *responsibility*, not licence. Neill expresses the difference between freedom and licence in his work *Summerhill* by saying that whereas the unfree home is that in which the child has *no* rights, and the spoiled home is that in which they have *all* the rights, the free home is that in which they have *equal* rights with others.[18] That said, it has often been held to be a less welcome consequence of their educational and therapeutic theory and practice that Lane and Neill supposed the only route to personal rehabilitation – after the repressive damage of coercion had been done – to be the removal of all forms of externally imposed authority or discipline in the interests of complete pupil

control of school life. Such radical freedom was conceived as the main therapeutic means to what Lane called 'the breaking of constellations':[19] until
troubled children had been liberated from the negative associations of (parental,
legal, educational or other) authority, it would be impossible for them to recognise the intrinsic life-enhancing purpose and utility of the norms of civilised life.
Consequently Lane and Neill appeared to let pupils at their schools do as they
pleased – to attend or stay away from lessons as they wished, to swear or even
destroy public property – in order to work psychologically though their acquired
resentment of authority. Despite this, the avowed aim of both educators was not
anarchy, but the promotion of responsible self-direction: in the course of doing
as they liked, pupils were meant to realise how intolerable life was without proper
rules of human association, and Lane and Neill sought to shift the burden of
responsibility for formulating and policing proper observance of such rules from
teachers to the pupils themselves. The ultimate aim of freedom was the promotion of authentic responsibility in a climate of mutual respect and trust.

Despite the fact that their theories have been widely dismissed and derided,
and that the practices they recommended and pursued are open to some question, I believe that the key works of both Lane and Neill – especially Lane's
insightful *Talks to Parents and Teachers* – are of enormous professional educational
interest, and that there is much of real value to be gained by students and
teachers from a sober and *critical* reading of them. To be sure, their ideas were
radical, and it should also be borne in mind that their often extreme measures
were forged in the fires of practical engagement with a specific educational clien-
tele of often deeply disturbed young people. From this viewpoint, it is arguable
that at least Neill makes a similar mistake to Freud in trying to give wider application to a rather special kind of explanation of human (mis)behaviour that is
only really called for in exceptional cases: just as Freud rather dubiously
extended to all humans a theory of personality formation he developed in order
to explain particular instances of neurotic personality, so Neill seems to have
been inclined to apply to all and sundry the kind of therapeutic techniques that
he and Lane first developed to understand and rehabilitate delinquent children.
On the other hand, however, the ideas of Lane and Neill on self-government,
and their explicit use of school democracy for the promotion of qualities of
responsible citizenship, are clearly not too far removed from those of other less
radically libertarian progressive educationalists. Thus, for example, although the
pragmatic or epistemological progressivism of Dewey and his followers is focused
less upon the development of personal psychological emancipation, and more on
the promotion of interpersonal and social qualities, it is fairly clear that the two
different progressive approaches have otherwise much in common. In the main,
Dewey's education for democracy, like Neill's education for freedom, is directed
towards the production of confident, self-assured and responsible young people
capable of the critical reflection that is above all needed for mature engagement
with the democratic processes of an open or liberal society. In both cases, it is
recognised that this can only be achieved in the sort of positive climate of reciprocal trust and respect in which young people are free from the manipulatory

pressures of social, political or other indoctrination, and to express their views without fear or anxiety.

The sources of authority

Traditionalists, however, are likely to regard this as all well and good, but easier said than done – not least in circumstances of extreme progressive freedom. Indeed, many contemporary traditionalists might be only too ready to agree with progressives – at least in the terms of extreme generality in which progressive aims have just been expressed – that it is the proper aim of education to produce responsible and critically reflective democratic citizens. It would clearly be a mistake – which some radical polemic on traditionalism has nevertheless sailed fairly close to committing – to suppose that traditionalists explicitly aim to produce insecure, neurotic and indoctrinated young people who are incapable of thinking for themselves. Where educational traditionalists disagree with progressives, however, is precisely over the question of how democratic citizenship and critical reflection are best cultivated – and, once again, this is less a technical question of the approriateness or otherwise of this or that pedagogical method, more a *normative* question of the proper educational balance of authority, discipline and freedom. From this viewpoint, although traditionalists may well agree with progressives in considering authority and discipline to be the very cornerstones of education, the apparent libertarianism of such psychological progressives as Neill has offered a ready target for criticism. To be sure, traditionalists may even here agree with such progressives that it is a mistake to suppose that the rules of good order need to be applied or enforced by coercive or authoritarian methods, and even with the progressive point that pupils might often be accorded more trust and responsibility, or be consulted more over the construction of school rules. But, in the light of fairly familiar considerations about the gradual emergence of human capacities for responsibility, it may also seem unrealistic if not irresponsible to place the entire burden of rule-making entirely on immature young shoulders. Moreover, although it is only to be expected that Neill's school was often a chaotic place, it is also not obvious that it always brought out the best in human nature, and so-called 'peer coercion' (perhaps no more than a euphemism for bullying) seems all too often to have been waiting to fill the gap left by the absence of adult authority.[20]

On a more traditionalist view, the key progressive mistake may be to regard the rules of good order as the arbitrary or subjective products of adult *or* pupil construction: insofar as the rules *are* rules of good order and responsible development, they are *objectively* justifiable and therefore in a real sense not of *any* mere human devising. From this viewpoint, good parents or teachers are arguably those who *kindly* but nevertheless *firmly* encourage children – irrespective of natural inclination – to internalise appropriate principles precisely in the name of those youngsters' own best interests. Although the principles, rules and virtues of honesty, self-control and respect have some source in the highest (social) impulses of human nature, they are not entirely natural, and young people need to appreciate that the discipline required to acquire such virtues is precisely a matter of submission to something beyond one's own natural impulses. To be sure, there may be exceptional circumstances in which loveless discipline can cause psychological damage, but there is no compelling reason to suppose that the bulk of kind parental direction towards the straight and narrow must have inevitable adverse consequences. However, these traditionalist reservations about the more extreme theories and practices of psychological progressives are not unrelated to a strong and longstanding traditionalist antipathy to the apparently more reasonable and less extreme pragmatist progressivism of Dewey and his many contemporary followers. In the United Kingdom, for example, Dewey has lately been the object of fairly strong obloquy for his alleged influence – previously noted in part II – on the postwar development of British primary education.[21] It has been said that Deweyan methodological emphases on integrated curricula, constructivist pedagogy and cooperative approaches to learning have greatly contributed to the (alleged) decline of academic standards – particularly of literacy and numeracy – and good school discipline across the state educational system. However, although the precise contribution of Dewey to such alleged educational malaise is a matter of some debate, there can be little doubt that the main target here is a set of ideas with which Dewey has been widely associated. It is likely that such 'back to basics' objections are concerned to defend a traditionalist faith in objectively grounded intellectual and moral discipline against a non-realist epistemology, and a morality of personal expression and/or social convenience, which seems to hold that we construct the world to our own preference rather than submit to what is required in the light of how things are. For many traditionalists, a pragmatist 'science' of knowledge and learning has appeared to be no less symptomatic of intellectual and moral decline than a libertarian progressive philosophy of self-fulfilment.

The key question for educational philosophy, of course, is that of how we should respond to these differences of perspective on the proper intellectual and moral direction of education and schooling – and this is no easy question. It is an enduring temptation to suppose that since some of these views are extreme, the best course may be to seek some suitable compromise between educational traditionalism and progressivism: that the answer, if there is one, lies in the middle. From this viewpoint, it would certainly seem reasonable to try to find some sensible middle way between the extreme authoritarianism of some traditionalist perspectives and the extreme libertarianism of some progressive views. However, even if we can find clear enough rational ground for dismissal of the extremes – for, after all, the philosophical issue is not whether they are wrong but *why* they are wrong – there may yet be much room for traditionalist versus progressive manoeuvre in the sane middle ground. We have already noticed that empirical method cannot settle the key issues in which traditional–progressive debates are often implicated – for example, that of the propriety or otherwise of punishment in education – for these are *normative* or moral not technical questions. To be sure, it also seems likely that some of the issues between traditionalists and progressives – that, for example, which separates more traditionalist or realist epistemology and pedagogy from pragmatist or constructivist conceptions – are *epistemological* more than moral: as such, there may in principle turn out to be better *theoretical* arguments for one position rather than the other – and I have in this work already expressed my own reservations about pragmatism and constructivism. That said, it is not quite so clear that the basic value conflicts as defined by the difference between greater traditional emphasis on disciplined learning of the academic 'basics', and progressive emphasis more on social learning and creative self-expression, would be susceptible even in principle of any such resolution by philosophical argument (or conceptual analysis) alone. In this respect, it could be that the differences between some traditionalists and some progressives over the place in human life of authority, discipline and freedom ultimately reflect diverse lifestyle preferences, and that no-one in a liberal-democratic society is well placed to decide for someone else whether they should have their child educated in an academic traditional school or under some more relaxed progressive dispensation. It may also be, given individual differences of personality and temperament, that it is not even wise to look for some general human developmental answer here. Sensitive parents of more than one child have ever appreciated that different offspring are liable to engender rather different disciplinary demands, and that what is appropriate to the upbringing of this child is not necessarily so for that. From this viewpoint, it may be appropriate for good parents and teachers to be intelligently sceptical with respect to those dogmatic developmental claims that have so often paraded in educational theory as universal truths of human flourishing. All the same, as we have argued in this work, it is also important to be appreciate that there are norms of human (moral and other) development and conduct which are more generally applicable in the interests of human flourishing as such: it is these norms that we ignore at our peril in any attempt to give free rein to personal preference or individual self-expression.

Possible tasks

(1) This chapter has suggested that the main difference between traditionalists and progressives is that whereas the former think that corrupt human nature needs to be controlled by social rules, the latter hold that potentially good human nature is apt to be corrupted by social repression. Attempt some critical evaluation of this conflict of perspective.

(2) Try to formulate a general strategy or policy for school discipline with respect to such issues as dress, punctuality, disobedience, respect for others, truancy, vandalism and failure to remain on task that is neither too repressive nor too libertarian, and that gives pupils proper scope for individual and/or collective responsibilty.

Chapter 15

Political dimensions
of education

Different senses of education as political

The aim of this last chapter is to examine the precise respects in which education
and teaching are implicated in *political* considerations and concerns. However,
insofar as it is nowadays often held that there are no significant non-political or
apolitical educational questions, it might be said that attention to the political
dimensions of education should have been the *first* rather than the last port of
call in any general survey of educational philosophy and theory of the present
kind. All the same, I believe the claim that all educational questions are political
is liable to serious overstatement, and probably stems from some overreaction to
what may now seem the rather dismissive attitude of early postwar analytical
educational philosophers towards the political context of education. Here,
indeed, it is not merely that first-generation analytical philosophers often
adopted a rather socio-politically *decontextualised* approach to the analysis of
educational concepts, but that some pioneers of analysis explicitly denied that
political considerations and imperatives could ever be relevant to the professional
determination or resolution of educational issues and policies.[1] Still, although I
believe there is something to these objections to earlier analytical approaches, it
may also be that they confuse two somewhat different issues – and, in fact, the
basic muddle may well be closely related to one upon which we have already
touched concerning aims of education and schooling. For, unless one defines
politics so loosely as to empty it utterly of meaning, it seems likely that there is a
significant distinction to be drawn between *education* and other processes of
human development and socialisation, which has no especial political import.
Any such distinction may be contested and contestable, and it may be that no-
one has yet drawn it in a satisfactory way; but it is far from clear that any form of
rational appreciation of this distinction would have to be *political* in any substantial sense. On the other hand, however, since schools are social institutions
provided by the state from public funds – and are therefore (at least in democratic polities) accountable to taxpayers – it is no less certain that reflection upon
the aims and purposes of *schooling* could hardly be *other than* political.

However, another factor that may have prompted some exaggeration of the
political character of educational questions is the recent preference – under the
explicit influence of currently fashionable non-analytical or social scientific intel-

lectual trends – for regarding *all* human institutions and practices, including schools and what they teach, as governed or shaped by normative constraints of a fundamentally *hegemonic* character. This view is again shot through with the most basic logical errors, and it is a continuing cause for concern that those who argue in this fashion will sooner attack careful philosophical analysis in the name of such blunders than employ responsible analysis in the interests of exposing the confusions. At all events, it is likely that the key error of new hegemonic analyses is a basic confusion between the *normative* and the political – or, at any rate, of assimilation of the former to the latter. A much revisited consideration in this work is the neo-idealist or communitarian (or, for that matter, 'critical realist') claim that concepts are (in some sense) culturally constructed, and therefore have social origins and histories which at least some previous approaches to philosophical analysis may have unhelpfully ignored. This point may be an interesting and significant one for some philosophical purposes – it may, for example, be of real philosophical importance to appreciate that people of past ages may not have construed ideas of justice, virtue or skill exactly as we do (although it is also not entirely clear what exactly such examples really do show about the general cultural character of concepts) – but it is far from evident that such considerations serve to support any general claim concerning the political or hegemonic character of culturally constructed concepts.

At the level of common sense, for example, it would appear that ideas of music, of its human value and of its educational potential, are culturally determined and matters of considerable cross-cultural controversy. Many educationalists, though not all, have held that music is humanly or culturally important enough to be included in the school curriculum, and have also advocated – on different grounds and from different perspectives – that this or that form of music should be promoted educationally. For example, although this author would argue that music *is* important, and that jazz is a significant form of music with which all pupils might be acquainted, it is also clear that many others would disagree. That said, it is far from clear how any resolution of questions about the educational importance of jazz and its place in the curriculum should be considered a *political* matter. Of course, one can see how the matter of whether or not jazz gets into the curriculum might be politically determined. I might live in an elitist society in which jazz is not regarded as part of the high culture – and therefore excluded from the national curriculum – or in another more culturally egalitarian liberal democracy in which it is considered politically correct for all forms of music to be represented in the curriculum of the common school. But it should be evident not only that both of these politically motivated reasons for including or excluding jazz from the curriculum are equally suspect (in fact, I believe they are both quite unacceptable), but also that no such political considerations could be of serious relevance to the question of whether jazz is good or worthwhile music, and therefore appropriate for curriculum inclusion. If this is a question for anyone, it is more one for experts in music and music education than politicians. Likewise, the even stronger assumption that the status or value of this or that human activity – and (in consequence) its place in the school curriculum – is entirely a function of its role in enabling some to control or wield power over others is just as implausible. In fact, we know that although this has *sometimes* been the case, it is no less evident that politicians and educationalists have often made explicit and strenuous effforts (successfully or otherwise) to reduce widespread inherited or other injustices, and to promote greater opportunities for the socially disadvantaged. Indeed, it is rather ironic that some contemporary educational philosophers and theorists influenced by poststructuralist or other hegemonic analyses of social institutions often seem to want to have it both ways by arguing that all educational and other social institutions are driven by considerations of power seeking, *and* that we should seek to establish a more just climate of inclusion. But if the former claim is true, it is not clear on what rational basis we might pursue any agenda of the latter kind.

The normative, the political and the hegemonic

Thus, extreme arguments to the effect that any and all deliberations about education must be political are prone to paradox or dilemma. On the one hand, if the point is simply that any and all conceptions of education are *normative*, and enshrine socio-culturally conditioned beliefs and values, this claim – though true – does not in the least serve to establish any very interesting or substantial conclusion about the *political* nature as such of education. Although it is reasonably clear from recent social and politial theory that human beliefs and values have cultural histories, it hardly follows from this that any and all deliberation with respect to them would have to be driven by political (as distinct from, say, moral, religious or aesthetic) considerations. Hence, any stronger claim to the effect that all educational deliberations and decisions are *nothing* but political seems implausible if not actually incoherent. Of course, any such stronger argument is itself susceptible of weaker and stronger versions. On the weaker interpretation, the point might be that in realms of normative inquiry socio-political motives and considerations are *basic*, and that what are generally thought of as moral, religious and aesthetic concerns are really political imperatives in disguise. Again, however, any such claim would seem to depend on some question-begging laundering of the term 'political' for which there is little clear warrant: the truth is that human lives and conduct are governed by many motives, considerations and concerns, some of which (such as voting, canvassing and protesting) are political, and some of which (such as praying, jogging and listening to jazz) are not – and it is little more than conceptual imperialism to insist that the latter must reduce to the former. However, the stronger claim that all normatively governed and constituted human enterprises and concerns are political in some more loaded *hegemonic* sense is prone to rather deeper incoherence. Both forms of the normative/political conflation run into the conceptual difficulty that if *everything* is political, then *nothing* is: if the reduction of the normative to the political blurs any and all familiar distinctions between the political, the moral, the religious, the aesthetic, and so on, then it is no longer clear what distinct sense we should continue to attach to 'political' (or, indeed, whether 'political' is the term we should persist in using following any such conflation).[2] But any further assimilation of the political to the hegemonic seems additionally problematic, for it is difficult to give any distinct sense to such assimilation other than in terms of a rather austere reading of the fact–value distinction. The point would now be that to whatever extent non-normative questions (recognising, of course, that some contemporary perspectives may not even accept the possibility of non-normative perspectives) can be settled in a rationally objective or value-neutral (perhaps evidence-based) way, normative questions – as matters of purely personal predilection – cannot be so settled. But then the consequence of construing normative questions first as political and secondly as hegemonic would seem to be to render them quite unsusceptible of any *rational* rather than non-rational resolution (by, for example, rhetorical persuasion, political lobbying or brute force) whatsoever. Hence, any meaningful claim that all questions of value are hegemonic amounts to a denial that reasoned argument can ever be of any real utility with regard to the clarification or justification of human values. But any and all such 'argument' is surely the ultimate counsel of philosophical (not to say philosophically self-defeating) despair – and, of course, quite absolves us of any *rational* obligation to respond to it.

It would be just as absurd, however, to deny there are any significant respects in which education and teaching are implicated in political issues and problems (or vice versa), and which involve neither wholesale assimilation of the normative to the political, nor any radical hegemonic construal of the political. Indeed, one such respect relates to an apparent general tension between (non-political) professional educational values and aspirations, and political aims and imperatives with regard to education and schooling. The point would be precisely that there are respects in which the professionally motivated concerns of teachers to provide young people with the best quality education must – by virtue of fact or practical necessity – conflict with the socio-political agendas or objectives of democratically or otherwise appointed offices and agents of government. Once again, one need not deny the inevitably *normative* character of what are here called 'non-political' or professional values or aspirations, or even that some of these aspirations are likely to be themselves coloured by the particular party-political allegiances of individual professionals. The point is rather that whatever the politics of particular professionals, they are nevertheless liable to find themselves – as professionals operating in a publicly accountable context of schooling – at variance with aims and objectives that have less to do with the quality of personal development of particular pupils, and more with the efficiency of an economically accountable social institution or system. From this viewpoint, career politicians and administrators may just be expected to have rather different goals from professional educationalists and teachers, and to be much more preoccupied with the socio-economic or other instrumental outcomes of schooling, or with the technical efficiency of any means adopted to achieve those outcomes, than with (say) ethical or other theoretical debates concerning the intrinsic aims of education and teaching. Indeed, assuming a general professional interest in providing the richest possible programme of education and development for pupils, and the inevitable concern of politicians with the management of tight financial budgets, regular clashes over money and resources between politicians and/or taxpayers and teachers and/or their professional (union and other) representatives are perhaps only to be expected. But the extensive literature of educational professionalism also bears witness to the more substantial differences of *educational* perspective that are likely to arise between those whose concern lies more with the overall instrumental benefits of an economically conceived system, and those who are more concerned with addressing issues of individual need and personal development.

But, of course, the professional practice of education and teaching may be rather more substantially implicated in political issues and concerns. Thus, notwithstanding that professionals of diverse political stripes might sometimes choose to unite in common opposition to the more general political instrumentalism just indicated, and although it is possible that some individuals might lack any specific political opinions, it is just as likely that many professionals will have developed political views, and that they will also be aware of the implications for education of the larger social goals and policies to which they are sympathetic as particular political agents. In short, insofar as education and teaching have inevitable social and political consequences, and professionals as political agents are committed to the promotion of some particular social vision, it may be expected that they will endorse those educational policies most conducive to that vision. From this viewpoint, it would seem reasonable to hold that particular party-political perspectives entail specific educational perspectives – or, conversely, that allegience to a given educational policy might commit one to a given party-political perspective. Indeed, I suspect that it is fairly widely held that it is possible to align different educational theories with diverse political perspectives in some such way. More precisely, it may well be that faith in such alignment reflects a rather dubious mapping of the lately explored contrast between educational traditionalism and progressivism onto a distinction between right- and left-of-centre politics. Thus, it often seems to be assumed that whereas educational traditionalism is a conservative or right-of-centre position, left-wing politics is more at home with an educationally progressive agenda. At all events, the remainder of this chapter will be devoted to a brief critical exploration of both of these more plausible connections between educational and political questions: first, of the idea of fundamental opposition between political and professional imperatives; secondly, of the idea that political perspectives have specific and distinct educational implications.

The political versus the professional

Significant opposition or antagonism between professional and official or administrative objectives has probably always been a feature of educational debate and controversy. Moreover, in the light of their explicit concern to enhance the general quality of teacher reflection and deliberation, postwar analytical philosophers of education seem to have elevated critique of official educational policy to the status of a professional duty, and criticism of official educational policy making has remained a large part of the stock-in-trade of even those latter-day professional educational philosophers and theorists who claim to draw inspiration from intellectual sources outside the analytical tradition. From this perspective, the extensive and ever-expanding contemporary literature of educational philosophy often seems to be largely – though certainly not entirely – defined by a certain enduring tension or opposition between professional and political interests and imperatives. To be fair, it would not be completely accurate to conceive this opposition as always and everywhere antagonistic, and professional theorists and policy makers have lately made admirable efforts in Britain and elsewhere to enter into collaborative and mutually respectful dialogue in the interests of more positive or productive movement on some of the issues that have often divided them.[3] That said, it remains hard to find clear cases in which familiar political and professional differences have been much mended by such open and friendly dialogue, and – in the light of the fundamental differences of pedagogical and administrative interest and concern earlier noted in this chapter – it may be overly optimistic to expect otherwise. Indeed, despite the extraordinary amount of ink spilt on the questions that divide educational professionals and politicians – and without in the least wishing to belittle the value and virtue of much of such effort (to which the author of this work has also often contributed) – any regular reader of the literature is liable to experience a certain wearying *déjà vu* about the overall drift of such debate. Although there is clearly much of both professional *and* political importance at stake in these matters, the often bitter debates between educational professionals and administrators seem seldom to achieve much more than an uneasy compromise between political and professional interests. Still, insofar as the price of professional freedom is wisdom and vigilance, to have noted the well-trodden nature of the debates is not in the least to doubt their worth, or to counsel apathy with regard to them. Indeed, resisting potential political or economic erosion of educational standards via frequent reiteration of well-rehearsed arguments probably just goes with the territory of responsible professional engagement, and the perennial need for such critical vigilance is also surely the principal justification for the broader 'theoretical' professional education that is so often vigorously resisted by (especially authoritarian) political dispensations.

All the same, the well-trodden nature of the terrain renders the present task of summarising the general issues of professional–political educational controversy rather easier than the volume of related literature might otherwise suggest. In the broadest terms, tensions or conflicts between professional and political interests and imperatives turn mainly on issues and problems of economic efficiency and accountability. In this regard, we should first note that professionals are no less interested in accountabilty and economically efficient educational practice than are politicians, and that professionals and politicians are both ultimately answerable to a common constituency – namely that wider public whose progeny actually attend schools and other educational institutions. But there is also clearly much scope for tension between the rather diverse ways in which politicians and professionals are publicly accountable, and between the rather differently grounded values and principles that inform political and professional accountability. On the one hand, politicians and public administrators are accountable to the public not just as parents, but also as voters and taxpayers: as such, the same parents who desire high-quality education for their children will often (though not always) want such education to be provided at the lowest possible financial cost to themselves, and they are also likely to want this without any significant reduction in quality of the other social and civic benefits – such as well-maintained roads, effective street lighting, safe civil engineering, adequate police protection, prompt medical attention – that they also expect to be funded from their taxes. In addition, however, politicians and officials face the considerable fiscal difficulty of ensuring that expenditure on public services does not outstrip available income: in short they have an obligation to balance the national budget, and many a government has run the national economy on the rocks by spending more on such welfare services as education than it could afford. From this viewpoint, governments faced with offering educational and other provision generally inferior to what the public desires may by that same token feel obligated to show as clearly as possible that what is on offer provides the best available value for money. However, to the extent that the more intangible qualitative benefits of education – those pertaining to enhanced personal growth – are harder to assess in any readily measurable way, there may be some understandable if not completely justifiable political tendency to focus on the more visibly productive aspects of education: by this light, good education is what produces measurable economic benefits.

On the other hand, educationalists are accountable to members of the public primarily in their roles as parents who want what they take to be the best possible quality of educational and other development for children – with especial regard to the needs and interests of their own children. Thus, parents are unlikely to regard their own children as mere cogs in the wheel of national productivity: on the contrary, they are much more likely to regard them – not least, perhaps, when they have remedial difficulties that may impede such effective productivity – as unique persons whose individual needs deserve the highest possible priority. Like politicians, however, teachers and other professional educationalists face the additional problem that the imperatives to which they owe primary allegiance often appear to be at odds with the aspirations of those – politicians, employers and parents – to whom they are also professionally accountable. Thus, just as it will often seem to politicians that they cannot *afford* to give the public what they want, it may often appear to educational professionals that there are principled reasons for not giving parents or other interested parties what they want. In this regard, indeed, one can certainly envisage circumstances in which the interests of external agencies in public schooling may not be in the best interests of individual children. One already noted example of such shortfall concerns past and present pressure from politicians, employers and training agencies to focus the content of the school curriculum more on instrumentally useful scientific and technical skills than upon personally formative cultural or expressive pursuits.[4] In such cases, a professional decision in favour of some balance between the personally formative and the economically useful (where these are not entirely beyond simultaneous achievement) may well be more rationally defensible than this or that instrumental official policy. But it is also likely that many parents who have the highest and best-intentioned hopes for their children may come to have a fairly skewed view of what is really in their children's best interests – by, for example, overemphasising academic achievement at the expense of other more personal and social aspects of development, or by forcing them in career directions that have more to do with frustrated parental ambitions than with what is dear to the hearts of their progeny. Thus, although it is not possible to give any brief summary of the higher values and principles to which professional educationalists owe primary allegiance, and while there is clearly much scope for individual diversity regarding more detailed conceptions of such values and principles, it is reasonable to suppose that they would turn upon a general commitment to truth, honesty and intellectual integrity (as opposed to mere expedience), and to justice as expressed in concerns for individual need and the common good (as opposed to mere self-interest or economic benefit). In this light, it is not hard to see how political and professional imperatives might conflict with respect to many issues of education and schooling.

Bones of professional–political contention

At all events, there would appear to be two main interrelated levels of concern about public educational provision that give rise to political/professional conflicts of accountability. First, there are (at what might be called the personal resource level) longstanding political and professional issues concerning the proper pre-service training, as well as subsequent in-service monitoring and appraisal, of state school teachers. The issues here turn mainly upon questions – upon which we have already touched in this work – regarding the proper relationship of theoretical or academic study to practical experience in training, and/or the extent to which teacher knowledge and expertise is a matter for professional deliberation and decision rather than top-down official prescription. Ignoring some implausibly extreme responses to the first question – namely some past professional overemphases on theoretical study at the expense of practice, and some more politically authoritarian claims to the effect that teachers do not need theoretical reflection at all[5] – these concerns very much converge in issues about the pros and cons of competence models of training, and about the proper character of ongoing teacher appraisal. In the case of competence models of training this may be less than obvious, since there are different anti-competence arguments, and it is not clear that all of these are opposed to top-down official prescription of teacher expertise. For example, to the extent that many such arguments are largely methodological, and focus more upon the technical psychological difficulties of identifying and measuring discrete teaching competences, it is not clear that such objections would have to be at odds with the idea that teachers need to be told what to do by others with greater theoretical expertise. Again, it is doubtful whether what appears to be the standard philosophical objection to competences – that they inevitably involve reduction of teacher expertise to routine behavioural skills – gets precisely to the heart of the matter;[6] indeed, many contemporary competence models claim, with some justice, that professional competences are intended to embrace knowledge, or intellectual as well as practical skills (although any such objection does invite the possible response that they cannot therefore be regarded as genuine competence models).[7] From this viewpoint, a more telling argument against competence models may be that what they purport to describe and prescribe as practical or intellectual skills are actually not specifiable skills at all, but rather variously interpretable values or problems susceptible of a wide range of professionally effective solutions. From this viewpoint, it is notable that the so-called 'theoretical' knowledge of competence models seldom ventures beyond required acquaintance with central or local directives, and certainly not so far as any explicit invitation to engage critically with the intellectual principles upon which competence prescriptions are themselves based.[8] This, of course, is hardly surprising – insofar as any serious invitation to question such principles could hardly be made from *within* a competence model. Thus, the key professional problem with competence models is that they seem wedded *in principle* to a top-down approach to the promulgation of teacher expertise; hence, it should occasion no great surprise that the main support for them has come from politicians and educational administrators concerned (understandably) with the regulation and control of teacher performance in accordance with demonstrable standards, and that the main opposition to them has come from educational theorists concerned to defend the professional necessity for free and open intellectual exploration of the fullest range of pedagogical possibility.[9]

Similar considerations affect the question of how, from a professional or administrative viewpoint, we may ensure that those who have been admitted to the teaching profession continue to maintain or develop their expertise in accordance with the highest professional standards. Once again, the main options would appear to lie in one or another form of either top-down or bottom-up approach to the appraisal of teacher performance. As might be expected, the official or administrative approach has invariably inclined towards more top-down or 'line-management' approaches to appraisal, which usually require teacher conduct to conform to certain externally imposed 'performance indicators'.[10] On this view, as positioned on the bottom rung of a complex hierarchy of educational line-management – rising through heads of department, deputy heads, headteachers, local directors of education, officially appointed inspectors, and so on – chalk-face teachers are directly accountable to standards handed down from on high. The key problem about any such approach, however, is that it is far from obvious that such official line-managers are better placed to advise teachers about the actual nitty-gritty of classroom practice than are the practitioners themselves. This explains why the responses of professionally experienced and respected classroom teachers to the advice of non-practising educational academics or officials are sometimes tinged with a certain animosity or resentment – which cannot simply be dismissed as mere anti-intellectualism or professional envy. The fact is that classroom teachers will sometimes have opted to remain in the classroom rather than to seek promotion to administrative posts precisely because they are good at and value what they do – and, from this viewpoint, even well-meaning advice from those at some remove from actual practice may be hard to stomach. Indeed, even on the assumption that those placed in authority over classroom teachers are privy to a better general grasp of the basic principles of practice, it may still be questioned whether they are better placed than those in the field to appreciate the particular challenges of the classroom situation: as the first nation American says, it may be hard (if not presumptuous) to judge a man until one has walked a mile in his moccasins. However, this broader problem of the value of 'outside' versus 'inside' educational knowledge and expertise looms larger in considering the more systemic dimensions of educational accountability and quality control.

Again, it should occasion little surprise that the problems of educational accountability and quality control arising at the institutional level largely reflect those at levels of personal resource. First, just as an issue has been raised about the control of individual practitioner quality to which competence models of practice and performance indicators have been advanced as official solutions, so an analogous issue has been raised about control and monitoring of the larger quality of schools. Thus, at a more systemic level, the idea of school effectiveness runs roughly parallel to that of competence models of professional preparation, and the general notion of school inspection may be regarded as the institutional analogue of teacher appraisal (although, of course, inspection can also be one form that teacher appraisal takes). At all events, the school effectiveness movement has lately gained much professional ground as well as official approval in response to contemporary concerns about the variable quality of state educational provision. At heart, the school effectiveness approach rests on the idea that general social scientific inquiry into the difference between 'successful' and 'unsuccessful' practice might serve to disclose certain universal features of the 'good' or effective school.[11] In short, the idea of school effectiveness is largely consistent with competence models in holding that principles of good educational practice are expressible in terms of something like causal generalities: the key idea is that precise conditions for the production of effective learning or desirable pupil behaviour might be disclosed by social scientific inquiry of a statistical or otherwise generalisable sort. On the face of it, however, school effectiveness inquiry thus conceived seems liable to much the same difficulties as competence models. For a start, there is the general problem that school effectiveness approaches, no less than competence models, are in danger of ignoring a significant element of legitimate value diversity in education and teaching: that schools and individual teachers are apt for judgement as good or bad in the light of different ideals, aims and goals. In Neill's school, Summerhill, discipline will certainly *look* different from, if not downright worse than, that of other schools;

but that may only be because the teachers in the school value a different sort of order or discipline. This, of course, is not to defend the disciplinary approaches of progressive education; it is only to insist that any judgement regarding the inferiority or superiority of Summerhill discipline would have to be normative or moral rather than *scientific*. Once again, it seems doubtful whether there could be any value-neutral *empirical* demonstration of a good school as such.

The grounds of professional knowledge

However, a rather different (albeit not unrelated) objection to the idea of school effectiveness turns upon the sort of considerations we have lately explored in connection with teacher appraisal by imposed performance indicators. For just as it is simply not clear whether such general indicators would or could be relevant to the situated needs and challenges of the field professional, so it is unclear whether all 'good' or effective schools could, would or should conform to such general criteria of school effectiveness. To take a previous, albeit hackneyed, example, it might be thought one plausible performance indicator of good (competent) teaching, or criterion of school effectiveness, that successful schools and teachers achieve impressive examination results. But not only is it less than obvious that achieving good examination results is the same as *good education* (since the former might be achieved by mindless drilling), it may also be that teachers in some schools are more concerned with the promotion of social and affective than (exclusive) cognitive and/or intellectual goals. Again, it is not just that different schools may have rather different concerns and aims, but that individual teachers of varying character, personality and ability in schools committed to the same broad aims may be faced with classes of variable social and/or psychological composition and needs. All of this suggests that field professionals require a much more particularised approach to the development of their practice, and renders it less likely that any overarching school effectiveness principles, rules or values would be of much widespread utility. From this viewpoint, one widely endorsed and professionally driven attempt to bring educational inquiry and reflection more into line with the particular needs of practice, and therefore to give teachers themselves more of a stakehold in the production of educational knowledge, has focused on so-called 'action research'.[12]

Action research, the conduct of systematic (empirically grounded) teacher inquiry into aspects of their classroom practice, has been widely recognised as a more professionally acceptable individual or collaborative approach to the requirements of both personal professional development and institutional effectiveness (or, as it goes under its more professionally approved title, *school improvement*). However, although the notion of action research has often been regarded as the perfect professionally focused solution to the kind of problems raised by more official and impositional approaches to educational quality control, it is not without difficulties of its own. One much noted problem is that *ex hypothesi* denial by some action researchers that such inquiry is answerable to *any* general criteria of a larger school effectiveness kind may suggest a somewhat idiosyncratic or subjectivist approach to professional practice: if the only ultimate justification that teachers can give for their practice is that it 'works for them', all things may seem permitted, and the baby of professional standards goes out with the bathwater of top-down prescription. A rather less often noticed problem about action research, however, is that it appears in its own empirically focused way to be no less technicist or instrumental in character than school effectiveness research; indeed, given its primary focus upon the immediate requirements of precisely situated classroom practice, it may appear to be not just instrumentalist but also narrowly pragmatist, if not actually anti-intellectual.[13] The trouble here is that it may ultimately be even more deprofessionalising to insulate the concerns and interests of the classroom teacher from the wider educational questions at least entertained by more general philosophical, sociological or psychological enquiries. In this light, action research may fall foul of the same dubious assumption – which we have sought to resist throughout this work – that educational inquiry is primarily conceivable as a form of scientific or empirical inquiry. In that case, action research may fail no less than school effectiveness research to appreciate that the professional wisdom of reflective practitioners is as much if not more a function of normative engagement with the wider moral, social and political implications of education than of the mastery of causal generalities conducive to the quasi-technical manipulation of processes (which is not, of course, to deny the relevance of causal knowledge and technique in their proper place).

However, we should not conclude this brief survey of tensions between political and professional educational imperatives without some comment on two other approaches to the quality control of education. The first of these concerns the monitoring of educational standards, or the quality of schooling, via official inspection. Although official school inspection has long been a cornerstone of educational quality control, conceptions of inspection have been subject to some radical contemporary development, and rather different approaches to inspection are apparent in the somewhat separately administered educational systems of present-day British schooling.[14] On the more traditional approach to inspection, school inspection is or was mainly (notwithstanding local advisory functions) the responsibility of civil servants located in a department of central government directly concerned with educational affairs. In recent days, however, a newer conception has emerged in England in which inspection, though still officially mandated, is more a matter of negotiated contract between schools and private agencies who stand to some extent apart from central or local government. As agents of a non-ministerial bureaucratic office separate from the Department of Education, so-called Ofsted (Office for Standards in Education) inspectors are not directly on the governmental payroll, anyone can train to be a school inspector, and teachers, university lecturers, advisors and other educational professionals are currently included among the ranks of Ofsted inspectorate. One arguable professional benefit of this approach is that although schools are required to budget for inspection from state or other sources of funding, privately contracted inspection teams might be held at least *in principle* accountable more to professionally independent standards of good educational practice than to patrons or paymasters of this or that political colour. On the face of it, then, one might expect private inspectors to observe greater professional neutrality and independence than the government agents of traditional inspection and to be therefore more acceptable to practising teachers. On the evidence, however, the new inspectorate seems to have been generally less popular than the old, and it would appear that (for example) the more traditionally modelled Scottish inspectorate is held in rather higher professional esteem than the new inspectors of England. That said, it may be that there are some fairly contingent reasons for this. For one thing, the new private inspectorate has never looked very politically independent: Ofsted was established under a markedly right-of-centre administration, has mostly proceeded to date under very conservative leadership, and has acquired something of reputation for high-handed authoritarianism.[15] Moreover, it is hard to ignore the fact that even the very idea of 'private' inspection has a politically right-of-centre flavour about it. This, moreover, brings us neatly to the last of the present issues of professional versus political accountability.

There can be no doubt that few educational issues have divided people quite so deeply as the question of the benefits or otherwise of relinquishing state control over education in favour of the privatisation of schools. Again, much has been said on this question, the jury is still out, and any short comment on this issue can hardly do justice to the complexity of the matter. In brief, however, it is beyond reasonable dispute that free-market educational initiatives have to date been not just politically motivated, but also driven by right-of-centre political perspectives.[16] They have also been generally linked to the cruder, more instrumental conceptions of schooling that mostly incline to reduce educational quality to productivity and commodity: one of the most criticised by-products of British market-led educational trends has been the publication of educational 'league tables' which force schools to compete with one another over the promotion of educational outcomes that are in turn largely (though not exclusively) measured in terms of examination success. One of the more frequently remarked suspect consequences of such competition is that schools that depend for market success on attracting paying customers are forced to concentrate on the achievement of academic or cognitive goals rather than upon those social and affective goals more suited to the needs of a range of variously disadvantaged children. This often means, for example, that schools may be forced to exclude children whose social and emotional (sometimes behaviourally disruptive) needs require the kind of labour-intensive attention which can impede the achievement of more commercially attractive academic goals. But it is arguably the key problem of market conceptions of educational provision that any concomitant commodification of education or schooling must give consumer interests and concerns final authority on what is educationally worthwhile: educational quality and value must ultimately turn on its being so regarded by this or that interest group. As we have seen, however, Socrates long ago argued that the customer is not always right, and that in their readiness to teach their educational clients whatever they might regard as congenial to their best interests the sophists were not always serving the highest (educational) interests of the soul.[17] From this viewpoint, it is arguable that any state concerned to ensure the best spiritual as well as economic welfare of its citizens should not shirk its responsibility to pursue – as far as possible – the highest Socratic educational benefits of wisdom and virtue for all young people, rather than encourage an unseemly scramble for positional goods in which not just already disadvantaged individuals, but society as a whole could ultimately turn out to be the poorer.

Educational principles and party-political allegiance

The final issue upon which we shall touch briefly in this last chapter is that of whether particular party-political affiliations have any specific implications or consequences for views about education and/or schooling. On the face of it, previous observations might suggest that this is indeed so: one might suppose, for example, that insofar as market conceptions of education are generally associated with the politics of the right, one would have to be politically conservative to support market policies, and/or that any opposition to such policies would entail commitment to a more left-of-centre political position. But this is fairly evidently not so. First, it is clear that a political conservative could readily reject a market conception of education, and it is perhaps to be expected that many more old-style (less 'neo-liberal') conservatives would indeed wish to do so. Equally, however, there seems to be no compelling reason why socialists would have to reject educational privatisation. Indeed, unless one falls into the 'conventionalist sulk'[18] of insisting that no-one who embraces market conceptions could ever be a *true* socialist, it should be apparent that socialists have lately and widely been drawn to market approaches in a wide variety of economic and welfare spheres. At all events, there is little reason to associate what we have called top-down approaches to quality control with right-wing politics, and bottom-up approaches with the left. On the one hand, top-down approaches incline to be a consequence, for reasons we have already examined, of all central initiatives – irrespective of party-political complexion – and the left-initiated attempt to impose comprehensive education on all sectors of British education in the 1960s was probably no less centralist or top-down than more recent conservative educational policies. On the other hand, of course, supporters of more bottom-up conceptions of professional preparation or school improvement are just as certainly distributed across a broad spectrum of political allegiance.

A general difficulty with respect to this question is that although the received nomenclature of political affiliation – 'right', 'left', 'socialist', 'conservative', 'liberal democrat', and so on – is by no means meaningless, these are seldom terms for anything very specific in the way of unitary or even coherent sets of socio-political perspectives and policies. Indeed, as the discernible contemporary

party-political difficulties of uniting diverse views under the headings of
'Labour', 'Conservative', 'Republican', 'Democrat' or whatever amply demonstrate, intra-party differences may extend to members of one party looking in
some respects more like members of allegedly opposed parties than members of
their own. Thus, although most British Conservatives are Euro-sceptics, not all
are – and they may be less so than some Labour supporters; and while many
British Labour supporters will be against free-market involvement in welfare
services, not all are – and some may in this respect be even more pro-market
than many Conservatives. In short, the standard labels for parties and affiliations
are portmanteau terms that refer mostly to loose constellations of policies and
perspectives united more by relations of family resemblance than strict logical
necessity. But since this applies no less, as we have already noticed, to such terms
of educational allegiance as 'traditional', 'progressive', 'child-centred',
'romantic', and so on, the problems facing any suggested alignment of 'traditional' with 'right-wing' or 'conservative', or 'progressive' with 'left-wing' or
'socialist', are merely compounded – despite perennial attempts to forge just such
associations. Indeed, perhaps the best known of such attempts in recent British
educational history to forge some such connection occured with the publication
of the notorious 'Black Papers' during the 1970s and 1980s.[19] Although the
Black Papers actually claimed support from a wide spectrum of (allegedly 'sane
and sensible') political opinion, they were widely interpreted – especially since
most of the editors and contributors were people of publicly recognised conservative views – as a blunderbuss right-of-centre attack on leftist educational views.
Despite this, the Black Papers opened somewhat indiscriminate fire on a
composite Aunt Sally of not obviously connected perspectives and policies –
comprehensive schooling, integrated curricula, non-didactic pedagogy, scepticism concerning psychometric methods, open-plan school architecture, too much
'theory' in teacher education, and so on – not all of which seemed clearly to be
of left-wing or socialist inspiration or provenance, or absolutely unacceptable to
conservatives.

To begin with, although comprehensive schooling and some general hostility
to selective education may be traced to broadly left-wing or socialist perspectives,
one might expect some of the rather different (perhaps especially economic)
arguments for comprehensive schools to be highly congenial to conservatives –
and, of course, there is no special connection between comprehensive schooling
and 'progressive' or 'child-centred' education or pedagogy. What, then, of the
suggested connection between progressive pedagogy and left-of-centre politics?
As we have seen, the difficulty is once more that progressivism seems to mean
rather different things. On the one hand, insofar as progressivism is associated
with a set of ideas about pedagogy which stresses more open and exploratory
modes of inquiry – the main emphasis of much British state progressivism in the
wake of the Plowden and other reports – there seems no obvious reason why
such methods should be at odds with more conservative perspectives and policies:
from this viewpoint, 1990s conservative critics of contemporary primary education did not oppose such more open methods *per se*, but only argued for a mixed

economy of teaching approaches in which didactic approaches might also have a proper place.[20] On the other hand, although we have seen another type of progressivism to have been more concerned with pupil freedom, and A.S. Neill as one famous advocate of individual freedom probably had generally social-democratic leanings, there are also some discernibly less than egalitarian tendencies in Neill's work[21] – and it is possible that many conservatives would be fairly comfortable with his emphasis on the development of more individual qualities of confidence and self-assertion. More particularly, any politically centralist opposition to Neillian or other educational experimentation might well be regarded as somewhat at odds with the modern right-of-centre neo-liberal emphasis on the importance of free choice between available alternatives, and more expressive of the totalitarian and levelling tendencies of some socialist rational planning. At any rate, there is certainly some irony in the fact that the same Black Paper conservatives who sought to defend alternative modes of education for children of different class, ability and personality[22] were so anxious to condemn the openness to experimentation generally characteristic of progressive approaches. However, if there is one Black Paper complaint that does seem to have been regularly associated with the authoritarian right, it is the hostility to theory and reflection in professional teacher education.[23] But even this may not be the sole preserve of right-wing (rather than left-wing) authoritarians, and it does not *have* to be a consequence of right-wing perspectives either. Indeed, although they may differ on many other issues, there is every reason for democratic conservatives and socialists to agree on the urgency of proper educational initiation of teachers into responsible professional reflection if there is to be much real hope for the future of democracy at all.

Possible tasks

(1) Consider the extent to which it might be possible to evade political bias in the school curriculum, with particular respect to the teaching of (i) history, (ii) music, (iii) social studies, (iv) moral education, (v) citizenship and (vi) sex education, (vii) gymnastics.

(2) Much political interference in the affairs of professional educationalists seems to be driven by a fear that, left to themselves, professionals would not be proper custodians of objective educational standards. Consider some possible strategies for the monitoring of educational standards that might be professionally more than politically controlled.

Glossary

Action research A form of educational or other empirical inquiry in which responsibility for the production of professional knowledge is given, or transferred from academic or otherwise externally located professional researchers, to situated field practitioners. The key idea is that practising professionals (such as teachers) are ultimately best placed to conduct the research most relevant to their own particular workplace needs.

Behaviourism

—— **Philosophical** The view that the ordinary 'folk-psychological' discourse of 'internal' or 'private' mental states, events and processes is in principle translatable without remainder into language about actual or potential public behaviour: that (crudely) 'John is afraid' means no more nor less than 'John is liable to tremble or run away'. The British philosopher Gilbert Ryle and the American W.V.O. Quine are (rightly or wrongly) two modern philosophers often associated with behaviourism.

—— **Psychological** The view that empirical psychology may be taken for all practical purposes to be the study of relations between animal or human behaviour (responses) and the environmental conditions (stimuli) that engender that behaviour: that, in short, it is not necessary to refer to any 'inner' states of mind or motivation in order to explain or predict behaviour. J.B Watson, E.L Thorndike and B.F. Skinner are celebrated modern psychological behaviourists. Behaviourism is also often just called 'Learning Theory'.

Care ethics Care ethics has its source in the reaction of certain psychoanalytic feminists to Freud's view of the Oedipal complex as the main mechanism of moral conscience formation (which seemed to imply that girls, since they do not experience the Oedipal phase, can never be truly moral). It is probably more familiar, however, through Carol Gilligan's arguments against the cognitive developmental morality of rules and principles that females have a different morality grounded more in relational states of affect (care and concern) than in the observance of rules. The educational implications of this idea have been further developed by Nel Noddings.

Cognitive developmentalism In general, cognitive developmentalism is the view that human mind, intelligence and reason are largely a function of the imposition on sensory experience of general structural principles, rules or categories of an essentially 'cognitive' (non-sensory) character. The modern origins of the view can almost certainly be traced to Kant's epistemology, but the Swiss experimental psychologist Jean Piaget is probably the best known modern exponent of cognitive developmentalism. However, Lawrence Kohlberg is also celebrated for his more particular application of cognitive developmentalism to problems of moral education.

Communitarianism A fairly loose constellation of views concerning the relationship of individual to society that regards social membership as a crucial precondition of individual identity: on this view, for example, moral beliefs are less a matter of autonomous rational construction (as on cognitive developmentalism) and more a matter of cultural inheritance. On a metaphysical reading of communitarianism, then, socio-culturally derived beliefs and values are identity-constitutive. However, on more political versions of communitarianism the individual is also subordinated to the collective authority of the community. Aristotle, Hegel, Marx, Alasdair MacIntyre and Charles Taylor are some past and present philosophers who exhibit distinct communitarian features.

Competences Greatly influenced by the reductive analyses of human behaviour of early theories of learning and scientific management, competence models of professional education and training attempt to reduce vocational conduct to repertoires of pre-specifiable intellectual and practical skills in the interests of the technically efficient management and quality monitoring of such skills. Despite the fact that advocates of competence models often try to give some place to theory, reflection and knowledge, the idea of pre-specification inevitably lends a distinctly top-down character to such models.

Comprehensive schooling By contrast with selective schooling, which undertakes to segregate young people for separate educational treatment on the basis of differences of race, intelligence, (broader) ability, class or gender, comprehensive schooling proposes to provide a common education for all irrespective of individual differences. However, motives for comprehensive schooling are diverse, and may be instrumental or economic as well as moral or egalitarian.

Conceptual analysis In one sense, all past and present approaches to philosophical inquiry may be regarded as concerned with the analysis of concepts: what else, after all, might they be concerned with? However, modern hostility to conceptual analysis often seems motivated (with some justice) by resistance to the rather narrow conceptions of semantic analysis that have often gone under this title. Some, for example, have attacked the exclusive focus on language of many conceptual analysts, emphasising that there can be forms or vehicles of meaning other than the 'linguistic'. Others (such as Wittgenstein) have attacked the rather too strict or formal conceptions of meaning (as fixed by necessary and sufficient conditions) and inference of bygone analytical philosophers.

Consensus theory   A social-theoretical view to the effect that the main principle of social cohesion is a body of rules, principles and values to which all
or most members of society can or do give voluntary assent. Insofar as
consensus theory more strongly implies that common agreement confers
authority or legitimacy upon such rules or principles, it can slide into social
or moral relativism. At all events, the views of Émile Durkheim may be
considered fairly representative of consensus theory, as can those of many
modern social and moral contractarians.

Consequentialism   A range of ethical perspectives generally characterised
by the idea that the moral goodness or badness, rightness or wrongness, of
actions is determinable by reference to the actual practical consequences of
those actions. Consequentialist theories are usually contrasted with deontological theories (according to which moral actions have worth irrespective of
their outcomes), and perhaps the best known type of consequentialist
perspective is utilitarianism.

Contractualism   The key idea of any form of contractualism is that the rules
by which society is or should be held together are best construed as matters
of actual or possible agreement. One may regard such rules as products of
rationally self-interested negotiation between individual social members in
prospect of some mutual benefit: for example, it is rational for me to agree
to be bound by a law preventing stealing if that law prevents others stealing
from me. Hobbes, Locke and Rousseau all defended types of contract
theory, and the idea also informs the contemporary social and political theories of Rawls and others.

Critical theory   Critical theory is principally influenced by Marxist philosophy, and critical theorists are sometimes referred to as post-Marxists. The
basic (Marxian) idea seems to be that since most if not all inherited socio-
cultural perspectives are a reflection of more or less unjust social hegemony
(and therefore represent forms of 'false consciousness'), the only road to
social justice lies in the development of a more critically impartial form of
rationality – for which critical theory seems mainly to have drawn on
Kantian resources. Leading critical theorists have included Habermas,
Horkheimer, Adorno and Marcuse.

Curriculum integration   Essentially the idea that cross- or multi-disci-
plinery topics or projects rather than subjects should be seen as the primary
focus of curriculum design and development. As an educational strategy,
curriculum integration owes much to Dewey's rejection of the 'passive spectator' epistemology of empiricism and of conceptions of knowledge as little
more than discretely packaged bodies of information. Dewey held that
genuine knowledge could only follow from active engagement with real
practical problems necessarily drawing for their solution on diverse (cross-
subject) rational strategies. W.H. Kilpatrick's 'project method' was an early
attempt to develop an integrated curriculum.

Curriculum theory   The systematic study of the school curriculum.
Although curriculum theory has always been of considerable interest to

social and political theorists and educational policy makers, much postwar curriculum theory has drawn upon philosophical insights in greater appreciation of the significant epistemological and ethical dimensions of principled curriculum theorising. Rather more philosophical curriculum theories have therefore been constructed around such epistemological notions as 'forms of knowledge' and 'ways of meaning'.

Deontology A general ethical perspective according to which moral conduct is principally action in accordance with duty. Although deontological views are usually contrasted with consequentialist views, the contrast is not always clear-cut insofar as some modern social-theoretical embodiments of deontology appear to have reduced moral duty to little more than social utility. However, on the purest versions of deontology (such as Kant's), moral duty is not reducible to any other instrumental or prudential considerations, and actions may only count as moral when performed for their own sake.

Deschooling Strongly influenced by Marxism, and associated with such postwar radicals as Illich, Goodman, Freire and Reimer, deschooling is basically the idea that modern institutionalised schooling is little more than an instrument for the indoctrination of pupils in values and beliefs of little real practical worth or moral value. Insofar as this is so, schooling is anti-educational and should therefore be abolished in favour of other (not very well-defined) community-based social practices and institutions for the initiation of young people into social or vocational knowledge of allegedly more emancipatory kinds.

Dualism (mind–body) Dualism is the view that mind and body constitute two metaphysically or ontologically separate and/or mutually irreducible entities or modes of existence. Dualism has probably exercised deepest influence on modern philosophy through the work of René Descartes, though it has had a wider impact on western society and culture through the influence of Plato on Christianity (notwithstanding the anti-dualist impact of Aristotle on Thomism). Dewey, Wittgenstein and Ryle have been important modern philosophical critics of dualism.

Empiricism The idea that experience – more specifically the deliverences of sense – is the only reliable basis of human knowledge. One problematic consequence of empiricism is that since only those human judgements that correspond to (or describe) sense-experience may be regarded as true, judgements that do not so correspond (such as judgements of moral, religious or aesthetic value) cannot count as true or false and therefore qualify as actual or potential knowledge. More extremely, however, since empiricists are hard put to accord significant epistemic status to anything beyond subjective experience, empiricism readily collapses into subjective idealism, phenomenalism or solipsism.

Epistemology The philosophical study of the grounds and logical character of human knowledge. Plato may be fairly regarded as the founding father of epistemology and his account of knowledge as justified true belief still grounds much contemporary epistemology. The two broad traditions of epistemology are rationalism and empiricism: rationalists holding that real or certain knowledge may only be had by the exercise of reason, and empiricists holding that sense-experience is the only reliable source of knowledge. Kant's epistemology may be regarded as the most significant (if not wholly successful) modern attempt to reconcile these two main epistemological traditions.

Ethics   The philosophical study of the logical, rational or other grounds of our moral conduct and judgements of moral value. Ethical theories fall into one or the other of three broad categories: (i) subjectivist theories which hold that moral judgements are largely non-rational personal preferences; (ii) relativist theories which hold that although moral judgements have no absolute validity, they have a certain limited objectivity in local social codes; (iii) objective or absolutist theories which hold that moral judgements are capable of universal and rationally demonstrable truth. Such great moral theorists as Plato, Aristotle, Kant and Mill have been moral objectivists and/or (albeit qualified) absolutists, although they have also given very different accounts of the rational basis of moral judgement.

Existentialism   A motley set of views deriving from the rather different worldviews of such past philosophical and other writers as Nietzsche, Dostoevsky, Kierkegaard and Kafka – as well as, in more recent days, Heidegger (who denied the label), Camus and (perhaps above all) Jean-Paul Sartre. Latter-day existentialism is much influenced by phenomenology and is sometimes expressed in the epigram 'existence precedes essence'. Perhaps the only common existentialist theme is a certain scepticism about the possibility of discerning any certain knowledge or truth in inherited human wisdom, and an emphasis on the need for 'authentic' action in the light of honest recognition of the basic 'absurdity' of human existence.

Extrinsic (educational) value   The idea that a subject or activity may be justified for inclusion in the school curriculum in terms of its extra-educational economic or social utility, rather than in terms of its own inherent educational worth. Although extrinsic construals of educational value have been explicitly defended in the writings of nineteenth-century and contemporary utilitarians, it has probably also been a common uncritical presupposition of much if not most past and present official educational policy making.

Forms of knowledge epistemology   The idea that human knowledge and understanding may, for many practical curricular purposes, be divided or categorised into a more or less fixed number (usually seven or eight) of logically discrete types. These have usually been held to include: mathematical and logical knowledge; empirical scientific knowledge; moral appreciation; understanding of the human (social) world; religious understanding; artistic and aesthetic appreciation; and philosophical understanding. Other philosophical conceptions of curriculum content, such as that of 'ways of meaning', seem to rest upon much the same idea of the logical divisibility of knowledge as forms of knowledge epistemology.

Idealism

—— **Subjective**   Basically the epistemological view that one cannot be certain that anything exists beyond the confines of one's own (private) mental experience, and that experience is therefore (to all theoretical and practical intents and purposes) exhausted by our subjective mental states of memory and perception. The Irish empiricist philosopher George Berkeley is often regarded as having held this view, which he expressed in the slogan 'esse est percipi': to be is to be perceived. Subjective idealism is virtually indistiguishable from what is sometimes called 'solipsism'.

—— **Conceptual**   What we have in this work called conceptual idealism would largely share subjectivist idealist scepticism about the possibility of any human knowledge of a mind-independent reality, and to this extent such idealism rejects that unconceptualised Kantian 'thing-in-itself' nevertheless supposed to give objectivity to our true knowledge claims. Like Kant, however, conceptual idealists would also reject subjective idealism as incoherent. For post-Kantian idealists, then, knowledge is crucially a matter of social and interpersonal rather than individual construction: the mind that makes the world is a collective mind expressed in public or social traditions of received wisdom.

—— **Absolute**   Since conceptual idealism rejects the idea of an unconceptualised order of reality, it cannot base knowledge claims – as do realist epistemologies – on any supposed correspondence to 'external' states of affairs. The key criterion of truth for conceptual idealists is therefore logical consistency rather than correspondence to fact. The problem now is that since rival or contradictory perspectives may be equally consistent, consistency alone cannot tell us which view we should rationally prefer. However, absolute idealists insist that conflicting historically conditioned social perspectives are nevertheless prone to negotiaton through a process of rational dialectic whose ultimate goal is an absolute 'God's-eye' view of the truth. The post-Kantian idealist G.W.F. Hegel seems to have held this view, as has (until fairly recently) the contemporary neo-idealist Alasdair MacIntyre.

Instrumentalism   A form of pragmatism especially associated with John Dewey by which human knowledge is conceived as a tool for the (technical or other) management, manipulation or exploitation of experience, rather than as a form of (passive) depiction or description of it. In this work, however, curriculum instrumentalists are those who would regard educational knowledge as valuable for some extrinsic (social or economic) end, rather than as worthwhile for its own sake.

Intrinsic (educational) value   The value that certain forms of knowledge of modes of human activity might be held to have for their own sake, rather than as means to the achievement of other externally related purposes. Liberal educationalists have often held that the school curriculum should be constructed around such intrinsically worthwhile forms of knowledge, and it seems reasonable to suppose (as we have argued in this work) that the teaching of such subjects or activities as history, poetry and dance is primarily justifiable in terms of the intrinsic or personally formative character of such subjects.

Liberalism A general normative conception of moral, social and political association that gives priority to individual freedom, to the political and legal protection of individual rights, and to the tolerance of differences of value and perspective. Generally, liberals regard the state as at the service of the individual, rather than the individual as at the service of the state, and argue for minimal state control of individual enterprise and initiative. John Stuart Mill, the nineteenth-century high priest of liberalism, argued in his essay *On Liberty* that the only rational justification for any restriction of individual thought or activity was potential or actual harm or violence to others. The great seventeenth-century empiricist John Locke, however, may be regarded as the founder of modern liberalism.

Marketisation (of schooling) The general tendency of recent right-of-centre or neo-liberal administration in Britain and elsewhere to structure educational provision around market mechanisms for the quality control of public schooling. Educational marketeers hold that a combination of more consumer-related arrangements for the funding of schools, greater scope for parental choice, and the competition engendered between schools by 'school league tables' will engender greater efficiency in the educational system in terms of the flourishing of good (high academically achieving) schools and the elimination of bad (low achieving) schools.

Marxism Those socio-economic and political views associated with or significantly influenced by the work of the nineteenth-century German economist and political theorist Karl Marx. Marx's views were themselves a materialist or economic reworking of those of the great German idealist G.W.F. Hegel – though for Marx, unlike Hegel, the apparent historical evolution of human culture is a manifestation of *economic* (rather than divine or spiritual) progress towards a highly corporate or collectivist conception of moral and political association. Despite this, some of the most significant of Marxian influences have been on philosophers (critical theorists or post-Marxists) who have sought to give a more liberal interpretation to central Marxian insights.

Metaphysics The philosophical study of the allegedly essential or necessary structure or order of reality. Although metaphysics has been regarded as a legitimate enterprise by the very greatest of past philosophers (for example, Plato, Aristotle, Descartes, Kant and Hegel), it has always been regarded more sceptically by philosophers drawn to more empiricist and/or social-theoretical perspectives on the origins of human knowledge. Indeed, twentieth-century interest in metaphysical inquiry undoubtedly suffered under the two-fold pressure of an empiricism broadly in the tradition of Hume, and an anti-realism derived from idealist and pragmatist sources, both of which take a largely dim view of any ideas of necessary or non-accidental truth. Many of these influences, via the poststructuralist rejection of structuralist essentialism, have also fuelled postmodern antipathy to meta-physics.

Naturalism (ethical)   Generally, any ethical theory that takes our moral judgements or responses to be grounded in or logically related to the allegedly natural facts or circumstances of human harm or flourishing. In defining good action as that which is conducive to pleasure or happiness and bad action as that which is productive of pain or harm, utilitarianism may be regarded as one influential form of modern naturalism. However, the recent revival of an Aristotelian virtue ethics identifying moral responses with certain principled dispositions of human character – the virtues – represents a perhaps more sophisticated latter-day development of natu-ralism.

Non-cognitivism   Generally, any moral theory that – unlike ethical natu-ralism – denies the alleged logical connection between moral value judgements and supposed natural facts or circumstances of human harm or flourishing, and/or that observes a strict distinction between fact and values. On extreme versions of non-cognitivism, defended in the spirit of Hume by modern emotivists, moral judgements are basically expressions of affect and have no rational basis whatsoever. On the more sophisticated versions of non-cognitivism defended by prescriptivists, reason or principle plays some part in the formation of moral perspectives regarded as essentially consis-tent commitments. More recent non-cognitivist views have included quasi-realism and error theory.

Non-realism   A loose constellation of views largely concerned to deny that there is any natural order of reality beyond individual or collective experi-ence of which human knowledge claims might be said to be truly descriptive or representative. On such views, there is no naturally ordered world 'out there' beyond human conception, and all knowledge is a matter of indi-vidual or (more usually) social construction. On such views, empirical knowledge or truth cannot be a matter of correspondence to conception-independent facts, since there are no such facts. The most influential forms of non-realism or anti-realism derive from the nineteenth-century idealist rejection of the Kantian epistemological objectivism of 'things-in-them-selves', and take the form of some or other version of social (epistemic) constructivism. Pragmatism is one widely influential contemporary form of non-realism.

Particularism   Broadly the view that the kind of practical reason that human agents employ in contexts of professional or other interpersonal practice cannot be captured or expressed in the impersonal generalities of (natural scientific) theoretical or technical rationality. On this view, effective profes-sional judgement and practice is a function more of sensitivity to the contextualised particularities of actual occasions of engagement, than of the crude application of general technical rules. Perhaps the most suggestive source of this idea is to be found in Aristotle's pioneering distinction (in the *Nicomachean Ethics*) between *techne* and *phronesis*, and recent educational philosophers have drawn widely on Aristotle's account of moral wisdom in their attempts to understand the particularity of teacher judgement.

Phenomenology   Specifically, a method of philosophical analysis pioneered by the nineteenth-century German philosopher Edmund Husserl which seems to suppose that any truly objective knowledge or understanding of the nature of things is possible only by means of some sort of unmediated contact between the mind and an (in some sense unconceptualised) experience. On this view, in order to have an authentic understanding of this or that aspect of experience, the mind must (somehow) bypass or 'bracket out' the familiar or received concepts and categories of human thought in which it has come to be expressed. Phenomenology has exercised a strong influence on contemporary existentialism and post-structuralism, mainly through the work of Husserl's most famous pupil, Martin Heidegger.

Postmodernism   Since postmodernism is more of a cultural movement than a philosophical view, it is hard to give it any precise philosophical definition, and hazardous to associate any leading contemporary philosophers with this label. Roughly, however, philosophical postmodernism draws upon such other modern philosophical movements as pragmatism, communitarianism, post-Marxism and post-structuralism. It shares pragmatist scepticism about the possibility of an external reality against which human conceptions might be judged, it agrees with the communitarian view of our values as socio-culturally constructed, and it also largely follows post-structuralism and post-Marxism in regarding values as hegemonically rather than rationally grounded. The French philosopher Jean-François Lyotard is commonly regarded as a philosophical postmodernist, and it may be that the influential work of the American philosopher Richard Rorty marks the point at which pragmatism shades into postmodernism.

Post-structuralism   Briefly, poststructuralists reject the structuralist claim that there are any universal, ahistorical and transcultural concepts or categories of human thought or understanding lying beneath the diverse socio-culturally conditioned forms of thought and discourse studied by social scientists. In short, all is cultural contingency and – in the light of that philosophical-historical inquiry sometimes called *genealogy* – past conceptualisations express no more than transient local and/or ethnocentric conditions and concerns. Strongly influenced by such nineteenth-century theorists of knowledge as power as Marx and Nietzsche, however, post-structuralists also argue that received conceptual frameworks have a hegemonic basis and are expressions more of will to power than of human reason. Michel Foucault, Jacques Derrida and Gilles Deleuze may be regarded as leading post-structuralists.

Pragmatism   A predominantly American school of philosophical thought stemming mainly from the work of C.S. Peirce, William James and John Dewey, pragmatism is a form of non-realism or anti-realism that shares post-Kantian idealist antipathy to the Kantian epistemic objectivism of 'things-in-themselves'. Moreover, since pragmatists also share idealist rejection of Kant's distinction between concepts and intuitions – insisting that there can be no sensorily experienced reality that is theory-free or prior to human conceptualisation – they are also given to denial of any real distinction between philosophical and empirical inquiry. However, whereas the acid test of knowledge for nineteenth-century idealists is coherence rather than correspondence, pragmatists find this inadequate (for a coherent theory may still be false), and therefore regard usefulness or utility as the key criterion of knowledge. On this view, knowledge is always provisional and truth is no more than (current) 'warranted assertability'. Dewey's 'instrumental pragmatism' has had great educational influence in America and Britain.

Prescriptivism A key form of ethical non-cognitivism devised by the Oxford philosopher R.M. Hare, which combines (not altogether congruously) elements of Humean and Kantian moral theory. Prescriptivism agrees with emotivists in observing the fact–value distinction and in maintaining that moral action must ultimately be more affectively than rationally motivated. Unlike emotivists, however, prescriptivists do not regard moral values as merely expressions of liking, and find a role for reason in the transformation (via Kantian universalisation) of preferences into moral principle. The actions we regard as 'good' are those that we are inclined to commend on the basis of consistent commitment.

Progressivism (educational) The source of progressivism is to be found in Rousseau's eighteenth-century rejection of a fairly common traditional or conventional view of education as the transmission of society's culture and values from one generation to another. Whereas traditionalists are inclined to hold that human nature is essentially corrupt and only improved or redeemed by educational initiation into civil or civilised society, Rousseau held that the considerable human potential for good is actually spoiled by such initiation: hence, he argued in his work *Émile* that the best education is one in which individuals are protected from the corrupting influences of society via a largely asocial education. There are, however, different brands or schools of progressivism:

—— **Pragmatic** What is called in this work pragmatic progressivism is mainly traceable to the educational thought and experimentation of the American pragmatist philosopher John Dewey. Although Deweyan progressivism does not share Rousseau's antipathy to the social, it is nevertheless profoundly opposed to traditionalist conceptions of education as the transmission of received values and convinctions. Deweyan progressivism is therefore mainly epistemic, and focused on the development of forms of (individual *and* social) learning that conduce to the development of critical and questioning attitudes to received wisdom.

—— **Psychological** What is called in this work psychological progressivism is mainly traceable to the psychoanalytically influenced work of the American educator and therapist Homer Lane and his (more) famous British disciple A.S. Neill. Unlike Dewey or Rousseau, Lane and Neill had small interest in the development of curriculum and pedagogy, but they did have a broadly Rousseauian interest in the liberation of the human mind and spirit from the indoctrination they descried in traditional child-rearing and schooling. Hence, Lane, Neill and their disciples have mainly sought to promote freedom from repression in the particular contexts of open and democratic schooling (of, for example, Lane's Little Commonwealth and Neill's Summerhill).

Psychoanalysis   Together with behaviourism and cognitive psychology, psychoanalysis is one of the principal modern quasi-scientific approaches to the study of the human mind. Originally pioneered by Sigmund Freud, psychoanalytic method rests on the idea that much if not most human character and personality development is the psychodynamic outcome of early conflict between infantile desires and the processes of socialisation which seek to control those desires. Such conflict invariably leads to emotional repression, and to the formation of unconscious mental structures or archetypes that can have beneficial or detrimental consequences for adult behaviour. In the course of exploring such repression, psychoanalysis makes ingenious use of human myth, giving rise (particularly in Jungian analysis) to suggestive connections between psychology and the studies of religion, mythology and art. Psychoanalysis has been more influential on (particularly continental European) philosophy than on educational theory, although psychoanalytic influences are discernible in the psychological progressivism of Lane and Neill and in the ethics of care of Carol Gilligan and Nel Noddings.

Psychometry   Psychometry is a branch of modern empirical psychology that has – as the name suggests – been mainly concerned to define and measure processes of human intelligence. The French psychologist Alfred Binet, the British psychologist Sir Cyril Burt and – in more recent times – the British psychologist Hans Eysenck may be considered key figures in the development of psychometry. Although psychometricians have usually taken intelligence to be a function of both genetic inheritance *and* environmental influences, they have usually placed most emphasis on the former, and modern psychometry has fallen into fairly bad academic and public odour as a result of suspect attempts to suggest a racial genetic basis for inequalities of intelligence. Psychometry has also more recently been the butt of criticism by proponents of alternative and affective intelligence.

Radical education   Although the line between radical education and educational progressivism is not hard and fast, and some famous modern anti-traditionalists such as A.S. Neill have preferred the label 'radical' to that of 'progressive', there are grounds for distinguishing between progressives like Neill and Dewey and such mid-twentieth-century 'radical' educationalists as Ivan Illich, Paul Goodman, John Holt, Everett Reimer and Paulo Freire. One key difference is that while most progressives (including Neill) are not notably opposed to ideas of institutionalised schooling and professional teaching, radicals regard both as profoundly counter-educational, and are therefore largely in favour of their abolition.

Realism Esssentially the view, opposed to non-realism, that true human knowledge claims may be regarded as more or less accurately descriptive of an inherently ordered external reality. Epistemic realists are therefore more or less committed to holding that there is a world of objective mind-independent facts to which human knowledge claims do or do not faithfully refer – although they are not committed to holding (as critical realists do not) that extant human theories and hypotheses offer anything more than a provisional and/or fallible picture of that reality. Again, although scientific realism is also compatible with moral non-realism – since it is possible to hold that whereas empirical judgements describe the world, value judgements do not – some philosophers have also been moral realists and have held that true moral judgements are descriptive of special moral facts.

Relativism (social and moral) If a social constructivist epistemology is combined with epistemic non-realism, it can readily slide into general epistemic relativism or the view that the rules and conventions by which one social constituency constructs reality may differ to the point of mutual contradiction from those of another constituency. Still, given that societies may appear to differ more in their moral than empirical beliefs, such constructivist relativism is most plausibly maintained in connection with the normative or moral codes or principles of human social groups. Despite common confusion between the positions, however, it is also important to distinguish moral relativism from moral subjectivism. Whereas a moral subjectivist holds that moral judgements are simply (probably non-rational) expressions of personal preference, a moral relativist holds that there are good objective or interpersonally valid (albeit local) reasons for abiding by one set of moral rules rather than another.

School effectiveness The school effectiveness movement is associated with a widespread contemporary programme of official and professional research designed to establish the defining managerial and pedagogical characteristics of the 'good' school. One obvious objection to this general strategy, however, is that – since 'good' is an evaluative term – what counts as a 'good' school cannot be determined by empirical research alone. A related 'particularist' objection is that there cannot be any general features of effective schooling, since good practice will be determined by contextual features that vary considerably from one school to another. Since school effectiveness research has also been associated with politically motivated 'top-down' or interventionist strategies for saving failing schools, it has also not been popular with professionals.

Semantic theory Basically the philosophical study of meaning or signification. Although the problem of meaning has inevitably been a key interest of all great philosophers from classical antiquity to the present, attention to questions of meaning received an enormous boost in modern analytical philosophy with the radical reconstruction of traditional logic by the German logician Gottlob Frege at the beginning of the twentieth century.

Structuralism   Although major pioneers of structuralism have often hailed from such fields of empirical (or quasi-empirical) inquiry as psychology, anthropology and linguistics, the central concerns of structuralism are clearly epistemic, and the most obvious intellectual influence on structuralist approaches to understanding human meaning-making is Kantian epistemology. Like Kant, structuralists reject empiricist attempts to reduce human knowledge and understanding to some habitual association of sense-impressions, and insist that knowledge requires the imposition on sensory experience of rules and principles that are in some sense necessary and/or culturally invariant. Key structuralists have included the anthropologist Claude Lévi-Strauss, the linguist Noam Chomsky and such psychologists as Jean Piaget, Jerome Bruner and Lawrence Kohlberg.

Subjectivism (moral)   Despite some widespread popular confusion with moral relativism, moral subjectivism is strictly the view that moral judgements (and perhaps value judgements in general) are essentially non-rational expressions of personal preference or taste. However, insofar as moral relativists believe that moral values are social rules that are (at least locally) justifiable by appeal to public reasons, moral subjectivism and relativism would seem to be not just distinguishable but actually incompatible views. Some ancient sophists (for example, Protagoras) may have been moral subjectivists, and there is certainly a strong subjectivist element in Hume and in the post-Humean ethics of emotivism.

Technicism   Technicism is generally the view that the empirical experimental methods of natural science (and/or of social science regarded as continuous with natural science) are broadly appropriate to the study of individual or social human life, and that moral and other practical problems of human association can be addressed by the application of social or human scientific (therapeutic or managerial) techniques. A good example of technicism is provided by B.F. Skinner's utopian proposal in *Beyond Freedom and Dignity* to improve human society by wholesale behavioural conditioning. The key problem of any such technicist attempt to settle normative problems scientifically, of course, is apparent once we ask in accordance with which or whose values such conditioning should proceed.

Teleology   In general, teleology and/or teleological explanation is explanation in terms of reasons or purposes, and Aristotle's final causes were explanations of this sort. Teleological explanation fell from modern favour with the rise of science and of a scientific reductionism that purported to explain everything in the mechanistic or statistical terms of efficient causation: whereas the faithful might hold that animal species are as they are because God designed them that way, Darwinian evolutionists could insist that they were so due to the mechanisms of natural selection. All the same, it is quite natural to explain human agency and its acts in terms of practical reasoning, and explanation in terms of practical reasoning is essentially teleological explanation. Hence, teleology has been subject to something of a modern revival among (especially Aristotelean) philosophers of human and social science.

Traditionalism (educational) Educational traditionalism is probably best defined as a culture-transmission or social-reproduction conception of the aims of education and schooling. Indeed, traditionalism has probably received its most succinct definition in Matthew Arnold's account of education as the transmission of culture, and culture as 'the best that has been thought and said in the world'. Although there is a general tendency among traditionalists to a rather pessimistic view of untutored human nature, the general position is also subject to some modern variation:

—— **Conservative** Those referred to in this work as conservative traditionalists are apt to regard the main function of schooling as the reproduction of traditional social structures and hierarchies. Plato, Matthew Arnold, T.S. Eliot, D.H. Lawrence and the modern British educationalist G.H. Bantock all seem to have been in this sense conservative traditionalists, and to have held that rather different sorts of educational provision are appropriate to the needs of different social castes or classes.

—— **Liberal** Those referred to in this work as liberal traditionalists are inclined to regard the personally formative and mind-enhancing benefits of a traditional liberal education as appropriate to all and not just some (the most gifted of socially privileged) citizens of a liberal-democratic polity. Many if not most liberal traditionalists are therefore inclined to defend equal educational access, a common curriculum and/or non-selective or comprehensive schooling against the various alternative curricula and segregated schooling proposals of conservative traditionalism.

Use theory An approach to the philosophy of meaning associated with such mid-twentieth-century Oxbridge philosophers as Ludwig Wittgenstein, J.L. Austin and Gilbert Ryle. Theorists of meaning-as-use basically rejected the decontextualised analysis of terms adopted by most (Frege- and Russell-influenced) linguistic philosophers of their day. They were inclined to deny that such philosophically significant terms as 'mind', 'knowledge' and 'goodness' had single or fixed senses, and to hold that attention to particular context-sensitive nuance was needed for any proper understanding of the meaning of this or that term or expression.

Utilitarianism Probably the best known and most common type of consequentialist ethic, utilitarianism holds that the moral goodness or badness, rightness or wrongness, of actions is a function of conduciveness to the production of pleasure or pain (Bentham), happiness or harm (J.S. Mill). Perhaps the most conspicuous objections to utilitarianism are that there is no common agreement about what constitutes human flourishing and harm, and that it is hard to predict precisely what the long- or even short-term consequences of one's actions are likely to be. Utilitarianisms may also involves some rather counter-intuitive laundering of received moral usage: according to utilitarians, if a murder is productive of good consequences, it would no longer count as a bad action.

Virtue ethics Basically a development of Aristotelian ethics, modern virtue ethics may be regarded as the chief contemporary rival of Kantian deontology and utilitarianism. Virtue ethics differs largely from its rivals in regarding the development of character more than any intellectual grasp of general moral principles (of duty or utility) as the key to moral virtue. Although virtue ethics does recognise a place for moral absolutes, it also sees the practical reason of moral wisdom (**phronesis**) as expressed more in particularistic judgement rather than in universal rules. There are two main types of contemporary virtue ethicist: some (like MacIntyre in *After Virtue*) have regarded virtues as specific to local cultural contexts; others (like Nussbaum) have regarded virtues as more universal or cross-cultural moral responses.

Notes

1 Education, persons and schooling

1 For key papers on the idea of the essentially contestability of social concepts, see: W.B. Gallie, 'Essentially contested concepts', *Proceedings of the Aristotelian Society*, vol. 56, 1955–6, pp. 167–98; and A.C. MacIntyre, 'The essential contestability of some social concepts', *Ethics*, vol. 84, 1973–4, pp. 1–9.

2 Radical ('deschooling') literature expressing scepticism about the educational value of schooling is extensive: see, for example, I. Illich, *Deschooling Society*, Harmondsworth, Penguin, 1973, *Celebration of Awareness*, Harmondsworth, Penguin, 1973, and 'Disabling professions', in *Disabling Professions*, London, Marion Boyars, 1977; P. Goodman, *Growing Up Absurd*, London, Gollancz, 1960, and *Compulsory Miseducation*, Harmondsworth, Penguin, 1971; N. Postman and C. Weingartner, *Teaching as a Subversive Activity*, Harmondsworth, Penguin, 1971; and E. Reimer, *School is Dead*, Harmondsworth, Penguin, 1971.

3 This point needs careful stating, for I have found that people often take considerable offence at the suggestion that there might be humans who are not regarded as persons. The point, however, is a purely conceptual, not a moral or practical, one, and it is only that some such possibility is *conceivable* in the light of the fact that person is more a normative than a biological concept. That said, it also seems likely (and I would personally want to argue) that the only *defensible* moral stance is one that regards all other humans as (potential, actual or late) persons, regardless of other considerations. Indeed, the widespread human tendency to accord to others of their species personal respect and dignity in health, sickness and even (and perhaps not least) in death is probably the definitive feature of that quality of personhood we refer to as moral agency.

4 See Descartes's *Meditations and Discourses*, in G.E.M. Anscombe and P.T. Geach (eds), *Descartes: Philosophical Writings*, London, Nelson, 1954.

5 Important modern critiques of Cartesian dualism of Ryle and Wittgenstein are to be found in: G. Ryle, *The Concept of Mind*, London, Hutchinson, 1949; and (more implicitly) in L. Wittgenstein, *Philosophical Investigations*, trans. G.E.M. Anscombe, Oxford, Blackwell, 1953.

6 See I. Kant: *The Critique of Pure Reason*, trans. N. Kemp Smith, London, Macmillan, 1968; and *The Critique of Practical Reasoning and Other Works on the Theory of Ethics*, trans. T.K. Abbott, London, Longman, 1967.

7 Arguably, the first philosopher to appreciate this gap and to reject scientific reductionism was Plato. See, for example, Plato's *Phaedo*, in E. Hamilton and H. Cairns (eds), *Plato: The Collected Dialogues*, Princeton, Princeton University Press, 1961.

8 See: M. Arnold, 'Preface to *Literature and Dogma*', in J. Gribble (ed.), *Matthew Arnold*, Educational Thinkers Series, London, Collier-Macmillan, 1967, p. 150.

9 The slogan 'education, education, education' was used by British prime minister Tony Blair to mark the high priority that his government pledged to give to educational issues and concerns at the time of the first New Labour landslide of the mid-nineties.

10 The philosophical literature on the moral value of physical education is now extensive. See, for example: D. Aspin, 'Ethical aspects of sports and games, and physical education', *Proceedings of the Philosophy of Education Society of Great Britain*, vol. 9, 1975, pp. 48–71; C. Bailey: 'Games, winning and education', *Cambridge Journal of Education*, vol. 5, 1975, pp. 40–50, D. Meakin, 'Physical education: an agency of moral education?' *Journal of Philosophy of Education*, vol. 15, 1981, pp. 241–53; and D. Carr, 'What moral-educational significance has physical education? A question in need of disambiguation', in M. McNamee and J. Parry (eds), *Ethics and Sport*, London, E. & F.N. Spon, 1998.

11 Utilitarian calculation is assessment of the goodness or badness of an action in terms of its consequences for human happiness or pleasure. For a classical account of the doctrine, see J.S. Mill's *Utilitarianism*, in M. Warnock (ed.), *Utilitarianism*, London, Collins, Fontana Library, 1970.

12 See, on broadly related issues and questions, D. Carr, 'Freud and sexual ethics', *Philosophy*, vol. 62, 1987, pp. 361–73.

13 See especially R.S. Peters: 'Aims of education', in R.S. Peters (ed.), *The Philosophy of Education*, Oxford, Oxford University Press, 1973; and *Ethics and Education*, London, George Allen and Unwin, 1966, chapter 1, section 2b, pp. 27–30.

14 For the postwar educational philosophical distinction between intrinsic and extrinsic worth, see in general: Peters, *Ethics and Education*.

15 For this point about the logical dependency of extrinsic on intrinsic worth, see: J.P. White, *Towards a Compulsory Curriculum*, London, Routledge and Kegan Paul, 1973.

16 For this attempt to conjoin intrinsic worth and intrinsic motivation, see: Peters, *Ethics and Education*, especially chapter 5.

17 See: R.S. Peters, 'Mental health as an aim of education', in T.H.B. Hollins (ed.), *Aims of Education: The Philosophical Approach*, Manchester, Manchester University Press, 1964, p. 85.

18 This important idea about the aims of education should perhaps be called the Peters point. See Peters: *Ethics and Education* and 'Aims of education'.

19 For Arnold's non-instrumentalism, see: Arnold, 'Preface to *Literature and Dogma*', p. 150.

20 See: P.H. Hirst, 'The curriculum: educational implications of social and economic change', *Schools Council Working Paper No. 12*, London, HMSO, 1967.

21 See: P.H. Hirst, 'Liberal education and the nature of knowledge', in *Knowledge and the Curriculum*, London: Routledge and Kegan Paul, 1974, p. 32.

22 For arguments to the effect that physical education has no intrinsic value, see: Peters, *Ethics and Education*, chapter 5, section 4. For an early attempt to show that it has, see: R. Carlisle, 'The concept of physical education I', *Proceedings of the Philosophy of Education Society of Great Britain*, vol. 3, 1969, pp. 5–22.

23 For some influential educational sociological work largely unsympatheic to the non-instrumentalism of liberal educationalists, see: M.F.D. Young (ed.), *Knowledge and Control*, London, Collier-Macmillan, 1971.

24 For an influential neo-utilitarian critique of non-instrumentalsim, see: R. Barrow, *Plato, Utilitarianism and Education*, London. Routledge and Kegan Paul, 1975.

25 For an exploration of confusions between education and schooling, see: D. Carr, 'The dichotomy of liberal versus vocational education: some basic conceptual geography', in A. Nieman (ed.), *Philosophy of Education 1995*, Urbana, Ill., Philosophy of Education Society, 1996.

26 For radical scepticism about the educational value of schooling, see the sources in note 2 above.

27 Once again, Peters' work largely goes the way of these conflations. See: Peters, *Ethics and Education*, especially chapters 1, 2 and 5.

28 For Hirst's subsequent revision of his earlier forms of knowledge thesis, see: P.H. Hirst, 'Education, knowledge and practices', in R. Barrow and P. White (eds), *Beyond Liberal Education: Essays in Honour of Paul H. Hirst*, London, Routledge, 1993.

29 This idea was quite central to a British report of the 1990s on the contemporary state of British education that was first televised and later published as *Every Child in Britain* (London, Channel 4, 1991). Such local educational luminaries as A.H. Halsey, Neville Postlethwaite, S.J. Prais, Alan Smithers and Hilary Steedman criticised British secondary education for its failure to take seriously the idea of a 'practical education'.

2 The complex character of teaching

1 I have explored some of these points in: *Professionalism and Ethical Issues in Teaching*, Routledge Professional Ethics Series, London, Routledge, 2000; 'Is teaching a skill?', in R. Curren (ed.), *Philosophy of Education 1999*, Urbana, Ill., Philosophy of Education Society, 2000; and 'Educational philosophy, theory and research: a psychiatric autobiography', *Journal of Philosophy of Education*, vol. 35, 2001, pp. 461–76. For a very fine pioneering work on the philosophy of teaching, however, see J. Passmore, *The Philosophy of Teaching*, London, Duckworth, 1980.

2 Socratic criticisms of the sophistic pedagogy are to be found in numerous Platonic dialogues. See, in particular: Plato's *Gorgias*, in E. Hamilton and H. Cairns (eds), *Plato: The Collected Dialogues*, Princeton, Princeton University Press, 1961. See also: S. Johnson, 'Skills, Socrates and the Sophists: learning from history', *British Journal of Educational Studies*, vol. 46, 1998, pp. 201–14. Criticisms of the pharisees of Jesus and also of St John the Baptist are, of course, to be found throughout the four New Testament Gospels.

3 The philosopher Ludwig Wittgenstein would appear to have been, by some accounts, one such example of a famous teacher with some pedagogical shortcomings.

4 For the basic definition of teaching as the intentional bringing about of learning, see: P.H. Hirst, 'The logical and psychological aspects of teaching a subject', in *Knowledge and the Curriculum*, London, Routledge and Kegan Paul, 1974.

5 This broad approach to understanding teaching is generally characteristic of the literature of 'teaching styles'. See: D. Carr, 'Education, professionalism and theories of teaching', *Journal of Philosophy of Education*, vol. 20, 1986, pp. 113–21, for some criticism of this approach.

6 For Russell and Dewey's evident enthusiasm for behaviourism, see: L.R. Perry, *Bertrand Russell, A.S. Neill, Homer Lane, W.H. Kilpatrick: Four Progressive Educators*, Educational Thinkers Series, London, Collier-Macmillan, 1967.

7 For competence models of teaching, see various articles in J.W. Burke (ed.), *Competency Based Education and Training*, Lewes, Falmer Press, 1989; Department of Education and Science, *Reform of Initial Teacher Training: A Consultative Document*, London, HMSO, 1992; Scottish Office Education Department, *Guidelines for Teacher Training Courses*, Edinburgh, SOED, 1993. For a critical account of competence models, see T. Hyland, 'Competence, knowledge and education', *Journal of Philosophy of Education*, vol. 27, 1993, pp. 57–68, and also *Competence, Education and NVQ's: Dissenting Perspectives*, London, Cassell, 1994.

8 For some well-known British empirical research into pedagogy, see: N. Bennett, *Teaching Styles and Pupil Progress*, London, Open Books, 1976; and R. Alexander, J. Rose and C. Woodhead (eds), *Curriculum Organization and Classroom Practice in Primary School*, London: Department of Education and Science, 1992.

9 John Elliott is one well-known critic of more general and decontextualised approaches to educational research. See his: 'Educational theory, practical philosophy and action research', *British Journal of Educational Studies*, vol. 35, 1987, pp. 149–69;

'Educational theory and the professional learning of teachers: an overview', *Cambridge Journal of Education*, vol. 19, 1989, pp. 81–101; and 'School effectiveness research and its critics', *Cambridge Journal of Education*, vol. 26, 1996, pp. 199–224.

10 For some consideration of the respects in which the learning of skills is apt to bypass understanding, see: D. Carr, 'Dance education, skill and behavioural objectives', *Journal of Aesthetic Education*, vol. 18, 1984, pp. 67–76.

11 Growing interest in the pedagogical as well as the academic dimensions of higher education in Britain and elsewhere has prompted various initiatives designed to improve or control the quality of university and other teachers. These have included the establishment in Britain of the Institute for Learning and Teaching in Higher Education (ILT), which seems to have its sights set upon eventual mandatory professional registration for teachers in higher education. The ILT is also associated with an academic journal entitled *Academic Learning in Higher Education*, published by Paul Chapman, Sage. However, although any attempt to improve the general quality of university teaching is to be welcomed, one may see potential dangers here of confusing the goals and standards required of higher education with those required of elementary education.

12 For the connection between character and moral appraisal in (Aristotelian) virtue ethics, see: D. Carr and J. Steutel (eds), *Virtue Ethics and Moral Education*, London, Routledge, 1999.

13 For Aristotle's comparison of virtues with skills, see: Aristotle's *Nicomachean Ethics*, in R. McKeon (ed.), *The Basic Works of Aristotle*, New York, Random House, 1941, book 2, section 1.

14 For Aristotle's contrast of virtues with skills, see: ibid., book 6, section 5.

15 For Aristotle on the specific contrast between intentional and non-intentional mistakes in virtue and art, see: ibid., p. 1027.

16 For one source of thinking about school discipline in terms of 'management skills', see: Elton Report, *Discipline in Schools*, Department of Education and Science and the Welsh Office, London, HMSO, 1989. But such thinking seems generally characteristic of competence models of professional teacher education and training.

17 For a recent fine exploration of the relevance of *phronesis* to educational philosophy, see: J. Dunne, *Back to the Rough Ground: 'Phronesis' and 'Techne' in Modern Philosophy and in Aristotle*, Notre Dame, Ind., University of Notre Dame Press, 1993: also, for a pioneering article in this direction, W. Carr, 'What is an educational practice?' *Journal of Philosophy of Education*, vol. 21, 1987, pp. 163–75.

3 The complex role of the teacher

1 These issues are explored rather more fully in: D. Carr, *Professionalism and Ethical Issues in Teaching*, Routledge Professional Ethics Series, London, Routledge, 2000.

2 See D. Carr, 'Professional education and professional ethics', *Journal of Applied Philosophy*, vol. 16, 1999, pp. 33–46.

3 See I. Kant, *Groundwork of the Metaphysic of Morals*, in H.J. Paton (ed.), *The Moral Law*, London, Hutchinson, 1948.

4 A strong case for teaching as a profession is made in: G. Kirk, *Teacher Education and Professional Development*, Edinburgh, Scottish Academic Press, 1988.

5 For examples of extreme scepticism about the value of educational theory in professional training, see: C.B. Cox and R. Boyson (eds), *The Black Papers*, London, Dent and Sons, 1975; S. Lawlor, *Teachers Mistaught*, London, Centre for Policy Studies, 1990; A. O'Hear, *Who Teaches the Teacher?*, Research Report 10, London, Social Affairs Unit, 1988; and M. Phillips, *All Must Have Prizes*, London, Little, Brown and Company, 1996.

6 This sort of criticism seems especially characteristic of the work of Melanie Phillips. See, again: Phillips, *All Must Have Prizes*. However, see also essays by Phillips, Lord

Alton and other contributors to J. Haldane (ed.), *Philosophy and Public Affairs*, Cambridge, Cambridge University Press, 2000.

7 Such complaints are just below the surface of much recent policy documentation on moral and spiritual education. For some recent British policy documentation that broadly implicates teachers in such wider social and moral responsibility, see National Curriculum Council, *Spiritual and Moral Education: A Discussion Paper*, NCC, UK, York, 1993; Ofsted, *Spiritual, Moral, Social and Cultural Development: An Ofsted Discussion Paper*, Office for Standards in Education, UK, London, 1994; Schools Curriculum and Assessment Authority, *Spiritual and Moral Development*, SCAA, UK, Discussion Paper No. 3, London, 1995, and *Education for Adult and Moral Life*, SCAA, UK, Discussion Paper No. 6, London, 1996. For some critical comment on such approaches see: A. Skillen, 'Can virtue be taught, especially these days?', *Journal of Philosophy of Education*, vol. 31, 1997, pp. 375–93; See also some of the contributions to R. Smith and P. Standish (eds), *Teaching Right and Wrong: Moral Education in the Balance*, London, Trentham Books, 1997.

8 For Aristotle on the practical wisdom of *phronesis*, see: Aristotle's *Nicomachean Ethics*, in R. McKeon (ed.), *The Basic Works of Aristotle*, New York, Random House, 1941, especially book 6.

9 For Aristotle on the affective dimensions of *phronesis*, see: ibid., especially book 2; also D. Carr, 'Two kinds of virtue', *Proceedings of the Aristotelian Society*, vol. 84, 1984–5, pp. 47–61.

10 For Aristotle's view of the proportionality of justice and equality, see: Aristotle's *Politics*, in McKeon (ed.), *The Basic Works of Aristotle*, book 3, section 9; and *Nicomachean Ethics*, book 5, section 3.

11 For ideas of multiple and emotional intelligence, see: H. Gardner, *Frames of Mind: The Theory of Multiple Intelligences*, New York, Basic Books, 1985, and *The Theory of Multiple Intelligences: The Theory in Practice*, New York, Basic Books, 1993; D. Goleman, *Emotional Intelligence: Why It Can Matter More Than IQ*, London, Bloomsbury, 1996. For some criticism of concepts of emotional intelligence, see: D. Carr, 'Feelings in moral conflict and the hazards of emotional intelligence', *Ethical Theory and Moral Practice*, vol. 5, 2002, pp. 3–21.

12 For some of the extensive radical literature enshrining scepticism about educational professionalism of this kind, see the sources in chapter 1, note 2 above.

13 The idea of 'being on the side of pupils' is central to the work of A.S. Neill. See: A.S. Neill, *Summerhill*, Harmondsworth, Penguin, 1968.

14 On the idea of semi-professions, see: A. Etzioni (ed.), *The Semi-Professions and Their Organization: Teachers, Nurses and Social Workers*, London, Collier-Macmillan, 1969.

4 Educational theory and practice

1 For some overdue recent critical reflection on the idea of reflective practice, see: T.H. McLaughlin, 'Beyond the reflective teacher', *Educational Philosophy and Theory*, vol. 31, 1999, pp. 9–25.

2 For a good example of an official attempt to apply the competence approach to professional education and training: Scottish Office Education Department, *Guidelines for Teacher Training Courses*, Edinburgh, SOED, 1993. For some defence of such approaches from the academic philosophical side, see: D. Bridges, 'Competence-based education and training: progress or villainy?', *Journal of the Philosophy of Education*, vol. 30, 1996, pp. 361–75.

3 For a classic modern discussion of the relationship of theory to practice, and of the place of knowledge in practice, see: G. Ryle, *The Concept of Mind*, London, Hutchinson, 1949. See also, on these issues D. Carr: 'The logic of knowing how and ability', *Mind*, vol. 88, 1979, pp. 394–409; and 'Knowledge in practice', *American Philosophical Quarterly*, vol. 18, 1981, pp. 53–61.

4 For a new postwar view of the role of educational theory in the professional education and training of teachers, see: R.S. Peters, *Ethics and Education*, London, George Allen and Unwin, 1966, pp. 309–10. See also: P.H. Hirst, Educational theory', in P.H. Hirst (ed.), *Educational Theory and Its Foundation Disciplines*, London, Routledge and Kegan Paul, 1983.

5 For a spirited defence of action research against school effectiveness research, see: J. Elliott, 'School effectiveness research and its critics', *Cambridge Journal of Education*, vol. 26, 1996, pp. 199–224.

6 I seem to recall encountering this striking critical remark on the misguidedness of much social scientific inquiry and research in the course of previous extensive reading of the works of C.S. Lewis. Despite all endeavour, however, I have not since been able to track down the precise source of this observation.

7 For the rather dubious idea of 'practical theory', see P. H. Hirst: 'The theory and practice relationship in teacher training', in M. Booth, J. Furlong and M. Wilkin (eds), *Partnership in Initial Teacher Training: The Way Forward*, London, Cassell, 1990; and 'The demands of professional practice and preparation of teachers', in J. Furlong and R. Smith (eds), *The Role of Higher Education in Initial Teacher Training*, London, Kogan Page, 1996. See also, more recently, J. Furlong, *Higher Education and the New Professionalism of Teachers: Realising the Potential of Partnership*, London, CVCP, 2000.

8 The comment on 'barmy theory' in teacher education was made by Kenneth Clarke when he was education minister in a previous Thatcher (UK) administration, see: K. Clarke, *Primary Education: A Statement*, London, Department of Education and Science, 1991.

9 For G.E. Moore's classic account of the naturalistic fallacy, see: G.E. Moore, *Principia Ethica*, Cambridge: Cambridge University Press, 1960.

10 For the notion of defeasibility in practical reasoning, see: P.T. Geach, *Reason and Argument*, Oxford, Blackwell, 1976, chapter 19.

11 For an interesting exploration of so-called 'objectivist' and 'relativist' fantasies in education, see: J. Wilson, *Fantasy and Common Sense in Education*, Oxford, Martin Robertson, 1979.

12 Recent works of Alasdair MacIntyre have done much to promote this view in social, moral and educational theory. See, for example: *After Virtue*, Notre Dame, Ind., University of Notre Dame Press, 1981; 'The idea of an educated public', in G. Haydon (ed.), *Education and Values: The Richard Peters Lectures*, Institute of Education, University of London, 1987; *Whose Justice, Which Rationality?*, Notre Dame, Ind., University of Notre Dame Press, 1987; 'How to appear virtuous without actually being so', in J.M. Halstead and T.H. McLaughlin (eds), *Education in Morality*, London: Routledge, 1999; and *Three Rival Versions of Moral Enquiry*, Notre Dame, Ind., University of Notre Dame Press, 1992.

13 For an important modern defence of ethical naturalism and of the idea of natural goodness, see P. Foot: *Virtues and Vices*, Oxford, Blackwell, 1978; and *Natural Goodness*, Oxford, Oxford University Press, 2001.

14 For what may well have been Socrates' own account of his mistaken mission, see: Plato's *Apology*, in E. Hamilton and H. Cairns (eds), *Plato: The Collected Dialogues*, Princeton, Princeton University Press, 1961.

15 For Aristotle on the moral wisdom of phronesis, see: Aristotle's *Nicomachean Ethics*, in R. McKeon (ed.), *The Basic Works of Aristotle*, New York, Random House, 1941, especially book 6. See also: J. Dunne, *Back to the Rough Ground: 'Phronesis' and 'Techne' in Modern Philosophy and in Aristotle*, Notre Dame, Ind., University of Notre Dame Press, 1993.

5 Wider moral implications of education

1 For significant critical discussion of postwar discourse of the neutral teacher, see: M. Warnock, 'The neutral teacher', and J. Wilson, 'Teaching and neutrality', both in M.

Taylor (ed.), *Progress and Problems in Moral Education*, Slough, Berks, NFER Publishing Co. Ltd., 1975, section II.

2 For such radical proposals, see again the sources in chapter 1, note 2 above.

3 Again, for suggestions of teacher accountability in this respect, see National Curriculum Council, *Spiritual and Moral Education: A Discussion Paper*, NCC, UK, York, 1993; Ofsted, *Spiritual, Moral, Social and Cultural Development: An Ofsted Discussion Paper*, Office for Standards in Education, UK, London, 1994; Schools Curriculum and Assessment Authority, *Spiritual and Moral Development*, SCAA, UK, Discussion Paper No. 3, London, 1995, and *Education for Adult and Moral Life*, SCAA, UK, Discussion Paper No. 6, London, 1996. And for another perspective see: A. Skillen, 'Can virtue be taught, especially these days?', *Journal of Philosophy of Education*, vol. 31, 1997, pp. 375–93. See also some of the contributions to R. Smith and P. Standish, *Teaching Right and Wrong: Moral Education in the Balance*, London, Trentham Books, 1997.

4 For a critical exploration of the personal–common values distinction, see: D. Carr 'Common and personal values in moral education', *Studies in Philosophy and Education*, Special Issue, vol. 17, 1998, pp. 303–12.

5 The liberal harm principle, of course, marks the limits of individual freedom in John Stuart Mill's liberalism. See: J.S. Mill, *On Liberty*, in M. Warnock (ed.), *Utilitarianism*, London, Collins, Fontana Library, 1970.

6 For the British Schools Curriculum and Assessment Authority's search for value consensus, see: Schools Curriculum and Assessment Authority, *Spiritual and Moral Development* and *Education for Adult and Moral Life*.

7 For critical comment on the kind of social control agenda that seems to characterise much contemporary official thinking about moral and values education, see: D. Carr, 'Cross questions and crooked answers: the modern problem of moral education', in J.M. Halstead and T.H. McLaughlin (eds), *Education in Morality*, London, Routledge, 1999; Skillen, 'Can virtue be taught, especially these days?'; and Smith and Standish (eds), *Teaching Right and Wrong*.

8 See: F. Nietzsche, 'The gay science', in R.J. Hollindale (ed.), *A Nietzsche Reader*, Harmondsworth, Penguin, 1977.

9 For modern consensualist views of ethics, see: É. Durkheim, *Moral Education: A Study in the Theory and Application of the Sociology of Education*, trans. E.K. Wilson and H. Schnurer, New York, Collier-Macmillan, 1961; and D. Gauthier, *Morals by Agreement*, Oxford, Clarendon Press, 1986.

10 For a broadly 'core plus options' conception of morality in contemporary educational policy documentation, see, for example: Scottish Office Education Department, *Religious and Moral Education 5–14*, Edinburgh, SOED, 1992.

11 The question of 'whose values?' has a central place in: Ofsted, *Spiritual, Moral, Social and Cultural Development*.

12 For Durkheim's account of the moral authority of 'Society', see: Durkheim, *Moral Education*.

13 See: Plato's *Gorgias*, in E. Hamilton and H. Cairns (eds), *Plato: The Collected Dialogues*, Princeton, Princeton University Press, 1961; and also S. Johnson, 'Skills, Socrates and the Sophists: learning from history', *British Journal of Educational Studies*, vol. 46, 1998, pp. 201–14.

14 For a discussion of the cardinal virtues, see: D. Carr, 'The cardinal virtues and Plato's moral psychology', *Philosophical Quarterly*, vol. 38, 1988, pp. 186–200.

15 See: Plato's *Republic*, in Hamilton and Cairns (eds), *Plato: The Collected Dialogues*.

16 For work on teacher's views on the moral role of teacher, see: D. Carr and J. Landon, 'Teachers and schools as agencies of values education: reflections on teachers' perceptions: part I: the role of the teacher', *Journal of Beliefs and Values*, vol. 19, 1998, pp. 165–76.

17 For some influential modern commentary on the importance of Aristotle's account of practical reasoning, see: G.E.M. Anscombe, *Intention*, Oxford, Blackwell, 1959.

18 For Rousseau on the moral law, see: J.J. Rousseau, *The Social Contract and Other Discourses*, trans. G.D.H. Cole, London, Dent, 1973, p. 210.
19 See: ibid., p. 181.
20 For a discussion of Kant's conception of personhood, see: D. Carr, 'Moral and personal identity', *International Journal of Education and Religion*, vol. 2, 2001, pp. 79–97.
21 See: Mill, *On Liberty*.
22 Modern liberal preference for a Kantian ethics is perhaps best exemplified in the highly influential modern work on moral theory of John Rawls: See especially: J. Rawls, *A Theory of Justice*, Cambridge, Mass., Harvard University Press, 1985.
23 Again, for good critical discussion of contemporary discourse of the neutral teacher, see: Warnock, 'The neutral teacher'; and Wilson, 'Teaching and neutrality'.
24 For MacIntyre on the problems of a common moral education in contemporary circumstances of value pluralism, see: A.C. MacIntyre, 'How to appear virtuous without actually being so', in Halstead and McLaughlin (eds), *Education in Morality*.
25 On the possibility of non-relative virtue ethics, see: M.C. Nussbaum, 'Non-relative virtues: an Aristotelian approach', in P.A. French, T.E. Uehling and H.K. Wettstein (eds), *Midwest Studies in Philosophy, Vol. 13: Ethical Theory, Character and Virtue*, Notre Dame, Ind., University of Notre Dame Press, 1988. Reprinted in M.C. Nussbaum and A. Sen (eds), *The Quality of Life*, Oxford, Oxford University Press, 1993. See also D. Carr, 'After Kohlberg: some implications of an ethics of virtue for the theory and practice of moral education', *Studies in Philosophy and Education*, vol. 15, 1996, pp. 353–70.
26 For some work by the author on virtues as expressive of positive affect, see: 'Two kinds of virtue', *Proceedings of the Aristotelian Society*, vol. 84, 1984–5, pp. 47–61, 'Emotional intelligence, PSE and self-esteem: a cautionary note', *Pastoral Care in Education*, vol. 18, 2000, pp. 27–33, but see also my 'Feelings in moral conflict and the hazards of emotional intelligence', *Ethical Theory and Moral Practice*, vol. 5, 2002, pp. 3–21.
27 For key works in the ethics of care, see: C. Gilligan, *In a Different Voice: Psychological Theory and Women's Development*, Cambridge, Mass., Harvard University Press, 1982; and N. Noddings, *Caring: A Feminist Approach to Ethics*, Berkeley, University of California Press, 1984.

6 Learning: behaviour, perception and cognition

1 For the key relevant works of these authors, see: Plato's *Phaedo*, in E. Mamilton and H. Cairns (eds), *Plato: The Collected Dialogues*, Princeton, Princeton University Press, 1961; Aristotle's *De Anima*, in R. McKeon (ed.), *The Basic Works of Aristotle*, New York, Random House, 1941; Descartes's *Meditations* and *Discourses*, in G.E.M. Anscombe, and P.T. Geach (eds), *Descartes: Philosophical Writings*, London, Nelson, 1954; T. Hobbes, *Leviathan*, Harmondsworth, Penguin, 1968; I. Kant, *The Critique of Pure Reason*, trans. N. Kemp Smith, London, Macmillan, 1968; J. Dewey, *Experience and Nature*, La Salle, Ill., Open Court, 1958; B. Russell, *The Problems of Philosophy*, Oxford, Oxford University Press, 1968; G. Ryle, *The Concept of Mind*, London, Hutchinson, 1949; L. Wittgenstein, *Philosophical Investigations*, trans. G.E.M. Anscombe, Oxford, Blackwell, 1953.
2 For different anti-dualist or anti-Cartesian approaches in Dewey, Ryle and Wittgenstein, see: Ryle, *The Concept of Mind*; Wittgenstein, *Philosophical Investigations*; Dewey, *Experience and Nature*.
3 For the idea that Platonic or Cartesian dualist approaches to the philosophy of mind rest on mistaken 'logical grammar', see again: Ryle, *The Concept of Mind*; and especially Wittgenstein, *Philosophical Investigations*.

4 For empiricist classics of associationism see: D. Hume, *A Treatise of Human Nature*, Harmondsworth, Penguin, 1969; and J.S. Mill, *A System of Logic*, London, Longman, 1961.

5 See: I.P. Pavlov, *Conditioned Reflexes*, trans. G.V. Anrep, New York, Dover, 1960.

6 See: J.B. Watson, *Behaviorism*, Chicago, University of Chicago Press, 1930.

7 See: E.L. Thorndyke, *The Psychology of Learning*, New York, Teachers College, 1913.

8 See: B.F. Skinner, *Science and Human Behavior*, New York, Macmillan, 1953; and for Skinner's influence on Quine, see: W.V.O.Quine, *Word and Object*, Cambridge, Mass., MIT Press, 1960.

9 See B.F. Skinner: *Walden II*, New York, Macmillan, 1948; and *Beyond Freedom and Dignity*, Harmondsworth, Penguin, 1973.

10 For a discussion of how skills learning may bypass meaningful understanding, see: D. Carr, 'Dance education, skill and behavioural objectives', *Journal of Aesthetic Education*, vol. 18, 1984, pp. 67–76.

11 For a very helpful discussion of the distinction between acting in accordance with a rule and following a rule, see: P. Winch, *The Idea of a Social Science and Its Relation to Philosophy*, London, Routledge and Kegan Paul, 1958.

12 For Kant on thoughts, content, intuitions and concepts, see: Kant, *The Critique of Pure Reason*, p. 93.

13 For some key works of 'Gestalt' psychology, see: K. Koffka, *The Principles of Gestalt Psychology*, New York, Harcourt, 1935; W. Köhler, *The Mentality of Apes*, trans. E. Winter, New York, Harcourt, 1925; and M. Wertheimer, *Productive Thinking*, New York, Harper, 1945.

14 For a useful collection of essays on the pschology of cognition containing reasonably short and accessible essays by Piaget and Bruner, see: P.C. Wason and P.N. Johnson-Laird (eds), *Thinking and Reasoning*, Harmondsworth, Penguin, 1968.

15 For a key work of Piagetian theory, see: J. Piaget, *The Psychology of Intelligence*, trans. M. Percy and D.E. Berlyne, London, Routledge, 1950.

16 For Kohlberg's important and influential work on moral development and education, see: L. Kohlberg, *Essays on Moral Development*, Vols I–III, New York, Harper and Row, 1984.

17 For an exploration of inconsistencies between cognitive theories, see: D. Carr, 'Knowledge and curriculum: four dogmas of child-centred education', *Journal of Philosophy of Education*, vol. 22, 1988, pp. 151–62.

18 For a critical account of Kohlberg's theory, see: D. Carr, 'Moral education and the perils of developmentalism', *Journal of Moral Education*, vol. 31, 2002, pp. 5–19.

7 Learning: meaning, language and culture

1 For Kant on thoughts, content, intuitions and concepts, see: I. Kant, *The Critique of Pure Reason*, trans. N. Kemp Smith, London, Macmillan, 1968, p. 93.

2 For some of Plato's difficulties over explaining the nature of concept-formation, see: Plato's *Republic* and *Parmenides*, in E. Hamilton and H. Cairns (eds), *Plato: The Collected Dialogues*, Princeton, Princeton University Press, 1961.

3 For some important modern arguments against abstractionist accounts of concept-formation, see: P.T. Geach, *Mental Acts*, London, Routledge and Kegan Paul, 1957.

4 For David Hume on problems of induction, see: D. Hume, *A Treatise of Human Nature*, Harmondsworth, Penguin, 1969.

5 For the linguistic theorist Noam Chomsky's innatism, see: N. Chomsky, *Language and Mind*, Harcourt, Brace and World, 1968.

6 For some interesting related points, see: D.E. Cooper, 'Grammar and the possession of concepts', *Proceedings of the Philosophy of Education Society of Great Britain*, vol. 7, 1973, pp. 204–22.

7 For John Locke's account of concept-formation, see: J. Locke, *An Essay Concerning Human Understanding*, Oxford, Oxford University Press, 1934.

8 For David Hume on impressions and ideas, see: Hume, *A Treatise of Human Nature*.

9 See: L. Wittgenstein, *Tractatus-Logico-Philosophicus*, trans. D.F. Pears and B. McGuinness, London, Routledge and Kegan Paul, 1961.

10 See: G. Berkeley, *A Treatise Concerning the Principles of Human Knowledge*, La Salle, Ill., Open Court, 1915.

11 For Kant's criticism of subjective idealism, see: Kant, *The Critique of Pure Reason*. Kant's argument against subjective idealism clearly pioneers the argument from polar opposites that is also explored by modern philosophers in, for example: G. Ryle, *Dilemmas*, Cambridge, Cambridge University Press, 1960, chapter 7; and J. Passmore, *Philosophical Reasoning*, London: Duckworth, 1970, chapter 6.

12 The German philosophers J.G. Fichte and G.W.F. Hegel may be considered key figures in the development of post-Kantian idealism. See, for example: J.G. Fichte, *The Vocation of Man*, trans. W. Smith, La Salle, Ill., Open Court, 1965; and G.W.F. Hegel, *The Phenomenology of Mind*, trans. J.B. Baillie, London, George Allen and Unwin, 1971. See also: C. Friedrich, *The Philosophy of Hegel*, New York, Random House, 1953.

13 See: L. Wittgenstein, *Philosophical Investigations*, trans. G.E.M. Anscombe, Oxford, Blackwell, 1953.

14 For Russell's philosophy of logical atomism, see: B. Russell, *Logic and Knowledge: Essays 1901–1950*, London, George Allen and Unwin, 1956.

15 For Frege's attempt to logicise mathematics, see: G. Frege, *The Foundations of Arithmetic: A Logico-Mathematical Enquiry into the Concept of Number*, trans. J.L. Austin, Oxford, Blackwell, 1978.

16 See: G. Frege, 'The thought', in P. Strawson (ed.), *Philosophical Logic*, Oxford, Oxford University Press, 1967.

17 See various essays in: P.T. Geach and M. Black (eds), *Translations from the Philosophical Writings of Gottlob Frege*, Oxford, Blackwell, 1966.

18 For a helpful discussion of some of the labyrinthine complexities of Frege's view of the referential status of concepts, see: A. Kenny, *Frege: An Introduction to the Founder of Modern Analytical Philosophy*, Harmondsworth, Penguin, 1995, especially chapters 6 and 7.

19 These ideas are also helpfully discusssed in: M. Luntley, *Contemporary Philosophy of Thought: Truth, World, Content*, Oxford, Blackwell, 1999.

20 For Frege's contextual criterion of meaning, see: Frege, *The Foundations of Arithmetic*, Introduction, p. xe.

21 For a very clear account of Wittgenstein's private-language argument, see: A. Kenny, *Wittgenstein*, London, Allen Lane: The Penguin Press, 1973.

22 For Plato's theory of forms, see: Plato's *Republic*.

23 See: Geach, *Mental Acts*.

24 However, for some trenchant criticism of so-called 'ascriptivist' accounts of meaning, see: P.T. Geach, *Logic Matters*, Oxford, Blackwell, 1972, section 8.

25 This point is made by Hilary Putnam. See H. Putnam: 'The meaning of meaning', in *Mind, Language and Reality*, Cambridge, Cambridge University Press, 1975; and *Reason, Truth and History*, Cambridge, Cambridge University Press, 1981.

26 For criticism of Piaget and Bruner in this connection, see: D. Carr, 'Knowledge and curriculum: four dogmas of child-centred education', *Journal of Philosophy of Education*, vol. 22, 1988, pp. 151–62.

27 On process and product, see: D. Carr, 'Education, learning and understanding: the process and the product', *Journal of Philosophy of Education*, vol. 26, 1992, pp. 215–25.

28 For suggestions that self-esteem and other processes might be regarded as aims of education, see: Scottish Office Education Department: *Personal and Social Education 5–14*, Edinburgh, SOED, 1993; and J. MacBeath, *Personal and Social Education*, Edinburgh, Scottish Academic Press, 1988. For some strong criticism of this idea, see:

D. Carr, 'Emotional intelligence, PSE and self-esteem: a cautionary note', *Pastoral Care in Education*, vol. 18, 2000, pp. 27–33.

29 For Wittgenstein's condemnation of empirical psychology, see: Wittgenstein, *Philosophical Investigations*, part II, p. 232.

30 On this issue, see: D. Carr, 'Educational enquiry and professional knowledge', *Educational Studies*, vol. 20, 1994, pp. 33–52.

8 Knowledge, explanation and understanding

1 For the anti-reductive perspectives of Plato and Aristotle, see: Plato's *Phaedo* and *Apology*, in E. Hamilton and H. Cairns (eds), *Plato: The Collected Dialogues*, Princeton, Princeton University Press, 1961; and Aristotle's *Nicomachean Ethics* and *De Anima* in R. McKeon (ed.), *The Basic Works of Aristotle*, New York, Random House, 1941.

2 For Socrates' critique of the Protagorean assimilation of knowledge to perception, see: Plato's *Theaetetus*, in Hamilton and Cairns (eds), *Plato: The Collected Dialogues*.

3 The term 'inert knowledge' was widely used by R.S. Peters to refer to more or less useless information. See: R.S. Peters, *Ethics and Education*, London, George Allen and Unwin, 1966.

4 For Aristotle's distinction of formal from efficient and other causes, see: Aristotle's *Physics* and *Metaphysics*, in McKeon (ed.), *The Basic Works of Aristotle*.

5 For a much-discussed critique of the Platonic definition of knowledge as justified belief, see: E.L. Gettier, 'Is justified true belief knowledge?', in A. Phillips-Griffiths (ed.), *Knowledge and Belief*, Oxford, Oxford University Press, 1967.

6 A fairly central role would appear to be given to the idea that knowledge is justified true belief in liberal educational accounts of autonomy, especially those focused on the educational epistemology of 'forms of knowledge'. See, for example: P.H. Hirst, 'Liberal education and the nature of knowledge', in *Knowledge and the Curriculum*, London, Routledge and Kegan Paul, 1974.

7 For Plato's famous cave allegory, see: Plato's *Republic*, in Hamilton and Cairns (eds), *Plato: The Collected Dialogues*.

8 See: R.S. Peters, *Authority, Responsibility and Education*, London, George Allen and Unwin, 1959, part iii, section 8, p. 104.

9 The idea of explaining necessity in terms of truth in all possible worlds seems to have been first suggested by the seventeenth-century philosopher Gottfried Leibniz. Significant modern developments of the idea, however, are to be found in: A. Plantinga, *The Nature of Necessity*, Oxford, Oxford University Press, 1974; and S. Kripke, *Naming and Necessity*, Oxford, Blackwell, 1980.

10 For the idea that God must be subject to logical and other constraints, see: P.T. Geach, *Providence and Evil*, Cambridge, Cambridge University Press, 1977, chapter 2.

11 For Wittgenstein's mathematical intuitionism (as opposed to Frege's realism) see: M. Dummett, 'Wittgenstein's philosophy of mathematics', in *Truth and Other Enigmas*, London, Duckworth, 1978.

12 Once again, Alasdair MacIntyre has been a key figure in promoting the communitarian conception of morality as local construction in educational philosophy as elsewhere. See the sources in chapter 4, note 12 above.

13 Once again, such philosophers as John Dewey and W.V.O. Quine may be regarded as key figures in the development of pragmatist philosophy of science. However, the more constructivist elements of pragmatist epistemology have been developed in a rather more radical direction by such more recent philosophers of science as Thomas Kuhn. See especially: T.S. Kuhn, *The Structure of Scientific Revolutions*, 2nd edition, Chicago, University of Chicago Press, 1970.

14 The work of the influential contemporary American philosopher Richard Rorty could be said to mark the point at which pragmatism turns into postmodernism. See especially: *Philosophy and the Mirror of Nature*, Princeton, Princeton University Press,

1979; and *Contingency, Irony and Solidarity*, Cambridge, Cambridge University Press, 1989.

15 See: J.-F. Lyotard, *The Postmodern Condition: A Report on Knowledge*, trans. G. Bennington and B. Massumi, Manchester, Manchester University Press, 1984.

16 The rejection of dualism runs throughout Dewey's mainstream and educational philosophy. See, for example: *Experience and Nature*, La Salle, Ill., Open Court, 1958; *Human Nature and Conduct*, New York, Random House, 1930; *Democracy and Education*, New York, Macmillan, 1916; *Experience and Education*, New York, Collier Books, 1938; and *The School and Society*, Chicago, University of Chicago Press, 1915.

17 For a useful collection of writings from Kilpatrick on curriculum and other topics, see: L.R. Perry, *Bertrand Russell, A.S. Neill, Homer Lane, W.H. Kilpatrick: Four Progressive Educators*, Educational Thinkers Series, London, Collier-Macmillan, 1967.

18 See: Plowden Report, *Children and Their Primary Schools*, London, HMSO, 1967; and Primary Memorandum, *Primary Education in Scotland*, Scottish Education Department, Edinburgh, HMSO, 1965.

19 For some fairly unguarded talk about personal meaning-making in recent British educational policy documentation, see: Scottish Consultative Committee on the Curriculum, *Education 10–14 in Scotland*, Scottish Curriculum Development Service, Dundee, 1986.

20 For a fairly heated British debate on the educational legacy of Dewey, see: A. O'Hear, 'Philosophy and educational policy', and A. Ryan, 'What did John Dewey want?', in J. Haldane (ed.), *Philosophy and Public Affairs*, Cambridge: Cambridge University Press, 2000.

21 See: Shakespeare's *Hamlet*, act II, scene 2, lines 248–50.

22 For Aristotle's critique of Plato's form of the good, see: Aristotle's *Nicomachean Ethics*, book 1, section 6.

23 For Aristotle on the limitations of precision, see: ibid., book 1, section 3.

24 On the contemporary neo-idealist insulation of moral principle from experience, see again various recent works of Alasdair MacIntyre as cited in chapter 4, note 12 above.

25 For the prescriptivist view that good is what we commend, see especially: R.M. Hare, *The Language of Morals*, Oxford, Oxford University Press, 1952.

26 See: L. Wittgenstein, *On Certainty*, trans. D. Paul and G.E.M. Anscombe, Oxford, Blackwell, 1969.

27 The source of the pragmatist idea that knowledge should be regarded as 'warranted assertability' is, of course, John Dewey. See, for example: *Experience and Nature* and *The Quest for Certainty*, New York, Milton Balch & Co., 1929.

28 For Aristotle's modest correspondence theory of truth, see: Aristotle's *Metaphysics*, book 4, section 7, p. 749.

29 Some such point seems central to a recent (Deweyan) pragmatist critique of allegedly traditional realist or foundationalist conceptions of education. See: R.A. Brosio, *Philosophical Scaffolding for the Construction of Democratic Education*, New York, Peter Lang Publishing Inc., 2000.

9   Curriculum: purpose, form and content

1 Some recent works in mainstream and educational philosophy in which reasonably clear distinctions are (variously) made between judgement and truth include: M. Luntley, *Reason, Truth and Self: The Postmodern Reconditioned*, London, Routledge, 1995; H. Siegel, *Educating Reason: Rationality, Critical Thinking and Education*, London, Routledge and Kegan Paul, 1988, and *Rationality Redeemed: Further Dialogues on an Educational Ideal*, New York, Routledge and Kegan Paul, 1997. See also, in a related vein: J. McDowell, *Mind and World*, Cambridge, Mass., Harvard University Press, 1996.

2 The idea here, of course, is that parents from some communities might regard initiation into some religious faith as the very bedrock of education, even on the understanding that it might be hard if not impossible to give a conclusive rational demonstration of the truth of that faith.

3 For an interesting recent discussion of 'whole child', see: T.H. McLaughlin, 'The education of the whole child', in R. Best (ed.), *Education, Spirituality and the Whole Child*, London, Cassell, 1996.

4 On this question, however, see: D. Carr, 'Knowledge and truth in religious education', *Journal of Philosophy of Education*, vol. 28, 1994, pp. 221–37.

5 The 'phenomenological' approach to religious education would appear to be derived from the work of Ninian Smart. See: N. Smart, *The Phenomenon of Religion*, London, Macmillan, 1973.

6 An official educational proposal to accord a fairly precise curricular time allocation to moral education is criticised in: D. Carr, '5–14: A Philosophical Critique', in G. Kirk and R. Glaister (eds), *5–14: Scotland's National Curriculum*, Edinburgh, Scottish Academic Press, 1994.

7 For the definitive statement of the 'forms of knowledge' thesis, see: P.H. Hirst, 'Liberal education and the nature of knowledge', in *Knowledge and the Curriculum*, London, Routledge and Kegan Paul, 1974.

8 For a very good example of some actual forms of knowledge curriculum planning in terms of core subjects plus options, see: Munn Report, *The Structure of the Curriculum in the Third and Fourth Years of the Secondary School*, Scottish Education Department, Edinburgh, HMSO, 1977.

9 For some general criticism of type-token forms of knowledge curriculum theorising, see: M. Warnock, *Schools of Thought*, London, Faber and Faber, 1977.

10 For some criticism of generalist forms of knowledge theorising about the arts, see: D. Best, 'Generic arts: an expedient myth', *Journal of Art and Design*, vol. 11, 1992, pp. 27–44.

11 For Wittgenstein on family resemblances, see: L. Wittgenstein, *Philosophical Investigations*, trans. G.E.M. Anscombe, Oxford, Blackwell, 1953, part I, section 67.

12 For the idea that the cultivation of 'one genuine enthusiasm' might be regarded as a criterion of educational development, see: M. Warnock, 'Towards a definition of quality in education', in R.S. Peters (ed.), *The Philosophy of Education*, Oxford, Oxford University Press, 1973.

13 For key sources of ideas of curriculum integration, see the extracts from Kilpatrick in: L.R. Perry, *Bertrand Russell, A.S. Neill, Homer Lane, W.H. Kilpatrick: Four Progressive Educators*, Educational Thinkers Series, London, Collier-Macmillan, 1967; also J. Dewey, *Experience and Education*, New York, Collier Books, 1938.

14 For a local British example of such integrated curriculum thinking, see: Scottish Consultative Committee on the Curriculum, *Environmental Studies: 5–14*, Edinburgh, Scottish Education Department, 1991.

15 For some considerable recent hostility to ideas of Deweyan or other progressive integration, see: A. O'Hear, 'Philosophy and educational policy', in J. Haldane (ed.), *Philosophy and Public Affairs*, Cambridge, Cambridge University Press, 2000.

16 For an explicit British 'progressive' attempt to address the problem of continuity between different traditions of primary and secondary curricula, see: Scottish Consultative Committee on the Curriculum, *Education 10–14 in Scotland*, Scottish Curriculum Development Service, Dundee, 1986.

17 On the apparent curriculum discontinuity between primary 'progressivism' and secondary 'traditionalism' see: D. Carr, 'Knowledge and curriculum: four dogmas of child-centred education', *Journal of Philosophy of Education*, vol. 22, 1988, pp. 151–62.

18 For some dissenting comments on a recent 'non-traditional' initiative for upper primary education, see the foreword by the then Scottish minister Michael Forsyth to: Scottish Consultative Committee on the Curriculum, *Environmental Studies: 5–14*.

19 See: J.S. Bruner, *The Process of Education*, Cambridge, Mass., Harvard University Press, 1960, and *The Relevance of Education*, London, Allen and Unwin, 1972.

10 Curriculum: process, product and appraisal

1 Again, for modern radical literature expressing scepticism about the educational value of schooling, see the sources cited in chapter 1, note 2 above.

2 For Plato's general interest in questions of knowledge, curriculum and learning, see generally: Plato's *Republic* and *Meno* in E. Hamilton and H. Cairns (eds), *Plato: The Collected Dialogues*, Princeton, Princeton University Press, 1961.

3 For Plato's meritocratic views on education, see generally: Plato's *Republic*. For a useful collection of essays on modern developments in psychometry, see: S. Wiseman (ed.), *Intelligence and Ability*, Harmondsworth, Penguin, 1967.

4 See: Plato's *Theaetetus*, in Hamilton and Cairns (eds), *Plato: The Collected Dialogues*.

5 For Plato's *Meno*, see note 2 above.

6 The modern literature of social scientific and other literature on educational assessment is enormous. However, for a very clear basic introduction to the key concepts by an educational philosopher, see: K. Williams, *Assessment: A Discussion Paper*, Ireland, Association of Secondary Teachers, 1992.

7 See: F.W. Taylor, *Principles of Scientific Management*, London, Harper and Row, 1911.

8 Some of these points seem less than helpfully run together in some texts on curriculum theory. See, for example: G. Blenkin and A.V. Kelly, *The Primary Curriculum: A Process Approach to Curriculum Planning*, London, Paul Chapman, 1987.

9 For Aristotle on the limits of precision, see: Aristotle's *Nicomachean Ethics*, in R. McKeon (ed.), *The Basic Works of Aristotle*, New York, Random House, 1941, book 1, section 3.

10 On questions of the balance of technique and free expression in arts education, see D. Best: 'Free expression or the teaching of techniques?', *British Journal of Educational Studies*, vol. 27, 1979, pp. 210–20; and 'Can creativity be taught?', *British Journal of Educational Studies*, vol. 30, 1982, pp. 280–94.

11 For the 'process' model of curriculum, see: Blenkin and Kelly, *The Primary Curriculum*.

12 See, for example: E.W. Eisner, 'Instructional and expressive educational objectives: their formulation and use in the curriculum', in W.J. Popham, E.W. Eisner, H.J. Sullivan and L.L. Tyler, *Instructional Objectives*, Chicago, Rand McNally, 1969.

13 For the recent British educational philosophical debate about assessment, see among other pieces: A. Davis 'Criterion-referenced assessment and the development of knowledge and understanding', *Journal of Philosophy of Education*, vol. 29, 1995, pp. 2–22, *The Limits of Educational Assessment*, Oxford, Blackwell, 1998, and *Educational Assessment: A Critique of Educational Policy*, Impact 1, Philosophy of Education Society of Great Britain, October 1999; C. Winch and G. Gingell, 'Educational assessment: reply to Andrew Davis', *Journal of Philosophy of Education*, vol. 30, 1996, pp. 377–88.

14 For the key works of Kant and Wittgenstein on the very possibility of human knowledge, see: I. Kant, *The Critique of Pure Reason*, trans. N. Kemp Smith, London, Macmillan, 1968; L. Wittgenstein, *Philosophical Investigations*, trans. G.E.M. Anscombe, Oxford, Blackwell, 1953.

15 For an amusing imaginative reconstruction of this incident, see: L. Goldstein, 'Wittgenstein's PhD. viva: a re-creation', *Philosophy*, vol. 74, 1999, pp. 499–513.

11 Liberalism, impartiality and liberal education

1 For classic early twentieth-century works of logical analysis, see: B. Russell, *Problems of Philosophy*, Oxford, Oxford University Press, 1968, and *Logic and Knowledge: Essays*

1901–1950, London, George Allen and Unwin, 1956; and A.J. Ayer, *Language, Truth and Logic*, London, Gollancz, 1967.

2 For key texts of so-called 'ordinary language' philosophy, see: J.L. Austin, *How to Do Things With Words*, Oxford, Oxford University Press, 1962; G. Ryle, *The Concept of Mind*, London, Hutchinson, 1949; L. Wittgenstein, *Philosophical Investigations*, trans. G.E.M. Anscombe, Oxford, Blackwell, 1953.

3 For a much celebrated pragmatist attack on the analytic–synthetic distinction by Quine, see: W.V.O. Quine, *From a Logical Point of View*, New York, Harper and Row, 1953.

4 See: J. Rawls, *A Theory of Justice*, Cambridge, Mass., Harvard University Press, 1985.

5 Such objections hailed mainly from the direction of radical and/or neo-Marxist sociological perspectives on curriculum theory. For a useful general critical survey of such perspectives, see: D. Lawton, *Class, Culture and the Curriculum*, London, Routledge and Kegan Paul, 1975.

6 For a fair example of a liberal traditionalist egalitarian position, see: J.P. White, *Towards a compulsory Curriculum*, London, Routledge and Kegan Paul, 1975.

7 See, for example: R. Nozick, *Anarchy, State and Utopia*, Oxford, Blackwell, 1974.

8 Again, for Alasdair MacIntyre's general critique of liberal social, moral and educational perspectives, see the sources cited in chapter 4, note 12 above.

9 The long-running debate between liberal and communitarians has virtually dominated social, moral and educational philosophy for the past couple of decades, and it would be impossible to document that debate here. However, one may gain a reasonably good sense of the issues that the debate has raised for educational philosophy in general and for issues about multi-culturalism in particular from the contributions to: Y. Tamir (ed.), *Multicultural Education in a Democratic State*, Oxford, Blackwell, 1995 (first published in 1995 as a Special Issue of *Journal of Philsophy of Education*).

10 See: T. Hobbes, *Leviathan*, Harmondsworth, Penguin, 1968.

11 See: K. Marx and F. Engels, *Selected Writings*, London, Lawrence and Wishart, 1968, p. 181.

12 For Aristotle's 'liberalism' versus Plato's collectivism, see: Aristotle's *Politics*, in R. McKeon (ed.), *The Basic Works of Aristotle*, New York, Random House, 1941. For an excellent recent exploration of the connections between Aristotle's political and educational views, see: R. Curren, *Aristotle on the Necessity of Public Education*, New York and London, Rowan & Littlefield Publishers Inc., 2000.

13 For Aristotle's point that practical moral reasoning is about means, see: Aristotle's *Nicomachean Ethics*, in McKeon (ed.), *The Basic Works of Aristotle*, book 3, section 3.

14 For Aeschylus' Prometheus trilogy, see: Aeschylus, *Prometheus Bound and Other Plays*, trans. P. Vellacott, Harmondsworth, Penguin, 1961.

15 See: Hobbes, *Leviathan*.

16 For the main source of Locke's liberal political views, see: J. Locke, *Two Treatises of Civil Government*, London, Dent Everyman, 1966.

17 See: J. Bentham, 'A critical examination of the declaration of rights', in *Anarchical Fallacies*, in J. Bowring (ed.), *The Works of Jeremy Bentham*, Vol. II, London, 1838.

18 For a key source in the development of deontic logic, see: G.H. von Wright, 'An essay in deontic logic and the general theory of action', *Acta Philosophica Fennica*, Fasc. XXI, Amsterdam, North Holland Publishing Company, 1961.

19 For the key works of Rousseau and Kant in this respect, see: J.J. Rousseau, *The Social Contract and Other Discourses*, trans. G.D.H. Cole, London: Dent, 1973; and I. Kant, *Groundwork of the Metaphysic of Morals*, in H.J. Paton (ed.), *The Moral Law*, London, Hutchinson, 1948.

20 See J.S. Mill's *On Liberty* and *Utilitarianism*, in M. Warnock (ed.), *Utilitarianism*, London, Collins, Fontana Library, 1970.

21 For some objections to utilitarianism, see: S. Scheffler (ed.), *Consequentialism and its Critics*, Oxford, Oxford University Press, 1988; and the contribution of Bernard Williams to J.J.C. Smart and B. Williams, *Utilitarianism: For and Against*, Cambridge, Cambridge University Press, 1973.

22 For Mill's critique of Kantian ethics, see: Mill, *Utilitarianism*, p. 254.

23 For some discussion of Kant's rejection of Rousseau's asocial approach to education in *Émile*, see: G.F. Munzel, *Kant's Conception of Moral Character: The Critical Link of Morality, Anthropology and Reflective Judgement*, Chicago and London, University of Chicago Press, 1999.

24 For the non-cognitivism of prescriptivism, see: R.M. Hare, *The Language of Morals*, Oxford, Oxford University Press, 1952; for non-cognitivism in cognitive developmentalism, see: L. Kohlberg, *Essays on Moral Development*, Vols I–III, New York, Harper and Row, 1984.

25 See: É. Durkheim, *Moral Education: A Study in the Theory and Application of the Sociology of Education*, trans. E.K. Wilson and H. Schnurer, New York, Collier-Macmillan, 1961.

26 See: Rawls, *A Theory of Justice*.

27 See: R.S. Peters, *Moral Education and Moral Development*, London, George Allen and Unwin, 1981; and S.I. Benn and R.S. Peters, *Social Principles and the Democratic State*, London, George Allen and Unwin, 1957.

28 See: P.H. Hirst, *Moral Education in a Secular Society*, London, London University Press, 1974.

29 See: Matthew 10: 34.

30 The problems of a 'core plus options' approach to moral education are discussed in: D. Carr, 'Common and personal values in moral education', *Studies in Philosophy and Education*, vol. 17, 1998, pp. 303–12.

31 For some discussion of such problems, see: ibid.; and D. Carr, 'Moral and religious education 5–14', *Scottish Educational Review*, vol. 24, 1992, pp. 111–17.

12 Community, identity and cultural inheritance

1 For the Marxist influence on critical theory and some handy short introductions to critical theorists, see: J. Lechte, *Fifty Key Contemporary Thinkers: From Structuralism to Postmodernity*, London, Routledge, 1994. For the connection between critical theory and education, see: T. Popkewitz and L. Fendler, *Critical Theories in Education*, London, Routledge, 1999.

2 For some key figures and themes in existentialism, see: H.J. Blackham, *Six Existentialist Thinkers*, London, Routledge, 1965.

3 For Freud and Freudian influences on modern thought, see: Lechte, *Fifty Key Contemporary Thinkers*.

4 For some key figures and themes in structuralism, see: ibid.

5 The pragmatist rejection of conceptual-empirical split is generally characteristic of Deweyan and other pragmatism, but see especially: W.V.O. Quine, *From a Logical Point of View*, New York, Harper and Row, 1953.

6 For the post-structuralist idea of genealogy, see: M. Foucault, *The Archaeology of Knowledge*, trans. A.M. Sheridan-Smith, London, Tavistock Press, 1974.

7 For the communitarian objection to the 'view from nowhere', see: M. Sandel, *Liberalism and the Limits of Justice*, New York, Cambridge University Press, 1982; and T. Nagel, *The View from Nowhere*, New York, Oxford University Press, 1986.

8 Aristotle's communitarian conception of the relationship of the individual to society is generally characteristic of: Aristotle's *Nicomachean Ethics* and *Politics*, in R. McKeon (ed.), *The Basic Works of Aristotle*, New York, Random House, 1941.

9 For Alasdair MacIntyre's specific views on education, see: 'The idea of an educated public', in G. Haydon (ed.), *Education and Values: The Richard Peters Lectures*, Institute of Education, University of London, 1987; and 'How to appear virtuous without

actually being so', in J.M. Halstead and T.H. McLaughlin (eds), *Education in Morality*, London, Routledge, 1999.

10 For some key works of Martha Nussbaum and Charles Taylor, see: C. Taylor, *Sources of the Self: The Making of the Modern Identity*, Cambridge, Cambridge University Press, 1989, and *Multiculturalism: Examining the Politics of Recognition*, in A. Gutmann (ed.), *Multiculturalism*, Princeton, Princeton University Press, 1994; M.C. Nussbaum, *The Fragility of Goodness: Luck and Ethics in Greek Philosophy*, Cambridge, Cambridge University Press, 1986, and *Love's Knowledge: Essays on Philosophy and Literature*, Oxford, Oxford University Press, 1990.

11 For relativist and other socio-political implications of MacIntyre's ideas, see: J. Horton and S. Mendus (eds), *After MacIntyre: Critical Perspectives on the Work of Alasdair MacIntyre*, Cambridge, Polity, 1996.

12 For an exploration of the professional implications of epistemology, see: D. Carr, 'Towards a re-evaluation of the role of educational epistemology in the professional education of teachers', in S. Tozer (ed.), *Philosophy of Education 1998*, Urbana, Ill., Philosophy of Education Society, 1999.

13 It has become something of a modern dogma that there can be no value-neutral science, and the work of Thomas Kuhn is one of the most commonly cited sources of this idea. See: T.S. Kuhn, *The Structure of Scientific Revolutions*, 2nd edition, Chicago, University of Chicago Press, 1970.

14 For Kohlbergian 'dilemmas', see: L. Kohlberg, *Essays on Moral Development*, Vols I–III, New York, Harper and Row, 1984.

15 For the idea of 'horizons of significance', see: Taylor, *Sources of the Self*.

16 For key works in the ethics of care, see: C. Gilligan, *In a Different Voice: Psychological Theory and Women's Development*, Cambridge, Mass., Harvard University Press, 1982; and N. Noddings, *Caring: A Feminist Approach to Ethics*, Berkeley, University of California Press, 1984.

17 See: A.C. MacIntyre, *After Virtue*, Notre Dame, Ind., University of Notre Dame Press, 1981.

18 Again, such 'absolute' idealism seems to be characteristic of the following works by MacIntyre: *After Virtue*; *Whose Justice, Which Rationality?*, Notre Dame, Ind., University of Notre Dame Press, 1987; and *Three Rival Versions of Moral Enquiry*, Notre Dame, Ind., University of Notre Dame Press, 1992. Interestingly, however, there would appear to be a shift towards a less idealist or more naturalist position in MacIntyre's more recent work. See: *Dependent Rational Animals: Why Human Beings Need the Virtues*, London, Duckworth, 1999.

19 See: K. Marx, 'Theses on Feuerbach', in K. Marx and F. Engels, *Selected Writings*, London, Lawrence and Wishart, 1968.

20 See: K. Marx and F. Engels, 'Manifesto of the Communist Party', in Marx and Engels, *Selected Writings*, p. 35.

21 See: ibid., p. 51.

22 One can only here give the briefest indication of the extraordinary extent of Marx's influence on modern philosophical, educational and other thought and practice. However, his influence is evident in all of the following works: P. Freire, *Pedagogy of the Oppressed*, trans. M. Bergman Ramos, Harmondsworth, Penguin, 1972; I. Illich, *Deschooling Society*, Harmondsworth, Penguin, 1973, and *Celebration of Awareness*, Harmondsworth, Penguin, 1973; M.F.D. Young (ed.), *Knowledge and Control*, London, Collier-Macmillan, 1971; J. Habermas, *The Theory of Communicative Action*, Vols 1 and 2, trans. T. McCarthy, Boston, Beacon Press, 1981; H. Marcuse, *One Dimensional Man*, London, Routledge, 1991; T.W. Adorno, *Negative Dialectics*, trans. E.B. Ashton, London, Routledge, 1990; H. Arendt, *The Human Condition*, Chicago, University of Chicago Press, 1958. See also: S. Sayers, *Marxism and Human Nature*, London, Routledge, 1998.

13 Justice, equality and difference

1 See: A.C. MacIntyre, 'How to appear virtuous without actually being so', in J.M. Halstead and T.H. McLaughlin (eds), *Education in Morality*, London, Routledge, 1999.
2 See: C. Taylor, *Multiculturalism: Examining the Politics of Recognition*, in A. Gutmann (ed.), *Multiculturalism*, Princeton, Princeton University Press, 1994.
3 See: J.J. Rousseau, *Émile*, trans. B. Foxley, London, Dent, 1974, chapter 5.
4 See: Plato's *Republic*, in E. Hamilton and H. Cairns (eds), *Plato: The Collected Dialogues*, Princeton, Princeton University Press, 1961.
5 The 1944 Education Act was something of a watershed in postwar British education. Despite its fundamentally egalitarian intent to provide secondary education for all young people irrespective of financial means or social background, it nevertheless proposed different levels of education on the basis of alleged psychometrically grounded differences of intelligence and ability, in a manner not unlike that of Plato's own inegalitarian and meritocratic proposals.
6 On issuess of sex and sexuality in education and the curriculum, see: D. Archard, *Sex Education*, Impact 7, Philosophy of Education Society of Great Britain, 2000. For a range of often contrasting perspectives, see also: M.J. Reiss and S.A. Mabud (eds), *Sex Education and Religion*, Cambridge, The Islamic Academy, 1998.
7 See: Plato's *Republic*.
8 For a useful collection of key essays on aspects of psychometry, See: S. Wiseman (ed.), *Intelligence and Ability*, Harmondsworth, Penguin, 1967.
9 For a classic text on comprehensive education, see: R. Pedley, *The Comprehensive School*, Harmondsworth, Penguin, 1963.
10 For a useful collection of essays on equality and problems of psychometry, see: D. Rubinstein (ed.), *Education and Equality*, Harmondsworth, Penguin, 1979.
11 For some philosophical arguments for the domain-specific nature of human ability, see: R. Dearden, 'What is general about general education?', in *Theory and Practice in Education*, London, Routledge and Kegan Paul, 1984.
12 For the work of a pioneer of the idea of multiple intelligence, see H. Gardner: *Frames of Mind: The Theory of Multiple Intelligences*, New York, Basic Books, 1985; and *The Theory of Multiple Intelligences: The Theory in Practice*, New York, Basic Books, 1993.
13 For champions of the idea of emotional intelligence, see: P. Salovey and J.D. Mayer, 'Emotional intelligence', *Imagination, Cognition and Personality*, vol. 9, 1990, pp. 185–211; and D. Goleman, *Emotional Intelligence: Why It Can Matter More Than IQ*, London, Bloomsbury, 1996.
14 See: Goleman, *Emotional Intelligence*, especially chapter 14.
15 See, in particular: B. Bernstein, 'Social class, language and socialization', in P.P. Giglioli (ed.), *Language and Social Context*, Harmondsworth, Penguin, 1972.
16 For the views of Eliot and Lawrence on education, see: G.H. Bantock, *T.S. Eliot and Education*, London, Faber and Faber, 1970; and J. and R. Williams (eds), *Lawrence on Education*, Harmondsworth, Penguin, 1973.
17 See: D.H. Lawrence, 'Education of the people', in Williams and Williams (eds), *Lawrence on Education*.
18 Ibid.
19 The British educational theorist G.H. Bantock was a key figure in the postwar development of the curricular implications of the conservative traditionalism of Eliot and Lawrence. For a short essay that succinctly captures Bantock's views, see: G.H. Bantock, 'Towards a theory of popular education', in R. Hooper (ed.), *The Curriculum: Context, Design and Development*, Edinburgh, Oliver and Boyd, 1973.
20 For a related argument in favour of the idea that ability in education should be regarded as 'more of a goal than a given', see: J.P. White, 'The curriculum mongers', in Hooper (ed.), *The Curriculum*.
21 For radical sociological criticisms along these lines, see: M.F.D. Young (ed.), *Knowledge and Control*, London, Collier-Macmillan, 1971.

14 Freedom, authority and discipline

1 See, for example: D. Carr, 'Traditionalism and progressivism: a perennial problematic of educational theory and policy', *Westminster Studies in Education*, vol. 21, 1998, pp. 47–55.

2 See: P.H. Hirst and R.S. Peters, *The Logic of Education*, London, Routledge and Kegan Paul, 1970.

3 See: A.S. Neill, *Summerhill*, Harmondsworth, Penguin, 1968.

4 This interpretation of the traditional–progressive distinction is really so prevalent in academic educational literature, policy documentation and media and other public discussions of education that it surely merits the status of the received view.

5 See: N. Bennett, *Teaching Styles and Pupil Progress*, London, Open Books, 1976.

6 See: R. Alexander, J. Rose and C. Woodhead (eds), *Curriculum Organization and Classroom Practice in Primary School*, London, Department of Education and Science, 1992.

7 On the basis of a report entitled 'Worlds Apart', which was commissioned by the British Office for Standards in Education (Ofsted) and co-authored by Professor David Reynolds and Shaun Farrell of Newcastle University in 1996 (and highlighted in a programme for BBC1's *Panorama*), Chief Inspector Chris Woodhead (as he then was) and others urged return to direct instructional 'whole-class' approaches to teaching (of particularly mathematics) of a kind allegedly conducive to economic advancement in such 'Pacific Rim' countries as Taiwan.

8 By 'structural functionalist sociology' I have in mind the sort of social analyses associated with social theorists such as Talcott Parsons. See, for example: T. Parsons, *The Structure of Social Action*, London, Free Press, 1949.

9 See J.J. Rousseau: *The Social Contract and Other Discourses*, trans. G.D.H. Cole, London, Dent, 1973; and *Émile*, trans. B. Foxley, London, Dent, 1974. For a very fine critical work on Rousseau that places *Émile* very much at the centre of his social theory, see: N.J.H. Dent, *Rousseau*, Oxford, Blackwell, 1988.

10 See: Rousseau, *Émile*.

11 See: J. Locke, *Two Treatises of Civil Government*, London, Dent, Everyman, 1966.

12 See: J.J. Rousseau, 'A discourse on the origin of inequality', in *The Social Contract and Other Discourses*, p. 84.

13 See: H. Lane, *Talks to Parents and Teachers*, London, Allen and Unwin, 1954.

14 There can be no doubt that, in Britain and elsewhere, increasing emphasis on and attention to the vital importance of early education in general and nursery education in particular for later educational development has been accompanied by a resurgence of essentially non-traditional or child-centred thinking about the sort of educational experience that might be most appropriate for early years. Much recent official and other early years policy documentation and wider academic and other literature is inclined to emphasise the importance of play and respect for the child's own interests, and the general inappropriateness of imposing any pre-specified formal curricular or other adult agenda on the child. In this respect, a fairly typical local British document is: Scottish Office, *A Curriculum Framework for Children 3 to 5*, Dundee, Scottish Consultative Council on the Curriculum, 1999.

15 For a fine comtemporary critical appreciation of progressive and child-centred ideas in general, see: J. Darling, *Child-Centred Education and Its Critics*, London, Paul Chapman, 1994.

16 See: Rousseau, *The Social Contract and Other Discourses*, p. 181.

17 Freud's 'traditionalist' view of the relationship of reason to feeling (or the rational to the irrational) arguably permeates his writings. See, for example: S. Freud, *Civilization and Its Discontents*, trans. J. Strachey, London, Hogarth, 1930. Certainly, despite his profoundly psychoanalytic perspective, A.S. Neill regarded Freud's views as too traditionalist for his own educational and therapeutic purposes, and turned rather to the works of Wilhelm Reich. The present author has also argued that Freud's views on

sexual ethics are inherently conservative; on this, see: D. Carr, 'Freud and sexual ethics', *Philosophy*, vol. 62, 1987, pp. 361–73. For broader discussion on Freud's views of the relationship of human nature to society, see: I. Dilman, *Freud and Human Nature*, Oxford, Blackwell, 1983.

18 See: Neill, *Summerhill*, p. 105.

19 See: Lane, *Talks to Parents and Teachers*, London, Allen and Unwin, 1954.

20 The general allegation that bullying replaced teacher authority in progressive schooling is explicitly made by R.S. Peters, in: R.S. Peters, *Ethics and Education*, London, George Allen and Unwin, 1966, p. 194.

21 For contemporary British philosophical debate on the educational influence of Dewey, see: A. O'Hear, 'Philosophy and educational policy', and A. Ryan, 'What did John Dewey want?', in J. Haldane (ed.), *Philosophy and Public Affairs*, Cambridge, Cambridge University Press, 2000.

15 Political dimensions of education

1 See: P.H. Hirst, 'Liberal education and the nature of knowledge', in *Knowledge and the Curriculum*, London, Routledge and Kegan Paul, 1974, p. 32.

2 Another argument from polar opposites of the kind employed in Kant's critique of subjective idealism in: I. Kant, *The Critique of Pure Reason*, trans. N. Kemp Smith, London, Macmillan, 1968. See again, for general discussion of argumentation of this kind: G. Ryle, *Dilemmas*, Cambridge, Cambridge University Press, 1960, chapter 7; and J. Passmore, *Philosophical Reasoning*, London, Duckworth, 1970, chapter 6.

3 The recent British 'Impact' series of essays on various philosophical aspects of aspects of educational policy and practice seems to have been very much motivated by a concern to generate positive exchange between policy makers and professional philosophers and theorists. See, for example: A. Davis, *Educational Assessment: A Critique of Current Policy*, Impact 1, October 1999; M. Luntley, *Performance Pay and Professionals: Measuring the Quality of Teaching. A Challenge to the Government's Proposals on Teacher's Pay*, Impact 2, January 2000; H. Brighouse, *Educational Equality and the New Selective Schooling*, Impact 3, 2000; and C. Winch, *New Labour and the Future of Training*, Impact 4, 2000. All volumes in the 'Impact' series are published by the Philosophy of Education Society of Great Britain.

4 For Matthew Arnold's arguments aginst nineteenth century educational instrumentalism, see: J. Gribble (ed.), *Matthew Arnold*, Educational Thinkers Series, London, Collier-Macmillan, 1967.

5 The present author has explored some of these points in: D. Carr, *Professionalism and Ethical Issues in Teaching*, Routledge Professional Ethics Series, London, Routledge, 2000.

6 For some recent strong philosophical opposition to competence models, see: T. Hyland: 'Competence, knowledge and education', *Journal of Philosophy of Education*, vol. 27, 1993, pp. 57–68; and *Competence, Education and NVQ's: Dissenting Perspectives*, London, Cassell, 1994.

7 For the defence of a place for theoretical reflection in competence models by advocates of competence, see: Scottish Office Education Department, *Guidelines for Teacher Training Courses*, Edinburgh, SOED, 1993; and D. Bridges, 'Competence-based education and training: progress or villainy?', *Journal of the Philosophy of Education*, vol. 30, 1996, pp. 361–75.

8 See: D. Carr, 'Guidelines for teacher training: the competency model', *Scottish Educational Review*, vol. 25, 1993, pp. 17–25.

9 See: Carr, *Professionalism and Ethical Issues in Teaching*, chapter 6.

10 For an excellent recent critique of the entire educational policy discourse of perfomativity, see: M. Bottery, *Education, Policy and Ethics*, London, Continuum, 2000.

11 For key British works of the school effectiveness movement, see: P. Mortimore, P. Sammons, R. Ecob and L. Stoll, *School Matters*, Salisbury, Open Books, 1988; and D. Reynolds, B. Creemers, P. Nesselrodt, E. Schaffer, S. Stringfield and C. Teddlie, *Advances in School Effectiveness Research and Practice*, Oxford, Pergamon, 1995.

12 The literature on action research as applied to education and teaching is truly enormous. For the idea in general see, for example: J. McNiff, *Action Research: Principles and Practice*, London, Routledge, 1988. The idea is not infrequently underpinned by an extreme 'particularist' conviction that the relatively abstract and decontextualised school research of educational academicians is largely irrelevant or insensitive to the actual contexts of practitioner engagement. This idea seems central to the highly influential work of John Elliott; see, for example, J. Elliott, 'Educational theory, practical philosophy and action research', *British Journal of Educational Studies*, vol. 35, 1987, pp. 149–69.

13 For some criticism of action research, see: D. Carr, 'Educational philosophy, theory and research: a psychiatric autobiography', *Journal of Philosophy of Education*, vol. 35, 2001, pp. 461–76.

14 On different styles of school inspection in England and other parts of the United Kingdom, see: T.H. McLaughlin, 'Four philosophical perspectives on school inspection: an introduction', *Journal of Philosophy of Education*, vol. 35, 2001, pp. 647–54.

15 For some idea of the professional unpopularity of Ofsted, see, for example, the following contributions to the *Journal of Philosophy of Education*, vol. 35, 2001: C. Richards, 'School inspection: a reappraisal' (pp. 655–66); C. Winch, 'Towards a non-punitive school inspection regime' (pp. 683–94); and M. Feilding, 'Ofsted inspection and the betrayal of democracy' (pp. 695–709). See also: Bottery, *Education, Policy and Ethics*.

16 For a useful recent collection on these pressing contemporary issues, see: D. Bridges and T.H. McLaughlin (eds), *Education and the Market*, Lewes, Falmer, 1994.

17 For Socrates' rejection of the commercialisation of education of his day, see: Plato's *Gorgias*, in E. Hamilton and H. Cairns (eds), *Plato: The Collected Dialogues*, Princeton, Princeton University Press, 1961.

18 Peter Geach attributes the dialectical strategy of the 'conventionalist sulk' to the philosopher Anthony Flew in: P.T. Geach, *God and the Soul*, London, Routledge and Kegan Paul, 1969, p. 3.

19 For the identification of progressive with 'left', see: C.B. Cox and R. Boyson (eds), *The Black Papers*, London, Dent and Sons, 1975.

20 See: Alexander *et al.* (eds), *Curriculum Organization and Classroom Practice in Primary School*, London, DES, 1992.

21 See: Neill, *Summerhill*.

22 See papers by Bantock and Eysenck and others on different educational approaches for different classes, abilities and personalities in: Cox and Boyson (eds), *The Black Papers*.

23 For some extreme hostility to theory in teacher education and training, see: ibid.

References

Adorno, T.W., *Negative Dialectics*, trans. E.B. Ashton, London, Routledge, 1990.

Aeschylus, *Prometheus Bound and Other Plays*, trans. P. Vellacott, Harmondsworth, Penguin, 1961.

Alexander, R., Rose, J. and Woodhead, C. (eds), *Curriculum Organization and Classroom Practice in Primary School*, London, Department of Education and Science, 1992.

Anscombe, G.E.M., *Intention*, Oxford, Blackwell, 1959.

Anscombe, G.E.M. and Geach, P.T. (eds), *Descartes: Philosophical Writings*, London, Nelson, 1954.

Archard, D., *Sex Education*, Impact 7, Philosophy of Education Society of Great Britain, 2000.

Arendt, H., *The Human Condition*, Chicago, University of Chicago Press, 1958.

Aspin, D., 'Ethical aspects of sports and games, and physical education', *Proceedings of the Philosophy of Education Society of Great Britain*, vol. 9, 1975, pp. 48–71.

Austin, J.L., *How to Do Things With Words*, Oxford, Oxford University Press, 1962.

Ayer, A.J., *Language, Truth and Logic*, London, Gollancz, 1967.

Bailey, C., 'Games, winning and education', *Cambridge Journal of Education*, vol. 5, 1975, pp. 40–50.

Bantock, G.H., *T.S. Eliot and Education*, London, Faber and Faber, 1970.

Bantock, G.H., 'Towards a theory of popular education', in R. Hooper (ed.), *The Curriculum: Context, Design and Development*, Edinburgh, Oliver and Boyd, 1973.

Barrow, R., *Plato, Utilitarianism and Education*, London, Routledge and Kegan Paul, 1975.

Benn, S.I. and Peters, R.S., *Social Principles and the Democratic State*, London, George Allen and Unwin, 1957.

Bennett, N., *Teaching Styles and Pupil Progress*, London, Open Books, 1976.

Bentham, J., 'A critical examination of the declaration of rights', in *Anarchical Fallacies*, in J. Bowring (ed.), *The Works of Jeremy Bentham*, Vol. II, London, 1838.

Berkeley, G., *A Treatise Concerning the Principles of Human Knowledge*, La Salle, Ill., Open Court, 1915.

Bernstein, B., 'Social class, language and socialization', in P.P. Giglioli (ed.), *Language and Social Context*, Harmondsworth, Penguin, 1972.

Best, D., 'Free expression or the teaching of techniques?', *British Journal of Educational Studies*, vol. 27, 1979, pp. 210–20.

Best, D., 'Can creativity be taught?', *British Journal of Educational Studies*, vol. 30, 1982, pp. 280–94.

Best, D., 'Generic arts: an expedient myth', *Journal of Art and Design*, vol. 11, 1992, pp. 27–44.

Blackham, H.J., *Six Existentialist Thinkers*, London, Routledge, 1965.

Blenkin, G. and Kelly, A.V., *The Primary Curriculum: A Process Approach to Curriculum Planning*, London, Paul Chapman, 1987.

Bottery, M., *Education, Policy and Ethics*, London, Continuum, 2000.

Bridges, D., 'Competence-based education and training: progress or villainy?', *Journal of the Philosophy of Education*, vol. 30, 1996, pp. 361–75.

Bridges, D. and McLaughlin, T. (eds), *Education and the Market*, Lewes, Falmer, 1994.

Brighouse, H., *Educational Equality and the New Selective Schooling*, Impact 3, Philosophy of Education Society of Great Britain, 2000.

Brosio, R.A., *Philosophical Scaffolding for the Construction of Democratic Education*, New York, Peter Lang Publishing Inc., 2000.

Bruner, J.S., *The Process of Education*, Cambridge, Mass., Harvard University Press, 1960.

Bruner, J.S., *The Relevance of Education*, London, Allen and Unwin, 1972.

Burke, J.W. (ed.), *Competency Based Education and Training*, Lewes, Falmer Press, 1989.

Carlisle, R., 'The concept of physical education I', *Proceedings of the Philosophy of Education Society of Great Britain*, vol. 3, 1969, pp. 5–22.

Carr, D., 'The logic of knowing how and ability', *Mind*, vol. 88, 1979, pp. 394–409.

Carr, D., 'Knowledge in practice', *American Philosophical Quarterly*, vol. 18, 1981, pp. 53–61.

Carr, D., 'Dance education, skill and behavioural objectives', *Journal of Aesthetic Education*, vol. 18, 1984, pp. 67–76.

Carr, D., 'Two kinds of virtue', *Proceedings of the Aristotelian Society*, vol. 84, 1984–5, pp. 47–61.

Carr, D., 'Education, professionalism and theories of teaching', *Journal of Philosophy of Education*, vol. 20, 1986, pp. 113–21.

Carr, D. 'Freud and sexual ethics', *Philosophy*, vol. 62, 1987, pp. 361–73.

Carr, D. 'The cardinal virtues and Plato's moral psychology', *Philosophical Quarterly*, vol. 38, 1988, pp.186–200.

Carr, D. 'Knowledge and curriculum: four dogmas of child-centred education', *Journal of Philosophy of Education*, vol. 22, 1988, pp. 151–62.

Carr, D., 'Education, learning and understanding: the process and the product', *Journal of Philosophy of Education*, vol. 26, 1992, pp. 215–25.

Carr, D., 'Moral and religious education 5–14', *Scottish Educational Review*, vol. 24, 1992, pp.111–17.

Carr, D., 'Guidelines for teacher training: the competency model', *Scottish Educational Review*, vol. 25, 1993, pp. 17–25.

Carr, D., 'Educational enquiry and professional knowledge', *Educational Studies*, vol. 20, 1994, pp. 33–52.

Carr, D., '5–14: A Philosophical Critique', in G. Kirk and R. Glaister (eds), *5–14: Scotland's National Curriculum*, Edinburgh, Scottish Academic Press, 1994.

Carr, D., 'Knowledge and truth in religious education', *Journal of Philosophy of Education*, vol. 28, 1994, pp. 221–37.

Carr, D. 'After Kohlberg: some implications of an ethics of virtue for the theory and practice of moral education', *Studies in Philosophy and Education*, vol. 15, 1996, pp. 353–70.

Carr, D., 'The dichotomy of liberal versus vocational education: some basic conceptual geography', in A. Nieman (ed.), *Philosophy of Education 1995*, Urbana, Ill., Philosophy of Education Society, 1996.

Carr, D., 'Common and personal values in moral education', *Studies in Philosophy and Education*, vol. 17, 1998, pp. 303–12.

Carr, D., 'Traditionalism and progressivism: a perennial problematic of educational theory and policy', *Westminster Studies in Education*, vol. 21, 1998, pp. 47–55.

Carr, D., 'What moral-educational significance has physical education? A question in need of disambiguation', in M. McNamee and J. Parry (eds), *Ethics and Sport*, London, E. & F.N. Spon, 1998.

Carr, D., 'Cross questions and crooked answers: the modern problem of moral education', in J.M. Halstead and T.H. McLaughlin (eds), *Education in Morality*, London: Routledge, 1999.

Carr, D., 'Professional education and professional ethics', *Journal of Applied Philosophy*, vol. 16, 1999, pp. 33–46.

Carr, D., 'Towards a re-evaluation of the role of educational epistemology in the professional education of teachers', in S. Tozer (ed.), *Philosophy of Education 1998*, Urban, Ill., Philosophy of Education Society, 1999.

Carr, D., 'Emotional intelligence, PSE and self esteem: a cautionary note', *Pastoral Care in Education*, vol. 18, 2000, pp. 27–33.

Carr, D., 'Is teaching a skill?', in R. Curren (ed.), *Philosophy of Education 1999*, Urbana, Ill., Philosophy of Education Society, 2000.

Carr, D., *Professionalism and Ethical Issues in Teaching*, Routledge Professional Ethics Series, London, Routledge, 2000.

Carr, D., 'Educational philosophy, theory and research: a psychiatric autobiography', *Journal of Philosophy of Education*, vol. 35, 2001, pp. 461–76.

Carr, D., 'Moral and personal identity', *International Journal of Education and Religion*, vol. 2, 2001, pp. 79–97.

Carr, D., 'Feelings in moral conflict and the hazards of emotional intelligence', *Ethical Theory and Moral Practice*, vol. 5, 2002, pp. 3–21.

Carr, D., 'Moral education and the perils of developmentalism', *Journal of Moral Education*, vol. 31, 2002, pp. 5–19.

Carr, D. and Landon, J., 'Teachers and schools as agencies of values education: reflections on teachers' perceptions: part I: the role of the teacher', *Journal of Beliefs and Values*, vol. 19, 1998, pp. 165–76.

Carr, D. and Steutel, J. (eds), *Virtue Ethics and Moral Education*, London: Routledge, 1999.

Carr, W., 'What is an educational practice?', *Journal of Philosophy of Education*, vol. 21, 1987, pp. 163–75.

Chomsky, N., *Language and Mind*, Harcourt, Brace and World, 1968.

Clarke, K., *Primary Education: A Statement*, London, Department of Education and Science, 1991.

Cooper, D.E., 'Grammar and the possession of concepts', *Proceedings of the Philosophy of Education Society of Great Britain*, vol. 7, 1973, pp. 204–22.

Cox, C.B. and Boyson, R. (eds), *The Black Papers*, London, Dent and Sons, 1975.

Curren, R., *Aristotle on the Necessity of Public Education*, New York and London, Rowman & Littlefield Publishers Inc., 2000.

Darling, J., *Child-Centred Education and Its Critics*, London, Paul Chapman, 1994.

Davis, A., 'Criterion-referenced assessment and the development of knowledge and understanding', *Journal of Philosophy of Education*, vol. 29, 1995, pp. 2–22.

Davis, A., *The Limits of Educational Assessment*, Oxford, Blackwell, 1998.

Davis, A., *Educational Assessment: A Critique of Educational Policy*, Impact 1, Philosophy of Education Society of Great Britain, October 1999.

Dearden, R., 'What is general about general education?', in *Theory and Practice in Education*, London, Routledge and Kegan Paul, 1984.

Dent, N.J.H., *Rousseau*, Oxford, Blackwell, 1988.

Department of Education and Science, *Reform of Initial Teacher Training: A Consultative Document*, London, HMSO, 1992.

Dewey, J., *The School and Society*, Chicago, University of Chicago Press, 1915.

Dewey, J., *Democracy and Education*, New York, Macmillan, 1916.

Dewey, J., *The Quest for Certainty*, New York, Milton Balch & Co., 1929.

Dewey, J., *Human Nature and Conduct*, New York, Random House, 1930.

Dewey, J., *Experience and Education*, New York, Collier Books, 1938.

Dewey, J. *Experience and Nature*, La Salle, Ill., Open Court, 1958.

Dilman, I., *Freud and Human Nature*, Oxford, Blackwell, 1983.

Dummett, M., 'Wittgenstein's philosophy of mathematics', in *Truth and Other Enigmas*, London, Duckworth, 1978.

Dunne, J., *Back to the Rough Ground: 'Phronesis' and 'Techne' in Modern Philosophy and in Aristotle*, Ind., Notre Dame, University of Notre Dame Press, 1993.

Durkheim, É., *Moral Education: A Study in the Theory and Application of the Sociology of Education*, trans. E.K. Wilson and H. Schnurer, New York, Collier-Macmillan, 1961.

Eisner, E.W., 'Instructional and expressive educational objectives: their formulation and use in the curriculum', in W.J. Popham, E.W. Eisner, H.J. Sullivan and L.L. Tyler, *Instructional Objectives*, Chicago, Rand McNally, 1969.

Elliott, J., 'Educational theory, practical philosophy and action research', *British Journal of Educational Studies*, vol. 35, 1987, pp. 149–69.

Elliott, J., 'Educational theory and the professional learning of teachers: an overview', *Cambridge Journal of Education*, vol. 19, 1989, pp. 81–101.

Elliott, J., 'School effectiveness research and its critics', *Cambridge Journal of Education*, vol. 26, 1996, pp. 199–224.

Elton Report, *Discipline in Schools*, Department of Education and the Welsh Office, London, HMSO, 1989.

Etzioni, A. (ed.), *The Semi-Professions and Their Organization: Teachers, Nurses and Social Workers*, London, Collier-Macmillan, 1969.

Feilding, M., 'Ofsted inspection and the betrayal of democracy', *Journal of Philosophy of Education*, vol. 35, 2001, pp. 695–709.

Fichte, J.G., *The Vocation of Man*, trans. W. Smith, La Salle, Ill., Open Court, 1965.

Foot, P., *Virtues and Vices*, Oxford, Blackwell, 1978.

Foot, P., *Natural Goodness*, Oxford, Oxford University Press, 2001.

Foucault, M., *The Archaeology of Knowledge*, trans. A.M. Sheridan-Smith, London, Tavistock Press, 1974.

Frege, G., 'The thought', in P. Strawson (ed.), *Philosophical Logic*, Oxford, Oxford University Press, 1967.

Frege, G., *The Foundations of Arithmetic: A Logico-Mathematical Enquiry into the Concept of Number*, trans. J.L. Austin, Oxford, Blackwell, 1978.

Freire, P., *Pedagogy of the Oppressed*, trans. M. Bergman Ramos, Harmondsworth, Penguin, 1972.

Freud, S., *Civilization and Its Discontents*, trans. J. Strachey, London, Hogarth, 1930.

Friedrich, C., *The Philosophy of Hegel*, New York, Random House, 1953.

Furlong, J., *Higher Education and the New Professionalism of Teachers: Realising the Potential of Partnership*, London, CVCP, 2000.

Gallie, W.B., 'Essentially contested concepts', *Proceeedings of the Aristotelian Society*, vol. 56, 1955–6, pp. 167–98.

Gardner, H., *Frames of Mind: The Theory of Multiple Intelligences*, New York, Basic Books, 1985.

Gardner, H., *The Theory of Multiple Intelligences: The Theory in Practice*, New York, Basic Books, 1993.

Gauthier, D., *Morals by Agreement*, Oxford, Clarendon Press, 1986.

Geach, P.T., *Mental Acts*, London, Routledge and Kegan Paul, 1957.

Geach, P.T., *God and the Soul*, London, Routledge and Kegan Paul, 1969.

Geach, P.T., *Logic Matters*, Oxford, Blackwell, 1972.

Geach, P.T., *Reason and Argument*, Oxford, Blackwell, 1976.

Geach, P.T., *Providence and Evil*, Cambridge, Cambridge University Press, 1977.

Geach, P.T. and Black, M. (eds), *Translations from the Philosophical Writings of Gottlob Frege*, Oxford, Blackwell, 1966.

Gettier, E.L., 'Is justified true belief knowledge?', in A. Phillips-Griffiths (ed.), *Knowledge and Belief*, Oxford, Oxford University Press, 1967.

Gilligan, C., *In a Different Voice: Psychological Theory and Women's Development*, Cambridge, Mass., Harvard University Press, 1982.

Goldstein, L., 'Wittgenstein's PhD. viva: a re-creation', *Philosophy*, vol. 74, 1999, pp.499–513.

Goleman, D., *Emotional Intelligence: Why It Can Matter More Than IQ*, London, Bloomsbury, 1996.

Goodman, P., *Growing Up Absurd*, London, Gollancz, 1960.

Goodman, P., *Compulsory Miseducation*, Harmondswoth, Penguin, 1971.

Gribble, J. (ed.), *Matthew Arnold*, Educational Thinkers Series, London, Collier Macmillan, 1967.

Habermas, J., *The Theory of Communicative Action*, Vols 1 and 2, trans. T. McCarthy, Boston, Beacon Press, 1981.

Hamilton, E. and Cairns, H. (eds), *Plato: The Collected Dialogues*, Princeton, Princeton University Press, 1961.

Hare, R.M., *The Language of Morals*, Oxford, Oxford University Press, 1952.

Hegel, G.W.F., *The Phenomenology of Mind*, trans. J.B. Baillie, London, George Allen and Unwin, 1971.

Hirst, P.H., 'The curriculum: educational implications of social and economic change', *Schools Council Working Paper No. 12*, London, HMSO, 1967.

Hirst, P.H., *Moral Education in a Secular Society*, London, London University Press, 1974.

Hirst, P.H., *Knowledge and the Curriculum*, London, Routledge and Kegan Paul, 1974.

Hirst, P.H. 'Educational theory', in P.H. Hirst (ed.), *Educational Theory and Its Foundation Disciplines*, London, Routledge and Kegan Paul, 1983.

Hirst, P H., 'The theory and practice relationship in teacher training', in M. Booth, J. Furlong and M. Wilkin (eds), *Partnership in Initial Teacher Training: The Way Forward*, London, Cassell, 1990.

Hirst, P.H., 'Education, knowledge and practices', in R. Barrow and P. White (eds), *Beyond Liberal Education: Essays in Honour of Paul H. Hirst*, London, Routledge, 1993.

Hirst, P.H., 'The demands of professional practice and preparation of teachers', in J. Furlong and R. Smith (eds), *The Role of Higher Education in Initial Teacher Training*, London, Kogan Page, 1996.

Hirst, P.H. and Peters, R.S., *The Logic of Education*, London, Routledge and Kegan Paul, 1970.

Hobbes, T., *Leviathan*, Harmondsworth, Penguin, 1968.

Horton, J. and Mendus, S. (eds), *After MacIntyre: Critical Perspectives on the Work of Alasdair MacIntyre*, Cambridge, Polity, 1996.

Hume, D., *A Treatise of Human Nature*, Harmondsworth, Penguin Books, 1969.

Hyland, T., 'Competence, knowledge and education', *Journal of Philosophy of Education*, vol. 27, 1993, pp. 57–68.

Hyland, T., *Competence, Education and NVQ's: Dissenting Perspectives*, London, Cassell, 1994.

Illich, I., *Celebration of Awareness*, Harmondsworth, Penguin, 1973.

Illich, I., *Deschooling Society*, Harmondsworth, Penguin, 1973.

Illich, I., 'Disabling professions', in *Disabling Professions*, London, Marion Boyars, 1977.

Johnson, S., 'Skills, Socrates and the Sophists: learning from history', *British Journal of Educational Studies*, vol. 46, 1998, pp. 201–14.

Kant, I., *Groundwork of the Metaphysic of Morals*, in H.J. Paton (ed.), *The Moral Law*, London, Hutchinson, 1948.

Kant, I., *The Critique of Practical Reasoning and Other Works on the Theory of Ethics*, trans. T.K. Abbott, London, Longmans, 1967.

Kant, I., *The Critique of Pure Reason*, trans. N. Kemp Smith, London, Macmillan, 1968.

Kenny, A., *Wittgenstein*, London, Allen Lane: The Penguin Press, 1973.

Kenny, A., *Frege: An Introduction to the Founder of Modern Analytical Philosophy*, Harmondsworth, Penguin, 1995.

Kirk, G., *Teacher Education and Professional Development*, Edinburgh, Scottish Academic Press, 1988.

Koffka, K., *The Principles of Gestalt Psychology*, New York, Harcourt, 1935.

Kohlberg, L., *Essays on Moral Development*, Vols I–III, New York, Harper and Row, 1984.

Köhler, W., *The Mentality of Apes*, trans. E. Winter, New York, Harcourt, 1925.

Kripke, S., *Naming and Necessity*, Oxford, Blackwell, 1980.

Kuhn, T.S., *The Structure of Scientific Revolutions*, 2nd edition, Chicago, University of Chicago Press, 1970.

Lane, H., *Talks to Parents and Teachers*, London, Allen and Unwin, 1954.

Lawlor, S., *Teachers Mistaught*, London, Centre for Policy Studies, 1990.

Lawton, D., *Class, Culture and the Curriculum*, London, Routledge and Kegan Paul, 1975.

Lechte, J., *Fifty Key Contemporary Thinkers: From Structuralism to Postmodernity*, London, Routledge, 1994.

Locke, J., *An Essay Concerning Human Understanding*, Oxford, Oxford University Press, 1934.

Locke, J., *Two Treatises of Civil Government*, London, Dent Everyman, 1966.

Luntley, M., *Reason, Truth and Self: The Postmodern Reconditioned*, London, Routledge, 1995.

Luntley. M., *Contemporary Philosophy of Thought: Truth, World, Content*, Oxford, Blackwell, 1999.

Luntley, M., *Performance Pay and Professionals: Measuring the Quality of Teaching. A Challenge to the Government's Proposals on Teacher's Pay*, Impact 2, Philosophy of Education Society of Great Britain, January 2000.

Lyotard, J.-F., *The Postmodern Condition: A Report on Knowledge*, trans. G. Bennington and B. Massumi, Manchester, Manchester University Press, 1984.

MacBeath, J., *Personal and Social Education*, Edinburgh, Scottish Academic Press, 1988.

McDowell, J., *Mind and World*, Cambridge, Mass., Harvard University Press, 1996.

MacIntyre, A.C., 'The essential contestability of some social concepts', *Ethics*, vol. 84, 1973–4, pp.1–9 .

MacIntyre, A.C., *After Virtue*, Notre Dame, Ind., University of Notre Dame University Press, 1981.

MacIntyre, A.C., 'The idea of an educated public', in G. Haydon (ed.), *Education and Values: The Richard Peters Lectures*, Institute of Education, University of London, 1987.

MacIntyre, A.C., *Whose Justice, Which Rationality?*, Notre Dame, Ind., University of Notre Dame Press, 1987.

MacIntyre, A.C., *Three Rival Versions of Moral Enquiry*, Notre Dame, Ind., University of Notre Dame Press, 1992.

MacIntyre, A.C. *Dependent Rational Animals: Why Human Beings Need the Virtues*, London, Duckworth, 1999.

MacIntyre, A.C., 'How to appear virtuous without actually being so', in J.M. Halstead and T.H. McLaughlin (eds), *Education in Morality*, London, Routledge, 1999.

McKeon, R. (ed.), *The Basic Works of Aristotle*, New York, Random House, 1941.

McLaughlin, T.H., 'The education of the whole child', in R. Best (ed.), *Education, Spirituality and the Whole Child*, London, Cassell, 1996.

McLaughlin, T.H., 'Beyond the reflective teacher', *Educational Philosophy and Theory*, vol. 31, 1999, pp. 9–25.

McLaughlin, T.H., 'Four philosophical perspectives on school inspection: an introduction', *Journal of Philosophy of Education*, vol. 35, 2001, pp. 647–54.

McNiff, J., *Action Research: Principles and Practice*, London: Routledge, 1988.

Marcuse, H., *One Dimensional Man*, London, Routledge, 1991.

Marx, K. and Engels, F., *Selected Writings*, London, Lawrence and Wishart, 1968.

Meakin, D., 'Physical education: an agency of moral education?', *Journal of Philosophy of Education*, vol. 15, 1981, pp. 241–53.

Mill, J.S., *A System of Logic*, London, Longmans, 1961.

Moore, G.E., *Principia Ethica*, Cambridge, Cambridge University Press, 1960.

Mortimore, P., Sammons, P., Ecob, R. and Stoll, L., *School Matters*, Salisbury, Open Books, 1988.

Munn Report, *The Structure of the Curriculum in the Third and Fourth Years of the Secondary School*, Scottish Education Department, Edinburgh, HMSO, 1977.

Munzel, G.F., *Kant's Conception of Moral Character: The Critical Link of Morality, Anthropology and Reflective Judgement*, Chicago and London, University of Chicago Press, 1999.

Nagel, T., *The View from Nowhere*, New York, Oxford University Press, 1986.

National Curriculum Council, *Spiritual and Moral Education: A Discussion Paper*, NCC, UK, York, 1993.

Neill, A.S., *Summerhill*, Harmondsworth, Penguin, 1968.

Nietzsche, F., 'The gay science', in R.J. Hollindale (ed.), *A Nietzsche Reader*, Harmondsworth, Penguin, 1977.

Noddings, N., *Caring: A Feminist Approach to Ethics*, Berkeley, University of California Press, 1984.

Nozick, R., *Anarchy, State and Utopia*, Oxford, Blackwell, 1974.

Nussbaum, M.C., *The Fragility of Goodness: Luck and Ethics in Greek Philosophy*, Cambridge, Cambridge University Press, 1986.

Nussbaum, M.C., *Love's Knowledge: Essays on Philosophy and Literature*, Oxford, Oxford University Press, 1990.

Nussbaum, M.C, 'Non-relative virtues: an Aristotelian approach', in P.A. French, T.E. Uehling and H.K. Wettstein (eds), *Midwest Studies in Philosophy, Volume 13: Ethical Theory, Character and Virtue*, Notre Dame, Ind., University of Notre Dame Press, 1988. Reprinted in M.C. Nussbaum and A. Sen (eds), *The Quality of Life*, Oxford, Oxford University Press, 1993.

Ofsted, *Spiritual, Moral, Social and Cultural Development: an Ofsted Discussion Paper*, Office for Standards in Education, UK, London, 1994.

O'Hear, A., *Who Teaches the Teacher?*, Research Report 10, London, Social Affairs Unit, 1988.

O'Hear, A., 'Philosophy and educational policy', in J. Haldane (ed.), *Philosophy and Public Affairs*, Cambridge, Cambridge University Press, 2000.

Parsons, T., *The Structure of Social Action*, London, Free Press, 1949.

Passmore, J., *Philosophical Reasoning*, London: Duckworth, 1970.

Passmore, J., *The Philosophy of Teaching*, London, Duckworth, 1980.

Pavlov, I.P., *Conditioned Reflexes*, trans. G.V. Anrep, New York, Dover, 1960.

Pedley, R., *The Comprehensive School*, Harmondsworth, Penguin, 1963.

Perry, L.R., *Bertrand Russell, A.S. Neill, Homer Lane, W.H. Kilpatrick: Four Progressive Educators*, Educational Thinkers Series, London, Collier-Macmillan, 1967.

Peters, R.S., *Authority, Responsibility and Education*, London, George Allen and Unwin, 1959.

Peters, R.S., 'Mental health as an aim of education', in T.H.B. Hollins ed.), *Aims of Education: The Philosophical Approach*, Manchester, Manchester University Press, 1964.

Peters, R.S., *Ethics and Education*, London, George Allen and Unwin, 1966.

Peters, R.S., 'Aims of education', in R.S. Peters (ed.), *The Philosophy of Education*, Oxford, Oxford University Press, 1973.

Peters, R.S., *Moral Education and Moral Development*, London, George Allen and Unwin, 1981.

Phillips, M., *All Must Have Prizes*, London, Little, Brown and Company, 1996.

Piaget, J., *The Psychology of Intelligence*, trans. Malcolm Piercy and D.E. Berlyne, London, Routledge, 1950.

Plantinga, A., *The Nature of Necessity*, Oxford, Oxford University Press, 1974.

Plowden Report, *Children and Their Primary Schools*, London, HMSO, 1967.

Popkewitz, T. and Fendler, L., *Critical Theories in Education*, London, Routledge, 1999.

Postman, N. and Weingartner, C., *Teaching as a Subversive Activity*, Harmondsworth, Penguin, 1971.

Primary Memorandum, *Primary Education in Scotland*, Scottish Education Department, Edinburgh, HMSO, 1965.

Putnam. H., 'The meaning of meaning', in *Mind, Language and Reality*, Cambridge, Cambridge University Press, 1975.

Putnam, H., *Reason, Truth and History*, Cambridge, Cambridge University Press, 1981.

Quine, W.V.O., *From a Logical Point of View*, New York, Harper and Row, 1953.

Quine, W.V.O., *Word and Object*, Cambridge, Mass., MIT Press, 1960.

Rawls, J., *A Theory of Justice*, Cambridge, Mass., Harvard University Press, 1985.

Reimer, E., *School is Dead*, Harmondsworth, Penguin, 1971.

Reiss, M.J. and Mabud, S.A. (eds), *Sex Education and Religion*, Cambridge, The Islamic Academy, 1998.

Reynolds, D., Creemers, B., Nesselrodt, P., Schaffer, E., Stringfield, S. and Teddlie, C., *Advances in School Effectiveness Research and Practice*, Oxford, Pergamon, 1995.

Richards, C., 'School inspection: a reappraisal', *Journal of Philosophy of Education*, vol. 35, 2001, pp. 655–66.

Rorty, R., *Philosophy and the Mirror of Nature*, Princeton, Princeton University Press, 1979.

Rorty, R., *Contingency, Irony and Solidarity*, Cambridge, Cambridge University Press, 1989.

Rousseau, J.J., *The Social Contract and Other Discourses*, trans. G.D.H. Cole, London, Dent, 1973.

Rousseau, J.J., *Émile*, trans. B. Foxley, London, Dent, 1974.

Rubinstein, D. (ed.), *Education and Equality*, Harmondsworth, Penguin, 1979.

Russell, B., *Logic and Knowledge: Essays 1901–1950*, London, George Allen and Unwin, 1956.

Russell, B., *The Problems of Philosophy*, Oxford, Oxford University Press, 1968.

Ryan, A., 'What did John Dewey want?', in J. Haldane(ed.), *Philosophy and Public Affairs*, Cambridge, Cambridge University Press, 2000.

Ryle, G., *The Concept of Mind*, London, Hutchinson, 1949.

Ryle, G., *Dilemmas*, Cambridge, Cambridge University Press, 1960.

Salovey, P. and Mayer, J.D., 'Emotional intelligence', *Imagination, Cognition and Personality*, vol. 9, 1990, pp. 185–211.

Sandel, M., *Liberalism and the Limits of Justice*, New York, Cambridge University Press, 1982.

Sayers, S., *Marxism and Human Nature*, London, Routledge, 1998.

Scheffler, S. (ed.), *Consequentialism and Its Critics*, Oxford, Oxford University Press, 1988.

Schools Curriculum and Assessment Authority, *Spiritual and Moral Development*, SCAA, UK, Discussion Paper No. 3, London, 1995.

Schools Curriculum and Assessment Authority, *Education for Adult and Moral Life*, SCAA, UK, Discussion Paper No. 6, London, 1996.

Scottish Consultative Committee on the Curriculum, *Education 10–14 in Scotland*, Scottish Curriculum Development Service, Dundee, 1986.

Scottish Consultative Committee on the Curriculum, *Environmental Studies: 5–14*, Edinburgh, Scottish Education Department, 1991.

Scottish Office, *A Curriculum Framework for Children 3 to 5*, Dundee, Scottish Consultative Council on the Curriculum, 1999.

Scottish Office Education Department, *Religious and Moral Education 5–14*, Edinburgh, SOED, 1992.

Scottish Office Education Department, *Guidelines for Teacher Training Courses*, Edinburgh, SOED, 1993.

Scottish Office Education Department, *Personal and Social Education 5–14*, Edinburgh, SOED, 1993.

Siegel, H., *Educating Reason: Rationality, Critical Thinking and Education*, London, Routledge and Kegan Paul, 1988.

Siegel, H., *Rationality Redeemed: Further Dialogues on an Educational Ideal*, New York, Routledge and Kegan Paul, 1997.

Skillen, A., 'Can virtue be taught, especially these days?', *Journal of Philosophy of Education*, vol. 31, 1997, pp. 375–93.

Skinner, B.F., *Walden II*, New York, Macmillan, 1948.

Skinner, B.F., *Science and Human Behavior*, New York, Macmillan, 1953.

Skinner, B.F., *Beyond Freedom and Dignity*, Harmondsworth, Penguin, 1973.

Smart. J.J.C. and Williams, B., *Utilitarianism: For and Against*, Cambridge, Cambridge University Press, 1973.

Smart, N., *The Phenomenon of Religion*, London, Macmillan, 1973.

Smith, R. and Standish, P. (eds), *Teaching Right and Wrong: Moral Education in the Balance*, London, Trentham Books, 1997.

Tamir, Y. (ed.), *Multicultural Education in a Democratic State*, Oxford, Blackwell, 1995.

Taylor, C., *Sources of the Self: The Making of the Modern Identity*, Cambridge, Cambridge University Press, 1989.

Taylor, C., *Multiculturalism: Examining the Politics of Recognition*, in A. Gutmann (ed.), *Multiculturalism*, Princeton, Princeton University Press, 1994.

Taylor, F.W., *Principles of Scientific Management*, London, Harper and Row, 1911.

Thorndyke, E.L., *The Psychology of Learning*, New York, Teachers College, 1913.

von Wright, G.H., 'An essay in deontic logic and the general theory of action', *Acta Philosophica Fennica*, Fasc. XXI, Amsterdam, North Holland Publishing Company, 1961.

Warnock, M. (ed.), *Utilitarianism*, London, Collins, Fontana Library, 1970.

Warnock, M., 'Towards a definition of quality in education', in R.S. Peters (ed.), *The Philosophy of Education*, Oxford, Oxford University Press, 1973.

Warnock, M., 'The neutral teacher', in M. Taylor (ed.), *Progress and Problems in Moral Education*, Slough, Berks, NFER Publishing Co. Ltd, 1975.

Warnock, M., *Schools of Thought*, London, Faber and Faber, 1977.

Wason, P.C. and Johnson-Laird, P.N. (eds), *Thinking and Reasoning*, Harmondsworth, Penguin, 1968.

Watson, J.B., *Behaviorism*, Chicago, University of Chicago Press, 1930.

Wertheimer, M., *Productive Thinking*, New York, Harper, 1945.

White, J.P., 'The curriculum mongers', in R. Hooper (ed.), *The Curriculum: Context, Design and Development*, Edinburgh, Oliver and Boyd, 1973.

White J.P., *Towards a Compulsory Curriculum*, London, Routledge and Kegan Paul, 1975.

Williams, J. and R. (eds), *Lawrence on Education*, Harmondsworth, Penguin, 1973.

Williams, K., *Assessment: A Discussion Paper*, Ireland, Association of Secondary Teachers, 1992.

Wilson, J., 'Teaching and neutrality', in M. Taylor (ed.), *Progress and Problems in Moral Education*, Slough, Berks, NFER Publishing Co. Ltd, 1975.

Wilson, J., *Fantasy and Common Sense in Education*, Oxford, Martin Robertson, 1979.

Winch, C., *New Labour and the Future of Training*, Impact 4, Philosophy of Education Society of Great Britain, 2000.

Winch, C., 'Towards a non-punitive school inspection regime', *Journal of Philosophy of Education*, vol. 35, 2001, pp. 683–94.

Winch, C. and Gingell, G., 'Educational assessment: reply to Andrew Davis', *Journal of Philosophy of Education*, vol. 30, 1996, pp. 377–88.

Winch, P., *The Idea of a Social Science and Its Relation to Philosophy*, London, Routledge and Kegan Paul, 1958.

Wiseman, S. (ed.), *Intelligence and Ability*, Harmondsworth, Penguin, 1967.

Wittgenstein, L., *Philosophical Investigations*, trans. G.E.M. Anscombe, Oxford, Blackwell, 1953.

Wittgenstein, L., *Tractatus-Logico-Philosophicus*, trans. D.F. Pears and B.F. McGuinness, London, Routledge and Kegan Paul, 1961.

Wittgenstein, L., *On Certainty*, trans. D. Paul and G.E.M. Anscombe, Oxford, Blackwell, 1969.

Young, M.F.D. (ed.), *Knowledge and Control*, London, Collier-MacMillan, 1971.

Index